Complete Guide to Film Scoring

The Art and Business of Writing Music for Movies and TV

2nd Edition

Richard Davis

berklee press

Complete Guide to Film Scoring
by Richard Davis

Edited by Jonathan Feist

BERKLEE PRESS
Dave Kusek, Director
Debbie Cavalier, Managing Editor
Ola Frank, Marketing Manager
Jonathan Feist, Senior Writer/Editor
David Franz, Contributing Editor

Cover Design: Moore Moscowitz
Book Design: Dancing Planet MediaWorks™

ISBN 978-0-87639-109-9

1140 Boylston St.
Boston, MA 02215-3693 USA
(617) 747-2146

Visit Berklee Press Online at:
www.berkleepress.com

DISTRIBUTED BY

HAL•LEONARD®
CORPORATION
7777 W. BLUEMOUND RD. P.O. BOX 13819
MILWAUKEE, WISCONSIN 53213

Visit Hal Leonard Online at:
www.halleonard.com

Praise for Richard Davis's
Complete Guide to Film Scoring

"From his technical discussions to his fascinating interviews, Richard's book is one of the best resources on film/television scoring I have ever read. I wish I'd read it twenty years ago. It should be mandatory reading for everyone in the business—newcomers, veterans, students, and movie buffs."
—*Mark Snow, Composer for the* X-Files *and* Millennium

"Richard Davis's book, *Complete Guide to Film Scoring*, is very concise and thorough. It is excellent both as a novice's introduction to the subject and as a reference for professionals."
—*Mark Isham, Academy Award nominated film composer and Grammy winning recording artist for* A River Runs Through It

"This book gets right down to business. Clear, concise, comprehensive, and up-to-date, this is the most well written book on the subject of film scoring. I highly recommend it to music students, lovers of film, or anyone who has an interest in film scoring."
—*Richard Stone, Emmy winning Musical Director of* Animaniacs *and* Pinky and the Brain

TABLE OF CONTENTS

Acknowledgements

No book is a solo effort, and there have been many who have given invaluable help to me on this project.

This book would not be the same without the participation of the composers, music editors, and agents who gladly offered their time. And I can't thank Nancy Knutsen of ASCAP and Doreen Ringer-Ross of BMI enough for the help they gave me in setting up many of the interviews.

In transcribing and preparing over 200 pages of interview transcripts, I had the very enthusiastic and gracious help of my student "elves": Haddon S. Kime, Michael Wasserman, Joseph Pondaco, Erica Weiss, Matt Koskenmaki, Sha-Ron Kushner, Daniel Davis, Marijke Van Niekerk, Alvin Abuelouf, Thanh Tran, Nina Edelman, Susan Lim, Jason Getzel, and Michael Albers. Their effort and feedback was wonderful. In Los Angeles, my former student, Alfonso Chavez was a great help in facilitating interviews, giving superior computer/technical advice and feedback on the manuscript. David Franz was the go-to details guy, efficiently helping with many different areas of production.

The Film Scoring Department at Berklee College of Music gave important feedback and guidance: Eric Reasoner, Jack Freeman, Don Wilkins, Michael Rendish, and Jon Klein. Also Richard Grant, creator of the Auricle software, helped steer me in the right direction on several issues.

In securing clearance to use copyrighted materials and photos I had the help of Jonathan Watkins of Fox Music Publishing, Carol Farhat of Fox TV Music, Antonia Coffman of *The Simpsons*, Stacey Robinson at Twentieth Century Fox Productions, and Richard Hassanian of Todd-AO Studios.

Finally, I'd like to thank the staff at Berklee Press. Managing Editor Jonathan Feist devoted countless hours to meticulously editing and assembling this manuscript. Jonathan, Dean of Continuing Education Debbie Cavalier, and Vice President of Berklee Media Dave Kusek all facilitated getting a huge project through the pipeline in a very short amount of time (not to mention gentle encouragement when I felt I'd never make it). And for additional help in proofing the manuscript, the eagle-eyed editor, Larry Davis.

—*Richard Davis*

PREFACE TO THE SECOND EDITION

In the time since the first edition of this book was published, the film-scoring world has changed drastically, and at the same time remained the same. It is the same in that there is still the opportunity to write and record great music that will be heard by millions of people. Composers and directors still must meet eye-to-eye and achieve the director's vision of a film. There are still improbably tight deadlines to meet, and a rocky political landscape to negotiate between director, producer, studio, and composer.

Where the change has come most significantly is in the area of technology, which influences every facet of the film composer's world, from how the music is written and realized, the way we interact with directors, the way our music is marketed, to the kinds of skills needed to be successful in this field. The advance of technology has changed the paradigm of composing for film from one of a solitary composer sitting at his desk or piano to one of a composer with at least one or more assistants in an electronic studio, racing against time to complete his or her score.

In addition, the Internet has changed the way we do business. Gone are the days of submitting cassettes, CDs, videotapes, or DVDs as the only way to show our wares. Today's composer has MySpace and Facebook pages as well as a personal Web site that a director, producer, or music supervisor may access to hear their music. Indeed, the Internet has enabled us to work long-distance, as both digital videos of scenes and audio files of music cues can be easily exchanged over the Internet.

Thus, I have reworked the original chapters having to do with finding work and presenting oneself in the business to make them more relevant to the film-scoring world as we know it today. There is a new chapter describing the evolution of technology in film scoring. And there are several other updates and revisions that will hopefully keep the book current for some time.

There are also two new and terrific interviews with Marc Shaiman and Harry Gregson-Williams, both of whom offer great insight as to how they work.

And on a sad note, I would like to acknowledge that several of the wonderful men and women who participated in the first round of this book are no longer with us. Elmer Bernstein, Michael Kamen, David Raksin, Richard Stone, and Shirley Walker are writing music in a different realm. Their original interviews and quotes have not been altered for this edition.

Finally, I would like to thank Alison Plante and Sheldon Mirowitz of the Berklee College of Music Film Scoring Department for their expertise and suggestions on how best to describe the development of technology as it relates to film scoring.

So, whether you are a composer interested in entering the field of film composing, a filmmaker, a student, or simply someone interested in film music, I hope that this second edition is relevant and helpful to your journey.

Richard Davis
January, 2010

Introduction

This book is for anyone interested in writing music for movies or television. It takes the reader step-by-step through the art of film scoring, from the history of the field, through the process of writing the score, and finally to an explanation of the music business as it pertains to film and television composers. As a composer myself, I have worked with some of the top people in the business. In preparing this book, I interviewed over 20 of my colleagues—composers, music editors, music supervisors, and agents—and included their observations and anecdotes.

Successful film scoring is not a matter of just writing good music; it is writing good music that supports a dramatic situation. After teaching film scoring for several years at the Berklee College of Music, I have realized that the most important thing for the beginning composer to learn is how to approach writing this kind of music. This means finding the heart of the film, the soul of the film, and expressing that in music. No one can get inside a composer's head and tell them which notes to write. Every musician brings his own personal experience and musical point of view to a composition. But they can be guided and pointed in a certain direction, either by a teacher, a director, or simply a gut reaction to a particular scene. I have found that the best creative guidance I can give is to help someone find that heart of the picture in order to know what they want to express about it. That expression can then combine with other skills—compositional, technical, creative, business, and communication skills—to make a successful film score and a successful composer.

This is our approach in the Film Scoring Program at Berklee, and there are several dimensions to our program that are reflected in the structure of this book. First, it is invaluable to have an appreciation of the masters of film scoring, past and present. The chapters on the history of the field give an overview, and hopefully will inspire the student of film music to further study.

Second, every composer hoping to work in film scoring must know the process of film making and the evolution of a film score. The chapters on topics such as spotting, syncing, and music editing will give the reader an understanding of this process that many established composers had to learn on the job.

Third, and the most difficult to impart in a book, are the chapters on creating the score. With the help of my composer colleagues, I focus on the important concepts in writing a film score. Again, my aim is to point the reader in the right direction, and hopefully the interested student of film scoring will take the advice of several of the composers in this book, and study, study, study.

The final chapters discuss an issue that is necessary to the livelihood of every professional musician: the music business. Royalties, agents, attorneys, copyrights, and other topics of the film music business are addressed at length. This provides a basic understanding for anyone entering the field.

The book concludes with 19 interviews with some of the top composers and agents in Hollywood. These interviews provide an illuminating glimpse into the careers of those who are successful in this field. Their relationships with directors, stories of how their careers began, the ups and downs along the way, anecdotes about how specific scenes were written, and many other issues are discussed.

How does this music end up on the silver screen? What does it take to be able to compose it? Who chooses the composer? Who chooses what the music should sound like? How long does it take? How do the finances work? This book answers these questions and many others about the art and business of film scoring.

—R.D., Boston, May 1999

The History of Film Music

PART I

CHAPTER 1

Early Films and Music: The Silent Movies

Music in film is a vital necessity, a living force.
—Bernard Herrmann[1]

Music and drama. Drama and music. Either way, these two branches of the performing arts have been linked together for thousands of years in many cultures around the world. There is Japanese Kibuki, Indian Bharatnatyam, and the Balinese Monkey Dance. The early Greeks and Romans used choruses and orchestras to accompany their dramatic plays. In Europe, during medieval times there were pagan festivals that used music to accompany stories of gods and heroes, as well as liturgical dramas that portrayed various biblical stories through singing and dramatic action. During the Renaissance, music was used in various scenes in the plays of Shakespeare and others. In the Baroque period of classical music we find early opera and ballet, forms of musical drama that continue today. And finally, in this century we have the huge popularity of Broadway plays and film music.

In all these examples, the music and drama can be separated into independent entities, but their combination as a whole is greater than the sum of their individual parts. Overtures and arias from Mozart's or Verdi's operas are often performed independently and are musically satisfying. Some of these same operas exist as plays or books. But hear the aria as part of the staged opera and the effect is profound in a way that the play or music by itself cannot approach. Music for film is similar. Certainly a film composer can write good music that stands up on its own without the film. John Williams' Suite from *E.T., The Extra-*

Terrestrial is frequently performed in concert to great acclaim. But when heard in conjunction with the visual of the film, it is awesome and the whole film takes on another dimension.

It is often difficult for modern audiences to appreciate the experience of the film audience of even the 1940s or 1950s, much less the moviegoers of the turn of the 20th century when the technology of moving pictures was new. But try, for a moment, to put yourself in the shoes of the filmgoer in 1895. The common forms of long-distance communication were letters and the telegraph. The cutting edge of communication technology was the telephone, and only a tiny percentage of city dwellers had one in their homes or had ever used one. Horses and trains were still the primary modes of travel; automobiles were about as common as telephones, and the flight of the first airplane was still 10 years away. Electric lights were only 15 years old and gas lamps were still the prevailing method of artificial light. Einstein had yet to propose his Theory of General Relativity. Stravinsky was only 13 years old and Schoenberg's twelve-tone system of music was more than two decades in the future; music lovers were most familiar with Brahms, Wagner, Mozart, Verdi, Beethoven, and other 18th and 19th century composers.

Imagine now that you enter a small theater, or even a café with curtains closed against the light. A very noisy machine in the middle of the room starts up, and across a screen in the front you see the images of people, animals, and buildings. To you, the almost turn-of-the-century filmgoer, this is like a miracle. And yet at the same time the images seem disembodied, for there is no accompanying sound. The mouths might move, the horse might gallop, the car spews its fumes, but there are no words, there is no clippity-clop, and there is no chugging and banging of the engine. All is left to your imagination, for the only sounds you hear are the loud and noisy rotations of the projector's motor.

However, imagine you are in the same room and there is a pianist or small group of musicians playing while the picture moves on the screen. This adds another dimension to your experience, and even if the music is just background music with no dramatic importance, your previous impression of empty, disembodied images is transformed into a more complete experience. There are still no words, no hooves, no automobile engine noises. But the addition of music somehow makes the images on the screen more complete and less like two-dimensional shadows.

From the very beginning, there were probably musical accompaniments to films, though the first documented incidents were in 1895 and 1896 when the Lumiére family screened some of its early films in Paris and London with musical accompaniment. These were a great success, and soon orchestras were accompanying films in the theaters.

At first, the music that went with these films was taken from anywhere: classical favorites, popular songs, folk songs, or café music. There was little or no attempt to give the music a dramatic importance; it was there to enliven the audience's experience.

As the film industry grew and became more sophisticated, music in the theaters grew as well. Depending on the size and location of the theater, there could be anywhere from one piano or organ to a small orchestra. The player or music director would choose various pieces from the already existing literature and prepare them for performances.

In 1908, again in France, Camille Saint-Saens was commissioned to write what is believed to be the first film score tailored for a specific film, *L'Assassinat du Duc de Guise*. This score was successful, but because of the added expense of commissioning a composer, preparing the music, and hiring the ensemble, the concept of scores specifically composed for a film did not take hold.

However, many people in the industry were becoming aware that there was a need for standardizing music for films, if not specifically composing for them. Music was not yet an integral part of the drama on the screen; it was still simply an adjunct with little or no dramatic significance. And because of the logistical problem of composing for as many different kinds of ensembles as there were theaters, scores were only rarely composed for specific films.

Music Fake Books

What did take hold, however, was a method of standardizing the musical experience of the audience, and a way of codifying what the musicians played. This happened with the publication of several books that provided many different pieces of music with different moods that could cover almost any dramatic situation. These books, of which the most well-known are the *Kinobibliothek* (or *Kinothek*) by Giuseppe Becce, *The Sam Fox Moving Picture Music Volumes* by J.S. Zamecnik, and *Motion Picture Moods,* by Erno Rapée, organized the musical selection to be played by dramatic category. The music director could simply determine the mood or general feeling of a particular scene, look up that idea in the book, and choose one of several possibilities. If, for example, he needed music for a very dramatic scene set in an evil castle, he might have seen these listings under "dramatic expression":

> Night: sinister mood
> Night: threatening mood
> Magic: apparition
> Impending doom
> Pursuit, flight
> Heroic combat
> Disturbed nature: fire, storm

In addition, there were many other moods and also other main categories: Love, Lyrical Expression, Nature, Nation & Society, and Church & State. (See Figs. 1.1, 1.2, 1.3.)

The use of these books could be a cumbersome process, especially if there was more than one musician playing. The music director in each theater would view the film several times with a stopwatch and time each scene. He then would choose the individual pieces to be played, knowing how many seconds each piece should run. Much was dependent on the ability of the conductor or player to anticipate a scene change and to be able to extend or compress a piece. One of the most problematic areas became the transitions between scenes that had different pieces of music. A change in key center, tempo,

MOTION PICTURE MOODS

For

Pianists and Organists

A Rapid-Reference Collection
of Selected Pieces

Arranged By

ERNO RAPÉE

**Adapted to Fifty-Two
Moods and Situations**

G. SCHIRMER, INC., NEW YORK

Fig. 1.1. Rapée.
Reprinted by Permission of G. Schirmer, Inc.

Table of Contents

[vi]

Fig. 1.2. Rapée.
Reprinted by Permission of G. Schirmer, Inc.

Agitato No. 3

(Suitable for *gruesome* or infernal scenes, witches, *etc.*)

Otto Langey

Allegro agitato

26262

Fig. 1.3. Rapée.
Reprinted by Permission of G. Schirmer, Inc.

instrumentation, or overall mood could be very awkward without a written-out transition. Therefore, many musical directors created such transitions themselves.

The fake books were successful since they created a set musical script that any musician could follow. However, their dramatic effectiveness was limited by the ability of each theater's musical director.

A concurrent system whose inception actually predates the use of fake books was developed by Max Winkler, a clerk at Carl Fischer Music Store and Publishing Company in New York. Winkler realized that if he could see the films before they were released, he could then make up what he called "cue sheets" for each film (similar to modern-day cue sheets or timing notes, but not to be confused with them). These cue sheets would lay out the choice of music and give timings for how long to play each piece, as well as present guidelines for interpretation, in order to stay synchronized. The publisher would preview the film, create a cue sheet, then organize and sell a book for each film that was provided to the musical director of a theater. This benefited the film maker, for it provided a set musical script with rough timings. It also benefited the publishers of the music, for they could make a profit selling or renting the music itself to the theaters. Here is the cue sheet for an imaginary film that Winkler drew up the night he got the idea:

Music Cue Sheet for
The Magic Valley
Selected and compiled by M. Winkler
Cue

1. Opening—play *Minuet No. 2 in G* by Beethoven for ninety seconds until title on screen "Follow me dear."

2. Play—"Dramatic Andante" by Vely for two minutes and ten seconds. Note: play soft during scene where mother enters. Play Cue No. 2 until scene "hero leaving room."

3. Play—"Love Theme" by Lorenze for one minute and twenty seconds. Note: Play soft and slow during conversations until title on screen "There they go."

4. Play—"Stampede" by Simon for fifty-five seconds. Note: Play fast and decrease or increase speed of gallop in accordance with action on the screen.

Copyright © Carl Fischer

This is clearly imprecise, with the effectiveness of the mood and the accuracy of the timings dependent on the pianist or conductor's ability to interpret these instructions. However, the response from producers and from musicians was overwhelmingly positive. It gave them a musical script to follow that ostensibly followed the wishes of the film makers.

In actuality, both the *Kinothek* and Max Winkler methods were destined for short lives. Winkler's system debuted in 1912 and the *Kinothek* was published in 1919. By the late 1920s the revolution of "talkies," the first movies with their characters actually speaking in synchronized sound, were being distributed. It was this technological advancement that began the modern use of music in movies.

CHAPTER 2

The First Talkies:
The Beginning of Synchronized Music

*There was a time in this business when they had the eyes of
the whole wide world. But that wasn't good enough for them,
oh no, they had to have the ears of the world, too. So they
opened their big mouths and out came talk. Talk! Talk!*
—Norma Desmond in Sunset Boulevard

The use of sound in films revolutionized the way movies were made. Not only was there an amazing new dimension to the audience's experience, but the way a story was communicated had to be completely rethought. Previously, when the actors were silent, the film maker often had to convey or amplify an emotion, or make a certain point by use of lighting or camera angles. Because the actors were now talking on-screen, directors felt that they had to highlight them with clear, bright light. In addition, the camera angles stayed more static in order to focus on the speakers and the reactions of those listening. (Actually, this was also a technological requirement because the cameras were still very noisy and had to be enclosed in bulky, soundproof cubicles that were cumbersome to move around the set.) The effect of all of this was that the dialogue became the focal point of the film. The imagination of the audience was curtailed as the actors explained everything happening.

This meant several things for the musicians. First, a composer could provide needed insight into the emotional and psychological drama through the music. Second, he could compose a piece of music that would accompany the film wherever it was shown. Third, the shift towards sound pictures meant that thousands of theater musicians would be put out of work.

One of the interesting side-stories to the development of the film industry is that in the late 1920s there were quite a few studio owners who believed that the talkies were a passing fad. However, there were others who saw the commercial possibilities of movies with synchronized dialogue. During the mid-1920s several different technologies were being experimented with to synchronize picture and dialogue. In 1925 and 1926, several shorts were screened to the public by the Warner Bros. Studio to gauge the audience reaction. These were not dramatic films; they simply showed opera singers, trains, or other mundane events that included synchronized sound.

In 1927, nervous Warner Bros. executives premiered *The Jazz Singer* in New York. Starring vaudeville singer Al Jolson, this film had several musical numbers featuring synchronized sound. With seventy years of hindsight, it is easy for us to think, "What was the big deal? Of course everyone would love this new technology." But the reality of the time is that no one knew how audiences would react after thirty years of silent pictures. Although much of the spoken dialogue was still silent and the story told by narration "cards," when Jolson sang "Blue Skies" and "My Mammy," and the sound appeared to come from his mouth, the audience was thrilled. *The Jazz Singer* did terrific box-office business and became the film that showed the industry the way to go. It opened up a whole new era.

For several reasons, both commercial and technical, many of the first successful talkies were to be musicals. For about three years, until about 1931, a steady stream of musicals was produced. This was probably because of the entertainment value of musicals; not only did the actors speak, they also sang and danced. In addition, there was the logistical advantage of having the musicians on the set and often on camera. However, as with any fad, after several years of a steady diet of musicals, the public's interest in them soon waned. When this happened many studio executives thought there was no longer a need for musicians, and many of the studio orchestras were laid off. A yearlong period of adjustment ensued until the same executives found out how much they really did need the music.

Adding music to films at this time was an expensive, cumbersome, and problematic process. In the very early days of talkies, there was no way to record the music separately from the rest of the production. All the musicians had to be present on the set, positioned in such a way as to be heard but not cover up the actors' lines. They could not make a mistake lest a whole take be ruined. This was a nightmare for all involved: musicians, actors, director, and soundmen. Sometimes a short song could take two or three days to record. In addition, there could be no edits afterward or the music would be ruined: the soundtrack would have jumps and blips.

The technology that was to free the music from the confines of the shooting set was the ability to record the music at a separate time, or "re-record" as it was known then. Developed about 1931, this allowed the music to be recorded on its own scoring "stage," so-called to distinguish the music recording building from the "sound stage" or film set building. It allowed the film maker to be able to put the music anywhere he wanted in the film, and it created the process we now call "dubbing," when the music, dialogue and sound effects are mixed together. Dubbing was yet another major technological advance, as it gave the director or producer control not only over where the music and sound effects would go, but also over how loud they would be in relation to the dialogue.

This new technology made the process of including music in films much more flexible and less expensive, and by the early 1930s, directors and producers began to accept that the film's underscore was a critical component. However, many still believed that the source of the music needed to be accounted for visually. Max Steiner, one of the giants of the early days of film scoring, described the situation:

> But they felt it was necessary to explain the music pictorially. For example, if they wanted music for a street scene, an organ grinder was shown. It was easy to use music in a nightclub, ballroom, or theater scene, as there the orchestras played a necessary part in the picture.

Many strange devices were used to introduce the music. For instance, a love scene might take place in the woods and in order to justify the music thought necessary to accompany it, a wandering violinist would be brought in for no reason at all. Or, again, a shepherd would be seen herding his sheep and playing his flute, to the accompaniment of a fifty-piece orchestra.[1]

Such examples show the naiveté of many film makers at that time. Audiences had been accepting music with no need for a visual justification from the beginning of films. However, it was a period when the industry was finding its way and discovering what worked and what did not work in these new sound movies.

To address the perceived necessity that all music be justified visually, two distinct and diametrically opposed solutions of music use came into vogue. One was the use of constant music—a score that started at the opening credits and did not stop until the picture ended. The other was no music at all. Neither of these solutions was ideal, and it took some trial and error on the part of film makers to find one that worked. Ultimately, a system of bringing the music in and out of the picture as the drama required became the standard practice, and still is adhered to today.

It is interesting to note that between these early days of talkies and the contemporary films of today there have been very few successful movies that had absolutely no music. A revealing anecdote is that of *The Lost Weekend*, a 1945 film starring Ray Milland. This intense film about an alcoholic on a weekend bender was originally released without any music at all. When first shown in the theaters, at the most dramatic scenes of Milland's descent into an alcoholic blur, the audience snickered and giggled—exactly the opposite of the film maker's intent. It was quickly pulled from circulation, and almost permanently shelved. However, composer Miklos Rozsa was brought in to do a score and the movie was re-released to great acclaim. It went on to win best actor, best picture, and best director, but the score was not acknowledged even though it was the only thing added to the original, failed version.

During the period of film music's infancy between 1927 and 1931, a clear progression can be seen. At first, the most common and obvious use of music in the talkies was as part of a musical with song and dance numbers. Upon the arrival of re-recording, producers went to the extremes and thought they didn't need music at all or had to have it all the time. Experiments were made with various kinds of *source music* (music that comes from a "source" on-screen), as in the Marlene Dietrich film, *The Blue Angel.* Theme songs were used, just as they are today, in order to promote the film and sell records and sheet music. And finally, directors began to play with the idea that music could come in and out of the soundtrack to support various types of scenes. Watching old films, you will notice that the concept of constant music was slow to die and was used in many films. However, the notion that music was a necessary part of film took hold and the underscore as we know it today began to take shape.

CHAPTER 3

The Studio System and The Studio Music Department

Music, one of our greatest art forms,
must be subjugated to the needs of the picture.
That's the nature of movie making.
—Sidney Lumet[1]

Much has been written about the Hollywood "studio system" in effect from the silent film era until the 1960s. Although we are primarily concerned with how this worked in relation to composers and musicians in general, it is worthwhile to briefly describe the overall "studio system."

In the early days of Hollywood, there were several large movie studios that produced the majority of films. These studios grew up during the days of the silent films, and the system of production they established then carried over to the talkies. Warner Bros. Studios, Metro-Goldwyn-Mayer (MGM), Universal Studios, Paramount Studios, RKO, Twentieth Century-Fox, and United Artists were the most productive and longest lasting. As still happens today, many of these entities were constantly shifting in ownership and had varying degrees of profitability. They were also each known for having certain kinds of films. For example, Warner Bros. was known for swashbuckling adventure stories, Universal for steady production of "B" horror and comedy movies, and MGM for grand dramas.

This was the most productive time in the history of the film business in terms of the sheer numbers of films produced. It has been said that in contemporary times Americans go to a movie, in the 1930s Americans went to the movies. Back then, people would frequently spend the afternoon seeing a double feature, whereas today going to the movies is an occasional evening out. In the 1930s approximately 80 million Americans (65% of the population) went to the movies *once a week*. Today, a much smaller percentage (under 10%) of the population goes to theaters regularly.[2]

In the summer of 1998 more people bought more tickets to movies (541.9 million) than any summer in history. However, since the population of the U.S. has grown so substantially since the 1940s, these statistics better reflect the movie-going public when expressed in terms of proportions to the general population.[3]

Because of the volume of films needed to satisfy the appetite of the movie-going public, the studios developed a system that was like an assembly line. It was efficient, streamlined, and somewhat insulated from the possibility of the temperamental manipulations of one creative individual. In other words, it was difficult for one person involved with the production, whether screenwriter, director, composer, editor, or others, to derail, hold up, or change the thrust of a production if they disagreed with the others. A new person would simply be brought in from the ranks of the studio staff, and work would continue. The only person with somewhat absolute power was the production executive, compared to whom even the stars had only limited power. If a particularly temperamental actor attempted to sabotage a production, the producer could control him by threatening not to give him any further projects for the remainder of his contract.

Each studio was a completely self-contained film-making factory where every aspect of the process was owned and controlled by the individual studio. The studio employed full-time contracted staffs of screenwriters, directors, producers, actors, extras, costume designers, hairdressers, carpenters, electricians, musicians, publicity agents, and others, spanning every possible job necessary to the making of a film. They had their own labs to develop the film and had complete post-production facilities for editing and dubbing. In addition, the individual studios also owned chains of theaters that showed only their films. The studio controlled not only the making of the film in every aspect, but also where, when and for how long it would be shown. (This ownership of the theaters was deemed illegal in 1949 and the studios were forced to sell off their theaters. It was only recently that Sony and others have found a way to own chains of movie theaters without violating U.S. antitrust laws.)

When a film started its journey through this studio assembly line, the producer pulled the strings and guided the process as it went through all the different departments. First, a group of writers would be assigned to create, complete, and polish the script. Note the operative word here is "group." Even though one writer would get screen credit, often it was a group effort. One person would write certain scenes, maybe love scenes. Another might write action scenes and yet another polish up the dialogue. There might also be a team of directors, each directing various scenes or different parts of the film. Various film editors would work on the project, as would teams of employees from the music, sound-effects, and costume departments. All of these workers were on staff at the studio. They could not work for any other studio, and they were obligated to follow the directions of the executives and supervisors of their departments.

The actors were also under contract to the studio, and especially at the beginning of their careers, had to do what they were told. Many stars were "groomed" by the studio; at a young age they were "discovered" and the studio would plan their careers and create roles specifically for them.

The producer and other studio executives were often involved in the creative process in a hands-on way. They would make creative decisions that might be in accord with the desire of the director(s), or they might be at odds. The producer's decision was the final word. The producer wielded much more power over creative decisions in those days of the studio system than they do today. In contemporary times, the director is responsible for delivering a final version of the film that is approved by the producers and/or studio. During the making of the film, the modern director has much more control over creative decisions than the director of the 1930s and '40s did, although his final cut of the film is still subject to approval.

Even though it seems impersonal, many great films were made by this process under the studio system. There were different styles to adhere to in film making: romances, melodramas, epic adventures, etc., and the different creative people learned to adapt to a certain style in order to maintain continuity throughout the film. The music, as well, was produced on an assembly-line basis, and many composers and orchestrators had to learn to adapt to the desired style. This is one of the reasons that so many clichés sprung up in the Hollywood films and music of the 1930s; the different departments had to use them to stay within the boundaries of the required style. For example, they produced soaring violins for the appropriate love scenes, and growling low brass or strings for the bad guys.

Another reason that so many clichés were in use had to do with the sheer volume of films produced—there was hardly time to work out fresh, original, creative ideas within the given time constraints. Finally, there was a prevailing attitude amongst producers that existed then as it does today, which is that "if it works, do it again." In other words, there was a general reluctance to try new things, and a conservative desire to use what was tried and proven both in film making and in music.

The Studio Music Department

Starting in the late 1920s, the studios had music departments that were self-contained so that every stage of the music could be done in-house. They had staffs of composers, orchestrators, songwriters, rehearsal pianists, orchestra musicians, conductors, choreographers, music copyists, proofreaders, music editors (then called "music cutters"), and music executives to oversee the process. These people usually worked under one roof in a music building that contained a music library and a recording studio.

The head of the music department was often a composer or conductor, like Alfred Newman, who headed the music department at Twentieth Century-Fox for many years during the forties and fifties. He also had to be an executive who interacted with the studio executives, producers, directors, accounting departments, recording specialists, costume directors when musicians were on-screen, and actors when they were singing or playing. He had to have a firm grasp of budgets and time schedules, and be an accurate evaluator of the skills, strengths, and weaknesses of the composers and performing musicians in his department.

The music department head would be aware of the production schedule of a film, and would know when it was about to be ready for music. If the film was a top feature, then he might assign one well-known composer to score the project. However, many of the second level, B-films, would be assigned a team of composers. These composers would screen the film with others on the music production staff. Perhaps the director would be there, perhaps not.

After the composers began writing, their sketches would go down the line to the orchestrators, copyists, proofreaders, and finally to the orchestra. If there were songs or dance numbers, there were rehearsal pianists on staff to take care of them. Everyone had his own job; it was all compartmentalized. In actuality, this is very similar in process to modern film-score production, with two major differences. Today there is only one composer on a project, and today everything is contracted outside of the studio. All the above roles and jobs still exist, but it is not in one place under one roof, and it is not controlled by the studio to the same degree of detail.

The deadlines and the pace of this process in the 1930s was frighteningly rapid, even by today's standards. Composer David Raksin began his career as a film composer working with Charlie Chaplin in 1935, and he describes this process:

> On the day when the new film was turned over to the Department for scoring, the staff gathered in our projection room. Present would be [the head of the music department], his assistant ... the composers ... two or three orchestrators, the head of Music Cutting and a couple of his assistants.
>
> By lunch we had "broken the film down" into sequences adjudged to call for music, determined what kinds of thematic material would be required and who would write it. After lunch, while the music cutters prepared the timing sheets that would enable us to

synchronize our music with the film, [the other composers] and I went off to our studios to compose whatever specific material had been assigned to us. We would shortly meet again, with several versions of each theme, to decide which ones in each category would best serve our purposes, which were usually quite clear— though never defined; these themes were Photostatted and each of us got a set of all the material for that film. By that time the timing sheets were ready, so we divided the work into three parts, and each man headed for home to compose his third....

Sometimes there was time to orchestrate one's own sequences, but usually the rush was so great that by the next morning we were already feeding sketches to the orchestrators, and by noon they were delivering pages of score to the copyists. On the morning of the fourth day the recording would begin; the Studio had a fine orchestra under contract, and available on very short notice....

On the fifth day a couple of days of re-recording (dubbing) would commence. After that, there might be a brief respite, and then the process started again ... It was wild, and we all enjoyed it.4

Five days to compose, record and dub a film is unbelievably quick. Today, a composer usually takes two to eight weeks to write the music and three to ten days to record it. Once his work is complete, three to four weeks are spent dubbing his music and the other sounds into the film, and soon after that, it is ready to hit the theaters. This means that the film will be released between five and thirteen weeks after the composer first receives the locked picture (see chapter 8).

David Raksin relates another anecdote about studio composing schedules:

We did tremendous amounts of music. For instance, when I composed the score for Forever Amber, that had about 110 minutes of music—about 100 of those I composed myself. The rest was music of the story's time. Originally I had twelve weeks to do that, but they were messing around with the movie, and by the time they got finished doing that I had eight and a half weeks to do that tremendous amount of music. And I did it!

The budget and importance of the project would determine quality of the music and the amount of time given to write it. B films were rushed through. If the film had major stars and was high profile, as in *Forever Amber*, there would be one "name" composer who would have more time to write the score. Still, the process that ensued once the score was written remained the same; the music went through the pipeline from composer to orchestrator to music preparation to the studio orchestra.

Chapter 4

Musical Styles ~1930 to 1950: The Golden Age of Hollywood

Study those who have preceded us: Korngold, Waxman,
Raksin, Steiner. Learn what they did. Learn why. Learn how.
Draw upon their genius, and your own understanding
of the marriage of music and film will deepen.
—David Spear

Between 1930 and 1950, an average of 500 films per year were produced. At this time Americans were attending movies more frequently than at any other time in history. For this reason, this time period is known as the "Golden Age of Hollywood." It was an exciting time to be in the movie business; opportunities were many, and technology and the industry itself were growing to maturity from the infancy of silent pictures, constantly making strides and innovations, both technically and creatively. Film music also grew up during this time, finding its way to a language and a technique that is the foundation for what is heard even today.

The musical film-scoring vocabulary of the 1930s and '40s is still familiar to modern audiences. The release of many of these older films on video and their airing on television has enabled even those of us born after this "golden age" of movies to recognize the lush, orchestral sound of the early film scores. Though this sound can seem "corny" to 21st century ears, if we understand where these composers and film makers were coming from, then we can appreciate their artistic accomplishments.

During the silent film era, the music that was most familiar to audiences and thus was commonly used in films was that of the 18th and like 19th century European classical composers, popular songs by composers such as Irving Berlin and George Gershwin, as well as some well-known folk songs. When sound became a part of films in the late 1920s, there arose a great need for accomplished composers who could write scores that would appeal to the contemporary audience, and be dramatically synchronized to enhance the action on-screen. At this time there was an influx of European born composers who came to Hollywood, many of whom were Jewish and were fleeing political upheaval and persecution in Austria, Germany, and Eastern Europe. They had conservatory training from their native lands in composition, conducting, and performance, and were therefore well versed in classical music styles—especially those of the 18th and 19th centuries. They had an in-depth knowledge of the operas of Verdi, Wagner, Strauss, and Puccini, and were intimately familiar with the concert and chamber works of Beethoven, Mozart, Brahms, Schubert, Berlioz, and many others.

Of these émigré composers, several were quick to set a high standard for the Hollywood music community. These included Max Steiner, Erich Korngold, Branislau Kaper, Miklos Rozsa, and Franz Waxman. A brief look at the musical achievements of two of these men, both before and during their Hollywood careers, will illustrate how the "sound" of the films during the Golden Age of Hollywood came to be.

Max Steiner (1888 to 1971) wrote over 300 film scores including *King Kong, Gone with the Wind, The Treasure of the Sierra Madre,* and *The Charge of the Light Brigade.* An Austrian immigrant who had written his first operetta at the age of fourteen, Steiner arrived in Hollywood in 1929. He was there as film music grew from infancy into a sophisticated art, and was one of the men that molded its growth. He became known for writing emotional, lyrical themes (as in *Gone With the Wind*), but was versatile and could provide any mood required. He used leitmotifs (themes, specific instruments, or both for a certain character or idea in the story) in many films, an idea borrowed from opera composers, especially Wagner. Most importantly, he was originally a composer of operettas, and so was well versed in the marriage of music and drama. It was this dramatic experience that gave him the sensitivity required to write effective film scores. And it was his training and foundation in 19th century composition that provided the necessary musical vocabulary.

[handwritten margin note: leitmotifs: themes, specific instruments, or for a certain character or idea / or both the story]

Erich Korngold was also an Austrian refugee who was trained in the Old World conservatory system. But where Steiner's background was in operetta, Korngold's was in grand opera. Korngold was a child prodigy in his hometown of Vienna, and by the time he was fourteen, his praises had been sung by Mahler, Puccini, and Richard Strauss. By the age of nineteen, he had written three operas and was considered to be one of the shining lights of Europe. He was well known, well liked, and well off financially by the time he was in his early twenties. Mostly his career consisted of conducting in various European cities while he continued to compose opera and concert pieces.

In 1934, Korngold was invited to come to Hollywood to arrange Mendelssohn's famous incidental music to *A Midsummer Night's Dream*. Although the producer of the project had probably never heard of Korngold, at that time Hollywood producers scored status points by successfully raiding the artistic world of Europe. So Korngold journeyed to California with his wife and children, and spent several months adapting Mendelssohn's music.

This trip proved successful, and Korngold was intrigued by the possibilities of film music. He was to return to America twice in the next few years, finally coming for good when he realized that the political climate in his native Austria was becoming dangerous for a Jew.

Korngold only scored eighteen films in twelve years, and he worked under the best conditions possible. He had the right to turn down any project, and was given as much time as he needed to write the music. As with Steiner, it was his early training in opera that gave him the ability to come up with appropriate musical solutions for Hollywood films. In addition, the musical vocabulary of his German opera writing and that required by Hollywood films was the same.

There were many other fine composers working in Hollywood during this time, but these two are representative of the ongoing style and trend. The strongest musical influences for them were 19th century late Romantics: Wagner, Brahms, Mahler, Verdi, Puccini, and Strauss. The musical vocabulary of these composers became the most common and fundamental language of the music in early Hollywood films.

Wagner, Brahms. Mahler, Verdi, Puccini, Strauss

Brahms, Third Symphony
Wagner, Parsifal
Tchaikowski, Sixth Symphony
Strauss, Till Eulenspiegel

Much has been said and written about why this happened. A question often posed is: Why did it take so many years for the more contemporary and modern sounds of Stravinsky, Bartók, Ravel, and Schoenberg to find their way into the dramatic expression of popular films? The answer is twofold. First, the late Romantic period of classical music was the most familiar to the film-going audience. In 1935, they were only 50 years removed from Brahms' *Third Symphony* and many other contemporaneous Romantic works including Wagner's *Parsifal*, Tchaikowski's *Sixth Symphony*, and Strauss's *Till Eulenspiegel*. The melodic thrust, the harmonic structure, and the overall thematic development were musical events that the average film audience could easily grasp. No matter what the dramatic need of a scene, whether it be lyrical or turbulent, it could be expressed musically in a way that was easily understood. This was an important requirement of popular films. They were not aimed at an intellectual or academic audience. They were not even aimed at the most educated audience. They were aimed at the great middle. And although many Hollywood films made philosophical, moral or psychological points in their stories, they were not to be confused with the more "arty" movies of film makers such as Fassbinder.

The background of men like Steiner, Korngold and Waxman made them perfectly suited to accomplish the musical need of the time. Essentially 19th century composers writing in a late 19th century and early 20th century style, they were able to bring quality music to films. They had an excellent grasp of harmony, melodic development, and other compositional techniques such as passacaglia and leitmotif. They understood form and thematic development so that they could spin out a melody when necessary, or fragment it and tease the audience. And perhaps most importantly, they had thorough knowledge of the music dramas, the operas of the 18th and 19th century.

When movies were silent, the composer or player was simply an adjunct to a moving picture. He could amplify an emotion, telegraphing danger or sweetening a love scene. But with sound films where the actors were talking, the role of the music changed significantly. The music had to interact with the dialogue of the actors and find a way to create the right mood, and at the same time stay out of the way of the voices. It needed to express and mirror the emotion of the actors as well as sometimes bring these emotions to a ringing conclusion. The music needed to develop as the story developed and move the plot along. The experience of the European composers in writing opera made them ideally suited to this task.

One listen to (or attendance at) a Wagner, Verdi, or Puccini opera would illuminate this point dramatically. The use of music from start to finish, the thinning out of the orchestra during recitative (dialogue), the grand crescendos and emotional outbursts at high points of the drama, and the use of leitmotif in opera are no different in concept from the marriage of music and film during the early days of Hollywood.

In opera, sometimes the same musical idea or phrase might keep returning to reinforce the audience's understanding and response to an idea or emotion in the film. Max Steiner's score to *Gone with the Wind* did just this. There were seven different motives or themes representing different characters or situations, and they return periodically throughout the film. Korngold's score to *The Adventures of Robin Hood* (1938) had a theme for the Merry Band, a theme for Marion, one for Robin Hood, and yet another for the Sheriff of Nottingham. (Note that this technique is still used in modern times, but with a more contemporary music language. John Williams' score to *E.T. The Extra-Terrestrial,* and Alan Silvestri's score to *Forrest Gump* are but two examples.)

In addition to thematic organization, as more and more scores were recorded over the years, certain conventions came to be used. This has always been the case and still is today, for it is really prevailing conventions that make up a given style. In the 1930s those conventions were numerous, and sometimes born out of necessity. Though all the composers, even those working on "B" films, were highly skilled, the time crunch they worked under was often outrageously short.

We chuckle today at some of these 1930s conventions, for they seem so dated. But every generation of films has had its musical style. There were love themes with soaring violins often in octaves, brass in fourths and fifths whenever there were Romans, Greeks, or medieval kings, and string sections seemingly ubiquitous throughout a film, providing a warm, rich, and lush blanket upon which both dialogue and acted-out emotions could sit. But in the eyes and ears of the 1930s audience, these conventions were as effective as the mournful Irish sounds in the score of *Titanic*.

New Ideas in Music

The 19th century romantic style of Korngold and Steiner was used in films through the 1950s. But during the 1940s, new ideas were introduced slowly. Composers like David Raksin and Bernard Herrmann were expanding the range of possibilities by introducing elements of jazz and contemporary 20th century music. Scores like *Laura* (1944) and *Citizen Kane* (1941) did much to open up the minds and ears of the movie industry to new sounds. For example, Raksin wrote a 12- tone score for *The Man with a Cloak* (1949).

David Raksin:

> Man with a Cloak *had a 12-tone row, the first five notes of which spelled E-D-G-A-R. The R became D♭ so it was still Re. I saw Johnny Green (head of music at MGM) the next day and he said, "Gee that's a remarkable score, what's that crazy god-damned tune you've got there?" And I said, "Johnny, it's a 12-tone row." He was astonished because it sounded so much like a theme and wanted to know why I used a row. I told him it was because in this picture you don't find out until the last 45 seconds or so that the hero, the man in the cloak, is really Edgar Allan Poe.*
>
> *I had a great time doing what I was doing. Sometimes I was motivated by jazz, sometimes by contemporary music. You would have to be crazy not to feel the enormous effect of the music of Stravinsky. For me it was Stravinsky and Berg. So I just wrote the way I thought I should be writing.*

Raksin also points out that as film music drew its influences from what musical styles were popular, it also influenced those styles. Contemporary music, or dissonant music that was not accepted by audiences for the concert stage, would be accepted in the appropriate scene of a film. Raksin again:

> If you have a really violent sequence and you write something that is really dissonant, they wouldn't like to hear that as a [concert] piece of music. But they will accept it if it is the right music for a film sequence.

New ideas, such as twelve-tone rows and other modern compositional techniques, were slow to gain popularity in film scores. However, producers, directors, and the composers themselves gradually saw the dramatic value of these methods, and musical styles in films began to change.

Composers:
Raskin *
Herrmann
Steiner*
Korngold*
Waxman
Kaper
Rozsa

Movies/Scores:
The Man with a Cloak
Laura
Citizen Kane
Gone with the Wind
The Adventures of Robin Hood
King Kong

↗ Synchronization of music

1930s - 50s: heavily influenced by Romantic composers, use of leitmotifs, conventions During the 40s, more contemporary techniques emerged, especially jazz.

CHAPTER 5

Musical Styles 1950 to 1975

*Putting music in a film is not an arbitrary thing.
There's a form and a shape, an overall
pattern of where you put music in.*
—Jerry Goldsmith[1]

In any discussion of artistic and historical styles and eras, it seems to be human nature to want to delineate and mark a specific date, year, or piece that ushers in the new era. But it is never really so cut and dry. Monteverdi did not wake up on the morning of January 1, 1600 and proclaim, "Ah-ha, let us begin the Baroque period of music!" Beethoven knew he was breaking away from the old classical style of Mozart and Haydn, but he was not consciously creating a new musical period called "Romanticism." Most new trends are the result of evolution, drawing upon the old and breaking ground for the new. Film scoring styles are no different. The Romantic style of Steiner, et al, remained prominent for about twenty years, from 1930 to 1950. But there were signs of experimentation, and certain scores written during that time seem to point to the future use of more dissonance, atonality, and eventually popular, jazz, and rock vocabulary in scores.

Remember that by the late 1930s the art of synchronizing music with film was quite new—only ten years old. Although composers, directors and producers were still heavily reliant on conventions that were tried and proven, there was always the occasional innovation that stood aside from the crowd. In 1941, in the midst of the Romantic style of Korngold and Steiner, a film was released that was to break the mold of the time, both visually and aurally. This was *Citizen Kane*, a film by Orson Welles with a score by Bernard Herrmann. Many of the more modern compositional techniques used by Herrmann in this film were not in common use until the 1950s—he was about ten years ahead of the pack. *Citizen Kane* pointed to the eventual use of contemporary new influences: Bartok, Stravinsky, Schoenberg; 20th c.

sounds and textures influenced by Bartók, Stravinsky, Schoenberg, and other 20th century composers. In addition, it presaged the rise of American-born composers in the film industry.

By the early 1950s, there were many conservatory-trained American musicians working for the studios as composers, orchestrators, pianists, songwriters, and arrangers. This included Bernard Herrmann, David Raksin, Alex North, George Antheil, Leonard Rosenman, Elmer Bernstein, André Previn, and Jerry Goldsmith. With a firm grounding in traditional harmony, theory, and counterpoint these men had not only studied the new music of Bartók, Schoenberg and Stravinsky—many of them also had a thorough knowledge of jazz styles.

Although Steiner, Korngold, Waxman, and others of the previous generation were often "genius" composers, they remained, for better or worse, heavily rooted in 19th century music and somewhat uninterested or even opposed to newer musical styles. When asked to comment about contemporary music, Max Steiner said: "I have no criticism. I can't criticize what I don't understand."[2] This comment really points out the difference between the old and new generations of film composers.

One composer working occasionally in films who was a great influence—not only on film music, but on all of classical composition—was Aaron Copland. By the time he scored his first film, *The Heiress*, in 1949, he was a world-renowned composer of ballet, symphonic, and chamber music. He only scored a few other films after that, including *The Red Pony* and *Of Mice and of Men*, but Copland left a large musical impression on all who followed. In fact, it was his ability to convey drama in the music to the ballets *Rodeo* and *Appalachian Spring* that brought him to the attention of Hollywood producers. He brought a new and fresh sensibility in his use of instrumentation and harmony. The instrumental textures in Copland's film scores are softer than the big Romantic scores of the time. He used smaller ensembles and avoided the big, overblown orchestral tuttis found in many films. His use of pandiatonic harmonies, polytonality, and controlled dissonance was imitated by many composers.

Golden Age: big dramatic orchestras
50s-75: Copland introduced idea of small ensembles

Aside from musical development and evolution in films, there were several other factors both in the kinds of films released and in American culture itself that must be taken into account when considering the sound of movie music in the 1950s. Perhaps the most important of these is the arrival of the invention of television. There was also the popularity of "rebel" films—films dealing with youth, rebellion and the darker issues of life including alcoholism and drug addiction. The McCarthy committee of the United States Congress, which instigated and led a witch hunt for Communists in many industries, and especially the entertainment industry, had an impact not only on who worked and who didn't, but also on the content of the films themselves. The rise of jazz—big-band swing and bebop—created a new musical culture, especially amongst the nation's youth. Add to all of these events and trends the birth of rock-and-roll music in the mid-fifties, and the need for new styles in film scoring can be clearly seen.

The Arrival of Television   40s

Beginning in the late 1940s television was readily available to the general public. As the cost of TV sets became more affordable, and as more programming was aired by the networks, more and more people made TV a regular part of their lives. At first, Hollywood studios looked down on this technology as someone might look askance at an unwanted relative who shows up uninvited for dinner. They refused to release their catalogue of movies to television stations, and did not produce shows for TV. In many cases, the studios hoped and believed television was going to be a passing fad. As we know today, they were quickly proven wrong.

In retrospect, it is not so difficult to see why many Hollywood people had a hard time accepting television. This new form of entertainment arrived only twenty years after the arrival of talkies. The studio system was powerful, smoothly oiled, and profitable, and many people were very comfortable with it. The "Golden Age" of films was generating millions and millions of dollars in profits from the millions of people that attended movies on a regular basis.

In 1946, an estimated revenue of 1.7 billion dollars was generated by theatrical movies. By 1962, this figure was down to 900 million dollars, just over half the 1946 amount. This was the effect that TV had on the movie business. It threw studios, executives, actors, and all the creative people into turmoil as a new playing field and a new ball game were created.

The period from 1955 to 1970 also saw the demise of the old studio system. Two factors were most important in contributing to this: the advent of television, and a court decision citing antitrust laws that required the studios to break up their chains of self-owned theaters. This was a true "double-whammy." First of all, the popularity of TV meant that many people stayed home and stopped attending movies in the theaters, causing a severe drop in revenues. Secondly, with the loss of the studio-owned theater chains, they no longer had the automatic distribution of a studio-produced film. Previously, a studio could make a film, and no matter how good or bad it was, release it to as many theaters as they wanted, for as long as they wanted to keep it in circulation. Under the new system, if a film was not accepted publicly, the independent theater owner could withdraw it. In addition, because the audience now had the option of staying home and watching TV, if the film wasn't of fairly high quality, or if it didn't strike a chord in the populace, it would fail in the theaters.

With a real pinch in the flow of cash, the studios could not afford to keep thousands of people under contract. So they had to let go of many employees: actors, directors, musicians, and even producers. In the space of a few short years, the dynamic of producing a film completely changed. Producers became independent, using studios to provide financing, a place to shoot, and a distribution network. No longer could the studio control everything from start to finish, though they could approve or disapprove the final product. But the process itself became removed from studio control. Those involved in the production could move from studio to studio as the projects required. This became the norm for all involved in film production, including the composers.

After a few years of refusing to show films originally released in the theaters on television, the studios finally relented in an attempt to gain at least some profit from the new technology. This gave rise to the TV shows that featured movies from the studio's catalogue, albeit frequently edited for length and content, and often interrupted for commercials. This marked the defeat of the anti-TV forces in Hollywood, and was the first step toward fully mobilizing the extensive studio machinery to include the production of television shows. It was only a short time before the studios were actively involved in producing sit-coms, dramas, and TV movies.

The New Music and the Composers Writing It

There are many films that contain excellent examples of the different kinds of scores written in the 1950s and 1960s. Several are worth mentioning because they broke new ground, or in some other way stand out from the rest.

One of the young composers making a mark on Hollywood was Alex North. Brought from New York to Hollywood by director Elia Kazan, his score to *A Streetcar Named Desire* (1951) was a landmark musical event. For the first time, a raw, edgy, and modern sounding score with many jazz elements was accompanying a popular film. It was not only the use of jazz but also the use of dissonance (influenced by modern classical composers) that gave this score a unique flavor. This opened the floodgates for other composers to incorporate jazz into their scores and a whole new musical style began.

In 1953, Kazan again gave an opportunity to a young composer. Juilliard-trained composer Leonard Rosenman wrote a score to *East of Eden*, starring James Dean. Another dissonant, edgy score accompanying a successful film with a popular star did much for establishing that dissonance as an acceptable sound both in the ears of the audience and the minds and pocketbooks of the producers.

jazz

dissonance

[handwritten margin notes: biblical movies still used the Romantic + conservative techniques]

In addition to the darker kinds of films that were being produced, there was also a great deal of activity in producing big epics, often based on biblical stories. These films, like *Ben-Hur, The Ten Commandments, Quo Vadis, El Cid*, and many others, required a more conservative score harkening back to the Romantic approach.

Some composers, such as Elmer Bernstein, had the facility to write a contemporary, edgy score like *The Man with the Golden Arm* and then switch gears and write a Romantic score to an epic or adventure film. Here is Elmer Bernstein speaking about creating the score to *The Ten Commandments* (1955) according to the musical tastes of director Cecil B. DeMille:

> *DeMille was a great Wagner lover. His concept of film scoring was utterly simple and very Wagnerian. Every character had to have a theme or motif. In addition to the characters having themes and leitmotifs, certain philosophical concepts had to have motifs too. God, good, and evil each had to have a theme. The idea was that whenever a particular character was on the screen, his theme had to be present as well. It was all very Wagnerian.*

Because of the leitmotif nature of the score and DeMille's desires, this score was more Romantic than modern in its musical language. That is what was necessary, and yet it didn't prevent Bernstein from being able to create a jazz score to *The Man with the Golden Arm* in the same year.

Another composer to take on scoring several epic films was Miklos Rozsa. A Hungarian-born composer with a doctorate in music, Rozsa had a passion for musicology. For films involving historical subjects, he did extensive research and tried to create a musical sound that was palatable to the average audience, yet based on real historical musical premises, motives, and instruments. His scores to *Ben-Hur, El Cid, Quo Vadis*, and others are large, grand and well thought out. They established a standard to which many composers writing these kinds of scores had to bear up.

Theme Songs and Rock 'n Roll

In every period of movies there has been the issue of the theme song, pop song, or end-title song. From the early days of sound films, producers realized the financial benefits of having a hit song. Not only could they entice more people into the theater to see the film, but they could sell more records (CDs in modern times) and sheet music. And because they owned the copyright to the song, they could collect on performance royalties if the song became a radio hit. This "theme song craze" has never really been a craze; it has always been present, only sometimes the frenzy has been slightly greater than others. Every era has had its hit songs, from the '30s and '40s onward to today and the success of "My Heart Will Go On" from *Titanic*.

A significant wave of theme songs began in the 1950s with the huge popularity of the song, "Do Not Forsake Me, Oh My Darlin'," written by Dimitri Tiomkin and Ned Washington for the movie *High Noon*. However, the popularity of this song doesn't come close to the ongoing success of Henry Mancini's 1961 hit, "Moon River," from the film *Breakfast at Tiffany's*, starring Audrey Hepburn.   ✳

Mancini was another Juilliard-trained composer with a strong jazz background. He had his first major success with the theme for the 1958 TV show, *Peter Gunn*. Then came "Moon River" followed the next year by "The Days of Wine and Roses" for the film of the same name. He went on to score dozens of films of every dramatic style, but remains best known to the general public for "Moon River," "The Days of Wine and Roses," and the scores to the Peter Sellers comedy series, *The Pink Panther*.

By this time, the early 1960s, producers could not get enough of the theme song. The producer of the film *Dr. Zhivago* was so enthralled with Maurice Jarre's melody to "Lara's Theme" that he basically discarded much of the original score and substituted tracks of the song melody. Later in the 1960s we get "Raindrops Keep Fallin' on My Head" in *Butch Cassidy and the Sundance Kid*, and "Mrs. Robinson" in *The Graduate*.

✳ examples of "theme songs"

used to *still more money* *animate more money*

#%%

These songs paved the way for a different use of songs in film. Instead of having the song be sung by a character on screen, or be part of the credits, all of a sudden a pop song, which is seemingly disembodied from the film, became an integral part of the soundtrack. The style evolved where a song was just "dropped in" to the movie soundtrack. Maybe the lyrics were applicable, maybe not. Maybe there was a dramatic reason to have a song, maybe not. For some producers, the only reason to have a song in the film was to hope it became a hit, generated lots of royalties, and caused people to go see the film. And as the popularity of theme songs grew, at least amongst Hollywood producers, more and more films came to rely on songs rather than specifically composed instrumental underscores.

Another factor contributing to this was the rock 'n' roll soundtrack. Beginning with the beach movies of the early 1960s, given a mighty push forward by the Beatles films, *A Hard Day's Night* and *Help!*, and coming to full fruition with the cult classic, *Easy Rider*, films consisting completely of rock songs as underscore became vogue. As the dark, edgy films of the '50s appealed to that audience, these rock 'n' roll films of the 1960s were aimed at the ever-expanding audience embracing the values of the "Woodstock generation." They were pertinent and popular. And truly, the use of songs was completely appropriate. How else to express the tone of those times but through the music of popular songs? The Grateful Dead. Simon and Garfunkel. Bob Dylan, Buffalo Springfield. Steppenwolf and The Flying Burrito Brothers were perfect for *Easy Rider.* This was absolutely the right music in the right place for certain films.

The problem that arises when this kind of trend hits is that producers and directors jump on the bandwagon rather blindly. When something new works in one movie, there are always several people doing imitations within a short period of time. So instead of choosing a style of music that serves the dramatic intent of the picture, they choose music that they believe is popular or will sell a lot of records. This was a problem in the 1960s, and it is still a problem today.

This is not to say that instrumental underscore in the 1960s became a lost art. Although some prevailing trends favored rock songs, and even jazzy underscores (*The Pink Panther*, some of the James Bond movies), there were many excellent orchestral-type scores. Elmer Bernstein's score for *To Kill a Mockingbird* is a beautiful example of the marriage of compositional structure and dramatic intent. Many other composers of note were active in keeping alive the orchestral vocabulary, including Jerry Goldsmith, Leonard Rosenman, John Barry, Georges Delerue, Maurice Jarre, and John Williams. The trends became parallel. One kind of movie still used traditional orchestral scores, another used pop and rock songs, another kind used jazz-influenced scores, and yet another used more dissonant and avant-garde twentieth century compositional techniques. The possibilities were expanding even as they were heavily weighted towards songs and jazz music during the 1960s.

influences:
- Bartok
- Stravinsky
- Schoenberg
- 20th c.
- Jazz
- pop
- Rock n Roll

Composers:
- Hermann *
- Raskin *
- North *
- Antheil
- Rosenman *
- Bernstein
- Previn
- Goldsmith
- Copland *
- Mancini *
- Barry
- Delerue
- Jarre
- Williams

movies:
- Citizen Kane *
- The Heiress *
- Of Mice and Men *
- The Red Pony
- A Streetcar Named Desire *
- East of Eden *
- The Man With the Golden Arm
- Breakfast At Tiffany's *
- The Pink Panther *
- Easy Rider *
- To Kill A Mockingbird

influences:
- Rock
- pop
- dissonance
- television
- 12 tone/atonal

composers:
- Mancini
- Schifrin
- Hefti
- Goldsmith *
- Williams*
- Vangelis
- Homer
- Poledouris
- Silvestri *
- Zimmer*
- Safan
- Kamen
- Horner
- Elfman*

movies:

TV {
- Peter Gunn
- Mission Impossible
- Batman
}
- Chinatown*
- Patton
- Jaws*
- Starwars*
- E.T.*
- Chariots of Fire
- Hoosier
- Witness
- Field of Dreams
- Conan the Barbarian
- Romancing the Stone

- Miami Vice
- Rain Man*
- Driving Miss Daisy
- The Lion King
- Beyond Rangoon
- Stand And Deliver*
- Lethal Weapon
- The Last Boy Scout
- Paris, Texas

CHAPTER 6

1975 to Today

I think music is one of the most effective ways of preparing an audience and reinforcing points that you wish to impose on it. The correct use of music, and this includes the non-use of music, is one of the greatest weapons that the film maker has at his disposal.
—Stanley Kubrick

During the 1960s and into the 1970s, as films incorporated scores of many different styles, audiences became accustomed to the pop/rock sound and modern dissonance instead of 19th-century-influenced orchestral underscore. This paved the way in the subconscious awareness of the public to accept what was coming down the road in the 1980s and '90s: the pop flavored orchestral score. But in the '60s and '70s, perhaps the biggest influence on what producers put in the theaters was television.

Many TV themes and underscores were heavily jazz and rock flavored. In an attempt to modernize the shows and make them different from "stuffy" film scores, the producers incorporated contemporary popular music. Mancini's *Peter Gunn*, Lalo Schifrin's *Mission Impossible*, Neil Hefti's *Batman*, and many others reflected this use of jazz and rock. In addition, twelve-tone and other methods of atonal composition began to be heavily used by television composers. In television, because the schedules and demands of a weekly series meant the composer had to work quickly and efficiently, twelve-tone became a valuable tool for writing tense or suspenseful scenes. Once again, in yet another way, audiences became accustomed to a new musical vocabulary. In the space of just fifteen or twenty years, from about 1950 onward, a whole new world of musical sounds became possible, and many composers took advantage of this.

One score that is representative of the new kinds of textures used by composers in the early 1970s was Jerry Goldsmith's *Chinatown*, starring Jack Nicholson. In this score, Goldsmith used four pianos, two harps, one trumpet, and strings. The pianos were often "prepared," a technique where various objects are put on the strings to change the sound; the piano is intentionally detuned, or the player actually plays the strings inside the piano rather than the keys. This created a uniquely dark and mysterious texture that dovetails beautifully with the rhythm of the film, the way the film is lit, and Jack Nicholson's acting.

In his score to *Patton*, Goldsmith used another unusual technique, that of sweetening, or adding an instrument after the main music tracks have been recorded. In this case he took a short motif on trumpet and recorded it several different ways with a lot of echo. This little idea was then dropped in wherever needed regardless of the harmonic and metrical consequences. It created a disjointed feeling, reflecting the odd and sometimes otherworldly aspect of the character of General George Patton.

These interesting and unusual devices were becoming more common in the early 1970s. As 19th century harmony, contemporary 20th century techniques, jazz, and rock collided together in the entertainment industry, a myriad of possibilities opened up. Audiences gradually became used to hearing strange dissonances, and even came to associate certain impending events with specific musical sounds. Add to this mix the new technology of multitrack recording (early 1960s), and the possibilities expand even more. The film composer's palette was larger and more varied than ever, but during the 1960s through the early 1970s, orchestral scores, though still used, had fallen somewhat out of favor. It was a succession of two scores—one melodramatic and suspenseful, the other big, dramatic and traditionally Romantic in style, that were to create a resurgence in orchestral scores.

Orchestral Scores Return to Stay

The year 1974 saw the release of the Stephen Spielberg film *Jaws*, which was to become one of the classics of suspense and drama. Spielberg and composer John Williams chose to use a more traditional orches-

Jaws helped the resurgence
of orchestral scores & Romantic
techniques

1975 to Today

tral sound for *Jaws,* and the success of this decision and the resulting score has often been credited with beginning a resurgence of the use of traditional orchestral sounds and a Romantic, or perhaps neo-Romantic musical vocabulary. However, even though *Jaws* was a milestone in the return of the use of a traditional orchestra, there was yet another John Williams score that made movie music come alive in the ears (and the eyes!) of the audience.

In early 1976, the first trailers (previews attached to other films) for the motion picture *Star Wars* appeared in American theaters. Believe it or not, those audiences laughed and jeered at the trailers, causing great consternation for George Lucas and the studio. However, when the film was released it became one of the all-time most popular films, making huge profits not only from ticket sales, but from ancillary merchandising as well. And many give the exciting score by John Williams a fair share of the credit for the film's success. From the moment the opening scroll gave the story background, and the bold *Star Wars* theme was heard, the audience knew that something special was about to happen.

According to Williams, when he first viewed the work-print, it had a temporary music track cut from the 1916 Gustav Holst piece, *The Planets.* He originally was asked to edit this well-known classical score, re-record it, and fit it to *Star Wars.* However, he convinced the producer and director that he could do something original in that style, and make it fit even better. The result is one we all know today: the wonderful themes for the Rebellion, the dark and ominous Darth Vader theme, Princess Leia's theme, and other fine musical moments are familiar to musicians and non-musicians alike. Using a large symphony orchestra and recording in London with the London Philharmonic, Williams brought back the symphonic score to the ears and eyes of filmgoers.

This was not exactly a return to the Romantic style of Korngold and Steiner. The score to *Star Wars* has many elements of Romantic musical language: lyrical themes, exciting brass tuttis, and delicate woodwind writing, but this new kind of orchestral score was not afraid to incorporate contemporary compositional techniques where necessary. John Williams was schooled at Juilliard and UCLA, and has a thorough knowledge of many different styles of composition, including jazz, 12-tone and atonal techniques. So the score to *Star Wars*, and many scores of Williams and others that followed this lead, fused elements of tonal 19th century writing with whatever textures or effects they wanted to use from the 20th century: Impressionism, jazz, rock, pandiatonicism, 12-tone, even aleatoric, or "chance" music.

None of this was new in film scoring; examples of all these techniques abound through the 1950s, 1960s, and 1970s. But something happened when *Stars Wars* was released that caused a shift in the way orchestras were perceived, in the acceptance by the audience of the music as a dramatic effect, and in the popularity of this music. It was one more milestone in the constantly developing art of film scoring.

In 1982, another Spielberg directed film with a John Williams score took the film-going world by storm. This was *E.T., The Extra-Terrestrial*, a magical film with an enchanting score that was loved by adults and children alike. Indeed, Spielberg has said, "John Williams *is* E.T.," emphasizing how important the music was to the emotional impact of that film. Again, as in *Star Wars*, Williams combined a lyrical, tonal style with elements of 20th century styles. (For examples of this modern influence, check out the scenes where E.T. drinks the beer from the refrigerator, and when the children take E.T. trick-or-treating.)

The popularity of these kinds of scores opened the door for many other composers to follow suit and incorporate any possible sound they wanted. But the film-scoring industry was about to undergo a massive infusion of new sounds and possibilities, and the whole business of film music was to shift yet again as it absorbed the new technologies of synthesizers and the personal computer.

Synthesizers and Computers: A Whole New Ballgame

It is ironic that only a few short years after the resurgence of the orchestral score, the score created entirely, or mostly, using electronic synthesizers became all the rage. Around the late 1970s, synthesizer technology had progressed to where keyboards were affordable. Previously synthesizers had been used in movies, but the ARP and Moog were

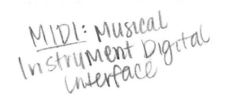

large, expensive, and cumbersome machines that required a huge amount of expertise to operate. The new technology quickly caught on, and the manufacturers were wise enough to create MIDI, Musical Instrument Digital Interface, a language that allowed synthesizers and computers of any manufacturer to interface or talk to each other.

The score that caught the public's attention, and made every producer in Hollywood want the same thing, was Vangelis's score to the 1981 film, *Chariots of Fire*. This score was entirely electronic, with no acoustic instruments at all. The synthesizer technology at the time was primitive compared to today. All Vangelis had to work with were analog synthesizers, since digital had yet to arrive. There was no sampling, digital editing, or hard-disk recording. The various synthesizer sounds were recorded to a multitrack analog tape machine in Vangelis's home studio.

The impact of this score cannot be overstated. It opened the ears of producers, directors, composers, and the general public to the possibility of using electronic sounds in a lyrical manner. Previously, synthesizer and other electronic sounds like the theremin were used in high intensity dramatic situations and science fiction films. They were usually part of a scary, spooky, or otherworldly musical landscape. Vangelis, in one stroke, showed the world that it could be otherwise.

Not only did this score make a huge impact on the success of the film, but it became a commercial hit, selling millions of records and tapes, and getting serious radio airplay. Of course, many producers jumped on the bandwagon and wanted a similar kind of sound for their films. Since Vangelis clearly could not do them all, it meant that other, more traditionally-minded composers would learn the new technology to one degree or another.

The availability and affordability of synthesizers in the mid-1980s was actually embraced by many composers, both the up-and-coming youngsters and the older generation. What open-minded musician could turn his back on the possibility of adding yet another entirely new dimension of sounds to his palette? Jerry Goldsmith, Maurice Jarre, Elmer Bernstein, and many others began to incorporate electronic sounds into their scores, or even compose scores that were completely electronic. Goldsmith's score to _Hoosiers_ and Jarre's score to _Witness_ are but two examples of traditionally-trained, established Hollywood composers writing scores that used electronic instruments exclusively. Younger composers like James Horner, Basil Poledouris, and Alan Silvestri began to incorporate synthesizer sounds in scores like _Field of Dreams_, _Conan the Barbarian_, and _Romancing the Stone._ Of course, some of this was necessary as producers were requesting it, but composers found that electronic instruments could aid them in creating new textures.

The swiftness of the rise of this technology was awesome. In a few short years the industry went from having access to only the most primitive electronic sound generators to having extremely sophisticated digital equipment at its fingertips. One downside of this was that for a period of time, many string, brass, and wind players faced a shortage of work. Although there were still many orchestral sessions in L.A. during this time, there were less than before because synthesizers were taking the place of the live musicians. In addition, many TV producers, influenced by the success of the score to _Miami Vice,_ also switched to completely or partially using synthesizers. The whole world of commercial music was shaken up and altered forever by the arrival of synthesizers and computers.

One of the consequences of this new medium was that because of the expertise needed to master the ever-expanding synthesizer and MIDI technology, an entirely new niche and a new kind of film composer was born: the specialist in electronic, synthesizer scores. These composers became experts in synthesizer sounds, sampling, MIDI technology and sequencing (the technique of using computers instead of analog tape to record the synthesizers or samplers). German born Hans Zimmer was one of the first to establish himself in this field, and has had many successful scores using either entirely electronically generated music or a combination of electronic and acoustical sounds. His scores to _Rain Man, Driving Miss Daisy, The Lion King_, and _Beyond Rangoon_ are just some examples of his work. Zimmer and his team have been on the cutting edge of developing new technology and creating new sounds with samplers and digital synthesizers.

[handwritten margin note: sequencing: the technique of using computers instead of analog tape to record the synthesizers or samplers]

Because of the affordability and relative ease of use of MIDI equipment, many young composers today are writing quality electronic scores for features, television, cable, and documentaries. This technology has become a necessary skill for film composers.

Even though the synthesizer craze hit hard and made a deep impact—not only on the sound and texture of film scores, but on the recording industry in general—the pendulum always swings back, as we have seen with other styles. In this case, after the initial rush to use electronic instruments a la Vangelis, many directors and producers began to recognize the cold and sometimes false sounding nature of these instruments. It was one thing to use synthesizers or samplers to create a new and unusual texture, or combine them with orchestral instruments, but the scores that used them to replace orchestral instruments tended to sound dry and phony. For example, if a string section or cello solo is playing beneath an action scene or under dialogue, then a really good sample can sometimes fool the audience. But if the same music is in an exposed place where there is little in the soundtrack to compete with it, even an inexperienced listener can often hear that it is electronically generated and not real.

The result of this was that composers began to use electronic instruments more as an adjunct to an orchestra, unless the director specified an electronic score. (Here, I am speaking of feature films. For television, cable, and low-budget films, often the film's music budget would not allow the use of an orchestra, and electronic instruments became a necessity.) In addition, many synthesizer specialists, such as Hans Zimmer, began to write scores that incorporated full orchestras. A middle ground was found, and it continues to this day as producers, directors, and composers continue to strive for appropriate uses of electronic sounds.

Pop Sounds, Jazz, and Rock 'n' Roll Composers

For many reasons, the language of rock and pop music has found its way into film scores in general. As we have seen, every style of film music has reflected, to some degree, the film-going audience. For example, in the '30s and '40s the audience understood 19th-century romanticism, and in the '50s and '60s they resonated with jazz-oriented scores. Today, the range of possibilities is the largest it has ever been.

As pop, rock, and jazz styles became more mainstream through the 1970s, their use in films grew. The influences that rock music brings to the world of film scoring are basically threefold: one, rock rhythms and grooves; two, a certain harmonic vocabulary spanning the traditional blues to progressive pop-, rock-, and jazz-influenced songwriting; and three, pop/rock melodic ideas.

Rock rhythms are the easiest to identify when they are used in film scores. This could be a traditional rhythm section of guitar, keyboard, bass, and drums; a hybrid combination of those instruments; or "world" music beats giving a hipper sound to the score. These kinds of sounds have been used in countless scores. In the 1980s, Hans Zimmer used a "world beat" kind of percussion groove in *Rain Man*, Craig Safan used a hip-hop groove for *Stand and Deliver*, and Alan Silvestri used synthesized drums in a quasi-Latin disco beat for *Romancing the Stone*. In the 1990s, Michael Kamen has used rock grooves in the *Lethal Weapon* series and *The Last Boy Scout*.

Many of the harmonic and melodic ideas used by film composers today draw upon pop melodic and harmonic ideas. This can be heard in the scores of those coming from the record industry as well as those coming from the conservatories. Anyone going into film music today knows that there is a fusion between orchestral styles and pop music. James Horner studied at the Royal Academy of Music in London, and Michael Kamen studied at Juilliard, but they can write a pop hit as well as a traditional sounding score. And this is no different from composers of the previous generation like Henry Mancini who did the same thing.

The one difference that exists today is that a composer can be a success in the film industry, and write orchestral scores without any, or minimal knowledge of the orchestra. This can happen because of two factors: one, orchestrators who assist and prepare a full score from a sketch or a tape, and two, the ease of using synthesizers and MIDI technology. Therefore, a talented rock or jazz musician who has some great creative ideas can realize a score that is beyond the scope of his actual orchestral ability.

In order to understand this trend fully, we must go back a few years. In the 1970s and 1980s yet another wrinkle was added to the film scoring community: the desire by some producers and directors to use well-known rock and jazz musicians to create a score for their films. In retrospect, the validity of this idea can be seen, but it seems to have had mixed success.

The impact of the popular music of the 1960s and 1970s cannot be underestimated. No other generation bought as many records, went to as many concerts, or looked to rock musicians for philosophical, political, and social leadership as did the Baby Boomers coming of age in the '60s and '70s. So it was logical that by the late '70s, the same Baby Boomers who were producing and directing films wanted to use the musicians they considered to be icons. The thinking was that these musicians would speak to the audience through the soundtrack as they did in concert or on records. This was a good idea in theory, but in practice it was dangerous for several reasons.

First, a film score requires the ability to create a musical structure that tells a story and remains harmonically and melodically interesting for about two hours. The average pop song is three or four minutes, and many of these artists do not have the expertise needed to sustain and develop their ideas in the way a film demands. Second, film scores need to have a well thought-out texture of sounds, and the experienced composer will draw upon a wide variety of instrumental possibilities. Most rock and jazz stars, although fine players in their own medium, are only able to execute a much narrower range of sounds and styles. If a film calls for this kind of narrow range, then a rock or jazz artist might be an appropriate choice. Finally, the successful film score comes from a composer knowing that he is a partner to the drama. There is a sensitivity that develops from working with many different pictures and different styles of music. The rock or jazz composer who only knows concert performance and CD recording is at a severe disadvantage when attempting to work in the unfamiliar medium of film.

This is not to say that there cannot be a successful rock or jazz score. It can and has happened. Eric Clapton has made fine contributions to the *Lethal Weapon* series. Ry Cooder has written some interesting scores including *Paris, Texas.* Jazz trumpet player Terence Blanchard has become a proficient composer and orchestrator.

One rock musician composer that has consistently stood out from the rest is Danny Elfman. Formerly with the L.A. band, Oingo Boingo, he began scoring films for director Tim Burton in the late 1980s. With *Pee Wee's Great Adventure*, *Batman*, and *The Nightmare Before Christmas*, Elfman established himself as someone very creative with melodies and sound textures, who caught the imagination of many. He showed a great ability to capture the mood of the different kinds of films he wrote for and has established a cult-like following amongst musicians and non-musicians alike.

There are many composers coming up in the ranks of pop and rock music that do not orchestrate, and occasionally there are stories of those who cannot even read music. This is a far cry from the Korngolds and Steiners, but it is the state of the industry today. But if a musician can create the right mood, and with the right musical support can appropriately heighten the drama of a film, is it a bad thing that they know nothing about an orchestra? This is an open-ended question that has proponents on both sides.

In addition to the many rock musicians who have limited orchestral skills, there are still those who have training in orchestration and composing. Today's film music is richer than ever. Part of this richness is due to rock and jazz composers who bring their own special kind of sound. Another aspect is the range of possibilities afforded from traditional symphony orchestras to electronic scores, and hybrids and fusions of the two. Today's composer can work in just about any sound medium he wants that will accomplish the director's vision of the film.

CHAPTER 7

Film-Scoring Technology

I was and still am to this day fascinated and excited by
the possibilities of using machines to make music.
—*Harry Gregson-Williams*

The film-scoring world is centered around the use of technology. Gone are the days of the lonely composer sitting in his or her studio with a piano and many blank pads of score paper. The modern film composer is surrounded by computers containing thousands of dollars' worth of software, various outboard devices, and often an assistant or two to help with MIDI programming and technical issues. This composer is expected to produce high quality demos, mock-ups, and final scores from this studio. While composers of the past were expected to be experts in composition, orchestration, and perhaps conducting, today's composer also needs to be expert in audio production and sequencing using sample libraries. Many films and most TV shows do not have the budget for live players, so all the music must be created "in the box:" the computer.

It is a wonderful thing to be able to put our hands on a computer keyboard, open up some software, make a few clicks of the mouse, and voilà! We hear an entire orchestra with just a few moments of work. Obviously, this was not always the case, and for today's computer-literate composer, it is important to understand the development and use of technology in scoring—important not just from a historical standpoint, but to understand how technology works and how it impacts one's own compositional process. In addition, it really is necessary for the contemporary film composer to have a broad knowledge of possible electronic sounds and samples ranging from the most current to older, "retro" analog synth sounds.

Film-Scoring Technology Timeline

From the very first primitive recording and playback machines to today's most sophisticated computers, we have relied on technology to offload music from our imaginations to the final mix that accompanies a film. What is truly stunning is the speed with which technological change has overtaken us. Analog recording was the standard for about fifty years, from the 1930s to the 1980s. Then the recording world was turned on its head with the advent of affordable analog and digital synths, digital recording techniques, the commercial success of CDs, and the explosive growth in both the power and affordability of computers.

The sum of all this technological change is that instead of needing to write music on paper, orchestrate it, and conduct it, the most basic skill set needed for today's composer is creative musicianship as well as facility and expertise with hardware and software. Of course, the composers who have applied themselves, studied all styles of music, and have skills in orchestration and composition will have a much deeper repertoire of musical ideas than those who are relying only on raw talent and technology. But there is room in the film-scoring world for many different composers with a wide range and variety of abilities.

Synthesizer Technology

The first synthesizers used in film music were analog instruments like the theremin, the ARP 2500, and the Moog. The theremin, created in 1928 by a Russian inventor named Leon Theremin, is instantly recognizable from dozens of scores to science fiction movies. Dmitri Shostakovitch used it as early as 1931 in *Odna*, and it has been heard in scores such as *Spellbound*, *The Day the Earth Stood Still*, *The Lost Weekend*, *The Ten Commandments*, and *Ed Wood*. (Though perhaps one of the most well-known usages of a theremin is the opening of the 1966 Beach Boys tune "Good Vibrations.")

 In the 1960s and 1970s, composers had access to much more sophisticated machines made by ARP and Moog. These were also analog synths, but gave the user the ability to combine tone generators, waveforms, and oscillators to create a huge palette of possible sounds.

These instruments were large and very complex and required very sophisticated skills, hence restricting a composer's ability to use them easily. Most composers hired synthesizer experts to program the instruments, though there are some, like Jerry Goldsmith, who owned one and could program it himself. The early ARP and Moog synthesizers can be heard on *Close Encounters of the Third Kind* (the mother ship), *Logan's Run, Sorcerer,* and *A Clockwork Orange* (the synthesized versions of Beethoven pieces produced by Wendy Carlos).

In the 1980s, we saw a big shift toward using synthesizers, either exclusively or combined with live instruments. This is when electronic instruments became user-friendly enough for the general musical public. The first of these synths, such as the Prophet-5 and Jupiter-8, were still analog but had a wide range of accessible sounds and were much easier to use than the early ARP and Moog synths. Then the first mass-market digital synthesizer, the Yamaha DX-7, was released in 1983 and allowed the use of more than one sound at the same time (known as polyphony). This was a huge advance and is still a technology basically used today.

Perhaps one of the most important technological advances was the development of MIDI, or Musical Instrument Digital Interface, in 1983. MIDI is a "language" in which musical notes are translated into digital information. At the time of its creation, MIDI was mainly used to control several synthesizers or samplers from one keyboard. Once the personal computer hit the market, however, the power of MIDI became even more evident, as the MIDI data could be recorded in a sequencing program, manipulated within the computer, and played back from small, portable files. It is important to note that one of the ways that MIDI is so powerful is that in representing musical notes as digital information, the size of the digital file really is quite small. This is in contrast to an audio file, which is a waveform of an actual note, and takes up a much larger amount of memory.

In terms of film scores during the 1980s, the scores by Vangelis for *Chariots of Fire* (1981) and *Blade Runner* (1982) were instrumental in bringing a synth sound to the general public. The soundtrack CD from *Chariots of Fire* became a huge hit and was the first electronic

Handwritten margin notes:

Polyphony: the use of more than one sound at a time

MIDI: a language in which musical notes are translated into digital info

57

score to win an Oscar. Many producers and directors followed the lead of this score and requested similar sounding scores for their films. *Witness* and *Hoosiers* are but two good examples out of dozens of 1980s synth scores.

In addition, during the 1980s, drum machines first became available and musically sophisticated enough to have many different possible combinations of sounds and beats. These became hugely popular for action films such as *Romancing the Stone* (1984). The early drum machines sounded slightly false and rhythmically too perfect, but created grooves and an ambience that sounded new and fresh at the time.

Samplers

The final piece of pre-desktop computer technology is that of samplers. These are electronic devices that use a digital recording of an instrument that can then be digitally reproduced and manipulated. The earliest samplers were outboard pieces of equipment, while today the sampler is usually a software program. In either case, the way it works is that the machine or software takes a "sample" (a digital recording) of one note or phrase from an actual instrument and plays it back at various pitches as instructed by a MIDI keyboard or instrument. So, for example, one note played on a violin could then be used as the basis for playing any note in the spectrum on the MIDI keyboard. However, this did not reproduce believable performances, and the end result often sounded phony. Today when reproducing, say, a violin, more than one sample will be used to accurately represent the total range and playing styles of the instrument.

Remember, at first, computers were not used to reproduce samples, instead this was done with hardware specifically designed for this purpose. Composers resorted to linking many samplers using MIDI. An old picture of Hans Zimmer's studio from the early 1990s shows a wall that had dozens of samplers capable of being used together to create an electronic orchestra. Each sampler was restricted to reproducing a small number of samples of an instrument or instrument group, like a solo French horn or a violin section. Although it worked, this was a cumbersome method with an extremely complex electronic setup.

[Handwritten margin note: Samplers: electronic devices that use of an instrument reproduced & manipulated. a digital recording of an instrument then be digitally reproduced & manipulated.]

(To give an idea of the state of technology at this time, around 1989, I did a project requiring the use of samples, which were to be added after a live session. I went to a studio where they had several Akai samplers, and had to sift through boxes of floppy disks—each disk containing one instrument sound! Then, to preview the sound, each disk had to be loaded into the sampler one at a time. Compare that with today's software and sample libraries in which there is not only instant preview on the computer, but the ability to play dozens of sample-based instruments at once.)

Package Deals and Home Studios

One interesting development during the 1980s is that because of the viability and popularity of synth scores, package deals (also called "all-in" deals) became desirable both for producers and composers. (Also see chapter 21) This is when the composer gets a flat fee and is then financially responsible for composing, recording, and producing the music. (When the composer gets a creative fee, the producer is then responsible for the production costs.) Because synthesizers were affordable and popular, more and more composers were setting up their own project studios using samples and synthesized sounds, though still mostly recording onto multitrack tape. This eliminated the expense and logistics of hiring live musicians, and composers could then negotiate a fee for creating *and* producing the music that was more than they would have received for just creating it, and less than the producer would have paid for the composing and live production.

It was in the mid-to-late 1990s that computer processors became powerful enough and fast enough to efficiently record audio on a personal computer. This was a huge shift toward cementing the home studio paradigm for composers. The final component of this shift was the technology that allowed samples to be stored on and accessed from computer hard drives. This allowed composers to buy one or more powerful computers and have a full virtual orchestra at their fingertips. This was a huge improvement over the previous methods.

Recording Technology

In the early days of film, music was recorded on wire spools, and eventually magnetic tape. Until the late 1950s – mid 1960s, this was always in mono. (Older scores tend to have a one-dimensional sound in addition to the low-fidelity recording quality, which is very poor by today's standards.) Therefore, until the late 1950s, when multitrack recording became an option, all music for both records and film had to be recorded live. If a take had a wrong note or other error in it, it was not usable. Different takes could be edited together by splicing the tape, but this was not always possible, either for deadline reasons or for musical and technical reasons. With the advent of multitrack recording, different instruments could be isolated and mistakes more easily fixed. The music could be layered, and no longer required all the players to be present at once.

However, it is important to point out that *as much as multitracking has been used in the record industry, it was not used very much for orchestral film scores until recent years.* This is because it is much more efficient and musical to record the entire orchestra at once. Deadlines are so demanding that there is no time to be lost doing overdubs. It was and is much more time-efficient to get everyone recorded at the same time. With the superlative quality of recording musicians in L.A., New York City, or London, it is routine to expect great live takes. (More on this later in this chapter.)

 The next advance beyond multitrack magnetic tape came in the 1980s with the advent of digital tape. This is when the music is converted to a digital signal of ones and zeros, and is recorded on magnetic tape. It is a step up in clarity and has a noticeable absence of noise compared to analog recording. But the common use of digital tape lasted only about twenty years (if that), and has been replaced by hard-disk recording. (Note that the use of analog tape has lingered, but is very rare, even though some in the recording industry prefer the "warmer" sound of tape as opposed to the drier, more defined sound of digital recording. However, very few studios are left that use multitrack tape, and the tape itself is becoming harder to purchase.)

Hard-disk recording, or recording directly into a computer or an external hard drive, is the next step and is what is current today. The first Mac desktop computers in the early 1990s had what were considered to be robust hard drives of 40 megabytes! When that went to 1 gigabyte, people in the techno world thought they were in memory heaven. However, it took until the end of that decade for hard drives to be large enough and fast enough to process the information that musical samples required, and for computer hard-disk recording to become a viable option. As of this writing, computers typically have a hard drive of at least 250 GB, and external hard drives can be much larger. A typical orchestral sample library can be 75 to 100 GB, and usually needs to be stored on an external hard drive.

The state of technology as of this writing is that everything is, at least initially, on the computer desktop or on external hard drives. Composers have access to recording and editing programs such as Pro Tools, Logic, and Digital Performer; sample libraries such a Vienna Symphony Library, Garritan Personal Orchestra, and East-West Quantum Leap Symphony Orchestra; and notation programs such as Finale and Sibelius. All it takes to have the capability to produce a high quality track is a minimum investment in a computer and software. The ramifications of this are large, as it also means that you do not have to be the world's most schooled or even talented musician to create a track with at least the audio fidelity that would be expected for film or TV.

Today's Multitracking Composer

If a score is to be acoustic or orchestral in style using live musicians, because of the nature of deadlines and the very large orchestral ensembles often used, it is preferable for film scores to be recorded live with no or few overdubs. With the use of sequences, however, there is often the need to record just a part of the orchestra, with the rest remaining electronic. What happens in this situation is that the composer brings the sequenced tracks to the session for the live players to hear. So if, for example, live French horns are being recorded, they would hear the strings, woodwinds, other brass, etc., as recorded originally in MIDI.

The economics of the film industry has meant the closing of many of the very large scoring stages capable of fitting 100 or more players, as well as the medium studios that could fit 50 or so players. That leaves only a few large scoring stages and a handful of medium size ones. If a studio is already booked during the desired recording time (remember that because of the film's release deadlines, there is often very little room for movement of dates here), then the next best option is to record music in pieces using smaller groups. The advantage is that you can have some flexibility in the schedule by choosing smaller studios, of which there are more options. Also, the composer can focus on one section of the orchestra at a time at the actual session. The disadvantage, as stated, is that the cohesiveness of the ensemble playing together can be lost.

The Composer's Setup

It has been mentioned that all a composer needs to create a professional sounding score is a computer and software. Although this is true to a large extent, there are many different variations on the kind of computer and the type of software used. And this is always changing, usually very rapidly.

The first question people ask is usually, "Do I need a Mac or a PC?" If this question was asked in the 1990s, the answer would have been an unequivocal, "Mac!" Today, however, Windows technology has developed to where some professional studios run PCs instead of Macs. However, because Mac was first in pro music applications, it still has the majority of users.

In terms of software, there are many viable recording and sequencing programs, with some having a larger market share and therefore more industry viability than others. The one program that almost everyone uses to some degree is <u>Pro Tools</u>. For many years Pro Tools has been the industry standard for hard-disk recording, editing, and post-production. Oftentimes, if a composer works in another software program, they will still bounce their stereo or surround-sound mixes to Pro Tools for their final delivery to the director. This is because most post-production for sound is done in Pro Tools.

Pro Tools

*Digital Performer

Other popular recording and sequencing programs are Logic and Digital Performer for Mac, and Sonar for PC. In terms of market share, since Apple bought and retooled Logic, it has become very popular, with many composers switching from programs they had used for years. Without going into the pros and cons, let it be said that each program has its very strong supporters and detractors. Go to any industry conference or Internet chat room where such things are discussed and experience the passion.

would sample library

Finally, the film composer needs powerful and multi-faceted sample libraries. There are too many libraries out there to enumerate, but just about every composer who is out there working will tell you that you can't have too many samples. Start with a core of a good orchestral library and a good ethnic instrument library, and build from there.

To sum up, the use of technology has in many ways aided the film-scoring process. It can help to communicate musical ideas to directors via a mock-up in a way that the composer playing the piano and humming a melody never could. Technology enables us to make great sounding scores for a small budget. And it has opened up the field to many talented people who do not have formal musical training.

There are also some down sides to the use of technology. One down side is that the technology is constantly changing, and there is really no way to keep up with the changes. Another down side is that using samples and hearing back the music one writes instantaneously can actually inhibit the musical imagination and puts a damper on learning about various instruments firsthand. In teaching many students over the years, one thing that continually comes up is the idea of instant gratification, and how students prefer to learn from a sample library as opposed to seeking out the real instruments. This fosters a lack of understanding of how various instruments work and sound in a real acoustical setting.

Technology is best used as a tool—as one dimension of a composer's total skill set. Composition, knowledge of instrumentation, and arranging skills are still key to writing film music that could demand any number of styles and genres from a composer. With both technological expertise and a strong foundation in music there are many and varied opportunities awaiting the aspiring composer.

Composers:
- Shostakovich

Movies:
- Odna
- Spellbound
- The Day the Earth Stood Still
- The Lost Weekend
- The Ten Commandments
- Ed Wood
- Close Encounters of the Third Kind
- Logan's Run
- Sorcerer
- A Clockwork Orange
- Blade Runner

Production

PART II

CHAPTER 8

The Film-Making Process

*That's the fun part about movie collaboration.
You work intensely with a lot of people who are
different from you and you learn a lot from them.*
—*Oliver Stone*[1]

The making of a major motion picture is an incredibly complex, costly, creative, and challenging endeavor. It requires people with all kinds of skills. One look at the credits of a film gives an idea of the wide range of expertise needed to pull it off: writers, painters, truck drivers, electricians, carpenters, cameramen, directors, musicians, special-effects designers and technicians, make-up artists, costume designers, publicists, directors' assistants, production assistants, assistants to the assistants, and on and on the credits roll while the music plays. The beauty of a production is that these seemingly disparate groups of people are all working in an organized way to achieve a common goal: the release of the film.

What the average filmgoer may not realize is that many of these groups operate separately, yet parallel to the whole operation. For example, principal photography (the shooting of the film) might be finishing up on location in New Mexico and at a studio in Los Angeles, while a team of special-effects wizards is beginning to work their computer magic in Northern California, the sound-effects people are working at yet another studio in L.A., and the lonely composer is sitting in his studio behind his home in Beverly Hills staring at the swimming pool waiting for the final version of the film.

Actually, this is both far from the truth and close to the truth. Hopefully, nobody will be wasting their time waiting for a film to be completed before they start writing the music because so many films take longer than originally planned. But the reality of the film-making *locked picture/fine cut: final version; given to composer to sync up music to action*

process is that the *music is the very last thing to be done*. The reason for this is that in order to sync up the music to the action, the composer must wait for the final version, or *locked picture*, also known as a *fine cut*. Before getting into what the composer does, though, let's take a look at the film-making process itself.

Decision Makers

There are several people involved in getting a film off the ground: the producer, director, writer, and possibly the talent (actors). These are the people whose creative, financial, and organizational skills actually drive the production.

Producer: oversees the financial and organizational aspects of the film.

The *producer* oversees the financial and organizational aspects of the film. This person supervises the hiring of everyone from director and actors to carpenters and electricians. He makes sure there is a workable schedule and ensures that all elements of the production are running smoothly, from the writing of the script to the feeding of the crew. The producer is responsible for the financial bottom line, and answers to the executives at the movie studio that will release the film.

Producer Darryl Zanuck:

> *People outside of Hollywood and New York don't really have a clear idea of what a producer is or what he does.... Most people think a producer is the person who puts up the money, which is wrong. If you're smart, you never put up the money yourself!*[2]

Even without putting up his own money, the responsibility for a producer can be enormous, as budgets for feature films climb higher and higher. To paraphrase one producer, a movie can be made for $50 million dollars and last one or two weeks in the theaters. But a huge skyscraper can be bought for the same amount of money and stand for decades. However, the producer does much more than just raise money. He is the one who must shepherd a project through the maze of production. This involves coordinating all the creative people, the technicians, the marketing experts, and the financial overseers.

Zanuck again:

> *Even with the right people, this isn't the furniture business or the car business. You have a lot of personalities and a lot of egos, so there are many factors at play.*
>
> *It's easy to go astray and very tough to carry the vision through completely every inch of the way, to make it all work. There's economic pressures, there's time pressures, and there are always personality conflicts when you put so many people together. Everyone works for the common cause, but it is an ego-driven business, and there's a lot of pushing and shoving going on.[3]*

The organization of the team is one of the producer's main jobs, and the three main components of that team are the writer, the director, and the actors. However, it is the director who is the most important day-to-day member of the team. Once the shooting begins, the producer often keeps his distance and lets the director achieve his vision for the film.

The *director* is the creative captain of the project. He has the overall vision for what the film will say and look like. He must also be able to communicate that vision to everyone working on the project and be strong enough to hold to that vision as the film makes its journey from script to silver screen. That means coordinating the creative efforts of many people. Director Ron Howard puts it this way:

> *The buck does stop with the director, but there are so many others involved. I think that the sooner we all see the same movie in our heads, the sooner the collaborative process works and the film benefits from the valuable ideas coming from all those different areas of expertise.[4]*

The director approves the script (sometimes writing it himself), and oversees all the design elements of the film including the cinematography (the camera angles, lighting, and overall "look of the film"), costumes, sets, props, hair, and make-up. The director is responsible for "directing" the actors on the set, deciding when a take is the right

[handwritten margin note: director: creative captain of the project; overall vision]

one, which scenes will be shot in which order, and keeping to the overall shooting schedule and budget. The director oversees the editing of the film after shooting is completed, and presents his version to the producer and studio executives for their approval. Except in the rare case of a director like Steven Spielberg or James Cameron, these higher-ups—the execs and producer—have the right to alter the film in any way they see fit. The director is often powerless to control the final version even though it represents months or even years of work.

The *writer, or scriptwriter* takes a story, an idea, a book or a play and makes it into a *screenplay,* or *script.* This person is responsible for creating a script that fits the director's and producer's desires for the film. This can mean that even if the writer is initially happy with a script, it might not be "finished" because of rewrites requested by the director or producer. The final version of the script that is used in the actual shooting of the film is called the *shooting script.*

The writer is responsible for creating an engaging story, making the characters believable, and writing dialogue that fits the characters and the tone of the film. Every line the actors speak, every scene, every part of the plot is considered and mulled over to make sure it is "just right." The screenplay then becomes a blueprint for the shooting of the film. Many people, including the director, producer, cinematographer, film editor, and the actors can have input on the script, both during the writing stage and during the shooting stage. This input can often make it even better as the collaborative process works its magic.

Sometimes several writers work on a film because a single author can't achieve the vision of the director or producer. On many films, "script doctors" are brought in to polish up either the whole thing, certain scenes, or lines of dialogue. Even with only one writer, a screenplay will go through many revisions before a final version, or shooting script, is ready. This process can take as short as a few weeks, or last as long as several years.

Putting It All Together

How does a film make its way from an idea in someone's head, a book, or a play to a multimillion-dollar production showing in your local theater? Depending on who comes up with the original idea for the movie, the process can unfold in different ways, and the people described come on board in a different order. There are three basic stages of this process: (1) getting the idea for the film, (2) obtaining financing, and (3) hiring the creative and organizational people to make the idea a reality. Often the process is from the top down; the producer gets an idea, receives a screenplay, or buys the rights to a book and then oversees the process from start to finish. However, there are many different ways the process can happen. Here are two possible alternatives to the scenario where the idea for the film originates with the producer:

Scenario 1: A director has an idea for a film, goes to a producer, and pitches a *treatment* (a short synopsis of the plot) to a producer. The producer agrees to undertake the project and begins arranging for financing. He hires a writer, usually with the director's approval. When the script is finished, the producer and director begin to contact actors for the lead roles. Important production roles, such as the cinematographer, film editor, and casting director are hired at this time. As the script nears completion, a production schedule is created and the rest of the crew is hired.

Scenario 2: An accomplished writer brings the first draft of a screenplay to a well-known director with whom he has an established relationship. The director loves the screenplay and agrees to direct it. The story calls for a strong action-hero type, so together they approach a well-known actor who also loves the idea. Next, this trio of proven professionals—writer, director, and movie star—presents a "package" to a producer. The packaged combination of talent, box-office draw, and exciting story line make the project irresistible, and the producer signs on quickly before they pitch the project elsewhere.

There can be many variations of this process, depending on who has the original idea and who that person's contacts might be. Many times an agent will get involved trying to package together two or more elements: writer and director, actor and director, producer, actor, and writer, etc. In the end, the process can be very political, with who-knows-whom being a big part of it. Sometimes it simply comes down to a matter of availability—an actor or director is just not available at the time this production would require him. And sometimes a project is pushed through by the sheer will of one of the parties involved because they believe in it. This is how the 1998 movie *The Apostle* got made. This film features Robert Duvall as actor, director, producer, and major financial backer. He invested several million of his own dollars because it was a project he believed in, and he wanted to see it get made. This is an example of one person performing several roles, putting his creative stamp on different aspects of the project. But whether it is one person filling multiple roles or many people dividing the roles, the making of a film is a huge, complicated, and enormously exciting process.

The Stages of a Film's Production

There are three stages of a film's production: *preproduction, production,* and *post-production.* Post-production can be divided into two parts: (1) editing and assembling the film, and (2) music, sound effects, and dubbing. Keep in mind that this business is a flexible one. Things are always changing and can happen in a different way or in a different order from what was originally projected. But these three main chronological divisions basically stay the same.

Preproduction is largely the process described in the previous section—the inception, planning, and development of an idea so that it can become an actual film.

Production: actual shooting of the movie [handwritten note in left margin]

☆ Preproduction involves:

- Conceiving the initial idea, or
- Obtaining the rights to a book, play or short story
- Writing the treatment
- Obtaining financing
- Writing the screenplay
- Hiring the principal creative people
- Casting (hiring the actors)
- Scheduling
- Scouting for locations (out-of-studio shooting)
- Hiring the crew

Production is the actual shooting of the movie. This can take weeks or months depending on the scale of the production. It is an exciting time when all the planning starts to become a physical reality. It is also a time when people are under a lot of pressure to meet deadlines, which can sometimes be affected by such diverse circumstances as the weather on the location, an actor's illness, or even a union work-stoppage. Production involves:

- Rehearsing the actors
- Shooting the film, either at the studio or on location
- Screening dailies (the scenes shot earlier that day, or the previous day)
- Special-effects photography/animation (continues into post-production)
- Film editors beginning review of footage and sometimes starting to assemble the film
- Dialogue soundtrack construction, sometimes including ADR (Automatic Dialogue Replacement, explained later in this chapter)

Post-production can be divided into two segments: _picture editing_ and _sound editing_. Picture editing involves assembling the film visually, while in sound editing, the dialogue, music, and sound effects are created and placed in the film. These tasks take place simultaneously for the first part of post-production; at this time the dialogue, sound effects, and music crews begin their work. However, it is not until the second part of the post-production process, after the editing is complete, that the real intensive production of the music, dialogue, and sound effects begins. This is because the film must be completed in order to synchronize these elements properly. (Note: A film is considered *locked* when the director and the producer have "signed off" on an edited version of the film and consider it completed.)

Digital technology is changing these distinctions. One may now edit the picture, music, sound effects, dialogue, and even visual special-effects at the click of a mouse. Before these computer systems were available, changes in the picture needed to be cut and spliced on a work print of the film; music recording tape had to be cut and spliced; sound-effects could not be edited so easily; and visual special-effects were primitive, if existent at all. Now, with powerful software, even after the film is supposedly "locked" and approved by the studio, the director can easily make minor or even major changes. This has led to many situations where the music is being recorded and the director "remembers" that he took out a few seconds of film and forgot to tell the composer. This creates havoc in the synchronization of music to picture. Unfortunately for composers, this is the way of the film-making world as we enter the 21st century.

Post-Production: Stage 1 — Picture Editing

Editing is when all the footage from production is assembled into a coherent film. This is done by the *film editor*. Often a director shoots several takes of the same scene, with different camera angles, that need to be put together in a natural way. This means matching shots, facial expressions, body language, and dialogue. Once the actual photography, or shooting, is completed, the film editor sifts through hours of footage and makes sure the story is being told in a coherent way, that there is no extraneous material, and that the cuts all make sense visually. It is a crucial task, because this process determines the overall pacing and dramatic impact of the film.

editing: when all the footage from production is assembled into a coherent film

The editorial phase of post-production includes:

- Assembling the rough cut (the working version of the film). The rough cut eventually becomes a fine cut, or locked picture.
- Music temp track
- Screening for studio execs
- Test screenings
- ADR

From the earliest days of film until the early 1990s, editing a film involved running a work print of the film through a projector over and over again. This projector is known as a Moviola, or flat-bed projector. Using foot-pedals, it allows the editor to go back and forth over a print of the film while synchronized with the dialogue track. The editor then decides where to make the edits, physically cuts pieces of film, and splices them together—hence the expression that a scene or line of dialogue ended up "on the cutting room floor." Once this work print is approved by the director, producer, and studio, a negative is cut and spliced in the exact same way. That negative is sent to the lab and copies are made for the theaters.

The method of film editing that uses Moviolas is now extinct. In today's world of computer technology, editing is done digitally. All the various takes are loaded into the computer, and the editor then cuts and pastes as he wishes. This also allows the director to easily view several options of a scene. However, after the editing is completed and the film is approved, a negative must still be physically edited to go to the lab.

Once the film is edited, it enters the stage involving the composer and the rest of the music crew, as well as the sound-effects crew. In a perfect world the composer would not begin writing music until there is a locked picture; changes in the picture would affect the planning and synchronization of the music. The exception to this is if songs are involved to which the actors sing or dance on-screen. Then, the music is usually recorded before shooting begins (prerecorded) so that the final version of the song or arrangement can be played back on the set. In addition to music, post-production is when sound effects are finalized and added.

Post-Production: Stage 2 — Sound Editing

Post-production involves:

Music	Non-Music
• Locked picture to composer	• Sound effects created
• Spotting session	• Foley
• Timing notes created	• ADR completed
• Music composition	• Special effects completed
• Orchestrations	• Dubbing
• Copying parts	• Answer print (preparation
• Song clearances	of physical film negative)
• Recording of music	• Distribution of film to
• Mixing music	theaters

Most of the technical terms listed above are explained in subsequent chapters of this book. However, some of these activities require a brief explanation here:

Foley is a process that creates sound effects through live recording. This can be as primitive as simulating horses hooves by clapping two coconut halves together, as in the old radio days, or it can be something like breaking windows or other glass to create the sound of a crash. There are many libraries of sound effects available today on CD, but often the sound-effects crew has a certain effect in mind that the CDs don't contain, so they must create it.

ADR or Automatic Dialogue Replacement, is when the actors go into a studio to redo any lines that were not recorded well or have extraneous noise on the production track. Often, the dialogue that is recorded on the set of a film is muddy, unclear, or tainted by unwanted sounds on the set. This is especially common with shooting on outdoor sets or location, when it is impossible to control noise such as airplanes, lawn mowers, sirens, and other sounds of modern life. In addition, the actor

76

[Handwritten margin notes:]
Foley: process that creates sound effects through live recording.
ADR: when actors go into a studio to redo any lines that were not recorded well.

may have garbled the line, the boom operator may not have gotten a good angle, or if wearing a body mike, the actor may have brushed it against an article of clothing. In ADR, the actors go into a studio, listen to and watch their original performance, and redo the line or lines until they are synced up exactly. This is quite common, and is an important part of the audio element of post-production.

The audio tracks are the very last element in the film's production. Once the music, sound effects, and dialogue have been added (the dubbing session), the film is ready to be printed, copied, and duplicated for release. The director sends the negative with the sound tracks to a lab that creates a copy of the film called an *answer print*. The director views this copy and ensures that all the colors were mixed properly at the lab, and that the look of the film is correct. Sometimes this is a one-step process; sometimes the director returns the print to the lab several times to get it right. Once the answer print is approved, it is ready for distribution.

This is a generalized overview of the film-making process. There are many other tasks that must be accomplished, ranging from financial accounting to building sets to feeding the crew—the list could go on and on.

One thing that cannot be emphasized enough is the pressure that can be placed on the composer because of the fact that he must wait for just about everything else to be finished before starting to write. Films are often behind schedule in production, but the release date cannot change; the composer may have less time to complete the score than originally scheduled. Remember our lonely composer sitting by the pool, waiting for a locked picture? Here is a story about post-production schedules:

Michael Kamen was the composer for the Kevin Costner film, *Robin Hood, Prince of Thieves*—a big-budget production of about $40 to $50 million. A huge amount of money had been spent for advertising, and by early spring, trailers, billboards, and buses around the country were announcing a June 6 release date.

Michael expected to receive the locked picture in March. However, production and editing got way behind schedule, and he did not receive the locked picture until the first week of April. This gave him only six weeks to write *and* record about 120 minutes of music for a 104 piece orchestra. (The last two weeks of May were given over to dubbing, color correction, duplication, and shipping of the film to the theaters.)

Now fortunately Michael was smart, and started working on his thematic material while he was waiting for the final cut, though he couldn't do any actual music cues. He remembered a ballet score he had written years before, and extracted a beautiful theme that became the love theme for the film, as well as the melody for the Bryan Adams song "Everything I Do, I Do It for You." He also worked on some of the action themes, preparing those for the time when he could synchronize them to the locked picture. When the locked picture finally arrived, he was ready and could work quickly and efficiently.

The stages of film production outlined here are not set in stone; this whole process involves a great deal of flexibility. For example, editing could begin during production. If enough footage for the beginning of the film has been shot, while the director is off shooting the ending of the picture, the film editor might assemble the first few minutes. Or parts of the script might be reworked even while the movie is being shot. The process is fluid, and the successful people are those who learn to honor that fluidity, and even harness it to improve the project.

CHAPTER 9

The Composer's Time Frame

Unfortunately, filming is all against the clock …
it's a constant battle between commerce and creativity.
—*Ridley Scott[1]*

The amount of time a composer gets to score a film can vary widely. In the previous anecdote there was only six weeks for an enormous amount of music, and although this sounds like an outrageously short amount of time, it is not all that unusual. Anything can happen during production that can cause the late delivery of a film; an actor gets ill and delays shooting, the weather on location won't cooperate, the director decides to make some changes, the studio doesn't like the ending and it has to be reshot. All a composer can do is go with it. Or, if the contract allows, refuse to take on the project if it is delivered later than a certain date.

A typical feature film will have from about 30 minutes of music to over 120 minutes. Each individual piece of music is called a *cue*. Each *cue* can be as short as just a few seconds, or as long as several minutes. A *cue* can be played by an orchestra, or it can be a song coming from a radio on-screen. Every new piece of music, regardless of its origin, is still called a *cue*.

The collection of cues making up all the music in the film is called the *score*. So if someone says, "I liked the *score* to that picture," they are referring to the music from beginning to end. If they say, "I really like that *cue*," they are talking about one isolated piece of music, often for a specific scene.

There is no rule of thumb as to how many minutes of music can be written in a certain amount of time. John Williams has said that he considers a good day to be two minutes of music composed. This means that in order to complete a *Star Wars* or *Indiana Jones* type of action film, with an average of 80 or 90 minutes of music, he needs about eight weeks to complete the writing. (Five-day-a-week schedules are often a luxury for composers; they are much more likely to go six or seven days a week for a few weeks and then take some time off.) A one-hour dramatic TV show such as *X-Files* can require as much as thirty or more minutes to be composed *and* recorded in one week. In addition, whether the music is for full orchestra or sequenced often determines the pace of writing and recording. Every composer has his own speed.

In most cases, the composer's first real involvement with the film is in post-production, after the film is locked. This is when the real composing begins. However, depending on what stage the film was in when he was hired, the composer might have had an earlier involvement. For example, if a certain composer is being considered during preproduction, the director might ask him to read the script and then informally discuss his ideas for the film. Some composers like to see the script in advance, for they like to start thinking about musical possibilities early in the process. Others prefer to wait until the picture is locked, or at least close to completed, because so much of what is composed is suggested by the actual visual images and pacing of the film.

There are also times when a director asks a composer to come to the set and observe the shooting of the film. As with reading the script, some composers are happy to participate in this early stage of making the film, but most prefer to wait until the film is completed before getting involved. This is because the shooting of a picture is a slow, painstaking, and sometimes tedious process where an enormous amount of imagination is required to envision the final product.

There are some instances when the composer gets involved with the film during preproduction or production. This is necessary when the film is a musical where characters sing on-screen (*Yentl, Mary Poppins*, etc.), or when the film contains scenes where the actors are dancing to live musicians or dancing to a song on the soundtrack. When any of these events are happening, the music must be planned in advance. The tempo must be chosen, and the music is prerecorded so that it can be played back on the set. If there are live musicians on-camera (called *sideline musicians*), they must be coordinated to appear to be playing. In modern film making, it is often the *music supervisor* who oversees this process.

The Spotting Session

In most cases, for a dramatic, or non-musical film, the composer's active involvement begins with post-production. First, he receives a locked version of the film. Very soon after receiving this tape, the composer attends the *spotting session*—the meeting between producer, director and composer where they decide how to use music in the film. The major decisions in this meeting are: where the music will begin and end for each cue, what it should sound like, and what role it will play in relation to the drama. Most composers like to view the film before going to the spotting session; it gives them a chance to think about it and get familiar with the film before discussing it with the director.

After the spotting session, the composer is really ready to get to work. The music editor prepares timing notes and the other technical aspects of synchronizing the music to the picture so that the composer can begin writing the music. The composer is acutely aware of the project's deadlines—most importantly, the delivery date for the music, the air date if it is for television, and the release date for a theatrical opening if it is a film. Many events are set in motion once the composer gets working on the film and has these deadlines. This includes hiring the orchestrators, studio musicians, booking the studio, etc. The composer must put himself on a disciplined timeline, or writing schedule, in order to make these deadlines. There can be as many as forty or fifty separate cues in a film, so there is a lot of music to keep track of. In order to complete this kind of output on time, the composer must write a certain amount per day.

The reality of this kind of schedule and the nature of the process of writing music combines to make this a solitary time for the composer despite all the necessary interaction with other members of the production team. Many hours a day must be set aside for writing, and this is something only the composer can accomplish. Through the years, film composers have commented on the lonely nature of their job, for once *[handwritten annotation at top: traditional approach: after spotting, Music editor makes timing notes; composer writes music w/ pencil & paper(maybe), generates sketch to send to an orchestrator]*

a project is begun they can be like hermits locked away in their studios for days at a time. However, it is a rewarding job and only this part of it is lonely. Another large aspect of the composer's job is interacting with interesting creative people—musicians, directors, writers, and others.

Different Working Styles

Every composer has a slightly different approach to the process of writing a film score. But there are two distinct styles that, for the purposes of this book, I will call the *traditional approach* and the *non-traditional approach*. In the traditional approach, after the composer spots the film, the music editor makes detailed timing notes. The composer then writes the music, usually with pencil and paper, ultimately generating a sketch that is sent to an orchestrator.

In the non-traditional approach, after the spotting session, the composer knows where each cue begins and ends, but often will not have any timing notes at all. That is because this composer plans to sequence his ideas by playing along with the film. In this method, often a team of people assists the composer. In addition to the music editor, there will be a recording engineer and sometimes a synthesizer expert. If a live orchestra is used, then eventually the sequenced music is sent to an orchestrator, who will create a written score.

Both methods are valid and used in Hollywood today. Some composers use one method exclusively, some use both, depending on the project. The non-traditional method is faster, and often must be used when the schedule is really tight.

An Ideal Schedule

For the purposes of this book, here is a generalized and ideal schedule from the time the composer receives a locked picture to the release of the film. Let's say that this film has 45 minutes of music, and the composer is using the "traditional" method:

[Handwritten margin note, top: nontraditional approach: after spotting, composer knows where each cue begins & ends but will not have timing ... because the [composer] ... to sequence his ideas by playing along w/ the film]

[Handwritten margin note, left: general idea of schedule using the traditional method]

Week 1

Composer receives the locked picture. Reviews at home. Spotting session with director, producer and music editor. Music editor begins preparing timing notes.

Weeks 2 to 5

Writing begins. Composer gives sketches to orchestrator. Orchestrations go to copyist as they are completed. Music editor finishes timing notes and prepares for synchronization.

Week 6

Recording the music: three to four days, six hours per day of recording. Approximately 18 minutes recorded each day. Mixing the music: two to three full days.

Weeks 7 to 8

Dubbing music with sound effects and dialogue.

Week 9

Film goes to lab for answer prints and color correction.

Week 12

Film delivered to theaters.

As with almost anything in this business, this timeline can morph in different directions. It can get shorter if there are delays in production or picture-editing, or there can even be the luxury of more time if things go smoothly during production, or if the release date gets pushed forward.

Mock-ups

[Handwritten note: Mockup: rough version of the cue recorded w/ synth & samplers to produce the sounds; sent to dir & producer]

As I have mentioned, there can be an enormous amount of pressure on the composer. There is also the added dimension of the pressure that comes from needing to please the director and producer. For this reason, in the age of MIDI, a composer often plays a sequenced *mock-up* of a cue for the powers-that-be. This is a rough version of the cue recorded with synthesizers and samplers to produce the sounds that eventually will be a real orchestra (unless it is an electronic or synthesizer score, in which case this version will not be so far from the final music). This is a dual-edged sword. On the one hand, it can give the director a good idea of where the composer is going with the cue, and the composer can be assured that the director's vision is being accomplished. The director can offer suggestions and comments, feel involved in the music process, and leave the composer's studio feeling secure that the music is going in the right direction. On the other hand, it can be very uncomfortable to have the director literally standing over one's shoulder making musical suggestions. In addition, on this rough version of the cue, the director might hear only the electronic-sounding synth strings and not-quite-real sounding French horn sample and think it is terrible, not having the musical ability to make the imaginary transfer to real instruments. Because he then focuses on the fake-sounding instruments instead of the actual musical ideas, he can mistakenly think that the cue itself doesn't work when all that is wrong is the use of electronic instruments substituting for real ones. It then becomes the composer's job to explain, or even "pitch" the music he conceived, and convince the director that it will work. Or he must change the cue and go in a different direction in order to please the director. Clear communication, and the ability to listen to a director and incorporate his ideas, is necessary.

Mark Isham illustrates this process, and discusses his experience in showing the director and producers the first version of the musical cues he wrote—the synthesized mock-up—for the movie, _Nell,_ starring Jodie Foster:

> As I remember, I wrote a whole bunch of music, and Michael Apted, the director, Jodie Foster, the star and co-producer, and Renée Missel, the other co-producer, were the team that would work with me. They came over to my studio and heard the first version. And they hated it! I honestly don't remember what it was about the first pass, except that I don't think it was mysterious enough. The thing I remember having to get— and it seems sort of obvious now because it really did help to align the movie a lot once I got it—was the sense of mystery. Where? How? Why? Who is this person? What could possibly have transpired to create a life for her like this?

Now Jodie Foster is one of the smartest people I've ever met in my whole life. And part of what makes her so smart is that she is really a good communicator. And Michael Apted is such an elegant gentleman. So in a meeting like that where they say, "We don't like it," it's never a feeling that you've been dealt this crushing blow and that you'll never rise up again. They don't scream and yell, "This is shit! How could you...!" It's not that at all. They have good reasons for why they don't feel it, and suggestions for where they would like it to go.

The balancing act a composer often performs is to write something that he is happy with, that fits the film, and satisfies the director's desires. Sometimes the composer disagrees with the director. Then it becomes a matter of discrimination whether or not to speak up and argue, or go with what is asked for. This will depend on several factors, including the composer's personal relationship with the director, the composer's track record and "clout," and sometimes how badly the composer wants to keep the job.

Alan Silvestri did the music for the 1998 film, _Practical Magic_, starring Sandra Bullock and Nicole Kidman, in just three weeks. He had to rely on experience and instinct in order to accomplish the task:

They [the production team] had a bit of a meltdown and they got in some trouble, scheduling-wise. I had to think long and deep about whether I was going to do this movie. I finally decided that if they could give me the time I felt I needed to accomplish a score, I would do it. It was about 60 minutes of music. I wrote it in 12 days, and recorded the entire score in three days of recording. They were dubbing, transferring, mixing, and printing the films while we were on the scoring stage. It was the deepest schedule hole I've ever seen. There may be projects that have been crazier, but for me, writing the entire score in 12 days, and recording it in three—those were consecutive days—and then the movie was out the following weekend ... that was really crazy.

Need: better sample libraries (handwritten)

A Digital World

The expectation of today's film-making world is not only that the music will be composed very quickly, but that it will sound great as a mock-up in the composer's studio. So today's composer must not just be literate in technology, but fairly expert. Huge sample libraries, facility with making instant changes, and the ability to create just about any style—world music, orchestral music, or the style of another composer—are requirements for the job.

In addition, because of digital technology, schedules are no longer as linear as they once were. First of all, the delivery of a film or TV show is always in a digital format, either QuickTime or digital video (DV). When editing the film, a director is no longer committed to an edit, as was the case when film was being spliced. Any edit can be undone or tweaked at the click of a mouse. What this means for the composer is that the "locked" picture can be unlocked at any time. Any music that was written for the original clip will then have to be tweaked, edited, or replaced. With schedules already very tight, this adds even more pressure on the composer, who is usually at the end of the film-making process facing the final deadline of the release of the film.

(For a more detailed discussion of the role of technology, please see chapter 7).

Although the entire process described in this section is based on the scoring of a full-length, large-budget feature film, the same principles apply to television shows and movies, cable and low-budget films, documentaries, and even student films. The composer does not begin writing until the editing of the movie is complete. There is then a spotting session and the use of music will be determined. (Note that in a TV series, also called *episodic television,* the director is often not involved in the spotting. This is because in TV, once shooting is complete, the director's job is finished. The producer then guides the rest of post-production.) There are still deadlines to make and the film makers still must be pleased with the final product. The scale is different, but the concept remains the same. It is still a collaborative effort. Clear communication and good listening skills are always necessary. Proper organization of one's time is crucial in order to meet deadlines. Time frames change, and sometimes the composer feels like he is in the middle of a swirling storm of deadlines and details. But the music must be written, and the deadlines met.

episodic television: TV series (handwritten, left margin)

CHAPTER 10

Spotting

*What you're trying to do is to catch the spirit of a picture.
And that means sometimes you go contrary to what's on the screen,
and sometimes you go with what's on the screen. It's a matter of
instinct; if your instincts are good, it's going to work for you.*
—David Raksin

Of the many elements that go into creating the music for a film, one of the most crucial is spotting. *Spotting* refers to where the music goes and what it will sound like. Frankly, one could have fabulous themes, sparkling orchestration, great players and a terrific creative relationship with the director, but if the music comes in and out at the wrong places, it can ruin a film. If a particular instrument enters in a way that is obtrusive, it can destroy the dramatic impact of a scene. If the overall sound and texture of the music is light and bright, but the film is dark and brooding, clearly that will not work. Psychologically, if the music does not fit like a glove in the way the costumes, lighting, and sets do, the audience can get distracted consciously or subconsciously. Therefore, the music's starts and stops, swells and retreats, and specific instrumentation and textures are carefully crafted to fulfill specific dramatic functions. This cannot be overemphasized. The point of the music is to further the story, to move the drama along, or tell us something about the characters or situation. In order to accomplish this, the music must be placed sensitively. When music is present in the film, it must be there for a reason, or it is probably not necessary.

The beginning composer should understand that effective spotting is a skill that comes with experience, so patience is in order. Many composers just starting out make the familiar mistakes of writing too many cues, over-writing the individual cue (as the Emperor said to Mozart: "Too many notes!"), and starting a cue too strongly (for example, using strings in a thick chord when a gentle unison would be better). Learning when to bring the music right in on a cut, and when you can be early or late, is a skill that comes with experience. In addition, as a composer becomes more experienced after scoring many different kinds of scenes, his insight becomes more finely tuned to what is on the screen and the intentions of the director. There are some general concepts that can guide this process:

1. *You are a partner in mixed media.* In most cues, music accompanies an actor's lines, creates a bridge from scene to scene, or gently helps to enhance the drama in a subtle way. In these scenes, the music is truly in the background. In a few situations, the music gets to stand out on its own—the action scenes, love scenes, and grand vistas of mountains or oceans. And these scenes also require sensitivity to how the music fits dramatically with what has happened and what is about to happen.

2. *Does there need to be music?* One must be absolutely sure that a given scene needs music. This surety can come in the form of a gut feeling, a plot driven need, or the director's request (whether or not you are in agreement). Points to consider include the dramatic needs, as well as what music has come just before or just after the scene in question.

3. *If there is music, what am I trying to say with it?* Asking this question helps keep the composer focused. It forces him to form an intent that gives an overall guideline for the emotional impact of the music. This goes beyond happy, sad, light, dark, etc. Similar questions are: Am I moving the drama forward? Am I expressing this character's thoughts or feelings appropriately? What instruments will accomplish these goals best?

Remembering these points helps keep the music a carefully considered element of the film, not just a composer's creative whim. If the composer is clear on why the music is there and what it is trying to accomplish, then his job is that much easier. The music then becomes a whole organic piece, not just a series of short musical sequences.

Elmer Bernstein speaks about how he begins conceiving music for a film:

I spot a film strictly as a dramatist. I'm not thinking of music at all when I spot a film. I look at a scene and say: Should this scene have music? Why should it have music? If it does have music, what is the music supposed to be doing? That's my process.

After the picture is locked, the composer meets with the director, music editor, and sometimes the producer and film editor. They review the film and discuss where the music will go, what it should sound like, and which dramatic situations to emphasize (or de-emphasize). This is called a *spotting session*. At this meeting the film is discussed scene by scene to determine the need for music, and to discuss what the music should sound like—what style, instruments, and emotions are musically necessary. The music editor takes notes for the composer regarding specific timings of cues and dramatic hits (see chapter 10). This meeting is the time when different approaches should be discussed, e.g., to play through a certain piece of action, to emphasize it, or to foreshadow an event or not. Keep in mind that most directors have no formal musical background and must speak in layman's terms, not musical terms. The composer must find a way to understand the director's desire and translate his words into musical ideas. The best way to do this is to discuss emotion and rhythm, or pulse. Avoid speaking in musical terms. Try to find out what emotion the director wants and how he wants the pacing of the scene to go.

Alan Silvestri has a wonderful relationship with several directors, and understands the pressure the director can feel, and how that pressure affects his relationship with the composer:

You've got to remember what you're doing here. You're working for somebody, and you, the composer, are not going to be the one called on the carpet when the movie was supposed to make $40 million this weekend and it only made $150,000 … You're probably off on your next movie, but there's somebody out there who's sitting in a chair right now with a bunch of people in suits standing around him, and he's having a real bad day. That person's called the director! So if you think for a minute that the director is not *going to have a whole lot to say about what kind of music goes into their film and how it sounds, you're kidding yourself.*

Spotting is the first step towards completing a successful score. It must be done carefully, sensitively, and with the understanding that the music is a partner with the drama, as the composer is a partner with the director. Sometimes this partnership is smooth with excellent give and take. There can also be considerable friction if the director (or producer) requests a certain style or musical idea that the composer finds objectionable. As mentioned previously, it is in these situations that the composer must decide whether to argue with the director, or to go along with his wishes. (This is often where the "temp track" can be useful. More about this in chapter 10.) Ultimately, the composer's job is twofold in nature: one, he must please those who have hired him, and two, he must do it in such a way that his musical integrity remains intact. Being a film composer involves an enormous amount of flexibility and sensitivity, with a handful of diplomacy thrown in for good measure. One must be a good communicator, and especially have the ability to listen and transfer into musical terms what a director is saying.

When I was scoring the TV series, *Monsters*, each episode had a different director. At one spotting session, the director said he wanted the opening to "float, like the beginning of *Citizen Kane*." Now, anyone who has seen this 1941 movie with that awesome Bernard Herrmann score will remember that the opening music features very low-end woodwinds playing non-functional harmonies. To me, it doesn't float; it actually is very heavy, and I feel "sinks" would be a better term. I had to translate what he was really saying. After looking at the show in question, I realized that the operative description was the director wanting the sound of Herrmann's score in *Citizen Kane*, not to the adjective "float." I wrote something low, dark, and ominous and it was just what he wanted.

Clear communication between composer and director is essential. The director's vision of the film is the most comprehensive, and his abstract ideas for cues may provide keen insight into the type of musical ideas that will make a score succeed. The composer must help these ideas evolve into actual music.

Elmer Bernstein reflects on conceiving the music for *The Rainmaker* as a result of conversations with director Francis Ford Coppola:

> *I have to credit Francis with the bluesy 6/8 idea in a roundabout way. What happened was, when I first got on The Rainmaker, Francis wasn't going to have a score as we know a score to be. At first, he was going to go the B.B King route—in other words, real Memphis stuff with some very minor connective things in scoring. But as he began to develop the film itself, he began to feel that he needed to depend more on score. So it was my decision to use the Hammond B3 organ, but it came out of his idea of Memphis ambience. Out of that ambience, I retained the three instruments you hear a great deal of: the Hammond B3, the muted trumpet, and the guitar. But that came out of Francis' original concept.*

> *When I came on Rainmaker it was in rough-cut form, and the version I finally recorded to was version #26. It went through some amazing changes. The interesting thing about Francis is that each time he changed the film it was for the better. He wasn't just fooling around, he was just "finding" the film, so to speak.*

The most important element of the *spotting session* is clear communication with the director. Once the composer and director share the same vision for the music, then the composer can get to work writing the score. However, there are still many spotting decisions to be made. The music can begin right on a cut, a few seconds before it, or even right after it. It can start immediately after an important line of dialogue, or it can wait and let that line sink in. It can foreshadow a dangerous situation, or play it more neutrally. There are countless spotting decisions to be made that will affect the drama, and the audience's experience of the story. How these decisions are made will be a combination of the composer's experience, his dramatic sensitivity, and the director's wishes.

CHAPTER 11

The Music Editor

Diplomatic skills. You've got a director sitting next to you, you're in a recording booth, the composer's out there, the music is being recorded, and the director says "What the hell is this music that I'm hearing?" Well, what do you say to that? Good luck! You hope that it's a long music cue so it will give you time to think of how to respond.
—Eric Reasoner, Music Editor

The people assisting the composer on a daily basis are the orchestrator (see chapter 12), the composer's assistant, and the *music editor*. The music editor is often an under-recognized member of the production team. He must have excellent music skills, thorough knowledge of various advanced software programs (Auricle, Cue, Digital Performer, and Pro Tools are common), and be a cool, calm, and collected diplomat in the service of both the composer and the director. The music editor is responsible for making spotting notes from the spotting session, creating timing notes, and preparing the film or software for synchronization of the music with the final version of the film.

Music editor Eric Reasoner:

> As a music editor, the more you know about music the better off you are. However, there are still a lot of music editors that have an instinctive sense—not that they studied music, but they really know and have quick instincts about cutting music. They are also good at dealing with pressure and handling a lot of different kinds of individuals, which is a big, big part of it.

In today's modern world of film making, most of the music editor's tasks are accomplished using computer software. However, there are still some physical tools and pieces of equipment that are used:

reel: the carousel that the film is loaded onto when it goes through the camera during shooting & through a projector

A *reel* is the carousel that the film is loaded onto when it goes through the camera during shooting and through a projector. Every reel used during production and post-production contains about 8 to 12 minutes of film, making about 10 to 14 reels for the average movie. However, when a film is delivered to the theater, every two reels are combined so that the theater receives 5 to 7 reels. The projectionist then makes *reel changes* at the appropriate points. At some of the more modern theaters, they can splice and load the film onto one giant reel, called a *platter*, which turns parallel to the floor, making reel changes unnecessary.

Magnetic sound film, also known as *mag film*, is film that is specially coated with a magnetic substance similar to audiotape. This is the kind of film that is used to record and edit sound to sync to picture. Film is used so that the music, dialogue, sound effects, and picture can run on similar machines, and the motors can be easily synchronized. *Mag film* is being used less and less as digital technology replaces it.

The *optical soundtrack* is the stripe on the edges of a finished film that contains the sound for the movie. Until recently, with the arrival of digital technology, this track was read by a light cell that converted the light-sensitive images into sound. Hence, it is called an optical soundtrack. This technology has changed very little from the inception of sound films to the 1990s, and is still used in many theaters today as the digital technology that will replace it is still being implemented. (See Fig. 11.1. 35mm Composite)

SMPTE is the time code that enables different computers, synthesizers, and video machines to talk to each other and synchronize music to video, or music to music. The letters stand for "Society of Motion Picture and Television Engineers," which developed this time code in the sixties.

Temp Tracks

Often, the first real involvement the music editor has in a film is towards the middle of post-production. At this time, as the work-print of the film is solidified, the director asks the music editor to prepare a *temp track*. This is a temporary track of music laid into the work-print

platter: giant reel

SMPTE: Society of Motion Picture & Television Engineers; time code that enables different computers, synths & video machines to talk to each other magnetic sound film: mag film; film that is specially coated with a magnetic substance used to record & edit sound to sync to picture

35mm Composite

optical soundtrack: the stripe on the edges of a finished film that contains the sound for the movie

Optical sound track

Frame

Frameline

Sprocket holes

temp track: temporary track of music laid into the work-print of the film

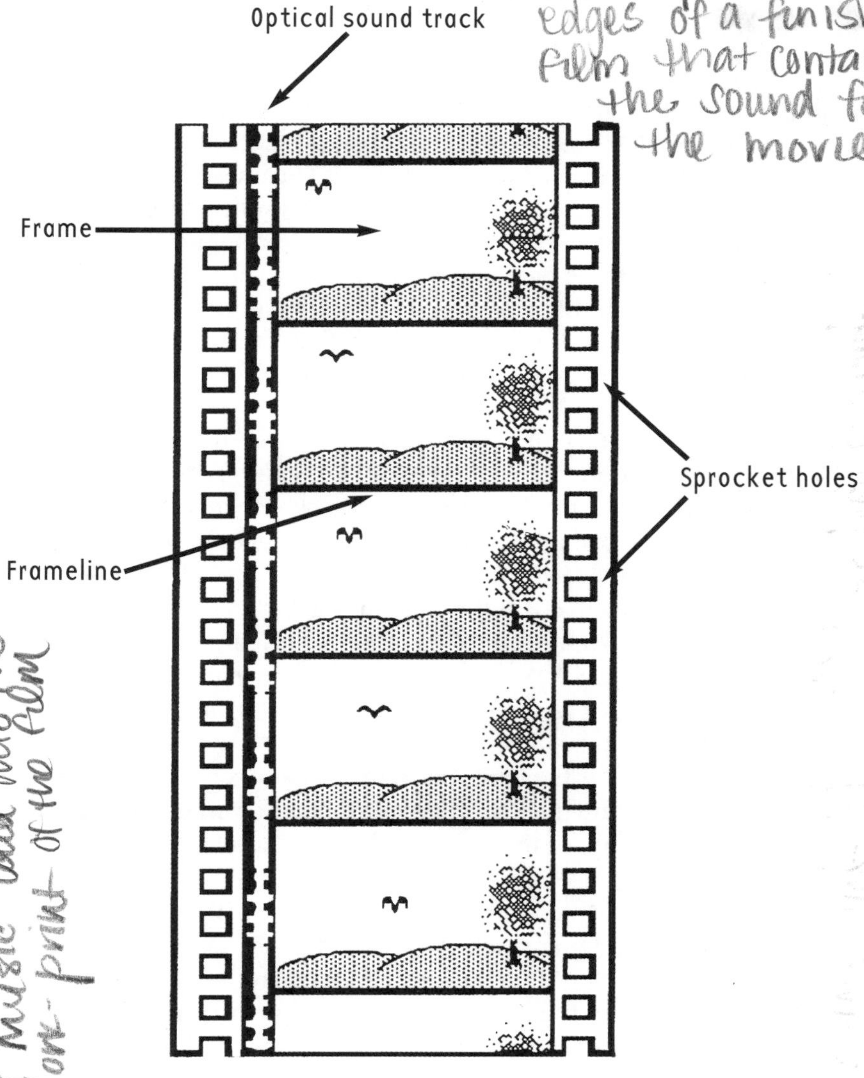

Fig. 11.1. 35mm Composite

of the film in order to give studio executives and test audiences an idea of what the film will be like once the final score is completed. Without any music at all, this work-print can be dry and lifeless, especially in action scenes. So the director gives the music editor some guidelines as to what kind of music to use (if not specific pieces), and the music editor snips and cuts these pieces to fit, not only dramatically, but also rhythmically and harmonically. In the old days, magnetic tape and film had to be spliced in order to accomplish this; today, Pro Tools or other digital audio software is employed. The music for the temp track can come from anywhere—from other soundtracks, from classical, pop, or jazz CDs—anything the music editor can find is fair game. No royalties need to be paid and no sync licenses agreed to because this temporary music will not be used in a version of the film that is shown to the public. It is only used in-house to show the producers, studio executives and test audiences to get their reaction.

Most contemporary films have temp tracks until the final scoring is completed. If one listens closely, often it can be discerned what the temp track was if the composer had to closely imitate it in order to please the director. For example, the temp track for *Titanic* was built from music recorded by the Irish singer Enya. Composer James Horner then had to adapt this kind of flowing, ethereal, New Age style to fit the action. Another good example is the temp track for *Star Wars*. This was Gustav Holst's 1917 classical piece *The Planets*. If the movie is a sequel, it's an easy call. For example, the temp track for *Lethal Weapon IV* was taken from *Lethal Weapon I, II,* and *III*. But no matter what the source of the temp track, music editors must work hard and long to edit a temp track to fit a picture, and they must have command of a huge selection of music from which to choose.

Music editors often use the term *tracking* to describe either the process of creating the temp-track, or to the task of laying-in preexisting music to a finished film. Tracking can refer to the process of creating the temp track for the work print, or to the use of preexisting music in the final version of the film. So, the use of music that is not written by the composer specifically for a scene, where it is taken from another source, is usually called tracking. Eric Reasoner discusses the process of creating temp tracks:

It depends on the relationship between the director, picture editors, and you [the music editor]. You may set up a traditional spotting session where you look at the film and discuss ideas for the temp track. Or you may just screen the film on your own and then converse with the director about styles and things like that, and then just begin searching for music. Sometimes, you have a real wide creative range to pick music that's appropriate, and you can just go your own way.

On The Three Musketeers, when [music editor] Michael Ryan and I were tracking that film, we had a two or three hour meeting with Steve Herek, the director, where we looked at different parts of the film, talking about style. He had already laid up some music against some scenes as examples, and from that session Michael and I went back to the office and just started searching through tons and tons of existing scores, soundtracks, and CDs, picking out music that fit within those guidelines.

Spotting Notes

The music editor's next responsibility, after cutting the temp track, is usually to go to the spotting session, take spotting notes, and then prepare the timing notes. *Spotting notes* are a generalized description of where the music begins and ends for each cue. Spotting notes also contain any special instructions discussed between the composer and director for a certain cue like bringing in a theme at a certain point, or hitting a specific piece of action. From the more general spotting notes, the music editor then prepares timing notes, which are very detailed descriptions of each scene with corresponding timings. (See Fig. 11.2. Spotting Notes from *The Simpsons*.)

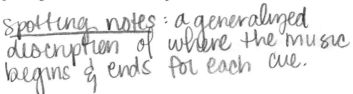

THE SIMPSONS #5F02 "Treehouse of Horror VIII" · Music Spotting Notes

Composer **Alf Clausen** / Music Editor **Chris Ledesma**

CUE #	START	STOP	LENGTH	DESCRIPTION
1M1	01:00:35:17	01:01:04:03	:29	Main Title starts as sword appears; low, change on stabs; play thru title and couch gag to out
1M2	01:01 19:03	01:01:22:14	:03	Open Act 1 - Homega Man - Sci-Fi; tail under Brockman dia
1M3	01:02:12 25	01:02:15:05	:02	Start on cut to military antique store; Homer goes to buy a bomb shelter; tail under next dia.
1M4	01:02:40 11	01:02:44:25	:04	On cut to estab shot of Paris; musette; happy until settle on military compound, then dark on settle; tail under next dia.
1M5	01:02:59 09	01:03:07:28	:09	On cut to Eiffel Tower splitting open; launch missile ominous and threatening; out on cut to outer space
1M6	01:03:11 08	01:03:23:00	:12	On EOL "What the hell was that?"; through snickering aliens; out on cut to missile headed for earth
1M7	01:03 24 17	01:03:42:10	:18	on cut to missile flying over Springfield; G.P. on comic book guy; resume on POV missile and out on explosion
1M8	01:03:55:14	01:03:59:00	:04	Spooky and creepy on overhead shot of car in traffic out on cut to back of Homer head leaning out of car
1M9	01:04:20:28	01:04:23:27	03	Sting the push-in on newspaper; out on cut to Homer
1M10	01:04:27:13	01:04:46:21	19	Eerie as Bart ghost appears; thru entire family until Maggie and others are out of frame; then sad as Homer cries; out just before "No, no, no!"
1M11	01:05:02:20	01:05:05:02	02	On cut to estab movie theater; happy Homer; tail on cut to int.
1M12	01:05:23:25	01:05:35:12	12	*SOURCE* -- Homer sings along with a boom box; "War" CD master
1M13	01:05:38:19	01:05 40:10	02	Start on cam settle on mutants; scary/dark; out as Homer shrieks
1M14	01:06 08 19	01:06.28:09	20	As Burns: "And now you must die"; dark and scary; then chase as they run after him; tail on cut to dead chauffeur; thru reveal of coffin and out
1M15	01:06 35 13	01:07:03:13	38	On cut to ext. on car; Car chase; tail on cut to int. house on relieved Homer
1M16	01 07 09 27	01:07 10:14	01	Sting on push-in on mutants; out on cut to reverse angle on Homer
1M17	01 07 22 04	01:07:24:26	03	Start on cut to back of Homer going to hug kids; tail under the mutants: "Awww."
1M18	01 07 56 23	01:08:00:03	03	Sincere Marge as cam pushes in on her during her speech; out to clear "NOW!"

Fig. 11.2. Spotting Notes from The Simpsons.
Used by Permission

Master Cue List

From these spotting notes the music editor creates a *master cue list*, or *music summary*—a list of all the cues and the corresponding places they appear in the film. Eventually, the composer gives every cue a verbal title, like "Billy Splits Quick," or "The Big Kiss." But at this stage, which is before the composer has begun writing, the music editor assigns every cue an alphanumerical designation, like "4M3," which indicates the reel and its location within that reel. The first number is the reel, "M" stands for music, and the last number is a sequential number indicating where that cue is placed in the reel. In this instance, 4M3 means the 4th reel, music cue number 3. Some reels might have several music cues, some might have none. But if a music editor sees 11M2, he knows that piece of music is the second cue in reel eleven.

Note that in television there are variations of this system. Because the shows are divided into "acts," instead of reels, the first number often corresponds to the act number. (An *act* is each segment of the show, divided by commercials.) So 3M2 means Act 3, music cue number 2. And sometimes, in television, the first number refers to the episode number for that particular season, and the second number is simply where the cue falls in the entire show. For example, 14M7 means the seventh cue in the fourteenth show of the year.

The master cue list shows every cue, assigns it an appropriate number, indicates how long it is, and gives the SMPTE time for when it begins. Cues are also called *starts*, meaning that the orchestra has to start a recording for each cue. It is often said, therefore, that the master cue list shows every start. (See Fig. 11.3. Master Cue Sheet from *The Simpsons*.)

music cue

4M3

Reel number

where cue is placed in reel

act: each segment of the show, divided by commercials

99

Simpsons 5F02
Alf Clausen

Mon 10/6/97 2:00 Pm O'Henry

CUE	CLIX	TIME	TITLE	Vln	Vla	Vc	Bs	1	2	3	4	Hns	Tpt	Tbn	Tba	Pno	Syn	Harp	Guitar	Drums	Perc	Arr
1m1	9 - 4	00:28	Halloween VIII	10	3	3	1	Fl	Ob	BcBc	CB	2	2	2		Syn	Syn	1			2	AC
1m2	10 - 1	00:08	The Homega Man	10	3	3	1	AF	Ob	Fl	Fl	2				Syn	Syn	1			1+El	DH
1m3	12 - 5	00:07	The Withstandinator.	10	3	3	1	Fl	Ob	Bc	Bn	3	2	2		Syn	Syn	1			2	DH
1m4	9 - 7	00:05	Cordon Bleu	10	3	3	1	Fl	Ob	Ob	CB	3				Syn	Syn	1	Gtr			DH
1m5	16 - 1	00:09	Rocket In The Pocket	10	3	3	1	Fl	Ob	Q	CB	3	2	2		Syn	Syn	1		1	2	DH
1m6	21 - 0	00:12	Kang & Kang	10	3	3	1			BcBc	CB	3				Syn	Syn	1			1	AC
1m7	9 - 3	00:18	Missie Whistle	10	3	3	1	Fl	Ob	Fl	Bn	3	2	2		Pro	Syn	1			2	DH
1m8	13 - 2	00:08	A Disarming Discourse	10	3	3	1	AF	Ob	Fl	Fl	2		2		Syn	Syn	1			1+El	DH
1m9	11 - 0	00:03	Oh, My Dog Sting	10	3	3	1	Fl	CB	Q	Bn	3	2	2		Pro	Syn	1			2	AC
1m10	15 - 2	00:19	Just Cos	10	3	3	1									Syn	Syn	1			2	AC
1m11	11 - 6	00:07	The Last Man Alive	10	3	3	1	Fl	Ob	Q	Bn	3		2		Pro	Syn	1			1	AC
1m13	16 - 6	00:02	A Mutation Sensation	10						BcBc						Syn	Syn	1			2	DH
1m14	10 - 6	00:20	Hearse Castle	10	3	3	1	Fl	Ob	Q	Bn	3	2	2		Syn	Syn	1			2	DH
1m15	9 - 5	00:28	Cloakie And Dagger	10	3	3	1	Fl	Ob	Q	Bn	2	2	2		Syn	Syn	1			2	DH
1m16	13 - 4	00:01	Sting De' Mutants	10	3	3	1	Fl	Ob	Q	Bn	2	2	2		Syn	Syn	1			2	DH
1m17	13 - 3	00:08	Brings A Tear To Your Eye Socket	10	3	3	1	Fl	Ob	Q	Bn	3		2		Pro		1			1	DH
1m18	19 - 4	00:03	Sharing Their Vision - Not	10	3	3	1	AF	Ob	Q	Bn	2					Syn	1			2	DH
1m19	11 - 3	00:11	That's The Marge I Married	10	3	3	1	Fl	Ob	Q	Bn	3	2	2		Pro	Syn	1			2	DH
2m1	14 - 3	00:06	Fly vs Fly Theme	10	3	3	1	Fl	Ob	Q	CB	3	2	2		Syn	Syn	1			2	DH
2m3	15 - 1	00:06	I Must Warn You	10	3			AF	BH	Q	Fl					Pro		1			2	AC
2m4	13 - 6	00:08	The Cat's On His Way Out		3	3	1	AF		Q	Fl	3		2		Syn	Syn	1			2	DH
2m5	10 - 1	00:11	Oh Dog, A New Look	10	3											Syn	Syn	1			2	AC
2m6	14 - 0	00:11	A Superfly Fantasy	10	3	3	1	Fl	Ob	Q	Bn	3	2	2		Pro	Syn	1			1+El	DH
2m7	18 - 4	00:17	Flee, Fly, Flo, Fun	10	3	3	1	Fl	Ob	BcBc	CB	3	2	2		Pro	Syn	1			2	DH
2m8	10 - 0	00:05	Big, Fat & Ugly	10	3	3	1	Fl	Ob	Q	CB	2	2	2		Pro	Syn	1			2	AC
2m9	9 - 5	00:05	A Little Night Music	10	3	3	1	Fl	Ob	Q	Fl	3				Syn		1			1	DH
2m10	14 - 2	00:04	Another Sucker Spidered	10	3	3	1	Fl	Ob	Q	CB	3	2	2		Syn	Syn	1			2	DH
2m11	15 - 7	00:05	Big, Ugly	10	3	3	1	Fl	Ob	Q	CB	3	2	2		Pro	Syn	1			2	AC
2m12	16 - 1	00:06	Fly-By Nite Visitor	10	3	3	1	AF		Q	Fl	3				Syn		1			1	DH
2m13	8 - 6	00:08	Ew, Gross!	10	3	3	1	Fl	Ob	Q	Bn	3	2	2		Pro	Syn	1			2	DH
2m14	16 - 1	00:17	Big Mistake, Flyboy!	10	3	3	1	AF	BH	Q	Fl	2	2	2		Pro	Syn	1			2	AC
2m15	17 - 1	00:12	Don't Trifle With Them	10	3	3	1	Fl	Ob	Q	Bn	3	2	2		Pro	Syn	1			2	DH
3m1	11 - 4	00:10	Easy Bake Coven Main Title	10	3			AF	BH	BcBc	Fl	3					Syn	1			1	DH
3m2	9 - 5	00:04	The Smoking Lamp Is Lit	10	3	3	1	Fl	Ob	Q	CB	3	2	2		Pro	Syn	1			1+El	DH
3m3	16 - 6	00:06	Which Is Witch?			3	1	Fl	Ob	Q	CB	3				Pro	Syn	1			2	DH
3m4	15 - 5	00:15	Falling Every Witch Way'	10	3	3	1	Fl		Q	Bn	3	2	2		Syn	Syn	1			1+El	AC
3m5	17 - 3	00:08	Witch Is Which!	10	3			AF	BH	Q	Bn	3				Pro	Syn	1			1+El	DH
3m6	11 - 1	00:21	Bats Entertainment	10	3	3	1	Fl	Ob	Q	Bn	2	2	2		Pro	Syn	1			2	AC
3m7	12 - 4	00:09	Frame Spotting	10	3			AF	BH	BcBc	Fl	3					Syn	1			1	DH
3m8	12 - 5	00:21	Witch Excitement	10	3	3	1	Fl	Ob	Q	CB	3	2	2		Pro	Syn	1			2	AC
3m9	13 - 4	00:01	Crossed-Witch			3	1	Fl	Ob	Q	CB	3		1		Pro	Syn	1			2	DH
3m10	15 - 6	00:05	That's Owl, Folks	10	3			Fl		Q		3				Pro	Syn	1			1	DH
3m11	16 - 0	00:26	The Story Of Caramel God	10	3	3	1	Fl	Ob	Q	Bn	3	2	2		Syn	Syn	1			2	AC
3m12	11 - 1	00:11	Which Witch Is Which?	10	3	3	1	Fl	Ob	Q	Bn	3	2	2		Pro	Syn	1			2	DH
3m13	8 - 2	00:40														Syn	Syn	1			2	AC
3m14	10 - 6	00:03	Gracie Logo													Pro	Syn	1				AC

Fig. 11.3. Master Cue Sheet and Orchestra Breakdown from The Simpsons.

timing notes | cue sheets: extremely detailed descriptions of every shot, every cut & every line of a dialogue in a scene, with timings to the hundredth of a second

The Music Editor

Timing Notes

Once the master cue list is done, the music editor makes timing notes for every cue. *Timing notes* (also sometimes called *cue sheets*) are extremely detailed descriptions of every shot, every cut, and every line of dialogue in a scene, with timings to the hundredth of a second. The composer uses these notes to find exact moments to synchronize the music, and also to choose appropriate tempos for the cues. Timing notes are usually prepared on software such as Cue or any word-processing software. (See Fig. 11.4. Timing Notes from *Hearts on Fire*.)

The sequence of the music editor's tasks just described—creating temp tracks, attending the spotting session, music summary, and creating timing notes—are considered the traditional order of events. However, this sequence is changing in today's world as more and more composers begin to digitally sequence their scores by playing along to the video. For these composers, timing notes that describe every single visual event and line of dialogue are not necessary. More common in this situation would be an abbreviated form of timing notes, with a list of any sync points (see chapter 15) the composer wishes to make. A music summary will always be necessary to keep track of the many cues in a score, but it is important to understand that the music editor's job responsibilities change from composer to composer and from director to director.

Syncing and Recording

The next job for the music editor is assisting the composer in synchronizing the music to the film. He prepares click tracks and punches and streamers (see chapter 15, "Syncing the Music to Picture") for the recording session, and makes sure that the music and the picture—either video or film—are locked. Also, at the session, the music editor keeps a log for every take of each cue. If a cue needs to be moved either by a few frames or even by a few seconds, the music editor assists the composer in making the timing changes. This can involve changing tempos, moving bar-lines, or changing the placement of punches and streamers.

In addition, if after the recording session the director asks for significant changes in the music, or wants to place a cue originally

Production: **HEARTS ON FIRE**   Production #: **R#3 Ver.4**   Episode: **Video Date: 4/1/98**
Cue: **3m2** "**DOWNTOWN CHASE**"
Begins at **c3:01:44:17** in Reel/Act 3

ABS. SMPTE #(29):	REL. TIME:		
			Cops FRANK, BILL and JOEY are leaving restaurant. FRANK sees 2 bad guys and:"Hey that's them, hold it!"
c3:01:44:17	0.00		MUSIC STARTS over CLOSE "SHOOTER" (1st bad guy) as he STARTS to RUN
c3:01:44:23	0.20	CUT	CLOSE FRANK and JOEY thru window
c3:01:45:02	0.50		FRANK RUNS
c3:01:45:05	0.60	CUT	CLOSE 2nd bad guy TURNS to RUN
c3:01:45:20	1.10		FRANK CROSSES in FG as bad guy runs away
c3:01:46:02	1.50	CUT	WIDE STREET as BAD GUYS RUN toward CAM
c3:01:47:16	2.97	CUT	MED FRANK RUNS out Restaurant DOORWAY
c3:01:47:27	3.34		OS BILL:"**Hey FRANK!**"
c3:01:48:12	3.84	CUT	MED WIDE STOREFRONT as FRANK RUNS and BILL follows
c3:01:49:09	4.74	CUT	MED CLOSE FRANK as CAM PANS and BILL:"**GET 'EM, HE'S THE SHOOTER**"
c3:01:50:22	6.17	CUT	WIDE STREET as bad guys run down sidewalk
c3:01:51:07	6.67		FRANK into view in BG
c3:01:52:25	8.27		SHOOTER STARTS TOWARD CAM behind VOLVO
c3:01:53:15	8.94	CUT	LONG SHOT STREET as bad guys RUN ACROSS between cars
c3:01:54:24	10.24		FRANK and JOEY START ACROSS as tires SCREACH
c3:01:55:03	10.54	CUT	MED BAD GUYS as they weave thru cars
c3:01:56:02	11.51		CAR SCREACHES as SHOOTER DARTS RIGHT
c3:01:56:10	11.78	CUT	WIDE STREET as FRANK and JOEY run thru cars
c3:01:56:28	12.38		FRANK JUMPS UP ON HOOD of car
c3:01:57:03	12.55	CUT	MED WIDE FRANK FLIPS OVER HOOD as Guys Run in FG
c3:01:57:20	13.11	CUT	MED FRANK lands on street as BILL appears in BG

TOTAL TIME · 13.11

Fig. 11.4. Timing Notes from Hearts on Fire.

slated for an early reel into a later one, it will fall to the music editor to accomplish this task. Although this usually happens at the dubbing stage (see fig. 13.2), sometimes the music editor will move, edit, or rebuild a cue to have it ready for dubbing. This is a time when the music editor's job gets interesting and creative. Taking material meant for one scene and reworking it to fit another requires both technical and musical skill. In addition, this is where the music editor's diplomatic skills come in handy, because at this point he is answering to the director, who may or may not have the ability to communicate musically.

Eric Reasoner:

> *Changes occur [at the recording session], and they're subject to tastes of producers or directors—whoever's there running the show. It may be multiple people and that's also frustrating for the composer and any of us that are working to make it right. Basically, you're there to help fix problems. If you're in the booth and the composer's out on the stage, a lot of times you hear things said that would never be said if the composer was in the room, and that's a kind of a nerve-racking experience. So it's basically, figure out if there are problems and figure out what the problems are. If they're simple fixes, like subtracting elements of the music—something that the director doesn't like, you have to find out what they don't like. If it's a sound, a color, or a particular instrument, you can just get rid of it. If it's the whole cue, or how it's structured, then you're really in trouble. The composer will make the musical changes for the orchestra from the podium. But moving bars, and changing the form of the piece creates problems for the synchronization, which is the music editor's department. So you assist the composer by restructuring, whether it's in the computer program or whatever you used to line up the streamers or clicks.*

Dubbing

Once the music is recorded, it is mixed to whatever format the film requires—stereo, stereo surround-sound, digital, etc. The music editor then prepares the cues for the final stage, the dubbing. *Dubbing* is

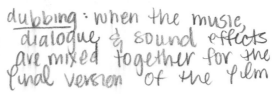
dubbing: when the music, dialogue & sound effects are mixed together for the final version of the film

when the music, dialogue and sound effects are mixed together for the final version of the film, a process that for an average film takes two to four weeks at the dubbing studio, or dubbing stage.

Until recently, the music editor would prepare reels of mag film with the final music cues that corresponded to reels of picture. Every cue would be placed in order, and if there were a few seconds or minutes of picture in between music cues, the music editor would insert blank film to fill the gaps. The mag film would then run simultaneously with the picture, sound effects, and dialogue at the dubbing stage.

Today, dubbing is done digitally, usually on Pro Tools. The music editor comes to the dubbing stage with a digital file of all the cues, and runs these digital files locked to picture, sound effects, and dialogue via SMPTE time code.

Dubbing happens in two stages. The first is called *pre-dubbing*. At about the same time that the music is being recorded and mixed, the dialogue engineers clean up the dialogue tracks and get them to sound strong and clear, independent of the sound effects and music. (Each voice and each component of a sound effect has its own separate audio "track" that can be controlled independently. Music usually has two to eight tracks depending on the format.) Concurrently, the sound-effects people are doing the same thing in their own studio. One of the reasons pre-dubbing is so important is because of the complexity of some of the tracks; sound effects alone can have over one hundred separate tracks!

When the sound effects, dialogue, and music are all ready (independent of each other), then it is time for the final dubbing sessions when they are all put together. The music editor attends these sessions and assists the dubbing engineers in placing the music at the proper spots. He also has input on the levels and eq of the music.

Also present at the dubbing are the director and sometimes the film editor. This is a critical process because the precise levels of music, dialogue, and sound effects must be found. If one is too loud or soft, it can be distracting or irritating. Also, depending on the format—stereo, stereo surround, digital, etc.—the mix is more or less complex. The director has the final say during this process.

It is at the dubbing session where a composer's music is most likely to be moved around. A director might not really like the cue the way it was designed, and will try a different cue in place of the original. Again, this is his prerogative and it is one that many directors utilize. Many cues from the best composers have been moved around on the dubbing stage. In the movie *Airplane!*, during the climactic crash-landing scene, Elmer Bernstein had written a cue with many stops and starts as the picture cut back and forth between the airport gate areas and the plane itself. This was because the humor was in the people waiting, who were running to successively higher gate numbers as the plane came in on its crazy course. Director Jim Abrahams apparently didn't like these stops and starts, so he had the music editor take a low-end ostinato from earlier in the cue and loop it—that is, they repeated the ostinato over and over so there was continuous music throughout the cue instead of the stops and starts Bernstein had written. Incidents like this are not unusual, and the music editor is the one who must accomplish such changes. (The composer does not often attend the dubbing sessions and at this point is usually out of the picture, his job having been completed.)

Eric Reasoner describes the process:

> *It's extremely tedious. You're going back and forth, back and forth, over the same area of sounds with a different focus each time, and if your area of sound isn't of concern at the moment, it's really tedious and you'd like to get out of that room. You may very well spend a 12- or 16-hour day mixing one reel of film—that's a 10-minute segment of film. In action films, when they're really loud, you walk out of there and your ears are just completely fatigued. I can remember going home from the dubbing stage on Die Hard With A Vengeance after an action reel. I got up the next morning, and got in the car to go back to the dubbing stage. I started up the car and the radio came on with the volume*

> *up to 11. I was thinking, oh my god, I was listening at this volume last night when I drove home! It just kind of shows you what your ears and your body can do, shutting down after a bit.*

Mark Isham tells how his music editor, Tom Carlson, works at the dubbing stage:

> *Tom understands the process very well, and he actually looks forward to being the knight in shining armor on the dubbing stage. He's got the patience. He knows how to hang with the guys—the mixers and the whole post-production crew. He's willing to put in those hours, and he's willing to wait until that tenth hour and say, "Can I hear it once with the music up?" And when the director says, "No," he'll just say, "Look, you're missing a chance to be more emotional." He fights the good fight and knows how to do it.*

Once the dubbing is completed, there is one more task for the music editor: preparing a finalized list of all the music in the film. This is called a *music clearance sheet*, or *cue sheet*. (Note: cue sheet is a term that has several different uses. Some composers refer to timing notes as cue sheets.) This list is submitted to the appropriate organizations for licensing the music so that royalties can be paid. (Fig. 11.5. Music Cue Sheet from *Die Hard with a Vengeance*.)

After the music clearance list is prepared, the music editor's job is finished. As you have seen, the music editor performs an interesting, important, and unheralded role in the making of a film. In addition, although his musical allegiance and bond may be to the composer, ultimately the music editor answers to the director. An ability to work quickly and accurately under pressure, and also to work with grace under people who are not always kind or gracious, is a must. But the role of music editor is an exciting one that is also crucial to the successful completion of the score and the film itself.

TWENTIETH CENTURY FOX FILM CORPORATION

Music Cue Sheet

(Revised July 1998)

PAGE 1

PRODUCTION: <u>DIE HARD WITH A VENGEANCE</u>   OB27

RELEASE DATE: <u>MAY 1995</u>   <u>WORLDWIDE RIGHTS</u>

1MA
COMPOSITION: TWENTIETH CENTURY FOX TRADEMARK   :21 INSTR BACKGROUND
COMPOSER: ALFRED NEWMAN
PUBLISHER: T C F Music Publishing, Inc. (ASCAP)

1MB
COMPOSITION: CINERGI LOGO   :20 INSTR BACKGROUND
COMPOSER: JERRY GOLDSMITH
PUBLISHER: CINERGI PICTURES ENTERTAINMENT INC. (BMI)

1MC
COMPOSITION: SUMMER IN THE CITY   :49 VOCAL BACKGROUND
COMPOSER: STEVE BOONE/MARK SEBASTIAN/JOHN SEBASTIAN
PUBLISHER: TRIO MUSIC CO. INC./ ALLEY MUSIC, INC. (BMI)

1M1
COMPOSITION: SIMON SAYS FIND MCCLANE   1:21 INSTR BACKGROUND
COMPOSER: MICHAEL KAMEN
PUBLISHER: FOX FILM MUSIC CORP. (BMI)

1MD
COMPOSITION: GIFT RAPPED   :14 INSTR BACKGROUND
COMPOSER: MARK MANGINI
PUBLISHER: T C F MUSIC PUBLISHING, INC. (ASCAP)

1ME
COMPOSITION: GOT IT GOIN ON   :38 VOCAL BACKGROUND
COMPOSER: TED SILBERT/RICHARD BAKER
PUBLISHER: SILBERT MUSIC/HIC-TOWN UNDERGROUND/(ASCAP)

1MF
COMPOSITION: THE FAT OUTRO   :38 VOCAL BACKGROUND
COMPOSER: D. LEE/J. OWENS
PUBLISHER: ZOMBA SONGS INC./BACK SLIDING MUSIC/
                   EIGHTY-SECOND SONGS (BMI)

2MA
COMPOSITION: WESTWOOD ON A FRIDAY NIGHT   :13 INSTR BACKGROUND
COMPOSER: MARK MANGINI
PUBLISHER: T C F MUSIC PUBLISHING, INC. (ASCAP)

2MB
COMPOSITION: OFF MINOR   1:29 INSTR BACKGROUND
COMPOSER: THELONIOUS MONK
PUBLISHER: EMBASSY MUSIC CORP. (BMI)

Fig. 11.5. Music Cue Sheet from Die Hard with a Vengeance.
Used by Permission

handwritten annotations in top margin:

like a map of the cue ←

Sketch: a condensed version of the cue, either written on paper or sequenced. Then the composer fills out the measures & bar lines according to the timings required in a scene

CHAPTER 12

The Music Team:
Orchestrators and Music Preparation

In today's world, film composing has become a team sport.
—William Ross

When writing for a large ensemble of instruments, a full score must be created. This is the version that has one line for every instrument—flutes, oboes, clarinets, French horns, trumpets, violins, etc.—and will be used by the conductor at the recording session. However, making this final score is very time consuming, and it is a job usually given to an orchestrator. So instead of filling in all the notes on a thirty- or forty-line piece of score paper, the composer writes a sketch of the music.

A *sketch* is a condensed version of the cue, either written on paper or sequenced, where the composer then fills out the measures and bar lines according to the timings required in a scene. The composer then fills in this sketch to varying degrees of completion. Whether eventually scoring for a full orchestra, a small ensemble, or even when sequencing, a sketch is like a map of the cue. It indicates the timings for each bar and shows the composer where the various dramatic events fall within the boundaries of the music. This sketch can be a simple 2-line piano style version or it can be as many as 10 or 12 staves. It can contain complete information for every melody, counter-melody, chord and even designate individual instruments, as in a John Williams sketch. Or it can be the barest bones, single-line melody with scant harmonic indications, the rest to be filled in by the orchestrator. This sketching process is a great time-saving device for the composer, and allows him to focus on getting the music written for each cue without getting lost in the details of notating the orchestration. It is important to note that many composers, especially the classically trained ones, are excellent orchestrators. Some composers, like Ennio Morricone, insist on having enough time on the film to be able to do their own orchestrations. However, they may still complete a sketch first, and then orchestrate from it. (See Fig. 12.1. Sketch example and finished score.)

In today's world of electronics, the sketch can also be generated as MIDI files. These MIDI files are given to an assistant to edit and make sure the printout matches the composer's music accurately. The orchestrator then works from the assistant's edited sketch. This is also known as a MIDI transcription. Some scores are electronic in the entire music preparation process; the composer generates a MIDI file, it is edited, the orchestrator orchestrates on a software program instead of by hand, and parts are generated automatically from the orchestrator's full score. All of these stages are often accomplished via the Internet, so no one leaves his home or studio until the recording session.

Orchestrators

Once the composer has completed the sketch, or the transcription is prepared, the next stage in the journey to the recording session is the orchestration. As I mentioned, many film composers are fine orchestrators in their own right. In fact, many of these composers started out in the film-scoring business by orchestrating for established composers. However, many very talented film composers, especially those who come from the ranks of rock, pop, and solo jazz music, are not trained in orchestration and rely on their orchestrators to help them achieve an appropriate sound.

*look into orchestrating

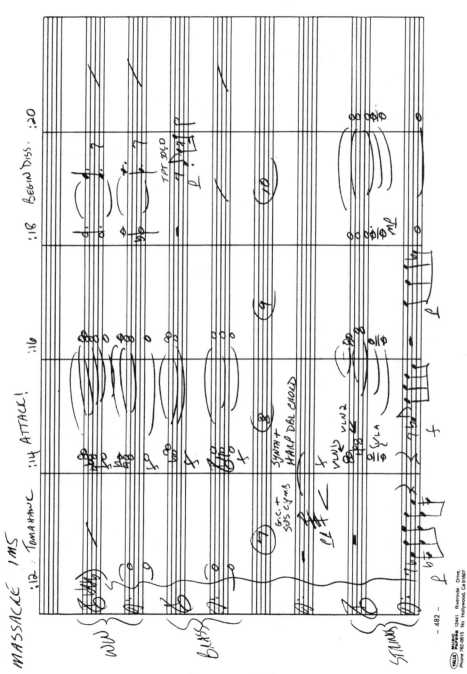

Fig. 12.1. p.1. Sketch.

Fig. 12.1. p.2. Finished score.

William Ross:

An orchestrator is a problem solver. Your best skill as an orchestrator is your ability to solve a problem, whether it's musical, psychological, economic—whatever it is. That's the mission: to solve these problems.

Orchestrators themselves can be from any background in music—classical, jazz, pop, country—but they must have studied composition and orchestration in depth in order to be able to execute what is required of them in a film score. Obviously, a full knowledge of many instruments is required: their high and low ranges, where they sound strong and where they sound weak, which rhythms sound natural and which ones sound awkward, whether there are any troublesome notes, and how they balance, overpower, or blend with other instruments. A thorough knowledge of composition is required since an orchestrator might be required to write a counterline, fill in a harmony, or voice-lead a series of chords.

[handwritten margin note: skills needed for orchestra]

When the sketch is ready, the composer usually meets with the orchestrator and discusses the cues. Depending on how complete the sketch is, the composer will give instructions as to who will play a certain part, or how loud or dissonant a specific measure might get. The orchestrator then goes home and begins working on the full score. Many orchestrators like to have a QuickTime video of the cue, as well as the timing notes so that they can know exactly what is happening in the scene and how the music fits. Oftentimes, the composer and orchestrator have an ongoing relationship, faxing and e-mailing sketches to each other and discussing cues over the phone. This saves a great deal of time so the orchestrator does not have to go back and forth to the composer's home or studio. Once the full score is completed, the orchestrator delivers it to the composer to be proofed, and either a messenger or the orchestrator sends an electronic file to the copyist.

How much the orchestrator has to add, change, or rewrite depends on the composer and the individual project. Often it is a matter of the orchestrator's ability to determine whether the passage in question should remain as it is on the sketch or whether it should be changed.

William Ross has orchestrated for over 100 films, and is also a composer in his own right. He explains the orchestrator's role:

> My job as an orchestrator is to assist the composer in getting the job done. Because of today's post-production schedules, it's very difficult for anyone to compose and orchestrate their own music.

Orchestrators work as independent contractors; they are basically freelance and go wherever their services are needed. The pay scale for an orchestrator is determined by the musicians union (the American Federation of Musicians, or AFM), and is calculated by the number of pages scored (four measures per page) and the number of staves on the page. Depending on the texture and complexity of the cue, this could take a few hours or an entire day. The difficult cues and the easier ones tend to balance each other out in the long run.

One final thought on orchestrators. It is sometimes said that an orchestrator or team of orchestrators has saved a composer. At times this can be true. But the bottom line is that the composer has a vision of the finished music, and even if he sketches only the bare minimum, he is the driving force behind a score. Composers count on the orchestrator's ability to make the music sound good. So if the composer's musical concept is a sound one for the project, then the orchestrator is really just amplifying this concept. If the concept is poor, then no amount of help by the orchestrator can make it succeed.

Music Preparation: Copyists

Once the orchestrator completes the full score it goes to a music preparation office. In the old days of Hollywood, every studio had its own music preparation office. In fact, *all* the music people were under contract and they worked only for that studio. So, the music would go down an in-house assembly line, from composer to orchestrator to

[handwritten margin note: Copyist = the person who makes the parts up for the individual instruments]

[handwritten margin note: proofreader checks the newly copied viola part against the master score for errors]

music preparation to orchestra, and never leave the studio lot. Nowadays, everything is contracted out to individuals or small companies that have offices in various locations.

When an orchestrated cue arrives at the music preparation office, it is checked off on a master chart. There can be as many as forty or fifty individual cues for a single film, so there is a lot to track. The head of this office assigns one or more copyists to work on each cue. The *copyist* is the person who makes the parts up for the individual instruments. In the past two years (1997 to 1998), most of the copying work has converted from being handwritten to computer software-generated, usually either Finale or Sibelius. An orchestrator can turn in either a handwritten score, or a score done in one of these programs, and the copyist can prepare and extract the parts for the orchestra.

Once the copyist finishes a part for a cue, say the viola part, he then gives it to a proofreader. The *proofreader* checks the newly copied viola part against the master score for errors. This is to ensure that these errors are not discovered on the scoring stage where they would take costly minutes to fix (time on a scoring stage can cost several hundred dollars per minute). Once the proofreader completes a part or a stack of parts, he gives them to the supervisor of the music preparation office who then goes to the master chart and checks off those parts that are complete.

The next person in line is the music librarian. This is a crucial job. The *music librarian* sees that every musician in the orchestra has the proper music on his music stand at the start of the session. There can be as many as forty or fifty cues being recorded over just a few days. The composer is in communication with the music preparation office to say what cues he wants to record on which days, and to find out which cues are actually ready. The music librarian consults the master chart to make sure the desired cues are completed, takes the music to the scoring stage, and places the music on the stands of the musicians.

By this point in the production process, the film is often behind schedule, and all these music people can be working under enormous time pressure. It is common for the music preparation office to be in full

[handwritten margin note: music librarian: sees that every musician in the orchestra has the proper music on his music stand @ the start of each session]

swing from 8:00 a.m. until after midnight, or even all night. All of these people are also musicians, and many of the copyists, proofreaders, and music librarians work their way to orchestrating and composing. These are all union jobs, jobs where the salary is dictated by the American Federation of Musicians, which also covers orchestrators and recording musicians. (Interestingly enough, composers do not have to belong.) Because the union has established good "scales" or rates, these music preparation jobs can be financially rewarding.

The Composer's Assistant

Crucial to the composer's team is the composer's assistant. This job has grown in the past decade from someone who was an administrative assistant to a musician with skills in technology, composition, and music editing, amongst others. The assistant is the "go-to person" that works side-by-side with the composer and is on call to take on whatever task is needed.

Please see chapter 25, "Finding Work," for more on the composer's assistant.

Because of the shortened schedules in modern post-production, the composer must rely on his team to get the score from conception to the big screen. This means having reliable people to assist with the myriad details of sequencing, orchestrating, copying, booking musicians, and so forth. The goal is to create a space where the composer can focus on composing, and everyone else does his part to accomplish that.

Fig. 13.1. Scoring Stage. Todd-AO Studios. Studio City, CA.

CHAPTER 13

The Recording Session and Mix

You forget and sometimes you have to pinch yourself and realize, "Oh my goodness, this is amazing!" These are the best players, definitely the best sight-readers in the world. Absolutely the best sight-readers. And, the mistakes-quotient is: there is hardly ever a mistake.
—Lolita Ritmanis

Finally the time has arrived when all the hours of work and preparation become a physical reality. There is nothing like walking onto the scoring stage and seeing dozens of musicians gathered there to play your music. It is the moment every composer waits for.

Present at the session are the composer, conductor (if the composer is not conducting), director, producer, music editor, musicians, recording engineers, and all kinds of assistants and on-lookers. The orchestrators are not required to be there, but often stop by to see how things are going. However, someone with score-reading abilities—usually an orchestrator—sits in the control room with the recording engineer and follows the score to check for errors that the conductor might not hear. This person also assists the engineer in determining which instruments are playing when (especially helpful if there is a solo of some kind). The music editor usually sits behind the conductor or in the control room at a table armed with all the timing notes, a copy of the score, and his computer(s).

This is also an exciting and sometimes anxiety-ridden moment for the film makers. They have put months or years of work into producing the film; all the writing, shooting and editing are complete and the music is the final element to be added. Stephen Spielberg has said that a film is "dry and lifeless" without music, and many agree with him. Even though the director and producer may have seen a sequenced mock-up of the cues, there is nothing like the real thing and there is an *music contractor/contractor: books studio, hires the musicians, takes care of union paperwork & payroll, oversees the sessions to make sure everything is on time & happening to union rules*

air of anticipation, even apprehension, as the session begins. The reality is that when a director hands over the film to a composer, he has just lost control of the film for the first time. What the composer decides to do with the music can literally make or break the film. So the moment of truth is the first day of recording.

In the days or weeks before the sessions begin, the composer and music contractor discuss personnel requirements. The *music contractor*, or simply the *contractor*, books the studio, hires the musicians, takes care of all the union paperwork and the payroll for the musicians, and oversees the sessions to make sure everything is on time and happening according to union rules. In their initial conversations, the composer and contractor discuss the numbers of players and the breakdown of the orchestra—how many strings, woodwinds, brass, rhythm section players, etc., are needed. They also discuss any specific musicians the composer requests, and alternates. Some chairs have very specific requirements. For example, a woodwind chair might need someone who can play flute, soprano sax, recorder, and oboe. It is up to the contractor to find the appropriate players.

The music does not have to be recorded in the order it appears in the film, so the composer decides in advance which cues will be recorded in what order, and the music preparation office, as well as the music editor, are informed. There are different methods of beginning a session. Some like to start with something easy to warm up the orchestra, some like to begin with something fairly challenging. Most composers agree that if there is recurring thematic material, it is good for the orchestra to start with a cue where that material is fairly complete—usually the first or second cue—so that the musicians can hear it and recognize any variations or permutations down the line. Often, this is the main-title cue, but it could also come from another place in the movie.

Sometimes a film requires the entire orchestra to play on every cue. However, many times there are smaller groups that play various cues throughout the film, such as strings only, or a small group of strings, guitar, and oboe that are featured in several cues. In this case, the composer records all the cues for the larger group at one time, and then lets most of the players leave while the smaller group records. This is efficient and cost-effective. The larger group is known as the "A" orchestra, the smaller combinations the "B" orchestra, the "C" orchestra, etc.

Because of an agreement with the musicians union, there are certain rules governing the recording session. For feature films, a maximum of nine minutes of music per three-hour session may be recorded. (Sessions are usually booked in three-hour blocks.) For episodic television (series) and TV movies, a maximum of fifteen minutes per three-hour block is allowed. This is so the producers cannot take advantage of the sight-reading abilities of the musicians and record a huge amount of music in a short amount of time. If the session goes into overtime then these formulas are prorated. In addition, there are other regulations, like taking a ten-minute break every hour, a meal break after a certain amount of hours recording, etc. The contractor, who is the liaison to the union, attends the session and assists the composer in keeping track of these rules.

Once the cue is recorded to the composer's satisfaction, he goes into the control room to join the director and producer, and watch a playback of the scene with the music synced to the film. At this point, the director either signs-off on the cue, or asks for changes. Minor changes can be made right on the spot. If a major rewrite is required, the composer puts that cue away to be fixed before the next session, and he proceeds to another cue.

Every once in a while a composer's score is disliked by the director, the producer, or the studio executives. This can create a situation where the score is thrown out and another composer is brought in to redo it. This is embarrassing for the original composer and frustrating, as he has just spent several very intense weeks of his life on the project. It is also costly for the production team; they must still pay the first composer his full fee, they have paid the musicians and the recording studio for their time, and they must then must hire a second composer and pay the music production costs all over again. It is uncomfortable for all involved, yet it has happened to almost every major feature film composer in Hollywood.

One very important thing to keep in mind is that just because a score is thrown out does not mean that the music is bad, or even inappropriate for that film. All it means is that someone with enough power didn't like it. It is entirely possible that this person (director, producer, studio exec) had his own musical concept and could not make the shift to the composer's different, yet dramatically effective, idea. Whenever a score is thrown out, it causes composers to wonder if they are really good enough, or what they did wrong. It is possible, of course, that the score was not what the production team wanted and the composer made a big error in concept even though the music was sound. But it is also possible that the score was thrown out for an irrational reason that has nothing to do with the quality of the music.

Most of the time, the recording session is an exciting and rewarding moment for the composer. Music representing weeks of work is finally heard and its effectiveness evaluated. Flexibility is a key attribute to have at the session, for changes are often requested. Sometimes the director wants a little more dissonance or less musical activity in a cue. Sometimes a cue needs to be lengthened or shortened. Sometimes everyone, including the composer, is in agreement about a certain change, and sometimes the composer disagrees. The bottom line is that the composer needs to be able to make changes quickly without being overly attached to what was already written. Making movies is a team exercise.

Overlaps and Segues

There are some instances when a composer wants to score a scene, and rather than doing the music in one piece, he records two separate cues and edits them together to create one longer, seamless cue. This is called an *overlap* or *segue*. A composer might do this is if the scene is very long, if there is a significant mood or tempo change, or if there are two completely different groups of instruments involved in each cue.

Most composers like to keep each cue under three to four minutes. This is largely due to the recording process. Although the professional musicians that play the top film scores and television shows are incredible sight-readers, they do occasionally make mistakes. It is very time consuming to stop the orchestra, go back to the start of the cue, reset the projection equipment if there are punches and streamers, and go for another take. In addition, at most sessions there is not true "separation" of the different players or sections of the orchestra in terms of multitrack recording. Although every section gets his own track, and soloists also get assigned a track, in the studio itself there is often bleed-through. So a composer or producer must be very careful about accepting a take and trying to "fix it in the mix." For this reason, it is common practice to try to get the best recording of the entire orchestra at once. (With digital editing, it is now easier to edit different takes together, but there is not always time for this.)

So, if a cue becomes too long, then many composers will find a spot to break it up into two or more cues that are recorded separately and edited together. This can be done seamlessly by matching harmonies, finding common tones from one cue to another, or matching instrumentation. The music editor reassembles the parts into one longer piece.

Such segues are planned when the composer writes the score. The composer constructs a segue from one cue to another so that the sonorities match, or don't match, as is necessary.

Recording Session and Mix

For a feature film, the orchestra is recorded using Pro Tools. Depending on the studio and engineer, there will also be multiple backups; the Pro Tools files will always be copied to other hard drives, and there may be a backup of the audio tracks in some other digital format such as digital tape.

After recording the tracks, the music needs to be mixed. This will usually happen in a mixdown studio, which is much smaller than the one used for recording. Depending on the project, the producer will ask for the music to be delivered in a specific format, or even more than one format such as stereo or surround sound. During the recording session, most engineers begin to set mix levels so that they have a head start when the mix session itself begins. A good film-score engineer can mix ten minutes or even more per day. Compare that to the pop-

STEMS: basically submixes of different groupings of the entire orchestra

Fig. 13.2. Dubbing Stage. Studio 1, Todd-AO Studios. Hollywood, CA.

music record mix, which is going very well if one or two four-minute songs per day are completed.

The mix of the music for films is usually done in _stems_. Stems are basically sub-mixes of different groupings of the entire orchestra. For example, a mixdown engineer might make five stems, which would be pre-mixes of the woodwinds, the strings, the brass, percussion, and everything else. Stems are a compromise between delivering a stereo or surround-sound track completely mixed versus delivering all of the many individual tracks unmixed. With stems, when the music is mixed in with the dialogue and sound effects, there is some flexibility to control these various sections of the orchestra without the complication of dealing with all the individual music tracks, or the restriction of dealing with an already mixed stereo track.

Ideally, the same person who engineers the recording session will do the mix. This person is the most familiar with the music, and thus can move fast. However, sometimes this is not possible. Oftentimes, the schedule is so tight that the music must be mixed as soon as it is recorded. This means that the mixing can overlap the recording. A recording session might begin on Tuesday; on Wednesday, the recording session continues, while Tuesday's tracks are mixed at a second studio.

Dubbing

After the music is mixed to the proper format, it goes to the dubbing stage. This is where the music, sound effects, and dialogue get mixed together for the final soundtrack (see chapter 11).

Reel by reel, scene by scene, line by line, and sometimes crash by crash, the dubbing team mixes, filters, eqs, pans, and generally tweaks the music, sound effects, and dialogue to blend together. Of course, the dialogue is the paramount force here. It always must be heard. But the music and sound effects have important roles as well. The toughest thing is when two sounds happen in the same frequency range. For example, a very high, sustained note in the violins could be cancelled out by the whine of a jet engine. Or a male actor's tender but somewhat throaty declaration of love could be challenged by a lyrical cello line. It is the job of those on the dubbing stage to make all of these things sound like one continuous whole. A sound palette that sounds natural and lets each voice or sound speak where necessary is the ultimate goal.

Dubbing is the next to last stage in the entire film-making process, and it is actually the final stage of the creative process. Nothing can be changed or altered after the dubbing, for the only stage left after this is "color correction"—when the film is processed and the director approves its colors and tints. In many ways, dubbing is the point of no return for the director, for at the various stages of production and post-production, changes can and will be made frequently. During the making of the film, the director makes many decisions, and commits to many paths of action, but the decisions made at the dubbing stage are the final commitment. For this reason, it is a detailed, painstaking process, and the feeling of completion is profound for all.

The Music

PART III

Handwritten annotations at top of page:
1. having a foundation of craft & knowledge of music
2. knowing what you want to say dramatically, emotionally & psychologically
3. knowing your own strengths, weaknesses & capacity to produce.

CHAPTER 14

Creating the Music

It's like anyone else. If the plumber doesn't take the wrench out of the bag, he's never going to get that pipe off, right? Well, if you don't sit down and play something or write something, you're never going to get it finished.
—Mark Isham

There are times when the most intimidating experience a composer can have is looking at a blank sheet of paper or computer screen. And there are other times when that same blank paper can be something he looks forward to filling with wonderful, exciting ideas. This is the reality of the creative process; there are ups and downs, there are times when the ideas just keep coming, and times when the stream is stone dry. For a composer working in films, there is usually no luxury of waiting until the juices start flowing. Often he must find a way to turn on the faucet himself.

Three Cornerstones of Composition

There are several important, yet simple concepts that can help in actually controlling and sometimes even jump-starting the creative process: first, having a foundation of craft and knowledge of music; second, knowing what you want to say dramatically, emotionally, and psychologically; and, third, knowing your own strengths, weaknesses, and capacity to produce. In the film-scoring business, these are all extremely important. As we have seen in other chapters, because the composer comes in at the end of the film-making process, the pressure to produce in a timely manner is often enormous. So a composer relies on his craft, the intent of what he wants to say, and knowledge of his own capacities to deliver the score on time.

① *Craft*

It is important to have developed your craft so you have as much technique as possible. If you write great romantic melodies, but that is all you do well, then obviously you are rather limited. If you are great at action/adventure films, what will you do if the project you accepted requires some scenes in the style of To Kill A Mockingbird? Will you find someone to ghost it?

The more you know about music, and the more different kinds of music you have analyzed extensively, the more tools you have at your disposal. Your musical vocabulary becomes larger and you can speak in many musical languages. Traditional orchestral, atonal, jazz oriented, or pop-music derived soundtracks will not intimidate you if you are thoroughly familiar with how these styles work.

For many, this is an ongoing life-long process that begins early. For every composer there are variations on the theme of musical learning and development. When you begin a project, if you can draw upon many different kinds of musical expressions, you are much better off. You will know the kinds of harmonies, rhythms, and melodies to write. As you watch a scene, or when you sit down to write, your familiarity with a style may start to suggest possibilities. Or if you are stuck, your knowledge of what it should sound like can bail you out. For example, if you know the director wants a particular scene to be heroic, there are certain rhythmic and melodic devices that you can draw from to create something of your own. On the other hand, if your background is narrow, and you are asked to write something outside of what you know, it can be difficult and time-consuming, if not flat-out impossible, to create something appropriate.

Study requires discipline and curiosity. If you are not interested in a particular style, if it doesn't make you sit up and take notice, curl your ears, or give you goose-bumps, then study that style as an academic exercise. This can be a necessary academic exercise for the aspiring film composer.

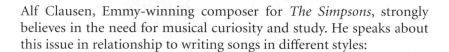

Alf Clausen, Emmy-winning composer for *The Simpsons*, strongly believes in the need for musical curiosity and study. He speaks about this issue in relationship to writing songs in different styles:

> [Students'] questions are always very pointed about "How do you do this, how do you do that, how do you write these styles, etc." My response is to ask, Have you dissected the popular songs of all the eras to find out what makes them work? Have you analyzed them to find out what the chord progressions are, what the melodic tricks are, what chord tones on what chords created a certain sound in a certain era? And can you sit down and write a song in that style because you have spent hundreds of hours dissecting those songs? And they say, "Not yet." Well, I have. I have spent thousands of hours dissecting and playing those songs. It's a matter of craft, it's a matter of study.

Intent and Concept

The intent of your music, or knowing what you want to say, is crucial. There is such a large range of emotion and feeling that can be expressed by music that it often takes a lot of thought, contemplation, and sometimes even prayer to figure out what to do with a particular film or scene. But to start writing without knowing what you want to say is like trying to swim without knowing the strokes; when you get in the water, you would just flail around and desperately try to stay afloat. It is important to take in a whole lot of information: the flow of the drama, the look of the film, and probably most important for the composer, the tempo of the scene. Every film and every scene has its own musical implications, and the composer must know what a film or scene means before beginning to write.

Elmer Bernstein has composed the scores to over 200 films, and is quite familiar with this process:

> The first thing I do is to spend a week just looking at the film without prejudice. When I say without prejudice, I say to myself, I'm not even going to try to think music during this week. I just want to look at the film until the film talks to me and the film

131

tells me things. What I want the film to tell me is what it's about, and that's not always on the surface. What is the film about? What is the function of music going to be in this film? Why are we having music in this film, what's it going to do? So I start with those kinds of thoughts—it's a kind of intellectual process rather than a composing process.

Now, I had a big problem with that in To Kill a Mockingbird, *because if you look at the film without music, all you're looking at is a film with a lot of kids in it. But you're also seeing a lot of adult problems—problems of racism, problems of injustice, death and violence, violence to children. So it took me the longest time to find where the music was going to go, how it was going to go, and what its specific use would be in the film. I determined after a long time—it took me six weeks—that the film is about the adult world seen through the eyes of children. All these problems, what we call adult problems, are seen as the children see them. Which led me to childlike things. For instance, playing the piano one note at a time, music box sounds, harp, bells, things of that sort. So what really got me into the film was the realization— at least, my realization—that it was a film about adult things seen through the eyes of children.*

Taking six weeks, as in *To Kill a Mockingbird*, to think about the approach to a film is a luxury most film composers don't have today. But they usually can take a few days, or perhaps a week, to come up with ideas. Once the concept becomes clear, ideas will often start to flow because the composer has a firm sense of direction.

Knowing Yourself

Dick Grove, a well-known music educator in Los Angeles, used to say, "We all think we're writing music to make money, or to move people. But what we're really doing, if we just take a look, is finding out about ourselves." When we sit down to write music, many things about ourselves come into play: How disciplined am I? How much do I trust my training and ability? How much do I believe in myself? Am I actually enjoying writing music, and having fun? Or is it a chore? Am I following the instructions of the client, or is my ego too big to listen to anyone other than my own infallible creative voice? On the other hand, am I too concerned with what people will think of me to stand up for my opinions, especially if someone asks for something I know is musically a bad idea?

These questions, and others, can come into play every time a composer accepts a gig. At some level in every writer's consciousness, there is an expression of one or more of these questions, whether they have acknowledged it or not. For example, are you the type that procrastinates until the last minute? If so, get a handle on it, for a film with 60 minutes of music won't get written the night before. Do you have a problem taking direction and/or feedback? Lose it, because as soon as you sign the contract, you are somebody's employee. Do you know you can write quickly and appropriately? Nurture that and utilize it. Are you very organized and structured? Stay organized, but don't forget to stay flexible.

When a composer sits down and starts to write, it is essential that he be brutally honest about these questions. He must know how many minutes a day he can produce, how many days there are before the recording session, which cues seem to be suggesting musical ideas, and which cues are tougher. There is very little time for second-guessing and extensive rewriting of any one cue, so confidence in one's technique is crucial. Being clear in ones communication with the director and a willingness to translate the director's requests into music are fundamental to this process.

Developing the Concept for the Score

In speaking with composers, the one thing that comes through again and again is that the most successful scores have a concept that drives the music. Then, once the concept for the whole score is set, each individual cue presents a particular problem to be solved. For example, just because the main concept for a film is big, orchestral, and Romantic doesn't mean that there cannot be a piano solo if the drama calls for it. But that piano solo must still feel like part of the rest of the score. In today's world, almost any musical language is part of the composer's palette, so the choices abound. But keeping to the overall concept keeps the sound focused.

Elliot Goldenthal is an accomplished composer of film scores, ballets, theatre, and concert works. He has found a way of approaching a score that produces a unique sound for each of his projects:

> Before I approach anything, I have a very strong concept of what I want to pull off, whether it works out or not. That might include limiting the choice of pitches or a very clear choice of orchestration. So I don't go into something and just start improvising, I find that if I do that, I just sort of waste my time. I stay away from the piano, away from the computer, away from the pencil. I think about the scene and I say, How can I achieve the dramatic effect that is necessary for the scene and have it still sound fresh? How can I make it sound like you haven't heard that before, you haven't lived that before? Sometimes the answer can be surprisingly simple. In Alien 3, for example, I used a solo piano to underline the scene with the little girl because I thought that having a piano way out in space would remind you of the most domestic of all instruments—it would remind you of home. Just things like that. That's a concept.

Sometimes a composer's concept for a film can be generated from a feeling or an idea that, in itself, is not musical. Many composers are very artistic in the way they look at the world; that is to say, they see the world in terms of emotional responses that eventually get translated into music. Clearly, this is a very valuable way to see things from the standpoint of writing music for the visual medium of film. Cliff Eidelman discusses his conception of the score to One True Thing:

> I had this idea of time changing, the changing of seasons. The feeling of wind passing through trees and then leaves blowing off in another direction. This wasn't music yet; it was just a feeling I wanted to add.

I set individual instruments apart from the orchestra, separated into their own isolation booths. Like three cellos in one room, or three violas with two woodwinds in another. They were off in their own rooms and the orchestra was in the center. Now, my concept was that the piano should be the main idea, accompanied by a small orchestra so that it felt intimate, and never too large. An introverted mood.

I also wanted it to feel like wind was carrying the music this way and out that way, creating different perspectives. The music wasn't just coming from the center of the room. It was coming from over here, and it shifted over there, and then it would come back over here.

So, early on, this conceptual approach merged with the themes. When I started producing musical ideas, my concepts worked their way in.

For me, the main thing is always the spine of the story. So, the first thing I do is look for that emotional core—that emotional spine of the story—within the soul of the music itself.

In *Forrest Gump*, Alan Silvestri had to come up with an opening music cue that would embody the whole film. He first discussed the opening shot, of the feather floating down from the sky and almost landing on Forrest, with director Robert Zemeckis:

[Zemeckis] didn't really go into a whole lot of detail, but the gist of what we did talk about was somehow, "This is the start of the movie. This is the start of this whole incredible odyssey we're about to go on." My take on it was ... I've got a couple of things to deal with now. One is, I've got physical things to deal with. I've got some events; the feather floats from the blue sky, makes an entrance into this town. It winds up almost landing on somebody's shoulder then at the last moment it's blown off. It's very symbolic, you know, if you're looking at this as something descending upon someone's life, that guy is not chosen right now. Then eventually the feather lands on Forrest; he's the chosen one.

So now we've got some physical things in terms of the image, and we've also got some events that are episodic in a sense. Coming from nowhere, blue sky, into this town, what does it mean? It's just a feather, then it almost lands on somebody, blows off. Now, there's some kind of dramatic context.

So now, what do you do? The invisible aspect of this is that somehow whatever you do also has to essentialize and embody this entire film. Right now. This cannot be "feather music." This cannot be "falling down music." This cannot be "missed opportunity music." This music somehow has to take everything, sentiment wise, that this film is about, and somehow essentialize it and present it. I'm thinking, at this point, if I can find that, I've got the key to this film. This theme will be all over the movie, and there will be a tremendous sense of cohesiveness for the overall tone of this film.

Now of course all of this is going on under the surface because I'm not sitting there making lists and treatises on 1M1. I know I've got to do something here. So I sit down at the piano, and I'm thinking, "This music has to deal with Forrest," and I start doodling at the piano. Literally in 20 minutes it's done! It's childlike, and it's simple, and yet it's not baby-like. It's innocent. It's what I'm feeling from Forrest. I look at this moment, where the feather moves away from this other guy. I make a key change there—an immediate unprepared key change there. We already planned that we're going to bring the orchestra in, with more sense of scope at this point.

That was the mission in Forrest. It had to be an honest attempt. Musically, as an actor, as a writer, as a cinematographer, don't get cute with this movie, or you'll sink the ship.

This anecdote embodies many of the principles outlined above with Silvestri's own personality and musical sensibility bringing it to its ultimate destination. He had a clear idea of what he needed to do, and what *not* to do dramatically. And having this understanding, he was able to sit down and create the theme that was just right for this film.

(Ironically, this theme was eventually used in only one other spot in the film: the ending where we see the feather again. Every time he tried to use it elsewhere, it just didn't work.)

One of the joys of film composing is this process of discovering a concept. Unlike writing concert works or pop songs, the film composer is responding to the visual images and the story on the screen. These images and story-lines suggest musical ideas and provide a framework within which the music can fit. Many composers have said that once they find the initial concept, the rest of the score writes itself. The trial and error, the thought, and contemplation often result in the stimulation of the composers imagination. Then he experiences the satisfaction of completing the director's vision of the film in the language of music.

CHAPTER 15

Technical Requirements of the Score

Nobody goes to the movies to listen to the score.
The score is simply assisting them in watching the film.
—Michael Kamen

Once a composer arrives at a concept for the score, he is ready to begin writing individual cues. However, there are many things to consider for each cue: its placement in the film, what kind of scene it is, whether or not there is dialogue, and how much of the story the music should express. These are just some of the many important considerations in structuring the score of a movie.

Perhaps the most important factor here is that a film can be anywhere from a short subject of just a few minutes to a full-length feature of over two hours. Either way, as the story unfolds on screen, the music must continually develop so that it stays interesting. Themes develop, instrumentation develops, and the overall emotional thrust of the music has an arch that matches the arch of the film. In addition, the music can affect the way the film has been put together; it can smooth out cuts, transitions, or dissolves. It can also help the audience understand shifts in location in time or place. Every cue has an impact that the composer and director are considering when placing it in the movie.

The first question that faces the composer is "What is this cue's dramatic function?" For the purposes of this discussion, I divide the various functions of film music into three broad categories: physical functions, psychological functions, and technical functions. As the interviews at the end of this book illustrate, every composer has a different working procedure. They each approach the task of writing a score and coming up with suitable material from a different angle.

Sometimes they intellectually analyze a scene and determine its musical requirements; sometimes they write from instinct. Frequently, some of the functions of the music overlap, or are vague, because every situation is different and can have more than one dramatic implication.

✳ Physical Functions

Music frequently functions in a way that impacts the physical action or location of the scene. This includes:

Setting the location of the film. If a movie takes place in an exotic location, often this setting is reflected in the music. For example, a movie that takes place in Ireland could use Uillean pipes and a pennywhistle. A movie that is set in the Appalachian Mountains of the United States might call for banjos and fiddles. How much this "ethnic" music is incorporated into the score will be a decision made by the composer and the director. They could decide to have the score sound authentic to the location, or simply incorporate one or two elements of the ethnic music into an orchestral score. (See chapter 15 for more on this.)

Setting the time period. If a movie takes place in another historical era, sometimes music of that time will be used. For example, if a film is set in 18th century Europe, a harpsichord can be used to give the audience an immediate association with that time. For movies set in medieval times, there are various ancient instruments like shawm, sackbutt, or psaltery that can be used. Again, as in *setting the location*, the composer may use a lot of these sounds, or just a hint.

Mickey-mousing. When the music mimics every little action on screen, it is called *mickey-mousing*. There is a difference, however between mickey-mousing and simply hitting various sync points. Mickey-mousing is a term reserved for hitting a lot of the action, not just one or two moments. It is often, though not exclusively, used as a comic device, as the music will imitate a character falling down the stairs, etc.

Intensifying the action. This musical technique is commonly used in action scenes. Chase scenes, fights, intense arguments between characters, and suspenseful moments are all heightened with appropriate

[handwritten margin note: Mickey mousing: when the music mimics every little action on screen]

music. To intensify the drama, composers might write music that closely follows the action onscreen, and often has many sync points. In this way, music partners with the drama very closely and accentuates what is seen, as opposed to bringing a different emotional element to the scene.

✳ Psychological Functions

Music can assist the psychological and emotional impact of the film in many ways. Sometimes it can be parallel to the drama and say basically the same thing as what is viewed on-screen. At other times, the music can add a new dimension, thought, or idea that is not expressed by dialogue or action. Some of the psychological functions of film music are:

Creating the psychological mood. Every film score must have a "sound" to be successful. If the movie is one that has psychological implications, then the overall mood of the score or any individual scene becomes very important. For example, in *What Dreams May Come*, a film that deals with death and the afterlife, a score was originally composed that was dark and somewhat serious. The production team decided that this approach did not work; it was too dark and needed to be lightened up. So they brought in Michael Kamen to redo the score three weeks before the release of the film.

Michael Kamen:

> *The original score was too serious. This film is about death and dying and it's a very serious film. I was asked to go the other way with it. I felt very close to the subject matter, as I had a real life experience at that time: my wife had just overcome a mortal illness. So I was able to respond to the film with joy and some sense of magic.*

There are countless examples of a change in the music altering the impact of a scene or an entire movie. The composer must continually be aware of the result of any musical moods, or even individual melodies or harmonies.

Revealing the unspoken thoughts and feelings of a character. Often, a director wants the audience to understand something about the character that is either not expressed verbally or not entirely clear from the visual action. The music can help to communicate these things because it can represent another dimension of the character's inner world—his thoughts, feelings and deepest emotions. A good example of this is the movie, *Thunderheart,* starring Val Kilmer. In this film, Kilmer plays an FBI agent sent to investigate a murder on an American Indian reservation. His father was half Indian and part of the plot deals with his character's struggle to understand his own heritage and ancestry. Towards the beginning of the film, when Kilmer's character first arrives in South Dakota, he sees an ancient Indian costume on display. The visual shows him simply staring at the costume, expressionless, but the music is tense and dark, representing his confused frame of mind.

Revealing unseen implications. How many times have we watched the good guy draw his gun and slowly walk down a deserted alley in search of the bad guys? Then the low strings come in with a sustained, swelling note, and we *know* they're out there somewhere! The music can tip us off to what is going to happen, both in a suspenseful way, and in a way that resolves a situation.

Deceiving the audience. In the same way as *revealing unseen implications,* the music can set us up to believe something will happen, but then a different event takes place. Sometimes known as a "reversal," in this case the music can simply be mirroring what we see on screen, or it can add another dimension to a scene that is visually neutral. This is most often used in suspenseful situations.

✳ Technical Functions

The technical functions are when the music aids the overall structure of the film:

Creating continuity from scene to scene. (Also known as "making a transition.") Music can help the viewer make a transition from one scene to another. This is a result of the way the human brain processes information. If we watch a scene that ends, and then we cut to another scene in a different location, obviously the eye is very aware of this change. Many times an abrupt visual change is appropriate, but sometimes it is desirable to soften this change. Music can help achieve this by beginning in the first scene, and carrying over to the second. In this way, both the eye and the ear are engaged; the eye takes in the abrupt scene change, and the ear hears a continuous piece of music. The total effect is one that is smooth; the music effectively overrides the visual aspect.

Creating continuity of the entire film. By using themes and textures that return throughout the film, the music can create a continuity of sound. These can be leitmotifs, where certain characters, emotions, or places have distinct musical motifs. There might also be one or several themes that appear in various instruments and harmonic settings. Or there could be a certain combination of instruments or sounds that carry through the entire film. By continually developing one or more elements of the music further, such as certain melodies or instrumentation, the composer can create a dramatic build. Here are three examples:

In *Fly Away Home*, Mark Isham uses a small ensemble featuring solo viola during much of the first part of the film. As the story grows and becomes more dramatic, so does the size of the orchestra. However, the same theme appears throughout, played by the different size groups. This creates a unity in the music even though the sonority grows in size.

In *E.T., The Extra-Terrestrial*, John Williams presents fragments of a particular theme throughout the film in various scenes. It is not until the climactic "flying scene" that these fragments come together as a complete musical statement. This is an example of the music developing with the plot. The basic musical idea is similar in several situations, but the audience doesn't hear it as a complete idea until the story line is also complete.

In *Speed*, Mark Mancina uses a combination of several metallic-sounding samples to create an electronic texture. This is used throughout the film as a sound "palette" that mirrors the urgency of the dramatic situation.

be sensitive to film's action & director's vision

Following the Drama

This is the part of writing a film score that separates those who really can from those who would like to. There are many composers who can write excellent music, but not all are sensitive to the film's action or the director's vision. Once the spotting is done, the director has given his input, the placement of themes has been decided, and the deadlines are clear, then all that is left is to choose which notes will sound and who will play them. These choices are inherently subjective. Every composer decides a scene's musical needs according to his own dramatic sensitivity and musical taste. Many choices contribute towards determining the shape and tone of the music in each scene. Remembering that the music is a partner to the drama also helps keep the focus of the music. Some of these choices are:

- Tempo. What is the rhythm of the film editing? How are the individual shots cut together? What is the overall pacing of the movie? Are there musical tempos implied by this?

Syncing
- Are there many sync points? Just one or two? Or is the music meant to just "wash" over the scene?

Is it needed
- Are there moments that require a musical comment?

Role
- How much is the music telling the story? Or is it more neutral and mood-setting?

- Is there source music in the beginning or end of the cue that needs to be taken into account in terms of key, tempo, etc.?

- What is this cue's placement in relation to the whole dramatic arch of the film?

- Where is this cue's placement in terms of other cues? Are they close in time? Do the keys have to match?

- Should the cue modulate for dramatic or musical reasons?

- Should there be orchestration changes accompanying the drama?

This list can go on, for the composer must answer many questions and make many choices. But this process is not always a conscious one. The more experienced a composer gets, the more his instincts get developed.

144

Many of the questions above are asked and answered on a subconscious level. However, it is important to look at every film and break down every scene from many angles in order to really make the music fit.

Writing for Dialogue

Writing for a scene with dialogue is one of the trickiest things for a composer. There is no one way to do it, for every situation is different. The approach to writing music under dialogue is determined by any number of factors, including the mood of the scene, the pacing of the scene, the amount of sound effects present, and the importance of the dialogue itself to the plot. And ultimately, the music will probably be dubbed, or mixed in, very low under the actors' lines. This is the natural fate of film music, for it is meant to accompany the action, and only infrequently does it take a starring role.

There are different schools of thought on the use of music under dialogue; some believe that it is good to move the music when the actors pause, and sustain the music when the actors are speaking. This is a technique used by many composers over the years. Some composers always write sustained tones during dialogue—this is another valid technique. However, it is best to consider every situation to be different, having its own musical requirements.

In order to determine the appropriate music for dialogue scenes, there are melodic, harmonic, and orchestrational factors to take into consideration. How active should the melody be? How thick should the chord be? What instruments should play? Here are several questions to consider when writing under dialogue:

What is being said? If the actors are declaring their undying love, or if some important element of the plot is being revealed, then the music must support that mood, and at the same time stay out of the way. One way to do this is to write a very transparent texture that allows the voices to cut through. However, sometimes a rich texture is appropriate; the theme could soar into the stratosphere while the actors are speaking, and the music will be mixed very low underneath the dialogue.

✳ *Who is speaking?* There are times when a particular register of a certain instrument conflicts with the actor's voice. For example, cello or French horn played between middle C and C an octave below share the same range as most male voices, and might fight for attention with the dialogue. Instruments between G below middle C, and G an octave higher might fight with a woman's speaking voice. However, whether or not such conflicts actually occur depends on the quality of the voice and the way the melody is constructed. The kinds of intervals used, the tempo, and the overall busyness or simplicity of the melody also contribute to the degree of conflict. Large melodic intervals, quicker tempos, syncopated rhythms, and busy melodies tend to draw the audience's attention to the music and away from the dialogue.

✳ *What is the pacing of the dialogue?* Are the lines spoken quickly, with urgency, or is the actor taking his time? Are there pauses between each line, or do they come rapid-fire, with each line overlapping the previous one? These considerations will help determine how fast the music moves. For example, the composer can accentuate quickly-spoken lines with very active music, or he can provide a cushion for those lines with long sustained tones.

✳ *What is the pacing, or tempo, of the film editing?* How the film is edited can provide another clue to finding appropriate music under dialogue. For example, as with the pacing of the actors lines, the composer can write music that mirrors a lot of fast cuts, or it can soften those cuts with a melody line of long tones.

Perhaps the most important point to make about writing music for dialogue is that the music should not draw too much attention to itself. Ninety-nine percent of the time, the dialogue reigns. If the music draws too much attention to itself, two things are likely: the cue will be rejected and the composer asked to redo it, or it will be dubbed very low in the mix. The best music under dialogue is that which reflects the dramatic situation, can be heard through the speaking, and allows the voices to be in the foreground without any aural conflict.

main title: music that is played at the beginning of the movie when the credits are rolling
end credits: when the film has ended & everyone is being named; usually a song to make money.

Technical Requirements of the Score

The Main Title

The music that is played at the beginning of the movie when the credits are rolling is called the *main title music*, or simply the *main title*. The goal of the main title music is to set the mood and tone of the film. The audience needs to know what kind of story they are about to experience, and the music should tell them. There are several different approaches to this music, which will be determined by the director's vision. If there are simply credits rolling and the names are all that is seen, then the music will probably be featured. Similarly, if the credits are rolling, and we are seeing footage of the location of the film, the music will also be featured. However, if there is dialogue while the credits are rolling, then the music takes a more subservient role; it will not be so much in the foreground, and act more as an underscore.

The main title music is often one of the few places where the composer can "stretch out" a little bit because there are often no dramatic moments to hit, and because the cue is usually about two to four minutes long. This is enough time to make a complete musical statement, especially if the theme has an "A" and "B" section, whereas in many cues during the movie there is not enough time to complete these ideas.

The End Credits

The *end credits* come when the film has ended, and all the people that worked on the film are being named. Often the music in this part of the film is a song, rather than instrumental music based on the underscore. The reason for this is usually pure commerce. Producers hope that because the song is the last thing heard, that it will stick in people's minds and make them want to buy the soundtrack album. This is a logical business decision, but often one that has very strange dramatic implications. It can feel like an intrusion when at the end of a two-hour movie with an orchestral underscore, a pop song with drum set, synthesizers, electric guitar, and electric bass suddenly begins.

However, there are many films that do use orchestral music to accompany the end credits. In this case, the composer usually develops themes presented during the film. Because of the length of the end credits, often five or six minutes, and the fact that the composer is free from dramatic considerations, he can write a piece that is more like a suite. Unfortunately, very few people remain in the theater to hear this music.

Composing with Synths vs. Pencil and Paper

There are two distinct approaches to actually writing the score; one school writes on a synthesizer and sequences the music, the other prefers writing with a pencil and paper. Both methods have adherents who have achieved great success, and there are those who practice both, depending on the kind of score required.

The pencil and paper method has the advantage of giving the composer a slow-motion experience of every note and every chord. There are no "happy accidents" where the hand just seems to find a particular voicing. This method forces the brain to consider every note and its placement because notes need to be specified one at a time. In addition, writing with pencil and paper requires a certain expertise and experience in being able to imagine the music and to hear what it will eventually sound like even though it is just dots and lines on a piece of paper.

The main advantage of using a sequencing program is that it can be faster. A composer can play his ideas, or play along to the video, and it is instantly recorded and notated. A transcriber can clean up the output from the sequencer and then give it to an orchestrator. So the composer can really churn out the music in a short amount of time, especially if he has a team of people helping.

For every composer, the reasons for choosing one method over another differ. Some can write in the traditional way if they want to but because of time pressures they use the sequencing method. Other composers are not as trained in music notation, so it is much easier for them to realize their ideas exclusively from a keyboard.

In addition, sometimes the film itself requires a score with strange textures that can best be designed and sampled at a keyboard, or played by unusual instruments that are layered one over the other. This is something that you can hire professional players to do, or learn yourself. Mark Mancina has had great success with pure sampling, sampling in combination with live orchestra, and designing sounds with unusual instruments.

Mark Mancina:

> *I was doing documentaries all through the '80s, and because of the budget, everything was done electronically, with MIDI. With the advent of samples, I could create something that sounded pretty good. It became, for some of the movies that I have done, a real advantage. For a movie like Speed it had to be done that way. The concept of that score for me was to take orchestral percussion and replace it with metallic and metal sounding percussion, which I sampled and set up specifically for that score using all sorts of tin cans and things. All of a sudden Speed became such a huge hit and a big movie that I kind of fell into the "electronic composer" category because I used rhythm and electronic sounds for that score.*

> *[Now] I'm very tired of MIDI, and I don't like anything in my scores that isn't played live. I don't like that electronic sound. It has worked on some movies that I've done, but I feel it doesn't work in a lot of movies, although now I hear it done a lot.*

As you have seen, there is never only one solution to a creative problem, and every composer has his own viewpoint and method of working. There are many variations on the same theme. When writing a score with many cues, there is a lot to consider. Some composers plan every cue for thematic content and key center. Some create as they go, and their basic musicianship enables them to make a unified musical statement as the movie unfolds. Whether you plan everything out or do it on the fly, understanding how the music functions in any situation is crucial to creating a successful score.

You may be wondering, "Once I've got my dramatic concept, how do I start writing?" Which notes to put on paper, on your sequencer, or on your hard disc recorder is something that cannot be taught, much less talked about in a book. It will be the sum of your musical *and* personal experience—your ability as a player, how much music you have absorbed over the years through listening and study, your musical philosophy, your life experience, and your personal outlook on life. No one can dictate taste and musical choices; that is what gives every composer a unique musical expression. The way to find yours is by doing it—by writing scores, playing gigs, listening, studying, making choices along the way, and learning what works for you.

CHAPTER 16

Syncing the Music to Picture

Scoring sessions are the greatest thing in making movies because the film is ... cut by then.... It's the first time you can sit back and watch the picture come together.[1]
—Stuart Baird

Like many technologies in today's modern digital world, the methods available to a composer for synchronizing music to picture are expanding. Traditionally, the composer waited to receive timing notes from the music editor before beginning to write individual cues. However, with today's technology, it is possible to score an entire film without ever creating any timing notes, and still sync the music to the picture. In fact, this is how many composers work, especially those that write directly into a sequencing program. This chapter discusses the various methods of syncing, beginning with the traditional way of using timing notes. First it is necessary to understand some basic mathematical ratios and terminology of film and music:

Frame:
A film is actually a strip of thousands of photographs passing through a lens, giving the illusion of movement. Each of these individual "photos" is called a frame.

24 frames per second:
The speed that 16- and 35-millimeter film (most feature films) run through the projector.

30 frames per second:
The speed that something originally shot in video will run through the VCR (in the United States).

⚸ Two to four frames :

The amount of error that the human eye can see if the music is out of sync. Remember those old black and white "B" movies where the actors' mouths and the actual words are out of sync? This could be a differential of as little as two frames for the viewer to discern the difference. Converted to seconds, two frames equals $\frac{1}{12}$ or .08 seconds. In terms of time, that is a tiny fraction of a second. But the eye, ear, and brain are fast and can pick up that small of a difference.

⚸ Sync point

A place in the action that a composer wants to accent. This can be the end of a line of dialogue, a cut from scene to scene, or a piece of physical action like a fight, a chase, or a kiss. (A sync point is also called a hit, the place where the music "hits" a certain piece of action or a cut.)

No matter which synchronization method is used, the first thing for a composer to do is view the cue several times. The most important thing at this point is to *get a feel for the tempo of the cue*. Often, the on-screen drama suggests certain rhythms, and the way the different shots have been edited together suggests a certain pacing. Sometimes the music goes against action on-screen. For example, there could be a chase scene where the music moves very slowly for a dramatic reason. Whatever the conclusion, the tempo of the music must be established before writing can begin.

Once an approximate tempo is reached, the composer decides where there should be sync points, if any. Reference to the spotting notes and any decisions or requests from the director are noted, and the composer arrives at a general musical concept for the cue. Some cues have no sync points, and the music just "washes" through the action, creating an overall mood or feel. Others, especially action cues, can have many sync points. When the music mimics the action exactly, it is called *mickey-mousing*, coming from the old cartoons when the music followed the action almost beat by beat (this term is used whether it happens in cartoons or not).

window burn: a rectangular box on the screen of the work print that shows the reel, mins, seconds, & either hundredths of a second or frame numbers; visual representation of SMPTE

The timing of sync points can also be determined from the _window burn_—a rectangular box on the screen of the work print that shows the reel, minutes, seconds, and either hundreths of a second or frame numbers. This is actually a visual representation of the SMPTE time code used to lock up the video equipment to the audio.

Fig. 16.1. Window Burn.

Once the composer determines the sync points, he figures out how to tailor the music so that these sync points come at logical places in the music, often at downbeats.

Then the composer decides which method of synchronization to use—click track, clock, or punches and streamers. If a cue has a lot of sync points, or if the music is fast and rhythmically difficult, then a click track would be appropriate. If the music calls for rubato and

Punches & Streamers: a technique needed to be developed where the composer/conductor could manipulate the music to synchronize exactly with the film

Complete Guide to Film Scoring

expressive passages, then punches and streamers or clock allow that kind of interpretation. If the cue is short, or if there are no sync points that need accurate timing, then the clock would be appropriate.

Punches and Streamers

In the early days of sound films, it was apparent that a technique needed to be developed where the composer/conductor could manipulate the music to synchronize exactly with the film. The first method that was developed was that of *punches and streamers*. It was realized that once the composer decided the exact timing of where he wanted a musical hit, at the recording session that exact frame could be anticipated and the music synchronized to it. The way this worked was that the music editor would literally punch a hole in that particular frame (of the work print, not the negative) so that when the film passed through the projector, that frame would come out as a flash of light instead of a visual image. But that flash, or punch, needed to have a preparation. So a system was developed where the music editor would literally scrape a line (a streamer) on the film for a certain length, usually 3, 4, or 5 feet, which equals 2, 2⅔, and 3⅓ seconds. The conductor would then see a vertical line move across the screen from left to right, ending in a flash of light at the exact frame with which the music should synchronize. (See Fig. 16.2. Punches and Streamers.)

When using punches and streamers, there are often *reference punches*, also known as *flutter punches*. These are punches that show the conductor if he is going too fast or too slow. They are often placed at every bar, or every other bar, as tempo guideposts. Before computers, a music editor would find the frame of film in which a composer wanted to see a flutter punch, and punch a hole in every other frame of a five-frame sequence. The appearance on the screen when these five frames go through the projector is of a "flutter" of light. These reference punches are not meant to be hard and fast sync points; they are simply guideposts telling the conductor to speed up or slow down a bit.

Today, the music editor no longer has to manually punch holes and prepare the actual film; punches and streamers are generated by computer programs. This is a great advantage, for in the old days, if a

*reference/flutter punches:
punches that show the
conductor if he is going
too fast or too slow*

Punch

Streamer (3)

Streamer (2)

Fig. 16.2. Punches and Streamers.

Streamer (1)

change in the music was requested after the punches and streamers were prepared, it could not be done right away, on the spot. The composer and music editor would have to redo the cue, often that night, and record it at another session. With a computer generating punches and streamers, it is possible to make extensive changes on the spot, as long as the composer is able to shift things musically and the music editor is skilled at programming the software.

Using punches and streamers is actually a very accurate method of synchronization, if the conductor is skilled. The advantages of conducting to punches and streamers are that the music can be very flexible and expressive because it is not locked to a metronome, or click track. Also, the conductor sees the film, so he can react to it. The disadvantages are that the technology is not always available, and that if there are a lot of sync points, if the music is fast and difficult rhythmically, or if there are many tempo changes, punches and streamers do not serve the music well.

Click Track

A *click track* provides the tempo the conductor and musicians hear during a recording. Whereas metronome markings are measured in *beats per minute* (BPM), traditionally, film click tracks have been measured in *frames per beat* (FPB). This enables precise synchronization of the music to the film.

Today, computers enable click tracks to be generated in either format, but for many years composers indicated click tempos in their score, marked as pairs of numbers: 24-0, 12-7, 18-3. This has its origins from the early days of film, before the age of computers, when music editors created click tracks by punching holes in loops of film. The hole would pass over the projector's optical sound head and cause a pop, or "click," at a regular interval determined by the length of the loop.

The two numbers represent how many frames, and divisions of the frame, at which the hole would be punched. Since film runs at 24 frames per second, 24-0 FPB indicates a tempo of one beat every 24 frames (one hole punched every 24 frames), or one beat per second

M
A
T
H

(corresponding to a traditional metronome marking of mm=60 BPM). Lower numbers indicate faster tempos. The indication 12-0 FPB means two beats per second, or mm=120. The loop of film was shorter and the punched holes moved through the projector with greater frequency, causing a faster click.

The second click-track number is a very small measurement. Composers and music editors realized early on that smaller increments than one whole frame were necessary, so they used the film's sprocket holes as guides for smaller subdivisions. There are four sprocket holes in each frame of film (see Fig. 10.1.), and a hole could be punched at one of these holes or in between them. This gave eight possible increments of click track tempo for each frame. If a composer wanted a tempo slightly faster than 60 beats per minute, instead of punching a hole every 24 frames for a 24-0 click, he might try 23-7, 23-6, or 23-5.

The human ear can't distinguish measurements that small, and short cues of just a few seconds don't require such precision. However, on cues lasting several minutes, these fractions add up, and the difference can mean hitting or missing an action on-screen at the end of the cue.

Funding the tempo

There are several mathematical formulas that can be used for finding a click tempo in frames per beat; these were used in the early days of film. Also, *click track books* list the timing on every beat at dozens of possible tempos.

In the 1950s a device called the Urei Digital Metronome was developed. This electronic metronome ended the need for film loops running through a synchronized projector, for it could generate any FPB click tempo electronically with the simple turn of a dial.

Nowadays, computers and sequencers are also used to find and generate click tracks. These easily express tempo markings in FPB and in BPM, which are now also divisible into tiny increments.

A click track is best used when the tempo is constant, when it is very fast, when the music is rhythmically complex, or when there are many sync points to catch. Some cues require a *variable click track*. This is

157

variable click track: same as regular click track but with one or more tempo changes

the same as a regular click track, only there are one or more tempo changes. These tempo changes can begin immediately at a new bar line, or can be prepared with warning clicks if the musicians are holding a long note or fermata. There can also be "ramps," or gradual accelerandos or ritardandos in the music. Some composers use very slight variations of click from measure to measure in order to make it sound more "real" and less mechanical. At the recording session, the music editor will have programmed the computer with the proper tempo changes, and monitors this process to ensure that the synchronization is accurate.

Clock

stopclock: conductor watches a giant clock

Another method of syncing music to film is the use of a *stopclock*, now simply called a *clock*. In this case, the conductor watches a large analog clock with a sweep hand (basically a large stopwatch about 12 inches in diameter). Using the clock method gives some flexibility in the music, but realistically, it is accurate for sync points only to plus or minus a third of a second. When using the clock, the music editor's job is fairly easy; he just has to know where the music is beginning and ending, and make sure that the conductor is accurate.

Wild

wild: recording w/o any kind of sync reference

There is one final way of recording a cue, and that is called recording *wild*. This is not when all the musicians go to the studio commissary and party down; it refers to recording without any kind of synchronization reference. A cue is recorded without clicks, punches and streamers, or the use of a clock. The music editor is then responsible for seeing that it is cut into the film at the proper point. This method is often used for very short cues, or cues where changes have been made at the recording studio and the previously prepared synchronization method is no longer valid. If the cue is longer than a few seconds, its success will depend on the skills of the conductor.

There are distinct advantages and disadvantages to each synchronization method:

Pros & Cons

Punches and streamers are great if the music needs to be free, flexible, or rubato. They are fun to conduct to! They can make your sync points accurate to the desired frame. They can facilitate tempo changes and be effective in any music where there are a lot of holds or fermatas. The disadvantages are they are difficult to use if the music is very fast, rhythmically complex, or has a lot of sync points. The effectiveness of punches and streamers depends on the ability of the conductor. Computers with software that can generate punches and streamers are not available in some studios.

Click tracks are great if you have a lot of sync points or if your music is fast or rhythmically difficult. They can give you spot-on accuracy in making sync points and can assist the players in staying together when there are difficult rhythmic patterns. A variable click track can give very secure tempo changes. The disadvantage to clicks is that they become robotic with a stiff and unmusical pulse. One way around this stiffness is for the studio to send the click into the headphones of the conductor, but not the musicians. This can improve the feel a bit.

Recording to clock is good for having flexibility in the music. It is a desirable method when punches and streamers are not available. It is good for shorter cues that don't require a lot of drama, like going to commercial in a TV show. The disadvantage is that using the clock is the least accurate of all the methods, so if you have any sync points that need to be dead-on, this method is not preferred. Using the clock is accurate to about one third of a second, or eight frames. Remember the rule of thumb that the human eye/ear connection can determine a differential of two to four frames.

Sequencing

Many composers do not use timing notes in the traditional way; they prefer to just play along with the video on a keyboard until they get an idea that they like. Sometimes they establish a specific click in advance because they know where they want to hit the action. But more often than not, they play without a tempo reference and sequence their ideas. If the sequence is going to be orchestrated and eventually recorded live, it then can fall to a music editor, or a composer's assistant, to construct a click track for the musicians to play along to at the recording session. This can be painstaking, and often results in the use of a variable click because of the natural variations of tempo that occur during live playing of the sequence. Sequencing programs allow the composers to "tweak" a sequence and move the tempo around; if the composer is a few frames early or late on a specific hit, that moment can be moved to be more exact. However, if a click is used while the composer is sequencing, that is easiest for the music editor, for it keeps the composer's tempo "honest."

Note that if a sequence is the final music for the project, then all of this is fairly straight-forward. All you must do is correctly edit and align the sequence to the places you want to hit. But if you are using the sequence as a mock-up of the cue, as a sketch, or as a way of generating some initial ideas, and the sequence is going to be orchestrated and then played live, then the process can be complicated. It may require a team of people: music editor, MIDI transcriber, and orchestrator to realize a synchronized cue.

Music editor Eric Reasoner describes working with composers who sequence, as well as those who use timing notes to prepare their score:

> There are a couple different modes of working. Some composers play stuff into a keyboard and sequencer while locked to picture. That's one mode of working, and that MIDI file then has to be deciphered. A click has to be laid up against what was played if the composer wasn't listening to a click, which happens a lot of times. They just play to picture, and then you have to figure out a click track so that they hit particular musical events where they want to on the picture.

> The other way is where the composer takes the timing notes that you've provided for them and utilizes that information. They do the math, they figure out how many bars, beats, and clicks. They figure out tempos, and lay out their score based upon that information. Then I see the score later and basically line it up with the picture. "Lining it up" means I create the click track and the

streamers and punches after the score is written, according to what timings I see above what measures, and what instructions are given. And that's relatively simple and fast, because they've taken care of it.

Once you choose your method of synchronization, you are ready to set up the score. Whether putting pencil to paper or sequencing, it is a good idea to lay out the entire score, locate all the sync points, and know whether any meters need to be adjusted, before beginning to write.

In beginning this composing process, several things must happen. First, watch the scene many times. Have a strong idea in your mind of what you want to say with the music. Should it be funny or should it heighten tension? Should it be somewhat neutral, or melodramatic? The mood or the emotion you want to express will suggest a tempo. Remember that the composer's role is to help move the story forward. It is of the utmost importance that you know why the music is in a certain scene, and what it is supposed to accomplish. Then your writing will be focused and appropriate dramatically.

CHAPTER 17

Television

The early television years were indispensable.
That was my learning process.
—Jerry Goldsmith[1]

Music for television is conceptually the same as music for feature films in that it underscores dramatic situations. However, the process of writing music for television, the scope of the music, and the sound of the music itself is often very different. The way television shows are produced leads to a very different use of music. In television, production schedules are tighter, budgets are much smaller, and live ensembles are smaller. There are commercial breaks to consider, and the look and feel of the shows is very different from features. Despite the differences in production, a composer must still write music that is dramatically appropriate and meets the requirements of the production team.

There are several different kinds of television shows and each one has different musical requirements. There are episodic series, TV movies, sports shows, news shows, documentaries, TV magazines, and daytime soap operas; each of these has a different need for music. There are commercials and network logos. Some shows use only synthesizers and samples, some use a live rhythm section, some use a live orchestra. There are those that are hip-hop, light rock, metal, or traditional orchestral in style.

This chapter is concerned with episodic series and TV movies—the shows with dramatic music. An *episodic series* (one that has a new show every week) can be a drama like *Grey's Anatomy*; a sit-com like *30 Rock,* or an animated comedy or dramatic series like *The Simpsons* or *Superman.*

[handwritten: episodic series: one that has a new show every week (Grey's Anatomy, 30 Rock, The Simpsons)]

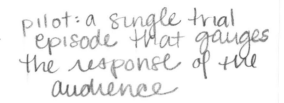
pilot: a single trial episode that gauges the response of the audience

The evolution of an episodic television show is similar to that of a film; the idea must be generated, and a producer and a network must be found. A _pilot_ is then made, and usually aired in the late spring or summer. The pilot is a single trial episode that gauges the response of the audience. If the pilot is well received, then the network may agree to a whole season, and the show is on its way.

Today there are only a handful of episodic shows that use any live musicians, much less a live studio orchestra. Because the budgets are smaller, if an orchestra is used, there are many less players than in the orchestra for a feature film. A typical television studio orchestra for a weekly show ranges from 20 to 35 players. (TV movies might use more.) Compare this to the orchestra used for feature films—usually 50 to 100 players or more. This is fitting because the scope of television is smaller in production value, as well as in the sheer size of the screen and audio speakers.

Evolving Styles of Television Music

As musical styles changed and evolved in the realm of feature films, so it has been with music for television. In the earliest days of TV, the music tended to be similar to that used in films, but with smaller ensembles. In the 1960s, many shows had a jazz flavor (_Peter Gunn, Batman, I Spy_), paralleling the trend in features. In the '70s, many shows added rock rhythm sections (_The A Team, The Greatest American Hero_). But in the mid to late '80s everything changed, with the introduction of synthesizers and the popularity of using songs instead of composed underscore. This is where we really see TV music gravitating more toward the pop world and away from the orchestral or jazz world. The downside to this is that there is no longer work as a musician playing for TV sessions on a regular basis. The upside is that one can find a wide range of styles in music for TV, ranging from a basically traditional orchestral sound (albeit, usually sequenced) to quirky groove-based music, to an even more quirky and surprising use of unusual sounds and colors, as in _Mad Men_ or _Glee_. In addition, the popularity of using songs has opened up many doors for songwriters and publishers to get their music placed on shows that are aired all over the world.

Schedules

When a show is contracted by a network, it is typically for 22 new episodes a year, running from about late September to May. The rest of the year is filled with reruns or alternative programming such as movies or news specials. (When a weekly show is bumped for a special movie or news show, it is said to be "preempted.") Production of these episodes usually takes place between late July and the end of April, with the period in between, May through July, referred to as "hiatus." It is during this time that production is "down" and many people take vacations. This is also the time when pilots are often produced.

Once a show starts weekly production and the first episode has been edited, the composer starts to work on the underscore. From this point on, the schedules are very demanding, for the turn-around is fast. Since new episodes are aired every week, the composer has very little time to write the music; every week a new episode rolls down the post-production assembly line and lands at his front door, ready for scoring.

An important production difference between films and television is that in television the director's role is somewhat diminished. Once the shooting is completed, the director's job is often finished. In television, the director is not involved in post-production, so the person that the composer communicates with is usually the producer or assistant producer.

Once receiving the final work-print of the show, the composer may have to spot, compose, and record anywhere from 10 to 30 minutes of music in a matter of days. And this is not a one-shot deal; he could be on a schedule that requires that much music every week, or every other week. If the composer is writing for a live orchestra, then this schedule gets even more compressed, for the music preparation pipeline of orchestrating and copying parts needs some time. If the composer is sequencing and doing the music electronically, then this kind of schedule is a little easier, but still grueling. In fact, some shows have multiple composers who rotate episodes every two or three weeks. When really in a jam, a composer will sometimes call a colleague to ghostwrite some of the music. This is when the main composer gets the screen credit, but others help by writing one or more cues. (Note: ghostwriting also occurs in features.)

Composer Shirley Walker mostly used live musicians. She describes working under the pressure associated with a weekly series:

> *The problem with a weekly show is that at a certain point it catches up with you because the schedule is crazy; every week you're turning out a show. Now, it doesn't go like that over the whole season because they plan hiatuses and preemptions and things like that. But inevitably you're going to have a three- or four-week span that hits you several times during the course of the 22 episodes where every week you have to be finishing a show. So you might start out on your first episode, and you've got three weeks, and then your second one you might have two weeks, and then pretty soon the weight of that whole thing is a snowball effect that starts really pounding you and pushing you from behind until every week you have to have finish anywhere from 25 to 45 minutes of music.*

For *X-Files*, Mark Snow composed all of the music electronically, only occasionally bringing in a live musician to his home studio. He usually had 20 to 30 minutes of music in every episode. In addition to scoring *X-Files*, he also wrote for *Millennium*, which required another 20 to 30 minutes per week. This enormous amount of music is possible only because the music is done electronically:

> *For X-Files I get about a week, seven days, but if I have to crunch it, I can do it in three days. If I get the episode on a Monday, I can have it ready for a Friday, which is when the producers come over to the house, listen to the music with the picture, and make their comments.*

> *The way I can do the two shows at once is because they usually, for some lucky reason, come at different times. Let's say they're done in the same week, I'd have three days on one, three days on another; it's doable. I'm used to the shows, I know the sounds and the textures and it's not about starting from scratch and walking around the house for days thinking, coming up with a theme or a palette of sounds. It's pretty easy.*

hook: the one most memorable lyric, melodic phrase, or part of the arrangement

I can go much faster than if I had to record with a TV orchestra. That would absolutely be out of the question. What I'd have to do then is have someone do a takedown, or send MIDI files to the copyists, have them copy the parts, assemble the orchestra, go to the session. It would just be impossible.

Alf Clausen does the music for *The Simpsons* with a live studio orchestra of about 20 to 30 players. His typical schedule is like this:

When we're on a week-to-week schedule, what I will normally do is spot an episode on Friday afternoon. The music editor will prepare my timing notes on Saturday and Sunday and then I'll start writing, usually Monday morning if it's a normal episode of 30 cues or less. If it's more than that, I'll sometimes start on Sunday to get a jump on things and then I'll put in probably four long days— Monday, Tuesday, Wednesday, Thursday—maybe nine in the morning until 11:30 or midnight every day. Then we spot the next week's episode Friday afternoon, and on Friday night starting at seven I'll record the cues that I've composed during the past week. We usually have anywhere from a three to a three-and-a-half hour recording session to do those 30 cues. Every week is different on The Simpsons, as you know. It really is dependent on whether it's straight underscore type of recording that I have to do or if I have to record vocals and do orchestral sweeteners of songs that I've written and already recorded. So it's never a dull moment.

Main Titles

The beginning part of the show where the opening credits are shown is called the *main title*, a term that is borrowed from feature films. The music for this opening is also called the main title by the music production team—a shortening of the phrase "main title music." For the television main title, the composer usually writes some kind of theme, or catchy music with a distinct *hook*. ("Hook" is a pop-song term that refers to the one most memorable lyric, melodic phrase, or part of the arrangement.) Actually, the composer of the main title is often different from the composer of the underscore on the weekly episodes. This is true especially if the main title music is a song with lyrics.

act: every segment of a television show/ TV movie, from commercial break to commercial break

For television, main titles are short—typically anywhere from 45 to 90 seconds—as opposed to feature films, where they can be three or four minutes long. In this amount of time, a strong statement about the show must be made that hopefully will be memorable. It is not enough time to develop a musical idea; any ideas presented should be concise and easily accessible to the audience.

Act-In/Act-Out

Every segment of a television show or TV movie, from commercial break to commercial break, is called an *act*. An act can be anywhere from 20 minutes long (the first act of a TV movie) to as short as five or six minutes. Often a composer is required to write a short cue, called an *act-in* or *act-out*, that brings us into the show after a commercial, or takes us out to a commercial. In the early days of TV, these transitions were used all the time. Today they are not automatic; their use depends on the show and the dramatic situation. Sometimes the theme for the show is used, sometimes new musical material or even a fragment of a song is introduced. An act-in or act-out can be as short as a few seconds, or it can be an extended cue. The important thing is that the act-in or act-out reflect the nature of the show and the story line.

Related to the act-in and act-out are the use of short bridges or transitions. A *bridge* is a music cue, usually of just a few seconds, that connects the story when it moves to another location or forward in time. This usually involves a cut or a dissolve to a new scene. Again, this is more typical of older dramatic shows, but is still used today in many comedies as well as dramas. The slap bass in *Seinfeld* is a typical use of music for both a bridge as well as act-in and act-out.

There are dozens of TV shows every week that use music, while there are fewer theatrical movies. There is a lot of opportunity for composers in television, and many top-notch composers are currently writing for television. There are also many composers now writing exclusively for features who got their start in television. In addition, television can sometimes be more lucrative for composers than feature films because the royalty payments compound when a show is aired and then goes into reruns. If a composer has shows airing on network TV, reruns on local stations and cable, the royalties add up quickly. (See chapter 22 for an in-depth discussion of royalties.)

Some of the most popular shows on television are animated series, such as *The Simpsons, South Park,* and *Teen-Age Mutant Ninja Turtles.* Although many of the compositional and scoring techniques are the same for animation as for live action television, there are also many differences. Such considerations are discussed in chapter 19, "Animation."

act in/ act out: a short cue that brings us into the show after a commercial or take us out to a commercial

bridge: music cue, usually just a few seconds, that connects the story when it moves to another location or forward in time.

CHAPTER 18

Ethnic and Period Music

*Motion picture art is different. It is realistic and factual. It not only
tries to capture the spirit of bygone eras, but it also tries to make believe
that it projects before the eyes of the spectator the real thing.*
—*Miklos Rozsa*[1]

Los Angeles is the entertainment capital of the world. And because
so many films are produced there, or in New York, their locale is
often set in these places. However, every year there are also countless
films where the story, or part of the story, takes place in other locations. These can be exotic and unusual locations anywhere on the
planet, such as Nepal, Congo, or backwoods Montana. Or they can be
large urban centers of the United States or Europe. Some of these locations have music that is instantly associated with them, some do not,
and the use of music to suggest a locale will be different from composer to composer, and director to director. The task is finding and
creating music that helps reflect the feeling of the location while being
effective dramatically.

In addition, sometimes there is the need to create a score for a period
film that takes place in historical Europe or America. This presents its
own set of problems, but the basic question, how to reflect the time
period while being appropriate dramatically, remains the same.

This discussion necessarily takes place from an ethnocentric viewpoint. In the world of film making, we are often dealing with a
situation where Hollywood is looking out at the rest of the world. The
philosophy is, "Everybody else is different, and those of us here in Los
Angeles are the norm." This is actually true for any culture or country—we see the world through our own prescription glasses.
Therefore, for the purposes of this book, I refer to "ethnic music" as
that which is not Western Classical or popular music. So with apologies

171

to readers from anywhere other than the United States, or Los Angeles in particular, let's look at how to approach "ethnic music," as well as music that describes a different European or American era.

Ethnic Music

Hollywood's approach to ethnic music has changed over the years. This is largely due to changes in film making itself, and to the shrinking "global village"—the fact that all corners of the planet are closer together due to ease of travel and the information technology that connects us.

Films have become much more "real" over the past decades. In the old films, killing was often an off-screen event, and blood was minimized. Cowboys wore fancy, fringed costumes and carried pearl-handled Colt 45s; they were always clean looking and freshly shaved. Today's cowboys are likely as not to be grungy, slightly ragged-looking and dirty, and if they kill someone, the blood flows bright red and freely. Probably this is closer to what it was really like. We not only see more "real" costumes, blood, gore, and violence in modern films, we also see more real emotions as well as special effects. Many films of past decades look dated to us; the younger generations often snicker at the "old" films. There are also situations where a director may ask that ethnic music or period music not be used at all. This is a creative decision that takes into account whether or not the experience of the audience will be enhanced by use of cultural instruments or scales. So the question becomes: If ethnic music is used at all, does it need to reflect a realism, and if so, to what degree?

This question has been answered in many different ways over the years, and part of the answer lies in the development of popular music. As popular music has become more sophisticated, the ears of its audience have developed in parallel. In the 1930s and '40s the audience was musically sophisticated when it came to Wagner, Brahms, Puccini, Duke Ellington, or Tommy Dorsey, but they were naive when it came to the music of other cultures. Today we have become more familiar with the many kinds of music heard in other countries; our global village shares resources, ideas, and technology. The composer must take more care in the way a country is represented musically.

There is also a psychological dimension of this process. We associate certain instruments with certain cultures, depending on our own experience. A mandolin played a specific way is definitely Italy; Flamenco style guitar can only be Spain. A banjo is the mountains or the Old South of the United States. But what about accordion, which is used in many countries? Or pan flute, which can be associated with Eastern Europe or South America? The composer must take care when designing a score with certain sounds that it is really suggesting the place he intends. There is no way to please everyone because different people have different musical associations. However, one way to make sure the music is accurate is to do research.

Research

When writing for a film that requires ethnic music, composers often do research. This can be done in many ways. It can be as simple as buying some CDs, or it can be as complex as spending time in a music library and corresponding with experts all over the world. The important thing is that the composer become familiar enough with the style of the music that he can create it in a way that is convincing dramatically. Oftentimes, he will just use one element of it, like a particular instrument blended in with an orchestra, or a scale derived from that culture. An ensemble of musicians from that country or culture can be used as a separate scoring entity, or it can be blended with the orchestra.

John Williams does this in the film, *Far and Away*, which follows the journey of an Irish couple from Ireland to the United States in the 1890s. Williams uses two Irish-derived melodies as the main themes; they are first heard in the main title, one played on pennywhistle, the other on pan flute. Both are accompanied by a symphonic orchestra. The effect is to achieve a "flavor" of the Irish location and characters, but not actually to be traditional Irish music. However, he also has scenes that are scored exclusively by The Chieftains, one of Ireland's premier groups that performs traditional Irish music. The Chieftains are often not accompanied by the orchestra, but because of the Irish nature of the orchestral sections, there is still continuity between the various kinds of textures.

One composer known for his love of musicology and investigating the music of other cultures was Miklos Rozsa. During the 1940s, '50s, and '60s, Rozsa wrote many scores, such as *El Cid, Ben-Hur, Quo Vadis*, and *Ivanhoe,* where he researched the music of the time and place, and incorporated it into his score. He was meticulous and immersed himself into the study of the music of the culture. For example, for the score to *El Cid*, he journeyed to Spain and studied with authorities on medieval Spanish and Moorish music. For *Quo Vadis*, he did a thorough investigation of Roman music and instruments.

Unfortunately, because of post-production schedules, composers today rarely have time for such efforts. However, research can be a valuable tool in enhancing the kinds of sounds and textures available to the composer. The deeper one gets into the music of another culture, the more it can be reflected in the original music for a film. Sometimes hours and hours can be spent researching, studying, and listening to the music of another culture, but very little specific music from that place is used in the score. But after this process, no matter how much ethnic music is used, the composer has an understanding, sometimes on a subconscious level, of the music he studied, which then comes through in his own music.

Cliff Eidelman speaks of the value of researching the music before beginning to write *Triumph of the Spirit,* a powerful 1989 film about Greek Jews in a Nazi concentration camp:

> *I went to the UCLA musicology department and I started listening to recordings of Sephardic Jewish folk music. Primarily pre-war music from Greece and Spain. As it turned out, a lot of what I was hearing was stuff that felt very second nature to me. I really connected to the kinds of feelings that were in that music. They were using mandolins, mandolas, a lot of tambourines, guitars, and drums. There was a certain raw feeling to it, but it was very warm.*
>
> *Then I read the script and started coming up with ideas. I wanted to incorporate some of those Eastern instruments into a Western orchestral setting. I took the liberty of adding an Indian*

instrument, the tamboura, which isn't a Sephardic Jewish instrument, but I liked the droning quality and I thought it was a nice color. Then I discovered quickly that the language they were speaking was Ladino, or at least a big part of what they were speaking was Ladino, which is a combination of Spanish and Hebrew and is essentially extinct today. When I realized I wanted to use a choir, I chose Ladino as the language for the text. In addition to that, I didn't want to use preexisting poems, I wanted to have poems written that were really more specific to the emotional context of what was going on in those scenes. I found a cantor who knew Ladino really well, and he was also a very good poet. I described the emotion, and he wrote poetry based on it. He translated the poems into Ladino, and that became the text for the score.

This story illustrates the kinds of research a composer can do in order to draw upon ethnic musical influences. Notice that Eidelman did not attempt to recreate the music of the Greek Jews; he simply tried to capture the feeling, even to the point of using an archaic language to represent the emotions of the film. Also, just for color, he used a tamboura, which has nothing to do with European Jews. This shows the creative license one can take. It is also interesting that no one outside a few people involved in the film would know that the language being sung was Ladino. But Eidelman and the director felt that the emotional content of this language would somehow transmit part of the experience of the people portrayed in the film. This is a subtle idea, yet one with a specific, if subconscious intent. Many composers and film makers rely on such subtleties to help complete the story.

Sometimes composers use ethnic instruments but inadvertently imply a different culture from the one in the film. This can happen for several reasons, not the least of which is the subjective nature of the audience's musical associations. An example of a film that reflects the exotic location, but perhaps inadvertently implies yet a second or even third different culture, is *Beyond Rangoon*. In this film Hans Zimmer uses a sampled ethnic sound reminiscent of Balinese gamelan, but also reflects instruments in the culture of Burma (now known as Myanmar), where the movie takes place. However, over the top of the texture that is glued together by this gamelan sound is a high wooden-flute sound. Many people who have heard this sound immediately associate it with Ireland, because the high flute sounds Irish in nature to them. However, upon hearing the music and seeing the picture, they concede that it works, that with the visuals of the Burmese countryside and rivers the ethnic association with Southeast Asia comes together, "Irish" flavor or not. This shows the power of combining the sound with images. When the music is isolated, one impression is conveyed. When it is married to the picture, a whole different set of associations can be conjured.

This illustrates the difficulty of writing ethnic music for a mass audience. It can be constructed in many different ways depending on the creative directions of the composer and the director, and it can be interpreted differently depending on the audience. The composer needs to have firmly in his mind how "real" the ethnic music needs to be. Does it need to be like source music, i.e., very real? Or can it just imply the culture? Sometimes the budget of the project determines how real the music gets. Bill Ross used ethnic music in *The Amazing Panda Adventure*, as well as on the television series *MacGyver*:

> The Amazing Panda Adventure *was set in China. [Director] Chris Cane wasn't sure what he wanted, so after thinking about it, I came up with the idea for this mellow Western approach with a kind of Chinese vibe. I did what I could to educate myself about some of the Chinese instruments, and wove them throughout with the Western-style orchestra. There were four cues where I wrote Chinese music as source music.*

> *In MacGyver, we used some ethnic instruments, but we didn't research them. There was no time and no budget to focus it in any more than a very general way. After a while it came down to large geographical distinctions—East or West, Europe, etc.—and a small group of corresponding instruments. The fortunate thing for a film—like* The Amazing Panda Adventure—*as opposed to television, is that you can afford to have the recording environment and the musicians to do what's necessary.*

Having the budget to do what is necessary is paramount. Hiring extra musicians who play specialized instruments can be expensive. Sometimes composers must make do with samples. But either way, the creative decision is to decide how much of the ethnic flavor is wanted. Most of the time, composers choose to incorporate ethnic instruments with the full palette of orchestral sounds available. This seems to be a solution that is pleasing to the ear of the modern audience, dramatically satisfying, and suggests psychological associations with certain cultures. It can mean simply adding one instrument like panpipes or koto, or a hint of a particular scale, or it can mean using a whole ensemble of ethnic musicians. A combination of research, good dramatic discrimination, and clear communications with the director usually provides the answer.

Period Western Music

Writing music for a film that takes place in historical Europe or America has always presented a problem for scoring. The question here is similar to the question regarding ethnic scoring: should the music reflect the time period? And the answer is also similar: it depends on the vision of the director and composer. More often than not, that vision is a combination of older, period sounds, and contemporary orchestra. The reason for this is the same as with ethnic music: audiences can most easily identify with a contemporary orchestra, yet a certain amount of realism is sometimes appropriate. An excellent example of this is *Anne of the Thousand Days*, with a score by Georges Delerue. In this score, shawms and other period instruments are blended with the orchestra.

Often, in both period and ethnic scores, realism can be achieved through the use of source music. Source music and underscore can often be combined and blended together to make a dramatically and musically satisfying effect. For example, in *Shakespeare in Love,* there are several instances where we hear 16th century source music, and then the underscore played by a modern orchestra actually grows out of the source music, eventually taking over. In *Shining Through*, a film about undercover spying in World War II, there is a scene at a party where the Glenn Miller arrangement of "Moonlight Serenade" is play-

source music

ing. Composer Michael Kamen effectively extends this '40s song by segueing to the underscore with a love theme that is thoroughly modern in sonority. These examples work because we accept the source music as representing the time period, and the orchestra as representing the dramatic situation.

Another example of a score that uses both period music as well as contemporary music as underscore is *Dangerous Liaisons*. In this film, which takes place amongst the aristocracy in 18th century Paris, George Fenton has constructed two distinct musical ideas that serve the drama well. In the main title, the first thing heard is a contemporary orchestra playing a very dramatic, tense and restless theme with a modern musical vocabulary. Then it segues to a harpsichord and a smaller Baroque sounding orchestra. These two contrasting sonorities provide ample material throughout the film; one reminds us of the time and place, the other is used in the more melodramatic moments.

The important concept in scoring ethnic or period films is to have a clear idea of how much of that music is necessary. This often depends on the director's vision, such as Francis Ford Coppola with *The Rainmaker* (see chapter 10). These situations call for the composer to find a solution that suggests time and place, and addresses dramatic needs.

This kind of scoring highlights what is essentially the psychology of combining music and visuals. Because the music addresses both visual and dramatic situations, the audience's attention is split. Their eyes must take in the picture, their ears take in the music. Composers are actually addressing this phenomenon every time they write a cue for any kind of film. The audience is having an experience on several sensory levels as well as several emotional levels. Music is just one part of this, although a big part. In films that use ethnic or period scores, we ask the audience to accept that we are not trying to create "authentic" music of the time or place, but simply add to the color of what they are already seeing. It is more important to be "real" in a visual sense; the music can *imply* the "reality" and still be accepted.

CHAPTER 19

Animation

The art of writing for animation is in keeping the music musical,
while hitting what needs to be hit without sounding choppy.
—*Richard Stone*

There are currently several different kinds of animated films and television shows. There are old-style cartoons, such as *Animaniacs* or *Tiny Toons,* dramatic action-hero animations such as *Justice League* or *Superman,* and comedies such as *The Simpsons, South Park, Rug Rats,* and *Teletubbies.* There is also the feature film animated musical such as *Pocahontas, Mulan,* or *The Little Mermaid.* The way the music is handled depends on the project's style, as well as the creative vision of the production team.

Note that films with real actors are referred to as *live-action films,* in order to distinguish them from *animation,* where the characters are drawn.

The Early Days of Animation

As discussed previously, film music styles were very different in the first decades of talkies from what they are today. In the 1930s, the music was likely to hit many pieces of action and comment on almost every emotion the actors showed. When the first cartoons came out, the musical approach was the same, though taken to an extreme. Almost every movement, whether the characters were falling in love or having a knock-down-drag-out fight, was reflected in the music. The term *mickey-mousing* refers to this style where the music mimics every little thing, as in the early Mickey Mouse cartoons.

Two of the most successful composers for cartoons in the early days of film were Scott Bradley, who did most of the *Tom and Jerry* cartoons, and Carl Stalling of Warner Bros. These men set the standard for the industry. At first, cartoon music was a thrown-together jumble of snatches of different melodies taken from other sources. Both Stalling and Bradley decided that something different could be done. Bradley describes his thinking:

> It seemed to me that almost anybody could collect a lot of nurs-ery jingles and fast-moving tunes, throw them together along with slide whistles and various noise makers and call that a car-toon score, but that didn't satisfy me and, I felt sure, wouldn't really satisfy the public. So I set about to work out musical scores that would add significance to the picture, that would be musi-cally sound and would be entertaining.[1]

So Bradley and Stalling went about finding a way to accompany the cartoons that was musical, interesting, and had integrity. The dilemma facing them (and composers today) was the sheer number of hits—as many as 30 or 40 in a 30-second cue—coupled with the fact that the action of the cartoons was irregular, in terms of musical beats. Somehow, a way had to be found to make the music *seem* regular. Mixed meters were a way to make musical accents come out on down-beats, yet cartoons had so many places where the music needed to hit the action that it was impossible to have every hit on a downbeat. One solution was the creation of a melody line that stretched over an entire sequence, and the hits in the music would be mostly in the accompa-niment to the melodic line. This was more elegant than simply stringing together bits of folksongs, nursery tunes, and arias, which tended to sound quite choppy.

In addition to mickey-mousing everything in the early cartoons, and despite the desire to achieve a more musical solution than simply link-ing familiar melodies, it became a convention to parody familiar pieces of music in a humorous way. This is probably a logical exten-sion of the way well-known tunes were used during the silent film era. For example, sunrise became the "Morning Mood" from Grieg's *Peer Gynt*, and if a character was drunk, something like "How Dry I Am" or "Little Brown Jug" would play. Many classical and popular pieces were quoted or parodied. To score these moments, composers still used the old silent-film fake books of Rapée or Becce, since these books provided dozens of excerpts of many different kinds of melodies. Books like these are still used as a reference by composers today.

The process for the composer in the early days of cartoons was different from today. Today, the composer receives a rough-cut of the film, the music editor creates timing notes, and the composer writes from the timing notes and the rough-cut. In the early days of animation, the composer often would not even see the film before the music was recorded. After a spotting session with the director, the composer would receive a "detail sheet," also called an "exposure sheet." (Note that the nomenclature varied from studio to studio.) Richard Stone describes the *exposure sheet*, as it was called at Warner Bros.:

> *These sheets laid out the action on paper and were a sort of mini-storyboard. The director would decide, for instance, how fast a character was walking, and would have this very elaborate sheet saying, "Daffy is walking across the street taking a step every eight frames." This information would be copied onto the exposure sheet giving Stalling a description of all the action and the frame measurements of all the action. That is what he wrote to.*

Once the composer had the "frame measurement," it was just a matter of math to figure out the rhythm and timings of these moments. The *exposure sheet* also had music staves below these verbal descriptions so the composer could fill in the sketched music.

Occasionally the composer would receive a "pencil reel" or a "storyboard" of the film. A *pencil reel* is a black and white rough-cut with line drawings as opposed to complete animation. This would be viewed by the composer on a Moviola. A *storyboard* is a series of boxes on a page, like a comic book, that sums up the story and the action and includes timings for each box.

Pencil reels, now called *pencil tests,* and storyboards are still used today. Animators often use line drawings in live-action films to roughly draw a sequence that ultimately gets computer-generated

pencil reel: b&w rough cut w/ line drawings (now called pencil test)

storyboard: a series of boxes on a page like a comic book that sums up the story & the action & includes timings

181

special effects. Storyboards are used during preproduction in animation, commercials, and occasionally in features.

The composers of the early cartoons were remarkable and often unappreciated. They had fine music skills in composition, orchestration, and conducting, and they were often self-taught. They had an innate sense of drama and what was needed in a film. And, of course, they had a great sense of humor.

Today's animations, except for many of those produced at Warner Bros., are very different. Let's look at the different kinds of contemporary animation one by one.

Warner Bros. Cartoons: The Old Style

In a world of modern computerized animation and musical trends that encompass Aaron Copland and ~~Kanye West~~, Warner Bros. has continued to use the musical style originally developed by Carl Stalling in the 1930s. Cartoon series like *Tiny Toons, Animaniacs,* and *The Sylvester & Tweety Mysteries* all use devices that were popular in the '30s, '40s and '50s: traditionally-based orchestras, mickey-mousing action to the smallest detail, and quotes from well-known songs and classical pieces. Creating this kind of show is demanding because the music is constant and there are so many hits. Richard Stone was the supervising composer of many of these Warner Bros. cartoons, and he describes the process:

> *It's like anything else. We still sit with the producer and have a spotting session. In our case, the music is wall to wall; the decisions are not where the music starts and stops, as in a feature film or a live-action television show. In our shows the music never stops. So the question at the spotting session is always about musical style, and what specific things we're going to hit— how loudly and with what instrumentation. We might talk about which public domain tunes we will use....*

What we do is an outgrowth of Carl Stalling's style, trying to stay in sync with as many things on screen as we can. Characters walking across the screen with pizzicato celli and a bassoon, if a boulder falls on somebody it will have a piano glissando on it, the xylophone eye-blink, and all the rest of those clichés. We also try to do musical puns with folk songs—PD tunes that we can use. We quote from the classical literature all the time.

A team of composers works on these shows; typically they rotate and do one show every two weeks. William Ross describes being one of several composers working on episodes for *Tiny Toons*:

They were about as hard as anything you want to do. It's like working inside this little tiny box because of the number of hits. Music has seams, let's say, and so the number of seams you have to do in cartoons is a lot. As a composer, I find that most of my time is spent making the seams seamless. Once I get a texture I like, it's easy to continue it for five, six, seven minutes. But every time I have to transition that texture to another one, it takes a lot of thought.

Tiny Toons *takes that to a whole new level. In the course of a few seconds, you may have ten hits. I know that sounds ridiculous, but there are lots and lots of hits, things you need to address where the music has to do something in these few seconds. So I would have a 30-second cue that had 40 things I had to hit. I tried to limit the number.*

It was difficult for any of the composers to take on an entire episode and finish it by themselves. It was essentially 19 minutes of music that had to be done in a week or two. It wasn't for the faint of heart. People would be on the floor trying to figure out how to get through this 19 minutes of music. Those that had arranging experience and could manipulate melodies seemed to fair well. I got to where I could do two minutes a day.

This honest assessment of the difficulty of writing for an old-style cartoon makes one appreciate the work of Stalling and Bradley even more. That they could crank out enormous amounts of music that worked effectively with the picture, day-in and day-out, shows the high degree of skill they had.

Animated Dramas: Action Heroes

Another type of animation that is very popular is the cartoon or animated drama with an action hero like *Superman* or *Batman*. These television shows or feature films are scored like regular live-action shows. The music does not mickey-mouse every move on screen; rather, it simply tries to support and enhance the visual action.

For animated dramas, the composer receives a work print of the show, and works exactly as he would for a live action show. There is a spotting session, timing notes if needed, and either a synthesized score or live orchestra. Whereas a series like *Tiny Toons* features wall-to-wall music, in an animated drama there is usually less music; it comes in and out as needed.

Animated Dramas: Comedies

One of the most difficult things to decide in any film, live action or animated, is when to be musically funny and when to be musically serious. In the *Tiny Toons* or *Animaniacs* type of show, the choice is obvious: the music must be as goofy as the drama. However, there are many comedies where it is much more effective to have the music be more serious or neutral, and let the comedy routines speak for themselves. *The Simpsons* is a great example of a show where the music does not mimic every piece of action; it simply comments where necessary. Composer Alf Clausen explains the concept:

> *Matt Groening [the producer and creator of* The Simpsons*] and company told me in our first meeting that "It's not a cartoon, it's a drama where the characters are drawn." And when in doubt, he said, score it like a drama, not like a cartoon, not to mickey-mouse everything. Matt was the one who made the request for the acoustic orchestra. He said, "I hate electronics, I think they cheapen the sound. I want the real orchestra."*

I have an old friend that came up with the phrase, "You can't vaudeville Vaudeville." That has also served me really well on The Simpsons. The producers keep saying, "We don't want the music to comment on the scene. We don't want the music itself to be funny." I'm always in agreement with that; we kind of joke in some of the spotting sessions about how the more serious I can play the music, according to the way the emotion is laid out, the more we pull the audience in and make them think that the situation is real. Then "boom," all of a sudden the gag comes and it becomes twice as funny than it would have if I had tried to set up something leading up to the fact that there was going to be a gag.

Musicals and Songs

Musicals, whether animated or live action, are extremely complex endeavors, from a production standpoint. The composer of the songs is involved during preproduction and writes the songs based on a script and conversations with the production team. There is a lot of back and forth between the songwriter and the production team regarding the musical feel and the lyrical content of the songs. This can be an efficient process or it can be drawn out, because in preproduction, people feel less pressured and take their time getting the music just how they want it. Finally, after everyone—the producer, director, songwriter—has agreed and signed off on them, the songs are recorded. The animators take the final recording of the song and synchronize the singing and movements of the animated characters. Finally, months, or even years later, when there is a locked version of the film, the underscore is written by either the same composer as the songs or by someone different. David Newman did the underscore to *Anastasia,* and talks about his experience from the composer's perspective:

I used all material from the songs because I thought that would be the right artistic choice for the movie. That's what my dad (Alfred Newman) would do with all those musicals, with all those Rodgers and Hammerstein musicals. I really liked that in shows like Carousel *and* The King and I. *He interwove the score right with the song, and then right out from the song back into the score. I approached* Anastasia *like that, just like it was a tra-*

ditional film. Steve Flaherty and Lynn Ahrens did the songs long before I began the underscore. Taking their themes and developing them in dramatic ways made the movie seem really unified.

Alf Clausen writes both underscore and the songs for *The Simpsons*. His process for these songs is exactly the same as if it were a feature film musical and not a half-hour television series. The songs need to be recorded before the animation is begun, months before the show aired. The process is very complex whenever music is done like this during preproduction, and requires a lot of planning:

The procedure is that normally I am given the script pages that have a lyric already written by one of the writers on staff. Then I'll have a conference with the writer and the producers about what they feel the thrust of the mood of the piece should be, and what the intent should be.

Then, once I've composed the song, I write out the rhythm-section parts, we do a demo of the song, and record the rhythm-section track first. If the song is going to be recorded by cast voices, then I'll record scratch vocals, which are thrown away eventually. They're just used for demo purposes so that we can make cassettes for all the cast members in order to learn the material before they go into the voice-record session. If the songs are not going to be sung by the cast members, and we're going to use our own vocalists, then normally we'll keep the vocals that we've recorded all the way to the end of the process.

The animators then animate to those tracks that are given to them with the rhythm section, the cast voices, and the click track. Nine months later, when the show is finished at the animation house, it comes back to us and hopefully they've left the songs alone and I don't have to do any major surgery.

So when I score the underscore cues for that particular episode, I'll also sweeten the song tracks that have come back, which means that I replace the rhythm section track with an orchestral track so it sounds as if the orchestra is accompanying the voices in the finished piece. So, there also needs to be new orchestrations written.

The composer's task in a musical is to weave songs and underscore together. When the music is continuous throughout the film, key relationships become very important from one cue to another, and between songs and underscore. There also must be a sonic unity between the songs and underscore. In addition, sometimes the animated story is about animals who need to be given human qualities, as in many of the Disney pictures. Mark Mancina produced many of the songs for *The Lion King,* and wrote the underscore—in addition to producing the songs written by Phil Collins—for *Tarzan:*

> *When you do an animated movie, it's hard because you're not only scoring the same way you score a normal movie, but you're having to bring a certain sense of realness and humanness to characters that are animated.*

Mancina also discusses the need for good collaboration with other musicians, as well as constant awareness of the flow between underscore and songs:

> *Key relationships between songs and underscore are tremendously important, especially in a movie where the music doesn't stop. Basically, in Tarzan, the music never stops. There needs to be continuity between the songs and the underscore. I don't like going to a movie, and when the song starts, I yawn, or I start going, "Oh God, here comes the song." I hate that. So does Phil (Collins). One of the ways we achieved a unity between the two elements was by me playing on his songs, and by him playing drums on some of my cues. That way the score and the songs can sound very similar. Not only the key relationships, but also the sonic relationships between cues.*

In addition to collaborating with other musicians, the process also involves collaboration with the production team. Because music is driving animated films, there is a whole team of people, from the director to the head of the studio, that gives input to the composer and songwriters. Mancina describes this:

> *There's not just one guy that comes in and listens to what I do; there's a group of guys. There's the director, the producer, the executive producer of music, the VP of theatrical, Michael Eisner, Joe Roth, the Chairman of the Board. All of 'em. They're all going to hear it! They're all going to have their own opinions on every note of the music, every frame of film—and they're all going to have something to say about it. Five of them might think it's the best cue they've ever heard me write, and three of them might say "I don't like it, and it's gonna have to be changed."*

Animation can be an interesting, fun, and grueling scoring assignment. There is the opportunity to have fun with the music, as well as write serious underscore. Depending on the project, the composer can use traditional instruments or electronic sounds. The creative scope is wide, and though the process is difficult at times, animation can be among the most inspiring and fun genres of film scoring.

CHAPTER 20

Songs, Soundtracks, and Source Music

If everyone on the movie, from the studio execs all the way down, is in sync and agrees we need a hit song for this movie, then it is a totally great situation because then everyone is shooting for the same goal. But that's never the case and I don't believe that will ever be the case. Even if it is, everyone's vision of what that hit song will be is going to be totally different.

—Jeff Carson

Many films use music besides the instrumental underscore. In addition to the kind of composed score that has been discussed so far, film scores frequently include songs. In musicals, as well as some dramatic films, the actors sing on-camera. Often there is *source music*, music that comes from a source on-screen that the actors can hear—a radio, stereo, live band, or someone singing or playing an instrument. A song can be used in place of instrumental underscore to heighten or comment on the dramatic action. For example, in the last scenes of *Michael Collins*, when Sinead O'Connor sings, "He Walked Through the Fair," the picture alternates between Michael Collins driving to what is ultimately his assassination and his fiancée trying on her wedding gown. This creates a poignant bridge between the two characters in their different locations. When the music for a film is mostly, if not completely, comprised of songs instead of underscore, as in *Pulp Fiction*, *Jerry McGuire*, or *The Big Chill*, it is called a *song score*, or *compilation score*.

There are several ways a song can end up in a film. If an established song is used in a new movie, the producer must obtain the right to use it, either in its original form, or by having a new version, or *cover*, recorded. Alternatively, the producer might commission a new song to be written for the film. Of course, if the movie is a musical, then several songs must be commissioned.

189

The composer's participation in a score that contains songs will vary from project to project. He may be involved in composing the songs, or he may only compose the underscore. For musicals, the songwriter might also write the underscore, as Alan Menken has done for many Disney films. If the songs are used as source music, then the composer is usually not involved, except when they are instrumentals and can be recorded at the same session as the underscore.

Regardless of whether or not the same composer is used for the underscore and the songs, there are always dramatic considerations to keep in mind when choosing or writing songs for a motion picture. Hopefully, the song will enhance the drama in some way, if it is used in place of underscore. But the hard reality of the entertainment business is that there is always a pull-and-tug between creative considerations and those of commerce and profit, and this duality has a large influence on the use of songs in a film. This chapter discusses the many aspects of using songs in movies and the process that lands a song in the film—from the featured songs in musicals to the more subtle and less memorable, but still dramatically important, songs used as source music.

Commissioned Songs

Many times a producer or director wants a song, or songs, to be written specifically for the film. The obvious case for this is a musical, where there are many songs that are essential to the plot. Another possibility is when a producer wants an individual song either for the main title or end credits, or for an important point in the film. Either way, there may be a music supervisor assigned to the project who assists the composer in facilitating the recording of the songs. The director is usually the decision-maker of what music appears in the film, including both songs and underscore. The director (sometimes the producer) is also involved in the process at the approval level, wanting to make sure the songs are appropriate both musically and lyrically.

Once it is determined that a commissioned song is required, a songwriter or songwriting team views a work print of the film. If the song is to be used in a particular scene, they watch that scene over and over.

They then come up with a tune and lyrics that specifically reflect the content of the film. If the composer of the score is also the composer of the song, the thematic material of the song will often be woven into the underscore. The song may use musical material written by the underscore composer (especially if the underscore composer and songwriter are the same person), or it may be a separate musical statement. The song may be used only in the main title or end-credits, or it could be featured as a dramatic statement in the body of the film. "How Do You Keep the Music Playing," from *Best Friends*, is organic to the score of the picture; Michel Legrand uses the theme in his underscore as well as in the song itself. Lyricist Alan Bergman (who writes as a team with his wife, Marilyn) describes the evolution of "How Do You Keep the Music Playing?":

> *This film has two people involved in a relationship. The woman overcomes the man's resistance to marry, and they go back East to meet their respective families. The visits don't go well, and by the time the honeymoon is over, the marriage is almost over. There is a sequence in which they are on a people-mover in the airport, separated and not talking to each other. It was a marvelous sequence for us [as songwriters] because there are no sound effects or dialogue. Here was an opportunity to find a new way to say, "How do you keep romance alive?"*
>
> *After viewing the entire film several times, we watched this scene over and over again. Then we said to [composer] Michel Legrand, "What if the first line of the song is 'How do you keep the music playing?'" And he said, "I like that." He wrote the whole melody from that line. We then wrote the rest of the lyrics to that melody.*

When writing a new song and tailoring it for a certain movie, writers try to reflect either a single dramatic or emotional moment of the film, or to make a statement about the entire film. In a situation like the one above, it is as close to putting words in the characters' mouths as possible without having them actually sing. This use of a song greatly enhances the story by reflecting exactly what the characters are feeling. In *Up Close and Personal*, the song, "Because You Loved Me," by Diane

Warren was commissioned for that film and used in the end credits. Even though it is not used dramatically in any scenes in the film, the song reflects the feelings of the film's main character, and articulates the emotional thrust of the film.

Sometimes a film maker uses songs containing lyrics that are close to what needs to be expressed, but are not exactly right on. There are many instances where songs are used because the title of the song fits the film, or part of the lyrics fit the film, but the rest does not. A good example of this is *The Big Chill*. This film's opening sequence is a montage where some old college buddies living in different cities find out that one of their old gang has committed suicide. Playing through this montage of several minutes is the original recording of Marvin Gaye singing "I Heard It Through the Grapevine." On the surface, these words fit the scene nicely, for we are seeing all the pals getting the news over the phone. However, these lyrics: *"I bet you're wondering how I knew, 'bout your plans to make me blue ..."* don't really fit the story; they are about a heart-broken guy singing to his girl. The only line that is really relevant is the title line, and this is one reason the song is in the film. Another reason is that it is a song many people know and love, so using it in a film preys upon the audience's familiarity with it—the feeling of nostalgia.

Musicals

Musicals are the ultimate genre where songs are tailored to fit a film. They must be, because the characters are singing them. The words must reflect the story and the music must fit with the overall musical style of the film. The process of writing songs for a musical, whether animated or live action, can be different from that for dramatic-action films. In a dramatic film the songwriters might not be involved until post-production; they probably do not see a script, and develop their ideas from a work print. However, for a musical, the songwriters are involved at an earlier stage. They read the script and discuss with the director where the songs shall go, what the feeling of a song should be, and what the lyric content will be. This is necessary because the songs must be completed before production begins. Then they write the songs, make demos for the production team to hear, make any requested changes, and make a final recording. The final recording is then played back on the set so that the actor(s) can lip-sync accurately. (It is called a *prerecord* when the music is recorded prior to shooting so it can be played back on the set.) This entire process, from writing to release of the film, can take anywhere from one to three years. Note that because all of the recording must be completed before the shooting of a scene, often the songs will be completed as long as a year before the release of the movie.

In writing a score for a musical, songwriters are usually involved with the screenwriters. Alan Bergman talks about the process of creating the music for *Yentl* with songwriting partners Marilyn Bergman and Michel Legrand, as well as Barbra Streisand—producer, director, and star of the film:

> *We agreed that this was a wonderful book for a musical. From the moment Yentl puts on the clothes of a boy and begins the masquerade, she cannot express to anyone her true feelings as a woman. This inner monologue was a perfect opportunity for music.*
>
> *So, first we spotted where the songs should be. Then we started writing. Michel is a dramatist; the best composers are dramatists. For one song, we said to him, "Yentl's father has just passed away. This is the first time she's been away from her village. It's a dark night in a forest and she is alone. In a way, she's pleading with her father." Michel wrote the melody that expressed in musical terms what our thoughts were for this song, and we wrote "Papa, Can You Hear Me."*
>
> *When he writes, or when anybody writes the music first, which we prefer, there are words on the tips of those notes and we have to find them. It's a search.*

Exploring, being a dramatist, finding just the right words to go with a character and a story are the jobs of the songwriter in a musical. These are the songs that are featured and are often the reason the audience goes to see the film.

Source Music

There are many, many instances of songs that are not featured and that are part of the background of the actual scene. *Source music* is any music that appears to be coming from a "source" on screen. Said another way, it is any music the actors in the scene can hear. Car radios, home stereos, bands in a nightclub, street musicians, and actors humming in the shower are all examples of source music. Source music can be familiar songs by known artists, songs by new artists, or music written by the composer specifically for the film. Source music can be strictly in the background as part of the aural landscape along with various sound effects, or it can become a strong dramatic statement.

Songs used as source music are usually chosen by the director, often with the assistance of the music supervisor. In the case of instrumental source music, it can be chosen from existing recordings, the composer can write or arrange something, or another composer can be brought in to do the source cues.

Dramatic Use of Source Music

Often, source music is mixed in the film at barely audible levels; it is frequently part of a room's ambient sound, far in the background. However, there are times when source music can play an important dramatic role in the film. The proper choice of songs can create an atmosphere that runs the gamut of dramatic possibilities. Composers often interweave the source music with the underscore in order to add to a dramatic situation.

For example, in *The Pelican Brief,* there is a scene where Julia Roberts leaves a hospital in fear of her life and ventures down a crowded New Orleans street, eventually ending up alone in a hotel room. The first thing we hear is James Horner's underscore consisting of piano and strings as she leaves the hospital. This fades into source cues as she goes down the street in a state of shock. These source cues consist of different kinds of rock or jazz music emanating from each nightclub she passes, and they blend one into the other as she weaves through the partying crowd. Finally, the underscore fades back in while the last piece of source music fades out (called *cross-fading*). This whole sequence has a continuity because of the way the music is structured. The source music reflects the craziness of the New Orleans nightlife, and as each song fades in and out, we experience what the actor is experiencing. The underscore gives the audience the sense of what she is actually feeling—fear, uncertainty, and confusion—helping to make the transition from the hospital to the street, and eventually to the hotel room.

Source Music to Establish Time or Place

In addition to dramatic usage, source music often establishes a time or place. By using source music that is indigenous to a culture, the feeling of that culture is placed in the mind of the audience. The underscore can then also use elements of the cultural music, or it can be a completely different entity.

There are also countless films that have used source music to establish a time in history, such as *Anne of the Thousand Days*, *The Madness of King George*, and *Shakespeare In Love* (see chapter 17).

The Composer and Source Music

The composer may or may not be involved in creating source music. It depends on the kind of underscore being written, and whether or not the composer has the musical background to write what is needed. If the movie needs source music describing a specific culture or time period, the composer must have the research and musical skills to write the appropriate music. If the underscore is closely related to the source music, or uses elements of it, it is best to have the composer also write the source music. However, if the source music is in a style unfamiliar to the composer, he will hire someone else to do those cues. In addition, if there are sequences like the one in *The Pelican Brief* described above, then the composer must at least be aware of the key, instrumentation, style and tempo of the source cues.

Whether or not the composer is involved in the source music also depends on dramatic considerations. Often, songs used as source music are taken from existing recordings and the composer is not part of the selection process. However, there are times when the composer is asked to write a source cue that is not a song, most likely an instrumental of some kind. The composer can utilize the players at the recording session for the underscore to record the source music. This is an efficient way to create source music without getting clearances and having extra recording sessions. In addition, if the composer writes the source music, then the theme for the film can be worked into it, as Alan Silvestri did during the fiesta scene in *Romancing the Stone*.

People often wonder why they don't remember hearing many of the songs on the CD soundtrack in the movie. The answer is, they probably did hear those songs, but they were source cues played for only a few seconds at a very low volume under dialogue. However, many record companies are quite content to have their artist's songs in the film as source cues, as long as they also appear on the soundtrack album. Soundtrack albums are now one of the biggest financial considerations in making a film.

Soundtrack Albums

At one point during the summer of 1998, three of the top five best-selling albums were movie soundtracks. And for the whole year of 1998, twenty-two of Billboard's top 200 albums were also soundtracks. The top selling album of 1998 was the soundtrack to *Titanic*, which grossed $26 million in sales for that year alone and spawned two subsequent *Titanic* soundtracks—one with more songs, and another with James Horner's underscore. During that same year, soundtrack album sales rose by an amazing 36 percent.[1]

With these kinds of numbers, it is no wonder that producers are all hopping on the soundtrack bandwagon, hoping to generate both profit and publicity for their films through the use of songs. This is not a new phenomenon, although the current sales numbers and profit levels are higher than ever. As discussed in chapter 5, from the earliest days of talkies, producers have used songs in films. In today's filmmaking world, this process is not so easy as simply commissioning a songwriter to create a tune for the film; there are many different elements to take into consideration. In an age where the record companies and film studios are often owned by the same conglomerates, there are several dimensions to the game. Financial considerations, not the creative ones, are often the overriding factors in making a soundtrack. Michael Greene, president of the National Academy of Arts and Sciences, which produces the Grammy awards, discusses this trend:

> *The connection between soundtracks and films has never been more vibrant. Not only have there been more soundtracks issued, but you have to back up and remember some of the reasons why—not the least of which is that many of the film companies are also the owners of the music companies. So they've found a good way to cross-promotionalize the music and films to everybody's advantage.* [2]

There are many films where the use of songs in the film is fabulous, entertaining, and totally appropriate. However, there are many that shoehorn songs into the film in order to get the song on the soundtrack album. The problem is that this often ignores the wishes of the film's creative team: the director, writer, editor, and composer. The people that win most often in the soundtrack game are the record companies, artists, and film producers. The lament frequently heard from those in the creative parts of the film industry is that the "suits," or businessmen, are making decisions that have nothing to do with the quality of the movie—only with the ability to "cross-promotionalize" and increase profits. Truth be told, this is a complaint that has echoed throughout the history of Hollywood, only at no time has it been so loud or futile. Film making is essentially a commercial enterprise, and with the kinds of profits that can be made, there is much motivation to exploit this burgeoning soundtrack market and little motivation to give creative considerations more weight. As music supervisor Jeff Carson says, "How do you make a hit movie *and* a hit soundtrack, and make them work together at the same time?" It is not easy. It can be done, and yet the mystery is that no one really knows which soundtracks will take off and which will be duds.

There are many different paths a particular song can take to find its way into a film. It can be commissioned by the producer; it can be requested by the director; it can be suggested by the film editor, music editor, or composer; or it can be part of the catalogue of the publishing company that the movie studio happens to own. The film could use the original performance, or record a new version. In all these instances, sync licenses need to be issued, clearances obtained, and royalty deals hammered out. If there are to be recording sessions for a song, someone must produce and oversee them. There are also budgets to adhere to. All of these elements are part of the complex process of bringing a song to a film, a process that is usually managed by the music supervisor.

Music Supervisor

The *music supervisor* is a role that has developed since the late 1970s into what we know today. It is a hybrid of many aspects of the music scoring business. Although there has often been someone with the title "music supervisor" since the earliest days of sound films, the tasks that today's music supervisor fulfills are vastly different from those of his counterpart fifty years ago.

The main job of the music supervisor is to oversee the process of placing songs in a film. These can be songs that are eventually used on the soundtrack album, or songs that are used strictly for source music. The music supervisor communicates with the composer, but does not oversee the composing of the underscore. Also, it is important to know that there are essentially two types of music supervisors: those that simply organize the choosing and clearance of the songs, and those that are musically trained and can produce a recording session as well.

The tasks that a music supervisor fulfills are as follows:

Creating and monitoring budgets. Since the music supervisor is often doing some of the actual business negotiations on behalf of the producer, he usually assists in creating a music budget for the film. This can involve budgeting only for the use of songs, if that is what the score is, and can also include overseeing the finances of recording the underscore and hiring the composer. It is also the music supervisor's job to oversee the day-to-day budgets in the recording studio during production of any songs.

Helping to pick the songs. This is often the largest part of the music supervisor's job. Which songs are chosen depends on many factors, including the budget, the director's wishes, the producer's wishes, instructions from the executives at the movie studio, which artists and publishers agree to allow use of their songs, and which artists are available for recording. It can be a difficult and politically complicated labyrinth to negotiate.

Getting clearance for songs. Before a song is used in a movie, permission must be obtained. First, the publisher must grant *sync rights,* the right to synchronize the song with the movie. If the producer or director wants to use the original version of a song, then a second permission must be granted by the owner of the original master-recording—usually the record company. The music supervisor either handles the negotiations for these clearances himself, or hires a music clearance company to do that work.

Record producing. No matter whether it is an old song being rere-corded or a song commissioned for the film, the music supervisor may produce the recording session. This job is often done by the film composer if he wrote or co-wrote the song, and sometimes an outside record producer is contracted. But even then, the music supervisor makes sure these sessions go smoothly and stay on budget. Whether old songs are re-recorded or not depends on how much money the record company wants for the use of the original master. Sometimes it is cheaper to use the master; sometimes it is cheaper to redo it.

Recommending the composer. Because the music supervisor is often involved in the project at an early date, often he is asked to recommend a composer he considers appropriate for the film, and who fits the budget.

Overseeing the temp track. Often the music supervisor is part of the team, with the music editor and director, that chooses the music and builds the temp track.

Overseeing music performed on camera. If there is a scene where the actors are singing or dancing, the music supervisor will be present to ensure that everything is going well. This means making sure the playback is correct and that the lip-syncing is accurate.

As mentioned above, helping to pick the songs for the film is a large part of the music supervisor's job. Although the process can sometimes go fairly smoothly, many, many problems can arise in the clearing of publishing rights, as well as clearing the use of original masters. In addition, there are often many different voices trying to influence the song selection process. Producers and directors often request specific songs; some are reasonable requests, some are out of the range of their budget, and some will not be released by the artist, record company, or publisher. There is the screenwriter, who may have written the idea for a specific song into the script. Then there is the movie studio, which might own a certain record company, and they want to promote its artists. The film editor, who has worked with the film for several months, has his own ideas. And there are even the spouses of these people that can get into the act, because *everyone* has an opinion about music and songs! This situation is familiar to music supervisor, Daniel Carlin:

> *It's not just picking any song that will work. Anybody that listens to the radio can do that. We've got to have a budget. We've got to think about a soundtrack deal, we've got to think about the politics. For example, say I go in and I put this great Mariah Carey song into a scene. What if the budget is $300,000 for 30 songs and I have just spent $100,000 of the budget? Because the director falls in love with it and will not have it any other way, that does not do anybody any good. Now everybody is fighting. The director is fighting with the studio, and somebody goes, "Who is the jerk that put this Mariah Carey song in there in the first place?" I don't what to be the guy who raises his hand.*

The music supervisor is often caught in the crossfire of these situations because he is the one handling the songs. And it often comes back to the idea that movie making is a balance, and not always a delicate one, between creativity and commerce. When so many different powers are trying to influence the use of songs, it can get diplomatically difficult for the music supervisor.

Jeff Carson:

> *Music supervision is kind of like trying to thread five needles at once, or hit five bulls-eyes all at once. It's very difficult to hit five bulls-eyes all at once. You're trying to accommodate the movie with the right music, you're trying to please the director, the producer, the studio executives, the studio's music department. Everybody.*

There is no one rule, or guide, for how much a song will cost. If it is going to be the title of the movie, obviously the owner of the copyright will ask for more money. If it is a well-known song by a well-known artist, then that will cost more than an unknown song by an up-and-coming artist. Daniel Carlin creates a hypothetical example of the kinds of negotiations that take place:

> *There is no law or rule about this stuff. You go to the publisher with hat in hand, and you say, "Here's our movie, here's our budget, and here's how much money we have to spend. Can you help us out?" And it depends. I mean if it's a one-hundred-million-dollar movie, they're not going to give you the song for eight thousand. But if you make a three-million-dollar movie, and you can them tell it's a labor of love for everybody, then they might say: "Here's what I'll do for you, I'll make a deal if you use five of our songs, and I'll give them to you for $6,500 each." And that way they get paid not only what I pay them for the songs, but then, when it goes on television, they get those residuals. Then it gets released overseas and gets more residuals. So they make up a package deal. The volume helps them, and it helps me too. And it also means that I'm not going to put in a competing singer. I'm gonna have five of their songs, and it makes everybody's life easier.*

As you can see, there are countless ways that songs can be used in a film, and many different motives for using them. The balance between creative and financial considerations is a tricky one that everyone in the film-making business experiences. Unfortunately, everyone involved rarely shares the same vision for the music, especially when there are songs involved. Because royalties and sales profits generated from songs and soundtrack albums are enormous, there are many interested people other than the film makers who try to sway the choices. The director might want it one way, the producer another, the movie studio a third, and an interested record company a fourth. There are often two conflicting goals in the choosing of what kind of music to have: the creative choice, based on the director's vision for the film; and the commercial choice, which is based on what will make the most money, both in soundtrack album sales and in helping to promote the popularity of the film. The music supervisor guides the process of choosing songs, whether they are intended for a soundtrack album or not. And hopefully he is able to guide the process towards serving the drama as well as serving the financial bottom line.

The
Business of
Film Scoring

PART IV

CHAPTER 21

Making the Deal:
Agents, Attorneys, and Contracts

When we need a lawyer to navigate through the complexities
of modern life, we want one who doesn't "miss a beat."
—*Don Campbell[1]*

Many musicians seem to want to avoid discussing the business aspect of film scoring. They would prefer to be *artistes* who can live in lofty heights above the humdrum, mundane world of money-changing hands. Some are simply scared at having to actually deal with making money doing music. But every artist, every creative person who works for himself, is also in business. Because of the freelance nature of our work, *we are in business for ourselves* and must learn to handle our financial affairs, deal with contracts, conduct ourselves in negotiations, and make the best deals possible. Many young composers have the impression that they will somehow get a gig writing music for films, be compensated handsomely for their music, and then someone else will handle the money. Unfortunately, this is far from the truth. Many composers have made a very good living writing film music for TV, cable, and documentaries and never have had an agent. Some are lucky enough to have an efficient and honest agent, but who oversees the composer's transactions with the agent? Ultimately, it comes down to every musician having control and being knowledgeable about his own business.

There are several key factors in controlling one's own business and one's own financial destiny. The first, as I mentioned, is knowledge. The more you know about your fee structure, royalties, budgets, expense accounts, taxes, and day-to-day expenses, the more informed are the decisions you make. This can be terribly dry stuff, but it is a part of a composer's livelihood.

② Another key factor is organization. Keep a file for all those receipts. When you come home from the music store with a new piece of equipment or book, file that receipt right away under "expenses." Paperwork can be a drag, but if you don't do it, it can come back to haunt you. Keep another file for all your royalty statements, another for tax papers, completed copyright forms, correspondence, etc. In addition, keep your phone numbers organized and don't throw any out! You never know when you will need that duduk player again, even though it has been five years since he played on your session.

Agents and Attorneys

③ A third key factor in keeping your business affairs in order is to have competent and honest people assist you. These are the attorneys, agents, and financial advisors who have expertise in specific areas.

Many film composers have agents who help the composer obtain jobs, and provide career management. The agent negotiates deals and sees that the terms of a contract are honored. An agent has thorough knowledge of projects in various stages of production, and contacts the producer or director to pitch one of his composers for a project. He constantly networks with people in every facet of the entertainment business, always looking for opportunities for his clients.

Agent David May of the Zomba Group:

> *What we depend on for our work is, number one, our relationships. This includes the music people out at the studios, the major production companies, and the major music supervisors. We are constantly calling them and they are constantly calling us about what they have on their plate and what they are looking for and who we have that might fit the bill. It's our business to be providing them with constant information about our clients, and also to suggest appropriate candidates wherever we can.*
>
> *You want to find out when projects are occurring, when they are going to be looking for a composer, who the key people are that will be influencing that decision, whether you are going through*

a music producer or music supervisor or directly to the director—just who do you deal with. So, at the appropriate time we can make the calls we need to make to that person, and get our people in there. And then, the next step—once we have some kind of entry, when we know what kind of person they are looking for and what kind of budget they have—we put together music or credits, whatever we can put together to hopefully make them interested in our client.

Most agents have a roster of composers, so the trick for the composer is to find the agent that works best for him. There is no way that an agent can give his full attention to one composer 100% of the time. For the agent, it is a constant juggling act that also involves an intuitive sense as to which of his clients to pitch for a job. So the composer must also be aggressive in searching out work, and then let the agent handle negotiations once the job is offered.

In 1991, composer Cliff Eidelman had already successfully scored several feature films including *Triumph of the Spirit* and *Crazy People*. He knew that a new *Star Trek* movie was in production, and decided he wanted a shot at it. Without the help of his agent he had a meeting with the director, read the script, and thoroughly notated places he thought music would happen. He also did a sequenced mock-up of several possible cues. His persistence, interest, and willingness to go the extra mile paid off and he got the job, leaving the particulars of the contract to his agent.

Agents welcome this kind of aggressive job seeking by a composer; it makes their job easier. But the good agent will always be looking out for your best interest. Also, the agent must be someone you can trust and count on to be honest and up-front with you.

David May:

> *It's a partnership between an agent and a composer. The theory is that if both of us are doing everything we can, and communicating as frequently as we can, then we're going to stand a much, much better chance in moving a composer's career forward.*

For new composers, it is difficult to get an agent. There is a catch-22: you must have done some work before they will take you on. And then, you are at the low end of the food chain, so to speak. It behooves the composer to pursue his own contacts and gigs as much as possible. When the gigs start coming in, this will get the agent's attention.

Attorneys

Perhaps the most important and most lampooned of all career advisors is the attorney. All shark jokes aside, a good attorney's advice (or an attorney's good advice) is invaluable. For a film score, after the agent negotiates the deal, the attorney reviews the terms of the contract. He may negotiate through your agent, or negotiate directly with movie producers. He also may make deals with publishers and record companies, and will often give career guidance. Your attorney will know exactly how much money you are making, how much you are paying in taxes and how much that new house just cost. Because of this, you need to find an attorney you can trust—someone who you feel is looking out for your best interest. One important thing to remember is *that you are paying this person.* For your hard-earned money, the attorney is performing the services mentioned above. If you don't like the way he conducts himself or his business, you can walk away and find someone else. Many people forget this and feel bound to one lawyer forever. The services of a lawyer are expensive and necessary, but you are the one doing the buying!

Despite all the negative stories we hear about attorneys and agents, there are many good ones out there. In our culture, bad news and negativity get the headlines. Yes, there are many attorneys and agents who are low-lifes, and there are some who get tempted by self-serving fortune, but there are also many who are honest and trustworthy. Use your instinct to find someone who works well for you.

One final note about agents and attorneys: any deal they strike with a producer, publisher, or other executive *must be approved and signed by you.* And that brings us full circle. In order to know that you are making the best decision for yourself, and sometimes for your family,

[handwritten annotation at top: deal memo = summarizes the terms the composer & production office have agreed upon & is the binding legal agreement until the final contract is completed by the attorneys.]

you must be informed and have a good grasp of the issues and items in your contract. Let the attorney and agent give you advice, but don't let them run your life.

[handwritten annotation: short form contract: a little more detailed than the deal memo, but not as detailed as the final contract]

Contracts

For a film composer, the financial bottom line is not just the fee received for writing a score, but also the royalties that can be generated for many years after the film is originally released. There are royalties for when the film is shown on TV or when the music from the film is played on the radio or in concert halls. There are royalties generated for music included on a soundtrack album. There are also additional royalties if the film is shown in foreign countries, either in theaters or on TV. If the composer writes or co-writes a song that is included in the film, it can generate another whole branch of the income river. One film score can generate royalties equal to several times the composer's original fee for writing the score. (Royalties are discussed in detail in chapter 22.)

How does this work? Where does all this money come from? Who keeps track of it? Before any music is written, before any money is generated, the composer signs a contract with the producer that specifies the services the composer will provide and the compensation the producer will pay. The terms of this contract coupled with the popularity of the film and its ability to generate royalty income determines how much the composer will make and where the money comes from.

After the composer is offered the gig, then either a *deal memo* or a *short-form contract* is drawn up. The deal memo summarizes the terms the composer and production office have agreed upon, and is the binding legal agreement until the final contract is completed by the attorneys. A short form contract is a little more detailed than the deal memo, but not as detailed as the final contract.

Agent David May:

> *Once we have verbal terms for whatever creative deal we finally come up with, I will typically generate a deal memo. If it's a*

studio, sometimes they will generate it, and different studios have different policies. Sony does a short form agreement first— they don't do deal memos—followed by a long form (contract). Others go straight to a long form, but I want to make sure that there is something on paper as quickly after the verbal agreement has been transacted as possible. Memories can be hazy, and it also is common for weeks, if not months, to go by between making a deal and actually getting a contract. So I don't want to be at that stage arguing with an attorney saying, "No, wait a second, your client agreed to half the publishing." And the attorney is saying, "Well, I don't have anything in my notes there."

Based on the deal memo, attorneys draw up a final *long-form contract*. Where the deal memo is a summary of the terms agreed upon, the final contract is a complex legal document. However, every composer should understand the basic items that are covered. There are many clauses in the film composer's contract that must be addressed and approved. Some of the important ones are:

- How much is the fee?
- How will the fee be paid?
- Is it a "package" or "all-in" deal?
- The length of time for composing the score
- Screen credit
- Advertising credit
- Copyright ownership
- Transportation and miscellaneous expenses
- Royalties for other use of the music (other than the film)
- Suspensions/terminations/defaults
- Royalty fees for underscore on soundtrack albums
- Royalties from video sales
- Exclusivity of the composer

screen credit: how your name appears on-screen
& where it is placed in the credits.

Making the Deal: Agents, Attorneys, and Contracts

Some of these items are fairly straightforward. *Screen credit* refers to how your name appears on-screen and where it is placed in the credits. Before the costume designer, after the cinematographer? Should it read:

Music by
Richard Davis

Or do you want the full treatment:

Music composed, conducted, and orchestrated by
Richard Mark Davis

Advertising credit is similar, referring to where and how your name is placed in newspaper, magazine, and billboard ads.

Transportation and expenses is for going out of town to record or do research. Will they fly you first class or coach? Will they pay for your spouse? How much per-diem? Many composers think this item is unnecessary, as they do all their work in Los Angeles or New York. But with many sessions happening outside of these cities for various reasons, this item needs to be negotiated up-front, and not left to see if it is actually needed.

Exclusivity of the composer means that the composer will not work on other projects during the time that he is committed to the one indicated in the contract. This is a protection for the producer to insure that they get your full attention. Composers are freelance and are always juggling schedules and projects, and the producer is investing a lot of money in your coming through for him. So it makes sense from the producers standpoint that you are working exclusively for him during the specified time. Another variation of this clause is *"non-exclusive, but first priority."* This means that the composer may work on other projects at the same time, but must give the other party of the contract first priority.

It is worth adding at this point that I believe in putting everything in writing, even when dealing with friends. There is nothing like a written agreement in the form of a contract or deal memo to prevent misunderstandings down the line. It is actually a protection for both parties in the event that one person has a different interpretation of

211

what was agreed upon several months before. Or in a worst-case scenario, if one party tries to deliberately misrepresent or distort the agreement, a written contract can settle the dispute. Gentleman's agreements are lovely, altruistic, and philosophically desirable—we all want to believe that our business partners are honorable. But in reality, verbal agreements sealed on a handshake can be somewhat quaint if not just plain bad business. If ever someone actually tries to avoid signing a written contract or a deal memo with you, walk out the door as fast as possible! This is a sure indication of a person who knows they cannot or will not honor the terms of your verbal agreement and just wants to take you for a ride.

The contract is a supremely important document. It is your security that certain terms have been agreed to by both sides. It must be clear, complete, and fully understandable by an unrelated third person (another attorney, etc.)

Two of the most important issues in the film composer's contract are the composer's fee, and package deals. There are several dimensions to both these items, and they require in-depth discussion.

Composer Fees

The first payment the composer receives on a film is the first installment of his composing fee. When we refer to a fee in this sense, it means that the producer is paying the composer for writing the music. If the composer accepts a straight fee, as opposed to a "package deal," then he is not responsible for any music production costs, e.g., studio time, orchestrators, musicians, etc. Fees for a feature film can cover a wide range, from about $25,000 for a low-budget film and a relatively unknown composer, to over $700,000 for a "name" composer on a big-budget feature. For TV, cable TV, documentaries, and cartoons, fees are less and depend on the total budget of the project.

Note: It used to be the rule of thumb that the complete music budget, including composer, musicians, music editors, recording studio, etc., would be a certain percentage of the film's overall budget, often in the range of 1.5 to 3%. If the film's total budget was $50 million, the music budget would be between $500,000 and $1.5 million. However, that practice is no longer in use. Some movie budgets are as high as $200 million, and music costs have not risen proportionately.

There are several ways the composer's fee can be paid. Often the fee is paid in three parts: the first when the spotting is completed and the composer begins writing, the second at the beginning of recording the music, and the third at the completion of the dubbing session. Sometimes a specific number of weeks are written in the contract, like *"the composer shall commence services on the spotting date of the picture and will complete the score within 12 consecutive weeks from that date."* Sometimes the completion date is tied into the post-production schedule. Other contracts give a specific month, day, and year by which the composer shall deliver the finished (recorded) score. If the composer is needed beyond the set time frame in the contract, there is another clause that provides additional compensation.

Package Deals

One of the newest wrinkles of the past decade, and most important factors in determining fees, fee payment schedules, and music delivery dates, is the *package deal*. Also known as the *all-in deal*, this is when the composer agrees to accept a certain amount of money in return for getting the music produced and recorded. Many low-budget films, cable and television films, and episodic television shows work this way. As opposed to receiving a fee for composing the music with the producer paying for all production-related costs, in the package deal, the composer is responsible for these costs with some possible exceptions.

Since the biggest cost outside of the composer's fee is hiring the musicians and recording studio, when a composer accepts a package deal, they are often planning on producing most, if not all of the music electronically. Many high profile composers now accept deals like this. For example, Mark Snow's music for the *X-Files* TV series is produced in his home studio with the occasional live musician (that *he* must pay). James Horner and Mark Isham are but two prominent composers who have recently done feature films as package deals. Many other composers with extensive electronic set-ups are happy to accept a package deal for they know how fast they can work, and what is financially viable for them.

The danger to the composer in a package deal is that if he miscalculates, the recording session, or other related costs, may escalate beyond his original budget. Then the composer can be responsible for paying the extra costs out-of-pocket in order to deliver the final music. However, there are often exclusions to what the composer is responsible for, and these vary from deal to deal. In lower-budget deals, the composer tends to be responsible for more of the music production costs than in major feature films. Some of these exclusions for which the feature film producer is normally responsible are:

- Music editing costs
- Licensing of songs if not written by the composer
- Reuse, new use, and other payments to union musicians
- Rescoring for creative reasons not due to the fault or omission of the composer

The final item on this list is extremely important. It protects the composer from directors or producers that make arbitrary, capricious, and frequent changes in the film, or ask for many changes in the music. Often a specific number of minutes of music will be agreed upon as a ceiling, and if this number is exceeded, the composer is entitled to extra fees.

The advantage to the composer of a package deal is that if he works quickly and enjoys working with synthesizers and samplers, a good profit can be made. And don't forget all those royalties coming down the road. The disadvantage is that the pressure of music production and the music budget is on the composer's shoulders. The reality of the film scoring business today is that in many instances, if a composer does not agree to the package deal, they will not get the job. The producer will simply find someone who will agree.

Mark Isham speaks about package deals:

A real important point for newcomers to understand is, because you're a newcomer you're probably going to get package-dealed from the beginning these days. It's very rare to just walk in and have someone say, "Here's a fee and we'll pay any costs you have." That's not going to happen unless you have a champion who says, "Look, I really want you to score this and I'll take care of it. Don't worry about a thing."

The important thing to remember is that everything is negotiable. You can negotiate for gross points. You can negotiate for album points. You can negotiate for publishing. You can negotiate for how many musicians you guarantee to employ. Every aspect of a package deal is negotiable. And make sure you do your homework, because if you miscalculate, and you agree contractually to supply 20 strings for 40 minutes of music, you better know what that's going to cost you. And you better do things like go to the director and say, "I will accept this on the terms that you sign off on everything that I play for you in demo form." Sometimes the director is sitting on the scoring stage and says, "What if this were faster?" Then you're looking at writing more music, changing your tempo, and somehow getting new music on the stand while the musicians are waiting for you. That could eat up your profit right there. So it's very crucial that you have a good line of communication with your director. Even if you can't get it in writing that they'll sign-off on the mock-ups, at least, man-to-man, get them to agree that this is a package deal, and you're going to try to help each other.

Agent and attorney David May also speaks to the package deal issue:

The package needs more definition and it needs to be more limited [than a "straight fee" deal]. Otherwise the composer can lose his shirt. What we'll do then is define what the package includes, and what it doesn't. What I try to do is limit it to certain number of minutes of music, limit to a certain number of live players, so if we agree to a package of $65,000 but for that there is no more *than 35 minutes of music, no more than ten live musicians. We try to limit it in every way possible so that they realize that if they want more than that, then they've got to pay more than the package amount. I really talk to the composer to make sure, before we agree to it, that the composer does a rough budget to make sure he can make what he wants to make. I'm always telling composers, you are in fact entitled to make a living at this.... But things happen, you want this, the director wants that, and that $30,000 profit ends up being whittled down to $17,000. I'm trying to avoid that.*

Package deals need to be approached with care and planning. Everything must be in writing, and communication with the director/production office must be clear. The best package-deal situation is when you are planning to produce most, if not all, of the music in your home studio. As soon as you venture into the world of studios, engineers, and live musicians, you are leaving yourself open to cost overruns for which you may or may not be protected contractually. But the package deal is a way of life, especially for low-budget features, episodic television, and television movies. Learn how to budget a package deal so you can make a reasonable amount of money when you get the opportunity.

CHAPTER 22

Publishing and Copyrights

One of the first lessons I learned in this business is you don't have the luxury of being a tortured artist. Go get a gig in the tortured artist venue. Hollywood has no time for that. It isn't allowed.
—Mark Isham

Publishing and copyrights is an area of the film composing business that is crucial to the composer's financial well being. *Most of the time, for feature films and television, film composers do not own their music due to a clause in their contract called "a work made for hire."* However, this is not always the case, and how your music is published, who owns the copyright, and in what proportions that ownership is divided between writer and publisher determines how much money in royalties you see down the road in the months and years to come after a film has been released. Royalties are discussed in depth in chapter 23, so first let's talk about what makes a work *published*, and what it means to have that work *copyrighted*.

What Is a Copyright?

Copyright refers to the ownership of a creative work—in this case music. (It could also be a book, a poem, a photograph, an artwork, etc.) It sounds somewhat circular, but copyright means "the right to copy," or the right to reproduce a certain work. The person who owns the copyright owns the rights to that work. Therefore, the person who owns the copyright controls how it will be published—that is, offered for sale to the public.

The history of copyright laws in the United States is a complex subject. Simply put, in the earliest days of the nation, laws were enacted that gave authors and publishers exclusive ownership of their creative works and protected them from theft of those works. In this century there have been three significant copyright laws enacted: in 1909, 1976, and in 1998.

The first copyright law in this century is the Copyright Act of 1909. This act set the length of the original copyright at twenty-eight years with a copyright renewal making the potential life of the copyright protection fifty-six years. After that fifty-six-year period, the work would enter the public domain (become PD) and no royalties would be paid to the copyright owners for use of the work. So, if someone wrote a song in 1910 and filed the renewal form in 1938, in 1966 the copyright would have expired and that song would enter the public domain. *Public domain* means that there is no ownership of a copyright, so anyone who wants to can reproduce or use the work in any way because there is no one to whom royalties must be paid. Older songs, folk songs with no known author, and classical music written before the earlier part of the century are examples of works in the public domain.

By the 1950s, this law had become outmoded and Congress began to look at ways to change it. It took until 1976 to enact a new law: the 1976 Copyright Revision Act. This law made the duration of the original copyright to be the life of the author plus fifty years. So, the copyright stayed in effect for fifty years after the composer or writer died.

The current law is this: In 1998, the U.S. Congress amended the Copyright Revision Act of 1976 to make the length of copyright protection *life plus seventy years.* This means that if a composer created a work in 1998 and lives to the year 2025, the copyright will continue to be in effect for his heirs or estate until the year 2095, a total of ninety-seven years. If the same composer creates a work in the year 2024, and passes away in 2025, the length of the copyright is only seventy-one years. This new law (beginning with the 1976 Revision act) is very beneficial for composers (and all artists) for it guarantees that as long as the creator is alive, his work will be protected by the copyright. Many composers outlived the previous fifty-six years protection of the 1909 law and saw their works enter the public domain while they were still alive. And some suffered the loss of copyright by forgetting to file the renewal forms, thus seeing the work enter the public domain after only twenty-eight years. This newest law insures the heirs or estate of the composer seventy years of copyright protection and potential income, whereas under the previous laws that protection was usually much shorter. And it also brings the United States into line with similar protection offered in European countries.

What Is a "Published" Work?

The legal definition of *publishing* according to United States copyright law is *"the distribution of copies or phonorecords of a work to the public by sale or other transfer of ownership, or by rental, lease, or lending."* In addition, a published work is one in which there has been *"an offering to distribute copies or phonorecords to a group of persons for purposes of further distribution, public performance, or public display."*

A work is considered to be published if it is offered for sale to the public. If a composer writes an incredible heart-stopping symphonic poem but leaves it on a shelf in his studio for years, that work is not considered to be published. However, if copies of the same work are printed and consequently offered for sale in a classical music store, that work is considered published. If a band makes a CD and just gives it away to friends, that work is not published. If the same CD is offered for sale at gigs and the local music store, that music is then considered to be published. When a film is released in theaters or shown on TV, that music is also considered to be published. (Note that in all the above examples, the works are protected by copyright whether or not they are published. More on this below.)

Once a work is published, royalties can be collected from performances of the work and from sales of recordings, sheet music, and songbooks. These royalties are divided into two portions: half goes to the publisher who is the owner of the copyright, and half goes to the writer (composer). In some cases the publisher and the writer are the same person, in some cases they are different. In addition, both the publishers' and the writers' portions can be divided into smaller parts if there are co-writers or co-publishers.

When a work is considered published, by natural implication, that work has a publisher. A publisher can be an individual, such as a film composer or songwriter, who is self-publishing their own catalogue of works, or it can be a large corporation with hundreds or even thousands of titles to oversee. The duties of the publisher are to register the copyright, oversee the financial administration of a work, collect royalties, negotiate new uses, and make sure that there is no infringement on the copyright.

Registering a Copyright

Registering a copyright is very easy. This is done through the United States Copyright Office, a branch of the Library of Congress in Washington, D.C. Most copyright registration is now done online. Go to copyright.gov and follow the link to the Electronic Copyright Office. You will fill out the form and upload a recording of the music to be registered along with the current fee. (There is also the option to register using a paper form and snail mail). After a period of about three weeks to three months, you will receive a copy of your completed form with a stamped seal of the U.S. Copyright Office indicating completed registration and full copyright protection. However, your protection begins on the day your form is received by the Copyright Office, as long as it is filled out correctly.

Copyright Protection

The questions are often raised: Should I bother to register my work? Is there any benefit to me in doing the paperwork and paying the fee? and, Am I not protected as soon as I create the work? The answers are yes, yes, and yes. But first, an explanation of how copyright protection works.

Whether or not a work is protected by copyright has to do with a term used by the writers of the law. This is where they refer to a work being *fixed*. This means that the work is set down, or fixed in some kind of tangible, physical form, like writing it down on paper or recording it. Here is the copyright law of 1976 defining what is fixed:

> *A work is "fixed" in a tangible medium of expression when its embodiment in a copy or phonorecord, by or under the authority of the author, is sufficiently permanent or stable to permit it to be perceived, reproduced, or otherwise communicated for a period of more than transitory duration. A work consisting of sounds, images, or both, that are being transmitted, is "fixed" for purposes of this title if a fixation of the work is being made simultaneously with its transmission.*

As soon as you begin to put the musical idea on paper or record it, it is considered to be fixed, and protected by copyright law. No registration needs to take place; no forms need to be filled out. If you are writing the work over a period of time, whether it is days, weeks, or years, the protection is in effect as you work. In addition, the last sentence of this excerpt of the law says that if an uncopyrighted work is transmitted or broadcast over TV or radio, and the author of the song has given permission for a recording of the initial broadcast, that work is considered to be "fixed" and protected by the copyright law.

This is actually the answer to the question above: Am I not protected as soon as I create the work? The answer is that you are protected in a technical and legal sense. However, strange things happen in a world of laws, attorneys, and courtrooms. If you created a work in the privacy of your home, the burden of proof as to when that work was created is on you. Unless you have witnesses, you could be hard-pressed to convince a judge or jury of the truth your story. If you are ever involved in a copyright infringement suit, you will want to have the most foolproof evidence of the origination of the copyright. This would be the stamped registration form you received from the Copyright Office. You would be kicking yourself if you lost a lawsuit you should have won because you did not want to pay a $20 fee and take ten minutes filling out the copyright registration form several years before.

One thing to remember is that as a film composer you often do not own the copyright—the producer of the film owns it (see *work made for hire* at the end of this chapter). In this case, the producer has the copyright registration form filled out and returned to him. However, on some projects you will retain the ownership of the copyright and will have to go through the registration process yourself. Either way, it is good to know the procedures.

The Rights of the Copyright Owner

What exactly does it mean to own a copyright? To sum it up, the owner of the copyright has the right to reproduce the copyrighted work, to distribute it through "phonorecords," and to perform the work publicly. (*Phonorecords* used to apply to just that—records that go on a turntable; now it legally means anything that reproduces sound. CDs, cassettes, prerecorded MiniDiscs, and any future invention of reproducing sound is covered by this term.) If you own the copyright to a piece of music, you have the exclusive right to decide how to initially reproduce copies of it, where and when the initial performance takes place, and who initially performs it.

Notice how that word "initially" snuck into those last few phrases. This is important since after the work is initially "offered to the public," or published, your ability to control the use of your copyrighted material changes. Remember that a copyrighted work is not necessarily a published work. A work can be under copyright but not yet be published. So if someone wants to use your music on their CD or perform it in public, and your music is copyrighted but not yet published, they need to get your permission. You have the right to decide about the initial performance or reproduction of copies. If your song or film score is yet to be published and another artist wants to record the entire work or a portion of it, they must get your permission first. However, if the work is already published, if you have already recorded and released it on a CD, or if it has been released in the theaters as a film score, then your permission is not necessary as long as they pay you a minimum royalty. This is a royalty paid at a rate established by the Copyright Royalty Tribunal (a five-person panel appointed by the President) called the *minimum statutory rate*. Or you could agree to a lower rate if it suits your interests. For songs, this minimum statutory rate is calculated by the song; currently it is set at 9.1 cents per song per unit sold. So if someone else records one song of yours, and their album sells 1,000,000 units, then the royalty would be $91,000. This is called a *mechanical royalty* that is paid to you by the record company for the privilege of using your music. If the music is instrumental film music, the royalty rate is calculated either by how many minutes in duration the piece is, or sometimes by how many selections appear on the album. For a film composer, this arrangement is one of the important items covered in his contract. (For more about royalties, see chapter 23.)

Copyright Infringement

Another question that often comes up is "What constitutes copyright infringement?" There are two types of copyright infringement: the unauthorized use of a copyrighted work, and the copying of substantial portions of a work.

The unauthorized use of a copyrighted work is the more clear-cut type of infringement. This is when someone records or performs copyrighted material without paying royalties to the owner of the copyright. This can happen if a performer records a copyrighted song, sells thousands of units and doesn't pay the appropriate royalty. Even though the copyright owner does not have to give permission for use of a published song, he must still be notified that the song will be used, and must be paid at least the statutory minimum royalty. In a film score, if a producer uses music from another film or recording but does not obtain a *sync license* (a license that gives permission to use the music and synchronize it to picture), that producer is guilty of copyright infringement; he has violated the copyright owner's exclusive rights.

The copying of substantial portions of a copyrighted work is a more difficult issue to determine. Many composers and songwriters are under the impression that you can copy up to four bars, or some other amount of actual music, before you are in danger of violating the copyright laws. This is a misconception. The copyright law says that you must have music that contains a "substantial similarity" to the copyrighted work before you are guilty of copyright infringement. In addition, the law says that for there to be infringement, the owner of the copyright must show "proof of access." In other words, if you are being accused of copying a substantial portion of a copyrighted work, the owner of the copyright must prove that somehow you had access to hearing the work in question.

For example, if this work has had substantial radio or TV airplay, then it is assumed that you had access to it. You cannot claim that because you do not own a TV, you never heard that sit-com theme song. The same applies for a film score. You cannot claim that you never saw the movie and therefore are not guilty of copyright infringement. If the music is widely disseminated to the public, either in theaters or on the radio or TV, then it is assumed that you had access to it.

On the other hand, say you have written a work that has only been performed locally in your city, Burlington, Vermont. Suppose that a composer based in Los Angeles comes out with a hit movie theme or song that sounds just like your song. In this case, you cannot claim copyright infringement, since you would be hard-pressed to prove that a composer from Los Angeles had access to your song that was only played in a nightclub in Burlington, Vermont. However, if you can prove that the composer in question had recently spent time in Burlington, and even was present at your gig, then you would have a case.

Copyright infringement is an area in which you should pray never to be involved. Be aware if you are subconsciously "borrowing" someone else's music. Try to always be original. These kinds of lawsuits can be messy, lengthy, and expensive. In our litigious society, there are people out there with no case at all who go after those they perceive as having deep pockets, hoping that they will at least get a settlement. This has happened to major performers including the Rolling Stones, the Beach Boys, and Sarah McLachlan. There are also cases where composers do unconsciously copy someone else's music. For example, this happened to George Harrison of the Beatles when he wrote "My Sweet Lord," which was obviously an unintentional rip-off of "He's So Fine" by the Chiffons. He was taken to court where he admitted that he unconsciously used this tune, and had to pay the writers and publisher a substantial settlement.

In songs, infringement could be based on musical or lyrical similarities. In film scores, there is only music. Actually, you often will hear similarities in two or more different scores of the same composer's work. For example, John Williams uses the interval of a fifth as the opening motive for the main themes of *Star Wars (1977)*, *Superman (1979)*, and *E.T. (1982)*. Is this copyright infringement on the part of the latter two scores? The answer is no, because the rest of the music after the opening interval in each of these scores continues on in different melodic, harmonic and rhythmic directions. One could find similar examples in the work of many of the top Hollywood composers, including Jerry Goldsmith, Ennio Morricone, James Horner, and others.

You will hear similarities in themes, harmonies, and instrumentation that run through almost every composer's work. One could dissect Mozart or Beethoven in this way and claim that they repeated themselves. Some self-repetition is bound to happen, since every composer has his own style. When it becomes copyright infringement (stealing from themselves) once again depends on whether the similar parts of the music are considered to have "substantial similarity," and whether or not someone has the desire to file a lawsuit.

Sync Licenses

There is an added dimension for film composers that makes its way into this discussion of copyrights and publishing. If a published work is going to be used for a film, television show, television commercial, or radio spot, the person desiring to use the copyrighted and published material must obtain a *sync license* from the publisher. This license allows the person to synchronize the music to their film, TV show, or commercial. Therefore, if you own the copyright to a song or film score and PepsiCo wants to use a portion of it for their next ad campaign, they must obtain a sync license from you allowing them to use the music for a specified amount of time, and for a specified amount of money.

Note that when you agree to write original music for a film, in the contract it will state that you are allowing the producer to use the music for that particular film, the promotion of that film, and purposes related to the marketing of the film. However, *under normal conditions, you will not own the music written for that film—the producer will.* You are still entitled to the writer's share of the royalties, but the producer controls the copyright because the standard agreement between composer and producer is that the composer is creating a "work made for hire."

Work Made for Hire

Work made for hire is yet another dimension for film composers in the complex, yet important area of copyrights and publishing. Many of the above hypothetical examples assume that the composer actually owns the copyright of his work. However, the usual conditions under which a film composer signs a contract and delivers the score is that he is completing a *work made for hire,* or simply, *work for hire.* This legal term describes a work, in this case a film score, that is created as a commission. The composer is hired to write the work by the producer, and while he is writing he is actually considered to be an employee of the producer. Once the work is completed and delivered, it belongs to the producer, who paid for it. The producer then owns the copyright and can decide how the music is to be used, both in the project it was composed for, and in the future. The composer still receives the "writer's share" of the royalties, but cannot control the reuse of the music. (Note: Future reuses are sometimes dependent on the agreement of the composer, depending on the kind of contract that was signed.) This is standard procedure, with some exceptions, in the film-scoring business.

Work for hire applies to both instrumental underscore as well as songs. If a composer is commissioned to write a song for a film (James Horner, "My Heart Will Go On," from *Titanic*; Michael Kamen, "Everything I Do, I Do It for You," from *Robin Hood, Prince of Thieves*), then that song is written as a work for hire. This is different from the song that is already in the composer's catalogue for which the producer must obtain a sync license from the publisher. When a song is written as a work for hire, the producer becomes the publisher.

Many composers have commented on the unfairness of this situation—that a person should spend weeks of his time using his creative talents and training to produce a unique product, only to turn over the ownership and future control of that product to someone else. This is not the case in the classical or concert music scene, where a composer usually retains the copyright ownership. In the film business, the future use of the music and potential royalties are often controlled by a producer who has no artistic interest in the music, only a financial one (sometimes not even that). As one producer's attorney said, "When we buy a score, it's as if we are buying a suit of clothes. If we want to hang it in the closet and just leave it there, that's our business."[1]

In addition to this hard-nosed attitude that the score will never see the light of day after the film is released, there is the possibility that the music will be used in a way that is creatively or morally reprehensible to the composer. To use a crass hypothetical example, a composer who has been a life-long vegetarian and animal-rights activist might not want his music to be used in a McDonalds commercial. And although he might reap tens of thousands of dollars in royalties, he still might not want his music to be used for that purpose. Yet, he may have no say in the matter.

Some composers have achieved a degree of success and enough clout in Hollywood that they can negotiate at least part ownership of their music. Once a composer is in demand, he has some bargaining power. If he is at the top of the field and has some choice over what projects he undertakes, he might be willing to turn down a project because the producer will not share the ownership of the music.

Composers have many horror stories as a result of a producer owning a copyright. Some involve the composer suffering significant loss of income because a producer or studio refuses to give permission for use of the score. Others instances are more benign but equally outrageous in the behavior of the studios. Writer Roy M. Prendergast relates two such stories:

> In 1971 composer Lalo Schifrin received a request to conduct the music from one of his films in connection with an appearance at

a university. He called the studio and asked for a score, but was perfunctorily informed that the music did not belong to him and that if he wanted to play it he would have to rent the music from the studio. Eventually the studio was gracious enough to lend him the music for nothing.

Another well-known film composer, Maurice Jarre, was asked by a major symphony orchestra to conduct his score for Dr. Zhivago. *Incredible as it may sound, when Jarre asked MGM for the score, he was told that it had been destroyed since MGM needed more storage space.*[2]

There is also a historical side to this issue that puts the disagreement between the composers and producers into another perspective. As mentioned earlier, in the early days of the movie studios, all the music at a given studio was done in-house. All the composers, orchestrators, and musicians were under contract to the studio. Under this system, the studio automatically owned any musical creation. Even though the origination of the studio system was in the 1930s, and the dissolution of this system came about in the 1950s, studios and producers today have resisted changing the nature of the ownership of the music. They know a good thing when they see it; a film score can generate thousands—or even millions—of dollars in royalties over several years. In addition, the producer or studio owns all the other creative elements of a film: the script, costumes, sets, etc. To them, the music is just one more "suit of clothes" for the closet.

Work for hire is a tricky subject, and for some it is an uncomfortable working situation. However, it is the reality of the film-scoring business, and all composers have to deal with it, from the newcomer fresh out of music school to the established old-timer.

One instance where a composer might want to try to negotiate out of the work-for-hire clause of his contract and retain the rights to his music is on certain low-budget projects. Occasionally on such projects the composer is offered a very low amount of money to do a package deal. If this is the case, you can attempt to negotiate retaining ownership of the music—or at least sharing the ownership—in exchange for an extremely low fee. In this way, you can make some extra money down the road collecting both writers and publishers royalties, especially if the film is ever shown on television. However, even low-budget producers are often resistant to giving up their ownership of the music.

Also, it is a good idea to attempt to retain ownership of the music if you are scoring a student film. Some universities do not allow this, but some do. Since most student films don't even pay for music production costs, you might as well attempt to keep the copyright ownership and be able to use the music somewhere down the road. The chances of a student film having a long theatrical life are nil, so it is a shame to write some good music that gets lost forever under the work-made-for-hire contract clause.

Keep in mind that you should never push too hard on this issue unless you are willing to walk away from the project if your demands are not met. It is standard procedure throughout the industry for a composer to write the music as a work for hire.

As a composer, I obviously have a bias about this issue. However, it is one of those unpleasant things, like taxes or telephone solicitations at dinner time, that is very difficult to change and is a part of life. Therefore, students and composers who are just starting should accept this arrangement at the beginning of their career as necessary. Once a composer has some degree of success, he is in a position to negotiate for part ownership of the copyright and be able to have more control over the use of his music.

CHAPTER 23

Royalties

It is a very special gift, this gift of being able to compose for film.
—Michael Gorfaine

When a composer writes a film score for a feature film, he can receive a fee that is anywhere from $25,000 to over $500,000. Either of these amounts is lot of money, but often the real income for the composer comes in the form of royalties. Money can be made for months or years after a film is completed from network and cable TV airings, soundtrack albums, use of the music for commercials, showings of the film overseas in foreign countries, use in a sports video, etc. Writing the score for a TV series especially can generate large amounts of royalties because of the number of episodes and reruns. There is a difference in the amount and the way money is generated between underscore or instrumental background music and the money generated in royalties from songs in a motion picture or television show. Although many modern composers are active in creating both underscore and songs, this chapter focuses on instrumental underscore. But first let's define what kind of royalties there are, where they come from, and who collects and distributes them.

Performance Royalties

There are two kinds of royalties to be collected: performance royalties and mechanical royalties. *Performance royalties* are those that you receive when a work has been performed. This covers some live performances, radio airplay, and television. These performances are monitored by the three performing rights societies in the United States: ASCAP, BMI, and SESAC, or a similar society in every country around the world. The three U.S. performing rights societies are affiliated with counterparts in foreign countries, so that if your music is performed overseas, the foreign society will report your earnings to ASCAP, BMI, or SESAC, who will distribute them to you.

These performing rights societies issue licenses to anyone who uses music in their catalogues. This includes TV and radio stations, restaurants, nightclubs, and Muzak-type companies that produce "elevator music." A yearly fee is paid to the performing rights society for a blanket use of the music in its catalogue. The performing rights society then determines the amount of royalties owed to the various writers and publishers that are its members, and distributes the money in quarterly statements.

Note that a writer can only belong to one of these societies and that his publisher must belong to the same one. Many publishers have several different companies under the same umbrella so that they can work with writers of any performing rights affiliation.

Small Rights and Grand Rights

There are two types of performance royalties: small rights and grand rights. *Small rights*, also called *non-dramatic rights*, are the ones previously mentioned—performances on radio, television, nightclubs, etc. *Grand rights*, or *dramatic performance rights*, are for performances in a dramatic setting—Broadway, ballet, or opera. The performing rights societies do not issue licenses for grand rights and do not monitor this type of performance. So if you write the music to a Broadway show or ballet, then either you or your publisher must negotiate the license for that music directly with the producer.

Most of the time, film scores fall under *small rights*, or non-dramatic rights. If a movie is shown on television (or is a TV show to begin with), or if the music is played on the radio, it is covered by a *small rights* license, and your performance royalties will be collected and distributed by ASCAP, BMI, or SESAC. However, if the same music from a film is adapted for a ballet, then the publisher must arrange for a *grand rights* license.

Royalties from Theatrical Performances of Films

The other thing to be aware of regarding royalty collection is that *in the United States no royalties are paid for the showing of the movie in theaters.* This is a situation that came about in the late 1940s. At that time, ASCAP was the predominant performing rights organization. BMI was just getting started and SESAC had yet to come into existence. In 1947, almost every film composer belonged to ASCAP and was receiving healthy royalties for his scores that were shown in theaters around the country. Every theater paid a yearly amount to ASCAP for the right to use copyrighted music, and ASCAP made quarterly distributions to the composers. However, in 1947, ASCAP tried to raise the fee substantially and the theater owners filed suit. On March 14, 1950, the judge handed down a decision in favor of the theater owners and against ASCAP, declaring that the raising of the fee was illegal. He also took this decision a step further, declaring that it was a violation of antitrust laws for ASCAP to demand *any kind of license* for the theatrical use of motion picture music. This meant that the theaters could show any movie with any music and not have to pay performance royalties at all.

This ruling was a blow to composers and greatly affected their royalty income. Unfortunately, it is still in effect today and is the reason why film composers do not collect royalties from the showing of films in America. However, most other countries do allow the issuing of licenses for theatrical performances, and if an American composer scores the music for a film that is released in theaters overseas, he will collect royalties through the foreign affiliate of his performance rights society.

The distribution of royalties from the performing rights societies is determined by complex formulas. For radio performances, it is based on a *sample survey.* The society takes a sample of radio airplay around the country, adds a multiplier to it, and comes up with a figure representing the total number of performances for that song. Then, the percentage of that song's performances is measured against all the other songs surveyed, the percentage is calculated with the total money received by the society, and the royalty is paid. What this amounts to is that you will receive royalties based on how often the song gets played, how many stations it is played on, and how long it stays on the charts. This can be an enormous amount of money, often as much as $250,000 in the first year alone for the writer of a number-one hit song.

For film composers, royalties from television performances are much more relevant. These are done by a *census survey*, meaning that everything that is performed in a given area, whether it be ABC, CBS, NBC, WB, HBO, TNT, etc., is counted and prorated, and then a royalty is paid. The size of the station, the time of day of the broadcast, and the kind of performance will determine how much the royalty actually will be. Performances on large, urban stations are weighed the heaviest. Prime time slots (7:00 p.m. to 1:00 a.m.) are the best time of day to have performances. The major networks, ABC, CBS, and NBC, still pay the most, with FOX, WB, UPN, and the others trailing behind. (The use of term *networks* can be confusing. Originally, there were only three TV networks: ABC, NBC, and CBS. With the advent of cable, there are now many smaller cable networks attempting to challenge the predominance of the three originals. This is a situation that is in flux, and future years will see the ultimate results. It may soon be anachronistic, but *networks* or *major networks* still generally refers to the original three: ABC, CBS, and NBC.)

Performances on television fall into the following categories, and each category gets paid a royalty at a different rate: visual vocal (songs sung on screen), background vocal, background instrumental, and theme songs. Visual vocals and themes get paid the most, and are paid per performance. That is, they get paid the same whether they were used for 30 seconds or 60 seconds. Background instrumental gets paid the least, and is paid on a *durational basis*, determined by the cue's length.

The way performances are tracked is that the producer or studio submits a summation of all the cues in a particular show or film to the royalty society, noting whether it is instrumental underscore, source music, or the main title to a TV show. This summary is called a *music cue sheet* (see fig. 10.5.). The performance royalty society knows when the show is aired, how many stations aired it, and how the music was used, and it will calculate the appropriate monetary distribution. Prime-time network TV pays the most, main-title theme music pays more than instrumental background music, and source music (songs) pays more than instrumental background music. Commercials have yet another formula, but that is beyond the scope of this book.

A lot of money can be made from hit theme music or background music for a television show. But before taking a look at the possible numbers, let's take a look at mechanical royalties—yet another source of income for the composer.

Mechanical Royalties

Mechanical royalties are those received from the sales of CDs, tapes, sheet music, music books, and sometimes videos. Although mechanical royalties are much more important to songwriters than film composers, they can create a sizeable royalty income for film composers as well. This is especially true in recent times with the explosion of the soundtrack market. Since the unanticipated success of the soundtrack from *Titanic*, the possibility of making major amounts of money in mechanical royalties has increased.

Mechanical royalties came about when, at the turn of this century, before radio, before stereo recordings, before long-playing 33-RPM records, even before 78s, the home music entertainment machines of choice were cylinder records, pianos, and player pianos. At this time, the 1909 Copyright Act was passed guaranteeing the writers and publishers of music a royalty for every record, piano roll, and piece of sheet music sold. Because these records and songs were reproduced on machines, they were called mechanical royalties. At that time, sheet music and piano rolls became the biggest income generators for composers and songwriters, with records running a distant second. As the technology changed over the years, records (of the various kinds), cassette tapes, and now CDs have replaced printed music as the primary source of mechanical royalty income.

There are actually two types of mechanical royalties. In the previous chapter we discussed how someone can perform and record your copyrighted material without receiving your permission as long as your work has been published (distributed or offered for sale to the public). When they do this, they are acting under a *compulsory mechanical license.* This license allows a person or company to use your published material without having to receive your permission, as long as they abide by certain rules, including:

- They agree to notify you within thirty days of making or distributing the work that they are using your copyrighted material,

- They will send you a monthly statement and payment of royalties earned, and

- They will pay the statutory mechanical rate based on the number of units manufactured.

The other kind of mechanical license is a *negotiated mechanical license,* which is very similar to a *compulsory mechanical license,* only it is more flexible. This license is simply referred to as a *mechanical license*—the license that is issued to someone who wants to use your music, and would like more lenient terms from you than those in the compulsory mechanical license. These terms usually involve the receipt of a quarterly statement instead of a monthly one, an agreed-upon lower rate than the statutory minimum, and the payment of royalties on units sold, as opposed to units actually manufactured. For film composers, the negotiated mechanical license is usually the one in effect.

Mechanical royalties are administered by the record companies, which keep track of how many units are sold and pay accordingly. For film composers who are not songwriters, until the late 1990s this was a significant, but not a huge, amount of money, for soundtrack albums traditionally sold small amounts compared to hit pop albums. However, as the soundtrack craze has taken off in recent years, enormous amounts of CDs are being sold that include not only songs, but also instrumental music from the film. This means more royalties for the composer of the score. Before this recent time, soundtracks that consisted of only the instrumental music from the film would sell 50,000 to 100,000 units at best. Now ten times that many can be sold from a mediocre film that does so-so at the box office.

Usually the film composer's contract specifies a dollar amount per album sold as his mechanical royalty. This is because film cues are not like songs; they can be much longer in duration, especially after the music editor is finished editing. This editing can involve cutting as many as fifteen short cues together to make eight or ten long selections for the CD. Remember, mechanical royalties for songs are based on the statutory minimum, 9.1 cents per song, or even lower if you negotiate a different rate. Therefore, if the film composer goes by that rate, for 10 selections on a CD that is actually a compilation of 15 or 20 cues, he will receive only 91 cents for every CD sold.

A typical amount of mechanical royalties for a film composer is usually between seventy-five cents and one dollar per unit if the album consists entirely of excerpts from the instrumental score. In addition, if the composer is also given credit as the producer of the album, another 5% of the retail price per unit will be paid in producer's royalties.

Real Dollars

Here is the nitty-gritty of royalties, and after reading this section you might be wetting your lips anticipating your pot of gold at the end of the royalty rainbow. Note that performance royalties are the main source of royalty income for film composers, so they take up the bulk of this discussion.

To sum up the previous section, when your music is aired on the radio or played on TV you are often going to receive royalties. If your music is played on television, either on network (ABC, NBC, or CBS) or cable, then you also will receive performance royalties. The amount of these television royalties depends on the length of the music, whether it is aired on network (more money) or cable (less money), what time of day the show is aired, and how the music is used.

Let's look at some of the possible numbers in performance royalties. The rates that the different performance royalty organizations pay are comparable, although they all have slightly different formulas for computing the rate. Currently, for background instrumental music on prime-time network television, the performance royalty rate is about $153 to $200 per minute. That means if you do twenty minutes of music for a show that is aired on ABC, CBS, NBC, or Fox between 7 P.M. and 1 A.M., you will receive between $3,060 and $4,000 in royalties. If you do twenty-two shows in a year, that is at least $67,320 a year in royalties. (Keep in mind that this is the writer's share; the producer is receiving an identical check for the publisher's share because you have created a work made-for-hire.) This is in addition to the fee you were already paid for composing the music.

After the initial twenty-two airings, many of those episodes will be shown during the summer rerun season. For this airing, you will also receive the prime-time royalty rate. A few years down the road, the producer will syndicate the show to local and cable stations, and you will continue to collect royalties, though at a lower rate. The initial year, or first year of the syndicated airing, is paid at one rate, while subsequent airings, or *strip syndication* (when the show is aired every day on various stations) royalties are paid at yet another rate.

If you have written the theme for this show, then that music is calculated at yet a different rate. For each performance of the theme, you will receive about $720, with a premium if the show is successful. That can boost the royalty to as much as $1,000 per performance. Since the theme is usually played at both the beginning and the end of the show, you will receive a minimum of $1,440 for each show. So for a season of twenty-two episodes, your performance royalty for the theme will be $31,680. Add to that the airing of the show in reruns, and the money keeps growing.

Note that songs played as background music (as in *Grey's Anatomy*) are considered the same as instrumental background. However, if someone is singing the song on-camera, that is considered a visual vocal, or featured performance, and the royalty rate is considerably higher.

Here is a sample list of the *approximate* royalty formulas in the spring of 2010. Remember that these numbers change frequently, depending on many factors at the performing rights societies. These figures are for prime time television.

Background instrumental

- ABC, CBS, NBC, FOX — $153 to $200 per minute
- CW — $114 per minute
- HBO — $12.73 per minute
- USA — $25.46 per minute
- TNT — $31.12 per minute
- Syndicated local TV — $1 to $40 per minute (depending on the size of the station)

Themes

- ABC, CBS, NBC — $720 to $1,000 per airing (regardless of length)

Featured performance (visual vocal)

- ABC, CBS, NBC, FOX — $766 to $1,000 per airing (45 seconds or more)

A glance at this (incomplete) list reveals that it is most desirable to have your music played by certain networks. They pay the most in licensing fees, so they generate the most weight in calculating royalty payments. As the audience share goes down (USA, HBO, etc.), the performance royalty rate gets lower. Note that the PROs are always in various cycles of negotiation with the various networks in order to obtain the best royalty rate for their members.

Finally, it is obvious from this list that if you have written a TV theme or have a song or performed on-camera in a television show, you get far more royalties than for background instrumental music. And if your theme is used in a background instrumental cue, then you get a part of the royalties from that cue—even if it is written by someone else. This happens frequently, and affects many composers' royalties because often the composer doing the week-to-week episodes is different from the one who wrote the theme.

Examples

Let's take a look at some hypothetical examples for feature films and television that take into account performance royalties from several possible sources, mechanical royalties from sales of CDs and downloads, as well as the composer's fee. Note that I am leaving out possible future revenue from commercials and other reuses. Also note that I am starting at the top and working my way down. That is, the first examples are for major feature films, next are network episodic television shows, and finally, network movies-of-the-week. And please make one final mental note that the following scenarios are hypothetical, although entirely possible.

Possible Scenario 1: Feature Film

Let's take a look at some of the possible numbers for music in a feature film that has 60 minutes of music, was a money maker with big stars, but was not a blockbuster hit. It is shown on cable six months after the theatrical release, and network TV one year later:

• Composer's fee	$500,000
• U.S. cable television (HBO), multiple broadcasts (60 minutes x $7 per minute x 50 showings)	$ 21,000
• Network broadcast, prime time (60 minutes x $180 per minute)	$ 10,800
• Foreign theatrical and other foreign performances (1st year)	$150,000
• U.S. and foreign local television performances (5 years)	$ 50,000
	$731,800

Now, keep in mind that this scenario excludes many possible future royalties such as more television performances, possible use in commercials, or even use in other films. In addition, a film can continue to earn performance royalties for the composer over many years of TV airings. (And remember that in the United States, there are no performance royalties when the film is shown in a theater, but there are for overseas theatrical performances).

Possible Scenario 2: Primetime TV Series

Here is how the money—fees and royalties—can add up for music in a network, prime-time TV series. Let's assume there are twenty minutes of music in each of twenty-two episodes, with each episode broadcast twice (the initial airing and reruns) on prime-time network over the course of one year:

- Composer's fee, twenty-two episodes:
  $10,000 x 22 $220,000
- First year, U.S. network prime time,
  initial airing, and summer reruns:
  44 shows x 20 minutes x $180 per minute $158,400
- Main title theme royalties:
  44 shows x $3000 $132,000
- First year, foreign television performances
  (1 year) $ 30,000
- First year syndication $ 50,000
- Strip syndication (1 year) $ 40,000
                                                       $630,400

You might have noticed that if the composer's fee is taken out of these examples, the TV series composer is making more money in TV royalties than the film composer. In real life this might be true, but there are several big differences. First of all, the TV composer is working steadily, maybe even six days a week for twenty-two weeks, whereas the film composer will probably spend four to twelve weeks on a feature film, and can score three or four films a year if he is really busy. In addition, there are creative benefits for the film composer. The budget for music on a film will be substantially higher, so the film composer is often writing for a large orchestra. And in many films, the acting, directing, and overall production value is higher, making the composer's job creatively more interesting.

Possible Scenario 3: Network TV Movie

- Composer's fee
  (or profit after package deal production costs): $30,000
- Prime time airing of film (45 minutes x $180) $ 8,100
- Foreign television performance: $10,000
- Re-airing on cable network: <u>$ 1,000</u>

   $ 49,100

Once we leave the area of feature films and episodic television, the numbers drop significantly. As you can see from the chart earlier in this chapter, when you have a film on HBO or local television, the royalties are paltry in comparison to other networks. So, it is important to get as much money as possible in the form of a fee. This is not to say HBO movies are not worth scoring. They can still be a good source of income, as well as a step towards bigger and better things.

Performance royalties are the film composer's great friend. They can provide steady income during slow times, and can add up to substantial amounts from all the different possible sources. In addition, the composer does almost no administrative work; the performing rights society takes care of it all. The only thing a composer must do is make sure that the cue sheets are filed properly with the performing rights society. Even that task is administered by the production office of the film; all the composer has to do is review the summary of cues.

The more work you do, the more you build up a catalogue, the more money will flow to you in the form of performance royalties. Shows or movies that you did ten years ago can still generate foreign or syndicated performances, so the more of these shows you have, the more income is generated. It can be like an annuity for retirement.

Internet Royalties

When music is sold over the Internet as a download, the writer and publisher of the music receive a royalty the same as if a CD was sold. Whether it is on iTunes, Amazon, or any other site, the rate is calculated the same as music that is on a CD. The publisher is paid by the Internet site, and the writer(s) are paid by the publisher.

If your music is being used as background music on a Web site, that is a different situation. Unfortunately, as of this writing, royalty payouts for music streamed on the Internet is a very murky issue. The Internet is such a new medium that policies covering how royalties are to be tracked and paid have not been developed and put into use. The PROs such as ASCAP and BMI are trying to create formulas where Web site companies pay for the use of music with very complicated formulas based on how active the Web site is and how much revenue it creates. But so far, it is a bit of a free-for-all. For that reason, many composers prefer to license their music by negotiating a buy-out. In that case, they give the Web site permission to use certain music in exchange for a fee. That fee is the only money the composer will receive—there will be no royalties—and it would be large enough to cover what the composer is guessing the royalties might reasonably amount to.

CHAPTER 24

Demos and Marketing

Life is a contact sport.

There comes a point when a dream can become a reality. The musician who has dreamt about working as a film composer is ready to live that dream when he has the appropriate composition and orchestration skills, has mastered dramatic synchronization, knows some basic sequencing, and above all, is ready to start making money writing music for movies. The questions are: How to get started? Where is the work? What materials are needed? Who should I call? Am I good enough? On and on these questions go, with many variations on these themes.

There is no one answer; there is no one best route to film-composing success and stardom. Every successful composer has a different story to tell. They all involve some combination of hard work, persistence, preparation, and sheer luck. Maybe the 347th door you knock on will be the one. You never know when a director will hear your new-age album and decide that your music is perfect for his film. You could knock on every door in Hollywood, Beverly Hills, and Century City for years, only to get into a fender-bender with a director who is looking for a composer. Maybe your charm and good looks will open many doors, even if your writing skills are minimal. So the best thing a composer can do is write a lot, get better at writing, be prepared, and be persistent.

There are hundreds of aspiring film composers living in Los Angeles right now, hoping to catch that big break. How can you hope to compete? It is part luck, and part self-effort.

Mark Snow puts the perseverance angle well:

> *You knock on every door and you're merciless, you keep persever-*
> *ing like crazy and pray, and 1 out of 10 guys who come to town*
> *make it. I don't know, maybe 1 out of 100. Maybe 1 out of 4.*

And Mark Isham talks about luck:

> *I never set out to be a film composer. I just happened to write*
> *music and other people said, "God, this would be great for film."*
> *And then somebody actually said, "I want you to do it for a film."*
> *And all of a sudden I had another career.*

There are many ways to get started in the film-composing business. You can move to Los Angeles and try to swim with the big boys. Or you can go to a smaller town, get some smaller projects, and gain experience and credibility. Either way, there are two things that must happen while you are getting started: first, you need to be actively involved in making or writing music on a regular basis, and second, you need to have your act together in terms of presenting yourself and your music. Take the time to organize your materials in a professional way. Remember that this is a business based on person-to-person relationships, and your demo, Web site, résumé, or bio could be the first step of this relationship. Create a logo and a company name, get stationery and business cards, make sure your answering machine is warm and welcoming—not goofy sounding. When you go to meetings, be appropriately dressed, arrive on time, and be confident. In short, create an aura about yourself that says to a producer or director, "This person has his act together, and I'd like to work with him."

Demos for Web Sites and CDs

The music that you present on your Web site or audio CD is an extension of your musical personality. People listening will be getting a sense of your creative ability, what kind of person you are, your sense of taste, and ability to interact professionally. So this music must sound great to the non-musical listener. It must be well produced and the package must be professional looking as it represents you as a film composer.

Recording quality. Make sure all the musical examples on your Web site are well recorded. Do not include projects played by students or amateurs if they have questionable intonation, or projects with poor mixes and less than terrific sound quality. A director may not know that the reason your wonderful composition sounds bad is because the clarinet is a quarter-tone flat or the shaker is too up-front in the mix. Use sample libraries and sequences instead of questionable live performances and have someone with experience check your mixes.

Composers have gone to various lengths to make great demos. Some have hired small orchestras to the tune of several thousand dollars in order to make the best presentation. There are demo orchestras that you can pay by the hour in Los Angeles and in Europe. Whether you go to this extent or sequence the orchestra on your desktop, the key is to make it sound as good as possible. This is the audio representation of who you are musically, so you must make it shine.

Make it thematic. Try to include as much material as possible that is thematic in nature. Cues with catchy melodic material are generally more interesting than cues that were originally conceived as underscore. Remember that most film music is background music, and as such is not meant to be listened to without also seeing the film. If there are sections in a cue that are really static, see if you can make an edit and just include the more interesting parts.

Film cues, not concert works. Choose pieces that are film-like in nature. Cues from film projects you have already worked on are best, but cues for an imaginary scene can work fine. Excerpts from classical concert pieces or jazz band arrangements are not recommended because they do not usually sound like film music. Classical ensembles and jazz bands have certain connotations in the ears of most people, and these are often not associated with film music. And it is important to note that although it may happen, not many films use these kinds of ensembles.

Variety. Have ready to include as many different styles of writing as you can. This can range from several different kinds of orchestral cues, like love themes, comedy, action cues, suspense cues, etc., to examples of world music cues, techno cues, and whatever styles you have written in. This will show your range of ability.

Include songs as a separate section. With the prevalence of compilation soundtracks today, many composers are also songwriters. This is a great skill to have and can expand your opportunities. It is best to keep your songs in a separate section of either your Web site or your audio CD demo. This helps the filmmaker separate out your skills as underscore composer and songwriter.

Web Site

The old cliché in commerce and marketing is that the key to success is "location, location, location." In the old days, if your business was on busy Main Street, that was a whole lot better than off on one of the lesser-used side streets. Today, a similar maxim applies, only it could be reworded to say, "presentation, presentation, presentation" and "Internet, Internet, Internet!"

The Internet is where a large portion of commerce and networking takes place these days. Having a terrific, professional looking, and easy to navigate Web site is absolutely necessary for today's composer. I will always emphasize personal relationships in the entertainment business, but the Internet has so changed the way we do business that I know composers who have been hired without ever meeting the director or producer because they had great stuff posted on a great Web site.

Today's Web site, Facebook, or MySpace page is a combination of yesterday's business card, résumé, and demo. It is the composer's public face, and is often the first impression a director or producer will have of you. Or it may be the second impression, after you get the opportunity to hand someone your business card at a networking event, and rather than calling you and chatting, that director checks out your Web page, and decides whether or not he or she likes your stuff. Here are some things to take into consideration when designing a Web site:

Presentation. Make your Web site professional and pleasant to look at. If you do not have the skills, have someone design it professionally. The graphics should be clear and have some flair. Not too dry, not too flamboyant. A sense of humor is great, but remember all different kinds of people might be checking it out, so go for the middle ground. Keep the language clean, and for those of you who are the "exuberant" type, keep a lid on the tendency to be goofy.

Organization and layout. The Web site should be easy to navigate and well organized. Make clear divisions in the options for pages that represent different facets of your career and who you are. For example, you might have different places to navigate to such as biography, credits, photos, film music samples, rock performances, song writing, concert music, director recommendations, contact information, etc. It is fine to have one Web site for everything you do as a musician. But another option is to create one Web site dedicated to music for film, and have another one for everything else, such as your work as a jazz pianist, for example. Both ways work.

Musical samples. First and foremost, if you are presenting more styles than just film scores, make sure you have made clear distinctions and options to the Web site visitor. The last thing you want is for a director to go to the heavy metal rock examples thinking that is all you do. This is where the clarity of your design is paramount. Make it easy to find the different pages that show your skills as a film composer as opposed to a concert composer. We've all had the experience of leaving a site because it is too busy, or the options are not clear.

In the "film cues" section of your Web site, because people can opt to surf through your presentation, include as many different examples with as wide a variety as you can. Try to keep the length at least thirty seconds long, at most two to three minutes long. (Cues can be longer, but wouldn't you rather someone hear an entire cue than constantly jumping to something else in the middle?) Make sure they all sound like film cues, not songs or concert pieces. Remember, those go elsewhere on your site. Have a variety of styles, like orchestral examples, world music, techno, rock, and whatever else you may have. Go ahead and label the cues, either with the original title, or with a descriptive title to entice the listener. For example, the cue that was originally titled "Sally Meets Bill" in a film could be re-titled "Love at First Sight." Or the action cue that was originally called "The Garbage Man" could become "Madison Avenue at 70 mph." In this way, the visitor gets a sense in advance of what they are about to hear. In addition, some composers with many examples break them down into sub-categories with several examples each of "action, love themes, mystery," etc. However you do it, remember that you want to make it as clear as possible to the Web site visitor.

Streaming video. Many composers stream video examples of scenes with their music. This is a great way to immediately show a film-maker that you are qualified. Make sure the section of your Web site that has these selections is clearly labeled. Some Web sites provide a choice in the "demos" section to link to either an audio sample or a video sample of the same cue. However you do it, make it easy to find and navigate to.

The Web site is a critical marketing tool for composers. It not only presents your music, but it gives a sense of who you are. Directors will often check out your site in lieu of listening to a CD in their car. Music supervisors looking for songs or music to track in a film will surf the Web to find the perfect music. So keeping a current and outstanding Web site is crucial.

Demo CDs and DVDs

It is still very important to be able to have great looking and sounding CD and DVD demos in addition to your Web site. Some directors, producers, or music supervisors will want to listen in their office, their car, or in the editing room. Make these discs look great with professional packaging, and as in the Web site demos, make sure that the sound quality is terrific.

Presentation. CD and DVD demos (or "reels" as they are often called, as in "I sent her my reel today") should have a nice design. *Never submit a disc with your name written with a Sharpie.* That labels you instantly as someone who is not yet in the game. There are two methods for making a nice looking label. One is to get an inexpensive software program ($20 to $40) that allows you to design and print labels that then stick on a disc. These can look great, and the software will come with a little round platform to allow you to center the label on the disc. The other way is to buy a printer that allows you to print directly on ink-jet ready discs. These are not necessarily expensive (start at about $100) and are made by several companies, including Epson and HP.

On the disc or jewel box insert, have a clear title. Make sure that your contact info is present on both the disc and the jewel box insert, and that that info includes e-mail address, phone number, and Web site. (If you do include a J-card insert for your jewel box, that should also be nicely designed, like the rest of the package.)

What music to include. Most composers have a generic demo that shows several different styles of music. One advantage of this is that you can have it commercially pressed if you run off, say, a minimum of 50 to 100 copies. However, there is often the need to create a more custom demo for a specific project that shows more examples in a certain style.

For audio CDs, keep the examples at least thirty seconds long, and no longer than three minutes. Try to keep the length to about one and a half to two minutes. This will minimize the listener's tendency to keep punching forward on the track list. It is often a good idea to edit a cue to tighten it up.

Songs are fine to include on the CD demo, but make sure they are clearly labeled. Some demos have all the instrumental music first, and then all the songs grouped together. The general rule of thumb is to remember who is listening and what type of music they need in their project. Hit them with the most pertinent material first, and then move to other dimensions of your writing.

DVD Demos

Some producers request DVD "reels" to show that you not only can write good music, but that you can write appropriate music for dramatic situations. For this reel, you might select cues that are different from the ones on a CD. Cues on the DVD demo should showcase your efforts that have really shone as a partner to the drama, which might be different from the cues with the biggest, most impressive musical ideas. In this case, the guideline of finding thematic material doesn't apply; just choose the cues that *look* the best and make the most impact on the visual. Make the demo ten to thirty minutes long with a variety of styles.

With a DVD, it is a good idea to begin with a "card" of your name, and your contact information. Visually slate each new cue with a card. The card should say the name of the cue, the project it was from, and any other brief, pertinent information such as the director, studio, TV network, or year of release. This can be easily done in Final Cut or even in iDVD.

Finally, as with the Web site and CD demo, make sure everything the director or producer looks at on the DVD demo is professionally done, and that all the graphics on the label, jewel box, etc. are well organized and printed.

Promo Package

Even though Web sites have become the composer's primary interface with potential employers, there is still the need for a mailable promo package. It is extremely important that you have materials that have a professional look, whether you do it yourself or hire a designer. The basics are business cards, stationary (for letters, credit lists, and résumés,) great demos, and well-designed CD/DVD labels. The graphics of these things should be uniform, so either create or have someone create for you a logo and a "look" for your personal name and/or your company name.

First, create a résumé, or if you are a little further along in your career, use a short bio with a list of credits. If you are just starting out and don't have significant credits, use the résumé format. This should reflect what you have done musically—projects completed, important gigs, awards, internships, teaching, software skills, and recordings. Also include prior work experience and your education. This tells the person reading it where you are coming from, and the scope and depth of your skills. Make the résumé look nice, with a pleasing font, and an easy-to-read and logical format. If possible, keep it to one page. The résumé is easily altered to fit different possible jobs. For example, use a different format, and include different items for a job as composer's assistant than for a piano teacher.

If you already have some credits, it is common to submit a short bio, accompanied by a list of credits. This is a more direct document than the résumé, for once you have had some experience, the person considering you for a project probably doesn't care where you went to school, or if you won any composition or scholarship awards. He wants proof of your credibility, to hear and see your competency, and to get to know you as a person.

Finally, have a folder or binder ready in which to package your materials. This should have a nice graphic with your contact info on the outside cover. Remember that everything you present to a director or producer says something about yourself and how you do business, so make it look really impressive.

To sum up, the key to success in presenting yourself to the film-scoring world is to look as good as possible in addition to sounding as good as possible. The competition is fierce, and your public face in the form of Web site, social networking page, logo, etc. will give you your own unique identity. Then when you go out looking for work you have a tangible image as well as your individual musical sound.

CHAPTER 25

Finding Work

The most important thing is a love for films,
and a fascination, a desire, a love, and feel for music.
—Mark Snow

Once you have all your materials together, you are ready to go out and get the gigs. That means meeting people anywhere you can, circulating, and knocking on doors. Be prepared for a lot of rejection that has nothing to do with your skills as a composer. Most of all, be prepared to talk, schmooze, and play the game.

The good news is that in the age of the Internet, cable television, computers, and sequencing programs, there is actually much more work than there ever has been, and quite a lot of opportunity for the film composer. The traditional jobs on network television, feature films, independent films, student films, and corporate films are still there. Yet now, there is also cable TV, video games, library music (used for low-budget films and TV), and music on the Internet. While there is a lot of competition, there is also plenty of well-paying work.

There are many avenues for the beginning composer, but the most important thing to do is to expand your circle of contacts. Whether you live in Los Angeles, New York, or anywhere else, find the places where film and music people gather. This could be trade organizations like ASCAP, BMI, or the Society of Composers and Lyricists. It could be like the Media Alliance in Boston, an organization with regular networking meetings that includes producers, directors, actors, composers, and many others associated with the entertainment business. Film festivals and screenings are also great places to meet people and to hang out with student filmmakers or people attending film-making seminars. Go to these events, take a stack of your business cards, and don't expect to get offered a gig; just meet some nice people, make some contacts, and then stay in touch with them. You'd be surprised how much fun you can have.

You could also get a job as an intern in a trade organization, at a recording studio, or at a production house. The Television Academy offers an internship every year, as does the Society of Composers and Lyricists. Opportunities like these are often posted at colleges or universities and on the Internet, but usually you will need to be resourceful. Make a list, and hit the phones! Put on your best, most confident telephone voice, and find out if a recording studio, composer, or post-production house ever needs interns or entry-level assistants. Keep a log of the responses including the names of all the people you talk to, even the receptionists. If they say, "No, but maybe in the future," wait a couple of months and call again. If they say, "No, we never hire unknowns," then cross them off the list.

Want ads were never a good way to find the rare film scoring related jobs, but now Craig's List has become the entertainment industry classified jobs site. People advertise internships, jobs as composer's assistants, and even put out a call for composers to submit music for a film. Check it frequently, even several times a day, as the competition for these jobs can be fierce. One former student of mine answered a Craig's List ad where an independent film company was looking for a composer to do sixty minutes of music *for free*. He responded within the first hour of the posting, and eventually made it to the final three. But he was told that they had received over three hundred inquiries by the end of the first day! That means that there were three hundred people who were at least willing to investigate a project where they could be spending dozens of hours working for nothing.

Composer's Assistant

With the continuing sophistication of technology, and the necessity for every composer to have an up-to-date electronic studio, the latest new job category is the composer's assistant. In the past, these jobs could include answering phones, making appointments, sequencing music, orchestrating, repairing equipment, doing transcriptions, and helping with paperwork. The job description would heavily emphasize the assistant's ability to sound professional over the phone, be able to meet and greet important people (directors, producers) and be very, very organized. Today, all these skills are still necessary, but there is yet another dimension that has equal priority to the people skills, and that is expertise in technology.

When an established composer is looking for an assistant, he or she is looking for someone to help relieve the pressure of short deadlines. That translates to someone who has superior technology skills, knowledge of both MIDI and traditional orchestration, or could help with some writing. And usually, it is the technology skills that come first. When applying for this kind of job, the typical skill set needed is expertise in Logic Pro, Pro Tools, Digital Performer, Reason, Kontakt, a multitude of sample libraries such as Vienna Symphony Library, software synths, and plug-ins. Which of these skills will be needed will vary from composer to composer, and of course, the actual duties performed by the assistant will differ depending on each composer's modus operandi.

The daily life of the composer's assistant can be very rich and varied, or it can be dry and dull. But most assistants report that it is interesting, intense, creative, and demanding. One day, the assistant could be answering phones and filing paperwork; the next day they could be orchestrating or composing a cue for a feature film or network TV show. Some composers have more than one assistant, especially as deadlines loom.

These are really terrific jobs, and although they are "entry-level," these opportunities immerse the budding composer in every aspect of the film-scoring process: making demos, mock-ups, spotting, meetings, deadlines, recording sessions, mixes, and dubs. It is both a mentoring situation as well as a real, usually well-paying job and can often lead to the composer recommending the assistant for a more prestigious job. Many young people working as composer's assistants network and stay in touch with each other. There is a kind of informal assistants network that starts humming as both long-term and short-term jobs open up.

Trailers and Music Libraries

Another avenue to explore for the emerging composer is to look into work composing for trailers or music libraries. There are several places that construct music for trailers, and these can be well-paying jobs. It often involves creating a sound-alike—a piece of music that sounds like something else. A director might have temped their movie with the score from *Brokeback Mountain* and want the trailer to sound like that score. If they are unable to obtain the rights to the original music, they will turn to the company that specializes in creating trailers, and their composers will come up with the desired style of music.

Music libraries can also be an opportunity for some income, though not so much one that will lead to bigger and better gigs. There are many library companies that license cues to TV and film producers. They have lists of genres that can be browsed, and they get paid according to the usage: how big the project is, where it will be shown, etc. The arrangement with the composer, however, is not so clear-cut and will depend on the company. Some libraries pay an up-front fee for the music, and the composer retains the writer's share of the royalties. Some libraries offer a buy-out, where the composer is forfeiting the writer's share and just receives a one-time, up-front payment. I heard of one library company that offered no money at all unless the cue was picked up by a producer, and then there was a small payment for the use of the cue as well as the composer keeping the writer's share of the royalties.

Cold Calls and Submissions

Another approach is to send your material to producers of low budget films, documentaries, and cable TV shows. Keep in mind that most unsolicited demos never get played. So the question becomes how to get your CD into the "solicited" mailbox. There are several ways to do this, but the best way is to somehow make personal contact with a producer or director. This can happen in any number of ways. You might meet someone at a party, at a seminar, or at an ASCAP or BMI function. You can call and ask the person's secretary if he or she is accepting any submissions from composers. Then you call again. And again. And again. Eventually, you might get through and make a pitch for the producer or director to hear your stuff.

Once you have sent your material, follow-up is extremely important. Wait about a week, and then call to "make sure that your package was received." This is not the only reason you will be calling. The other reason is to keep your name on their radar screen. Be careful here, though. There is a fine line between persistence and annoyance. People get busy. While it is sometimes important to remind them of your existence, it is also possible to become a pest and create a negative association with your name. Oftentimes, the response will be that the producer has not listened to your CD, or if he has, he is not interested. This is very difficult for some composers to hear because most of us want to believe that the world is waiting to hear our musical creations. However, finding work is often a form of self-promotion. The trick is to become thick-skinned, and not to take rejection as a reflection of your musical ability, personality, or worth as a human being. Take it as simply a result of where a particular person is at that particular day. Perhaps they really have no projects going. Perhaps they already have another composer. Perhaps they really didn't like your music. You need to have the confidence that someone else *will* like your music.

In order to survive in the entertainment business, you must develop a strong sense of who you are and what your music is about. Then all the rejections in the world will not phase you, and you can keep on plugging away. Artists in every aspect of the music industry face this same problem. Billy Joel was rejected from over twenty record labels before he got a shot from Columbia Records. Brian Epstein shopped the Beatles' demo to every label in London before he went back to EMI a second time and got George Martin to give them a try. In interviews for this book, composers such as Alan Silvestri, David Raksin, and Alf Clausen spoke about times when they could barely find work even after having had some degree of success and recognition.

Alf Clausen:

> *The common thread you will find with composers at any level is that we have all suffered a certain amount of abuse and hard knocks through the growth of a career. My own feeling is that the most successful careers are the ones that are able to keep those abuses in perspective and realize that it is only the music business. We are not looking for a cure for cancer. We can only do the best job we do, and hopefully, sometimes we will be lucky enough to be employed by people who like what we do. And sometimes, we might be lucky enough to be employed by people who we really like. It's not going to happen all the time.*

> *Try to keep a center to the vision. We deal in a product, and they are hiring us for our product. Unfortunately, that goes totally against art, it goes against the artistic tendency, and everything else. But it is part of the business, and as long as you learn how to deal with that, you will be much more successful on a daily basis.*

There are many projects involving music happening all over the country, yet the number is finite. And like every other segment of the entertainment industry, there are many more people trying to get work than there are jobs. Who gets what jobs often has nothing to do with who writes the best music or who is most experienced. The important thing is to enjoy writing music and even find a way to enjoy the constant search for work. Composer Lolita Ritmanis speaks about this issue:

> *It's hard to know why one person works and another doesn't. You have to stop wondering why because there's no point to it. There are great composers working on projects that have very little visibility. Their music might be brilliant. So why are they not scoring big studio films? It's often not fair, and worrying about it not being fair doesn't change a thing. I've seen quite a bit of disaster as well as success in this business. If you're only waiting for the big break, it can be a long wait and you can really get sick over it. You have to try and enjoy your life, and live a life too.*

One thing that young composers should be aware of is *that it takes some time to get established.* There are no overnight success stories; these are all a figment of publicists' imaginations. Every composer has paid his dues somewhere, whether it's as an orchestrator, as a studio player, as a rock musician, or as a waiter. If you are just starting out and you don't have the playing skills, or if your cutting-edge band hasn't provided enough income, then you must figure out a way to create an incoming cash flow. Although this might mean getting a "day job" in an office or a restaurant, it is important to create a cushion for yourself so that you can afford to make those demos and keep writing.

Shirley Walker:

> *You have to be able to afford to be a film composer. I think a lot of people come here to L.A. and they can't support the pursuit of their profession. And that's a hard thing to do. So if you have to make money being a film composer, it's going to be hard for you to get your career started because unless you're coming in at the very top, the beginning level isn't conducive to you supporting yourself.*

In addition to these economic realities, it is important to remember that the film business is based on personal relationships. Many composers at the top of the field tell stories about producers or directors that they met when they were just starting out. So nurture the relationships that you make all along the way. Enjoy people as human beings first, as business contacts second. The composer that is looking at everyone he meets as a possible "connection" or source of income is creating a lot of stress for himself, as well as very shallow relationships. If you treat people well, if you treat yourself well, then others will pick up on this and want to be around you. The entertainment business can be very difficult and even delusionary, so reaching out to others as people and having a strong personal center and confidence will carry you through the most difficult situations.

William Ross:

> *I approach it from the human point of view. Most people are driven to this business out of love for music and film. They're not out to get rich, at least not when they start. It's a hard thing to come out here to Los Angeles with the uncertainties of the business—to uproot yourself, to challenge yourself. To me, anyone who does that is a success, no matter what happens. I say that with utmost sincerity. I think we are in a business where you are a person first, and somewhere down the line you are a composer and you do all that. But the top of the list for me is what kind of person you are, how you treat people, how you get along with people. That's got to be in place.*

Finding work is not easy at any level of the entertainment business. Film scoring can be great work, wonderful work, rewarding work. If you love it, if there's nothing else in the world you would rather do, if you are willing to possibly endure several years of struggling and countless rejections, then go for it! There is no single road to the top; it can happen a million different ways. But you will never find out if you can get there until you try.

Interviews

PART V

Elmer Bernstein

Elmer Bernstein has scored over 200 movies, beginning in the early 1950s. He has worked with film makers of every generation, from Cecil B. DeMille to Francis Ford Coppola and Martin Scorsese. He has scored films of wide-ranging subject matter, from *The Ten Commandments* to *Animal House* and *Ghostbusters*. Some of his most well-known scores are *To Kill a Mockingbird*, *The Magnificent Seven*, *The Man with the Golden Arm*, *Airplane!*, and *My Left Foot*. Bernstein also teaches film composing at USC, and conducts performances of his film music with orchestras around the world.

HOW DID YOU FIRST GET INTERESTED IN FILM MUSIC?

I was a concert pianist, at first. I studied composition from the age of twelve, starting with Aaron Copland and finally with Stefan Wolpe. I was always interested in composition. Actually it was curious; I thought I'd be a composer but I never thought of composing for films. It was listening to the work of David Raksin and Bernard Herrmann in the forties—those two composers—that really made me sit up and take notice of what could be done with film music. I think the reason for that was that both Herrmann and Raksin had peculiarly American voices, and I found that voice appealing.

HOW DID YOU GET INTO JAZZ?

Well, the jazz thing came about in my own childhood. My father was a great jazz enthusiast, and I was brought up with the old Dixieland people like King Oliver and going on to people like Bix Beiderbecke and Louis Armstrong. There was a great presence in the house all the time, so I had a sort amateur interest in jazz. I myself was not a jazz player, but it was part of my upbringing.

HOW DO YOU APPROACH THE ACTUAL SCORING FOR A FILM?

Well, it differs from film to film. The first thing I do is spend a week just looking at the film without prejudice. When I say without prejudice, I say to myself, I'm not even going to try to think about music during this week. I just want to look at the film, I want to look at the film until the film talks to me and the film tells me things. So what I want the film to tell me is what it's about, and that's not always on the surface. What is the film about? What is the function of music going to be in this film? Why are we having music in this film and what's it going to do? So I start with those kinds of thoughts. It's a kind of intellectual process rather than a composing process. If the score's going to be based on highly thematic things, then I have to suffer out finding themes, so to speak [laughs]. Sometimes I get into the process and things are not going well for me, or I can't think of what I want to do. If I get desperate about time, I'll look at my 30 or 40 starts until I find a particular start that I can say, "I know what to do with this." Just sneak in the back door, so to speak.

DO YOU USE SYNTHESIZERS AT ALL?

I do. I think every score I've written in the last fifteen years has some synthesizers in it, but I don't use them as an end in themselves. I use them for the obvious factor: they make sounds that other instruments can't.

HOW DID YOU FEEL WHEN THEY FIRST STARTED TO CREEP INTO SCORES IN THE SIXTIES?

Well, oddly enough, I was one of the first people to use them, although people don't generally associate me with that. In the score for *Hawaii*, the very first sound you hear is a Moog synthesizer—way back in 1961.

IT'S REALLY EXPLODED NOW, SO ARE YOU FAIRLY SYNTH SAVVY? CAN YOU FIND YOUR WAY AROUND THEM A LITTLE BIT?

Not hands-on, no. I think about them; in other words, I will think of a use that I want to put a synthesizer to soundwise, and I will depend upon my people who do that kind of thing.

IN GENERAL, HOW DO YOU FEEL ABOUT THE USE OF SYNTHESIZERS IN TODAY'S SCORES?

At the risk of sounding arrogant, I will have to say that film scoring has descended to a lot of gadgetry, in our time. For most people, there are too many gadgets and not enough music.

COULD YOU SPEAK ABOUT THE CONCEPT BEHIND THE SCORE FOR TO KILL A MOCKINGBIRD?

Funny, before you were asking about the process and I said the first thing I do is to look at a film and try to determine what the role of the music is. Now, I had a big problem with that in *To Kill a Mockingbird*. If you look at the film without music, all you're looking at is a film with a lot of kids in it. But you're also seeing a lot of adult problems—problems of racism, problems of injustice, death and violence, violence to children. It took me the longest time to find where the music was going to go, how it was going to go, and what its specific use would be in the film. I determined, after a long time—it took me about six weeks—that the film is about the adult world seen through the eyes of children. All these problems—what we call adult problems—are seen as the children see them. This led me to childlike things: playing the piano one note at a time, music box sounds, harp, bells, things of that sort. So what really got me into the film was the realization that it was a film about adult issues seen through the eyes of children.

THERE'S SOMETHING ABOUT THAT SCORE THAT IS TIMELESS. IT COULD HAVE BEEN WRITTEN TODAY AS WELL AS ALMOST 40 YEARS AGO.

The thing about *Mockingbird*, and the reason that worked so well, is that it's a wonderful film. It is an absolutely wonderful film—the film is timeless. The film is absolutely timeless. Even though it's about real things, the film has a fable-like quality that makes it timeless. Every once in a while, you get to write a score for something like that.

WHAT ARE SOME MEMORABLE COLLABORATIONS YOU HAVE HAD?

To Kill a Mockingbird was a collaborative effort of director Robert Mulligan and the sadly late Alan Pakula. Those were really enjoyable relationships. I did about five films in a row for them. It was the kind of thing where we would talk about a project long before they even shot a roll of film. So I was constantly collaborating by just talking about it. That was an absolutely wonderful relationship.

If I had to pick the most outstanding relationship with a film maker, it would be with Martin Scorcese. I always said that I wish that every composer could have the privilege of doing at least one film with Scorsese. For him, film making is an art he respects. He's totally dedicated to what he's doing, with no phony ego stuff—no baggage of that kind. He has respect for other artists. It's just the most respectful and interesting collaboration because he's also very knowledgeable. When we were talking about *The Age of Innocence*, we decided that the sound or tenor of the score was sort of Brahmsian. Marty could then start talking about the Brahms sextet and stuff like that because he's so knowledgeable. That was a wonderful relationship—wonderful to work with. It was also wonderful to work with Francis Ford Coppola on *The Rainmaker*. Those were great collaborations.

WHOSE IDEA WAS IT FOR THE $^6/_8$ JAZZ ELEMENT WITH HAMMOND ORGAN IN THE RAINMAKER? WAS THAT YOU OR WAS THAT FRANCIS FORD COPPOLA?

I have to credit Francis with the bluesy $^6/_8$ idea in a roundabout way. What happened was, when I first got on *The Rainmaker*, Francis wasn't going to have a score, as we know a score to be. At first, he was going to go the B.B. King route—in other words, real Memphis stuff with some very minor connective things in scoring. But as he began to develop the film itself, he began to feel that he needed to depend more on score. So it was my decision to use the Hammond B3 organ, but it came out of his idea of Memphis ambience. I retained, out of that ambience, the three instruments you hear a great deal of: the Hammond B3, the muted trumpet, and the guitar. But that came out of Francis's original concept.

When I came on *Rainmaker*, it was in rough-cut form, and the version I finally recorded to was version #26. It went through some amazing changes. The interesting thing about Francis is that each time he changed the film, it was for the better. He wasn't just fooling around; he was just "finding" the film, so to speak.

HOW DO YOU HANDLE A SITUATION WHERE YOU'VE SIGNED ON AND YOU FIND OUT THERE'S A DIRECTOR THAT DOESN'T REALLY COMMUNICATE VERY WELL MUSICALLY?

Well, most directors do not communicate well musically. It's rare that they do. You kind of hope they'll let you do your thing, so to speak, and get on with life. But if they're ignorant and invasive you just have a miserable time. There's not much you can do. You try to be as diplomatic as possible, but sometimes you get your score tossed out or you walk out.

WHAT ABOUT WHEN YOU'RE SPOTTING A FILM—WHAT ARE THE KINDS OF THINGS YOU'RE REALLY LOOKING FOR?

I spot a film strictly as a dramatist. I'm not thinking of music at all when I spot a film. I look at the scene and say, Should this scene have music? Why should it have music? If it does have music, what is the music supposed to be doing? So that's my process.

WHAT IS YOUR ADVICE TO ASPIRING FILM COMPOSERS?

Learn everything you possibly can about all kinds of music—ethnic, pop, classical ... everything. Be prepared!

Terence Blanchard

Terence Blanchard has dual careers as film composer and jazz performer. He has composed original film scores for *Jungle Fever, Malcolm X, Clockers, Eve's Bayou, Gia, The Promised Land*, and *Till There Was You*, and played trumpet on *Mo' Better Blues* and *Malcolm X*. In addition to composing, he keeps a busy touring schedule, appearing around the world with his jazz group.

WHAT'S YOUR COMPOSITION BACKGROUND IN TERMS OF BOTH ORCHESTRAL AND JAZZ COMPOSITION?

I've studied composition and I'm still studying it. I studied when I was in high school and when I was playing with Art Blakey, although I never really had the chance to write for orchestra until I started working in film. But I would write piano pieces and stuff like that. And I was always writing for jazz ensembles.

Studying orchestral music is really great because it helps me understand the relationship between different musical lines, and how those lines define their own harmony. It's different than writing from a jazz perspective where the lines are related to certain chord changes.

HIGH SCHOOL WAS IN NEW ORLEANS?

Yes, I grew up in New Orleans. I moved away from home when I was eighteen and I went to college at Rutgers University. I played with Lionel Hampton while I was in college, joined Art Blakey's band when I was nineteen, and stayed in New York for fifteen years. And then I moved back home.

SO YOUR FIRST FILM-SCORING GIG HAPPENED IN NEW YORK?

Yes. What happened was, I was actually a session player on *Mo' Better Blues* and I had been coaching Denzel Washington. We had to do some pre-records so the actors could play along on the set. One day, while we were taking a break in the studio, I went to the piano and started playing one of my compositions. Spike [Lee] came over and said, "What is that?" And I said, "This is something I'm working on for one of my albums." He asked if he could use it, if I could write an orchestral arrangement for it. I said yes, even though I had never done one before. When he heard it, he said I had a future writing for film, and he called me to do *Jungle Fever*, which was my first film.

DID YOU KNOW WHAT TO DO ABOUT TIMINGS AND ALL THAT STUFF?

The interesting thing about *Jungle Fever* was that I didn't have a video to write to at the time. Spike didn't really want music to be specific to the scenes. He didn't like it when things happened right on point, right to the frame. There were some mistakes done in *Jungle Fever* in terms of the score because of that. There were certain things that would happen emotionally in the scene where things would shift, but I wasn't given those timings on the original sheets. But he recognized those problems, so for *Malcolm X*, I had a video.

I WAS WONDERING IF YOU COULD TALK A LITTLE BIT ABOUT THE FLASH-BACKS IN MALCOLM X, AND WHAT YOU WERE THINKING WHEN YOU HAD TO SCORE THOSE TYPES OF SCENES.

You know, the interesting thing about doing Spike's movies in general is that I never really have to worry too much about period stuff because he covers a lot of that with his source material. What I tried to do with those flashbacks was to have an essence of the period. That's why some of those arrangements are jazz arrangements, a couple of them are big band arrangements. And I tried to make sure that I had a blend of the period music along with the thematic material that we were using throughout the film. Spike is a guy who wants strong melodic content for his scores.

HOW SPECIFIC IS SPIKE IN GIVING YOU DIRECTION OF WHAT THE SOUND SHOULD BE?

In terms of what the sound should be, he's very specific. Spike is a very traditional film maker. He likes big lush orchestral scores. Let's use *Malcolm X* as an example. He said, "I keep hearing orchestra with a choir." So I said, "Okay, fine." And when we got to one of the jail scenes where the camera pans across the faces of the inmates, he said, "I just want to hear the voices right there." So he gives me that kind of direction, but he never really stands over my shoulder while I'm doing it.

AS I REMEMBER IT, THAT WAS A TRADITIONAL CLASSICAL MUSIC SOUND-ING CHOIR, NOT A GOSPEL SOUNDING CHOIR.

Right. You know, in Hollywood, and America in general, there's a very limited view of what African-American culture is all about. The thing that we've been always trying to do with Spike's movies is to broaden that, in terms of making people understand that there are many different facets to who we are as a people in this country. And one of the things that was great about that movie is that we used the Boys Choir of Harlem. They're really great. Really professional. Really on top of it.

WAS THAT YOU PLAYING TRUMPET IN MALCOLM X?

Yeah. I play on some of the stuff on *Malcolm X* because it really called for having some kind of jazz improvisation. Branford Marsalis plays on it as well.

WHAT'S YOUR COMPOSING PROCESS? DO YOU WRITE TO PAPER OR ARE YOU USING A SYNTH?

It really depends on how much time I have to write. Lately, I've been doing a bunch of television things, and television doesn't have the luxury of giving you the kind of time you have when you write for films. With television, I generally write from the keyboard because I only have a week and a half or two weeks to write maybe 60 minutes of music. If it's Spike's stuff, I like to use paper and pencil. I like looking at the music.

DO YOU ORCHESTRATE YOURSELF, OR DO YOU USE PEOPLE TO DO THAT?

To me, orchestration is the most joy I have in writing a score. Because coming up with thematic material is one thing, but to me real composition lies in the combination of instruments, creating the textures and colors of the sound. It's not just the notes. It's learning how to paint with those instruments. Whenever I'm writing a cue, I generally hear the orchestration in my head. I'll hear the cello playing the solo, or I'll hear violas carrying the lines in certain spots combined with a bassoon, or English horn—something like that.

DO YOU FIND THAT IT'S EASY TO SWITCH BACK AND FORTH BETWEEN A JAZZ STYLE AND A TRADITIONAL STYLE WHERE YOU'RE WRITING?

The two styles are really in the process of merging. I won't say that it's totally there yet, because I still feel that with my jazz writing there are some issues that I'm trying to work out in terms of form and structure. In terms of how to not be bound to a 32-bar form, a 12-bar blues form, or any of the traditional forms of jazz composition. I'm trying to get to the point where the melody lines really define the structure of the tune.

DO YOU FIND THAT YOU GET LABELED AN AFRICAN-AMERICAN COMPOSER? DOES THAT HAPPEN A LOT?

Yeah. It's a big problem. I suffer from that because the first thing that people wanted to know when I did *Malcolm X* was, "Is he black?" That's what they asked my agent at the time, which I thought was kind of an odd question. And when people began to realize that I am black, then I started to get called for a lot of those types of movies. I turned down a lot of those projects, because frankly, they just weren't things that interested me. I just didn't want to be labeled that. So my agents now have been working really hard to turn that around—which they are accomplishing. I've done a lot of different things like *The Tempest* with Peter Fonda, and *Gia*.

You know, it's not only race and gender, it's also cultural background. And that's the thing that I see that happens a lot in Hollywood, though I know people don't talk about it. I've noticed sometimes when I walk into a meeting, there's a certain kind of tension in the air already. And I'm not that kind of person. I consider myself to be a very easy-going kind of guy, easy to get along with. But I went into a meeting one time with another composer, and I saw immediately how he got hired. He was a great composer, don't get me wrong, but there was a certain type of cultural camaraderie that happened between the director and the composer that immediately made the director feel comfortable. I do understand it to a degree because there's a lot of money on the line in these projects. But at the same time, there's a lot of talented people out there who are probably not getting hired.

I WONDER, COULD IT GO BACK THE OTHER WAY? COULD A WHITE COMPOSER WORK WITH SPIKE?

Oh, I think so, because that's one of the big misconceptions about Spike. People think that Spike is so pro Afro-American that he doesn't hire other folks, but if you ever go to one of his sets you would see that is not true. One of the first things I noticed when I went to the set was the set wasn't full of black people. Not at all. And I was really amazed at that, and it made me feel really happy to be a part of that because it was so inclusive. I'm going to tell you a story. We were doing *Mo' Better Blues* and I had to be on the set everyday. There was a certain crew that didn't do their job and these guys were black. They were gone the next day. They were fired. Spike's thing is that he tries to give the best people the opportunity for the job.

ON ANOTHER NOTE, WHO ARE SOME OF YOUR FAVORITE FILM COMPOSERS?

Elmer Bernstein. I love John Williams. I love Thomas Newman, Jerry Goldsmith, Michael Kamen.

WHAT IS IT THAT MAKES THEIR SCORES SO GREAT?

To me, it's all about the sentiment. It's all about the emotional content and how it matches with the picture and the story. When I watch *Shawshank Redemption*, to me, Thomas Newman's score really elevated that movie. The thing that I always say that's great about Thomas is that he brings both the orchestral and electronic world together in a way that's unique. Because a lot of times, guys will use the electronic world to emulate the acoustic world, and that's a big mistake. He's one of the guys who really understands both worlds and understands that the electronic thing has its own strengths that can be utilized in a unique fashion.

WHAT ADVICE DO YOU HAVE FOR YOUNG COMPOSERS WHO ARE JUST STARTING OUT?

Pray, because everybody I know who got into this business fell into it backwards. You've got to be flexible. The biggest thing that you've got to do is put your ego aside. It's not like working in your own band, or having your own musical situation. The music is there to enhance and support a story. In some cases, the music is there to take a lead role, but more times than not it has a supportive role. You have to put your ego aside and understand the task that you have at hand. And you've got to study. You've got to listen. You've got to do your homework.

Alf Clausen

Alf Clausen began his career playing bass and French horn. He studied at North Dakota State, the University of Wisconsin, and Berklee College of Music before moving to Los Angeles. Well known since 1991 for his music in the television series *The Simpsons* (for which he received two Emmy awards), Clausen has also written the music for *Moonlighting*, *ALF*, *Fame*, *Harry*, *Police Story*, and *The Critic*. His compositions and orchestrations have appeared in feature films such as *Naked Gun*, *Mr. Mom*, *Splash*, *Airplane II: The Sequel*, and *Ferris Bueller's Day Off*. He is also very active as a jazz composer and arranger, with performances by the bands of Ray Charles, Stan Kenton, Buddy Rich, and Thad Jones & Mel Lewis.

LET'S TALK ABOUT YOUR BACKGROUND IN MUSIC, HOW YOU MADE THE JOURNEY FROM NORTH DAKOTA TO HOLLYWOOD.

I grew up in Jamestown, North Dakota. I came up through the concert band and concert choir programs in school as a French horn player. I was exposed at a very early age to some pretty high-quality musical taste, for which I am very, very thankful.

In addition to that, I was basically a rock 'n roller. I grew up with the early roots of rock 'n roll, loved rock 'n roll, loved r&b, I loved Chubby Checker. I loved Little Richard and Elvis Presley and all of those people forming the roots of that music.

I first majored in mechanical engineering at North Dakota State University in Fargo because my college entrance tests all told me that I should be a mechanical engineer! I eventually graduated with a BA degree in Music Theory. I started my master's degree at

Wisconsin, but didn't like it and wound up transferring to Berklee. So I packed my acoustic bass into my VW bug, got a U-Haul trailer for the rest of my belongings, and drove out from Madison to Boston. I didn't know a soul, but I decided that this was going to be the deal. I did all sorts of gigs, and taught at Berklee as well.

I eventually realized that if I was going to make the writing career happen the way I wanted it to, it was not going to happen in Boston. In Boston, you have to have three jobs to make ends meet. So my wife and I decided that L.A. would be a better place to raise kids than New York, and we moved out there. It turned out to be a fortuitous move because a lot of the work at that time was also moving out there. TV variety shows like *The Carol Burnett Show* and *The Merv Griffin Show* moved to L.A. This was the late '60s, when there was a lot of work going on, and I was at the front of the wave as everything started moving here.

So, when I got to Los Angeles, I started working all sorts of kinds of jobs. I played six nights a week playing bass in clubs, and worked as a music copyist quite a bit. I started doing some ghost arranging for a Vegas singer or show, I did some jingles. I just kind of kicked around doing all sorts of stuff.

DURING THAT TIME OF "KICKING AROUND," DID YOU EVER FEEL LIKE YOU WERE LOSING SIGHT OF THE ORIGINAL REASON FOR COMING TO LOS ANGELES?

There were many times when I felt like I was losing sight of why I had originally come here. When I first arrived, somebody had told me that you should give yourself five years and then evaluate your progress. I did re-evaluate, and I thought that maybe I should find another way of doing things. I had gotten some little things thrown my way here and there, but all of a sudden, five years went into ten years. I thought, it's coming along, it's coming along, but it's taking a lot longer than I expected. I just had a lot of faith that things would come the way I wanted them to. I developed a lot of patience and was willing to just wait for the next step to happen.

WHAT WAS THE FIRST SIGNIFICANT THING FOR YOU?

Through a series of strange circumstances I got a gig arranging for the *Donny & Marie Show*. After two seasons with that show, and a season with *The Mary Tyler Moore Variety Hour*, I decided I wanted to get into films. But no one would talk to me. I had gotten pegged as a variety-show arranger/conductor.

So I decided that I would play the game their way, and I would have to start from the bottom again. I had to work my way through the ranks, and start to orchestrate for whatever composer would take me on. I needed some experience, to learn the ropes and see how things were done in that segment of the industry.

Eventually, I started orchestrating for Bill Goldstein. I met him on a recording date where I was doing the booth work. Bill came over and introduced himself and asked me if I had done certain orchestrations. I said yes, and one thing led to another. It turned out he had two pictures going at that time and he asked me to orchestrate on both pictures.

Soon after that, he got the *Fame* series over at MGM, and I started working on that. I did a lot of orchestrating and ghost composing. At the same time, I did some ghost composing for David Rose on *Little House on the Prairie* and *Father Murphy*. One thing led to another. I started orchestrating for Lalo Schifrin and Lee Holdridge. Lee and I struck up a really, really close friendship, which still exists to this day. We worked together on many successful films, including *Splash*, and *Mr. Mom*. His focus with an orchestrator/composer is that if he finds a guy with some talent, he finds a way to help him work his way into the system and get his own gigs. His whole focus was to find a television series, write the theme, and then turn it over to me. This was without me asking!

He called me one day and said, "I've got this pilot over at ABC and it looks really, really good. What I'd like to do is have you orchestrate the pilot, and then let me introduce you to the executive producer so that you can do at least part of the series." This was

Moonlighting. And his plan worked. ABC was very high on the show, public acceptance was very, very good, and I soon ended up as the sole composer on the show. It was a major hit for four seasons. All of a sudden, my identity was established in the film scoring business. That's all it took. Even though I had been slaving away behind the scenes for years, it took the vision and aggressiveness of somebody like Lee to make it happen. I am eternally grateful to him for that.

How did The Simpsons begin for you? You've been doing that for how long now?

This is my ninth year. Actually, when *Moonlighting* and *ALF* stopped, my career stopped. I went for seven months without a show. Even though I had some income because those shows were in reruns, the cash flow was actually secondary. It was too quiet and I was not a happy camper. The creative mind likes to be busy, the creative mind likes to be assuming the responsibility and the challenge of regular projects. Because I love doing stuff.

Simpsons broke the drought. They had done 13 shows with Danny Elfman's theme and Richard Gibbs doing the underscore. During my dry spell, I was talking with a good friend of mind who is a percussionist, and coincidentally he said that he just had dinner with his nephew who was working on this new show, and they were looking for a different composer. So he gave his nephew my number, he called, we met, and then we spotted the next show— the very first "Treehouse of Horror" episode. I recorded it, and they loved what I did.

In that original meeting, what was the discussion like regarding the concept of the music for the show?

Matt Groening and company told me in that first meeting, "It's not a cartoon, it's a drama where the characters are drawn." And when in doubt, he said to score it like a drama, not like a cartoon, not to mickey-mouse everything. Matt was the one who made the request for the acoustic orchestra. He said, "I hate electronics, I think they cheapen the sound. I want the real orchestra."

WHAT DO YOU SAY TO MUSICIANS WHO ARE JUST GETTING STARTED IN FILM SCORING? DO THEY NEED TO BE IN L.A.?

My own way of doing it was to continue moving up rather than moving down. I started from very humble beginnings and took it step-by-step-by-step. Going from North Dakota to Wisconsin, going to Boston and then to Los Angeles. I know that if I had gone from North Dakota to Los Angeles, I would have been swallowed up, spit out, and I wouldn't have survived without putting in those dues beforehand.

There are a couple of schools of thought about how to get started as a film composer. One is move to where the action is and get involved in doing low-budget films under your own name as a composer. The other is to move to where the action is and start apprenticing with other composers, practicing your craft on a daily basis, which is what I did. I'm a firm believer in the second method. The thing I say to guys who want to do it the first way is: If you can you exist on one or two $500 dollar films a year and not practice your craft in the meantime, then be my guest. The guy who is going to practice his craft on a weekly basis, doing all kinds of stuff, to me is going to end up having much more of an advantage and much stronger chops in the long run.

Cliff Eidelman

After studying composition and orchestration at Santa Monica City College and USC, Cliff Eidelman received his first break at age 22, when he scored the feature film, *Magdalene*, starring Nastassja Kinski. He has gone on to score many feature films including, *One True Thing*, *Triumph of the Spirit*, *A Simple Twist of Fate*, and *Star Trek VI: The Undiscovered Country*. Also active as a composer and conductor of concert music, he has appeared with the Royal Scottish National Orchestra, The Munich Symphony and Chorus, and the Toronto Symphony Orchestra.

DO YOU RELY ON AN AGENT TO GET YOU WORK, OR DO YOU DO SOME LEGWORK YOURSELF?

My agent helps, but I also have to do my part in contacting people, having meetings, doing demos. But it's an odd thing, I've never gotten a gig by seeking it out initially. I may have to pitch my music, but someone always finds me; at least the first contact, they seek me out.

Sometimes I get the *Hollywood Reporter* and I circle the projects that look interesting. I may circle five of them, and I'll call my agent and say, "What's going on with this one ... this one ... that one ..." And then my agent will most likely say, "This one's taken ... this one's taken ... you don't have a chance at that one because the director has a long-standing relationship with another composer ... but I'll check on this one, I don't think anyone's on it." That's where it starts.

But I have never actually gotten a gig from doing that. Gigs have come because of other reasons. Because of a previous relationship, or because they heard a score of mine from a previous film, or somebody "temped" my music into some film, and they loved the temp and the next thing I know they're seeking me out. I personally have never had any luck with seeking out a film and getting it. It's always been the other way around.

For people at the very top of the field, like John Williams or Jerry Goldsmith, I think calls come in for them. Their agents are basically fielding calls, and presenting gigs to them. There is a point where they get offers all the time. But when you're in my position, where there has been some success and high profile projects, but not that one hit, blockbuster film, you really have to continue to pound the dirt yourself. It becomes one of those things where you have to just do the effort.

I think that in order to turn heads it takes a very great film where you can write a fabulous score that gets acknowledged. It has to be an association with a great film that gets great reviews and is also a good moneymaker. So it's a combination. All the pieces have to fit together right.

HOW DO YOU PREPARE YOUR SCORE? DO USE CUE OR AURICLE TO LAY OUT THE SCORE?

I use Auricle to lay out the tempos as I compose to picture. First, I conduct through it a few times with the video, feel the scene, and make sure that all the things that I want to hit are there. Then I create a click that is close to the slight variations of tempo that go with free conducting. If you were to look at my tempo map for a two-minute cue, you might see as many as 20 slight tempo changes. I am very particular about it, about those tempos and about the accelerations and the decelerations and all of that. The click is pushed slightly here, laid back slightly there. In fact, I've got some click maps where it could have been a 24-0 click. But instead, in order to achieve what I was feeling while I conducted to video, the tempo map might end up changing from 24-0 to 23-7, 23-5, 23-1, 24-7.

How do you determine what to hit and what to leave alone?

So much is by feeling. For me, it's whenever the chill occurs and however it's felt. In fact, I think it's detrimental to use a click for music that is more expressive or more lyrical. Especially when the musicians have the clicks in their ears while they're recording, there's a feeling of this perfect click going on. I think that that detracts from the emotion of the music and what the music really wants to do. So I try to conduct with streamers, for that kind of music. I know with *Triumph of the Spirit*, it was all by feel. If I was a little bit early to one streamer, I just knew I had to just slow down slightly so that three streamers later I'd be right on. And I knew it didn't really matter with that picture, because the music was floating, it wasn't commenting on anything specific, it was always floating above.

How do you feel about doing mock-ups?

In many ways they're helpful. If you can give the director mock-ups as you go, and get quick at laying out certain sounds—not flesh out every little detail, just give some good examples—I think that takes away the risk of disagreements when you're on the scoring stage. Mock-ups allow you to finish most of the work at home, and give the director the chance to have some input before the recording session.

What is your process in arriving at the concept for a score?

Dramatically, many of my ideas for a picture have to do with color and orchestration, which I have studied in depth. Orchestration is so much a part of music's conceptual design. First I compose the melodic themes, and once the melodies come to me, the orchestration begins to quickly reveal itself.

An example is what I did for the film, *One True Thing*. I had this idea of time changing, the changing of seasons. The feeling of wind passing through trees and then leaves blowing off in another direction. This wasn't music yet; it was just a feeling I wanted to add to the whole effect of the score.

I set individual instruments apart from the orchestra, separated into their own isolation booths. Like three cellos in one room, or three violas with two woodwinds in another. They were off in their own rooms and the orchestra was in the center. Now, my concept was that the piano should be the main idea, accompanied by a small orchestra so that it felt intimate, and never too large. An introverted mood.

I also wanted it to feel like wind was carrying the music this way and out that way, creating different perspectives. The music wasn't just coming from the center of the room. It was coming from over here, and it shifted over there, and then it would come back over here. So, early on, this conceptual approach merged with the themes.

HOW MUCH INPUT DID THE DIRECTOR HAVE AT THIS STAGE OF YOUR PROCESS?

Actually, the reason I got this particular job was because I demoed some thematic ideas for him. That was before I came up with this special idea. So the director was very involved in the creation of the broad emotional and thematic ideas, but less so in terms of the specifics of the orchestration. I mocked up a great many of the cues, but because the ultimate orchestration and setup of the musicians was so unusual, I really wasn't able to demonstrate the final orchestration that included the unique perspective of these isolated groups until we got on the scoring stage with the real players. I didn't want to blow it by trying to make that in my synth studio.

DID YOU EVER HAVE A PROBLEM SEEING EYE-TO-EYE WITH A DIRECTOR?

Did I ever have a real disagreement? I can think of two occasions, where it wasn't so much a disagreement as it was that a director had gotten so used to a temp score that he couldn't hear anything else. I was writing something that took us in a different direction. Once a temp score is thrown into a movie, what tends to happen is that the director gets used to it. To have him get unused to it and then used to something new is difficult. The temp process can be very detrimental. It can be the end of all possible creativity that could have come to that movie through music.

It's gotten to the point where some composers of the final score copy the composers whose music was used in the temp track, sometimes even ripping them off just because the production people get locked into the temp. I've heard thematic ideas from my scores used in other people's scores. It's infuriating. I honestly would never consciously sit there and rip someone off. I wouldn't be able to sleep at night.

WHAT KIND OF TIME FRAME DO YOU NORMALLY WORK UNDER?

I've actually been very lucky in that way. I've had to write a lot of music really fast only a few times. The kind of thing where I had to stay up and do twelve-hour days, seven days a week. On *One True Thing* I had two and half or three months to write it.

HOW WOULD YOU LIKE THE PRODUCTION TEAM TO VIEW YOUR PROCESS?

That they really understand the intense emotional self that I put into it. It's everything I have.

Photo: LM Jones

Danny Elfman

Danny Elfman comes to the world of film composing via the rock band Oingo Boingo. It was through Oingo Boingo that director Tim Burton first heard his music, and ultimately asked him to score *Pee Wee's Great Adventure*. Elfman has gone on to score over 30 films, including *Men in Black, Batman, The Nightmare Before Christmas, Mission: Impossible, Midnight Run,* and *Good Will Hunting*, which earned him an Academy Award nomination.

Let's talk about how you got started. Did you always want to write for films?

I was a big Bernard Hermann fan as a kid, in the '60s. I guess what you'd call kind of like a film-music nerd. My training was spending every weekend at the movie theater—I didn't play sports, I didn't really go out in the sun—I hated being out in the sun. I loved being inside a theater; it suited me well, and I lived around the block from one. I loved films and I loved film music. I knew that if Bernard Hermann did the music that it was going to be a great film.

What was your entree into scoring films?

It was a fluke, actually. I was with the Mystic Knights of the Oingo Boingo when we were still a musical theatrical troop, between '72 and '78. I was asked to score a midnight film, a cult film for my brother called *Forbidden Zone*, and that was my first time putting music to film, but it was far from a legitimate orchestral film score. It was performed by the Mystic Knights just before they retired, and the rock band Oingo Boingo began.

The fluke was getting asked to do *Pee Wee's Big Adventure*. [Director] Tim Burton was a fan of Oingo Boingo, and he just had a feeling that I could do more than I did with them. Paul Reubens was a fan of the *Forbidden Zone*, so when he heard that score he made a mental note to track me down. My name crossed paths between the two of them and it eventually all tied together.

COMING FROM A ROCK BACKGROUND, HOW DID YOU GO ABOUT DOING THE SCORE? WERE YOU SEQUENCING OR WRITING THINGS DOWN?

I wrote down everything, I didn't start using MIDI notation until '96. In a rock band like Oingo Boingo there's never any point to write music down. I mean, other than basically scribbling out a horn part every now and then, there was no writing involved because that's not the way rock bands work. On the other hand, the Mystic Knights did a lot of original material and it became necessary for me to learn how to notate. The Mystic Knights did a lot of kind of crazy ensemble stuff—real early jazz like Duke Ellington, Cab Calloway, and Django Reinhardt—and I began transcribing some of that stuff. That was my early ear training and from there I began to notate my own original compositions.

When I got offered *Pee Wee's Big Adventure* I knew I could create the music, but I also knew I would need help logistically with the orchestra. I knew what sounds I wanted because I loved orchestral music; I loved Stravinsky, I loved Prokofiev, I loved Charles Ives. So I called Steve Bartek, the guitar player from Oingo Boingo, and I asked him, "Have you ever orchestrated?" And he said, "Umm, I took some classes." And so I said, "Good, you'll do." And we both learned by doing it, as did Tim Burton. It was interesting, *Pee Wee* was Tim's first film, he'd never been to film school. It was my first score, I'd never been to composing school. And Steve orchestrating, he'd only taken a couple of orchestration classes at UCLA. We all learned our craft by doing it and the thing we had in common was we all applied ourselves really intensely to it, and we all had those kind of obsessive personalities. That "If I'm gonna do something, I'm gonna do it really, really well" kind of attitude.

Do you hear specific instruments as you write, or do you write something and then think about who could best play it?

I work both ways. Sometimes, when I'm hearing a melody, I'm also hearing the ensemble. In that instance, I look at a scene and I hear all the instruments right away. For example, in the opening sequence of *Mars Attacks*, I heard it dead-on the first time I saw the scene. I mean, I heard it almost note-for-note just like it was playing out of a radio in my head, and I ran home and I wrote it all down. I consider that one of the lucky moments. However, the more usual process of experimentation and working things out by degrees gets me more excited and involved. Although it is a lot more difficult, it can be more rewarding.

In those cases, at first I don't really hear exactly what I'm going to end up with; I get just a vague idea. First I see the film and then I start improvising. I start with a feeling, and I do maybe a dozen improvisations on piano without looking at the picture. Then I start going through the footage and I pull up different scenes to see how the improvisations work. Sometimes I improv for six, seven, eight minutes and then I pull out the ideas I like and focus on them.

And so, if there is any lesson I've learned over 35 scores, it's not to ignore the earliest impulses and not to lose anything. Because what early on seems like the most broad, poorly played, ill-conceived notion sometimes becomes what I'll look back on as one of my best ideas. You know, the raw material.

Do you enjoy working out the musical details of a big score?

It's great when I hit a certain section where things get really intricate, and there's a lot of detailing, and I'm satisfied with the way it comes out. That's the hardest work, and when it pays off, it feels really good. I also write songs, and when I'm writing songs, it's all inspiration based. It only takes a moment, once I get inspired to write a song. But writing an orchestral score takes so much time, and it's so easy to get it bungled and to get twisted up. When I start getting into the mode of detailing, and it doesn't turn into a cluttered mess, I'm really happy because I think my biggest weakness as a composer is sometimes I tend to overwrite. Sometimes I don't know when to stop and before I know it, what I thought was a good impulse or a good idea has become clouded into a big mess. I guess it's like when you're painting and you put a few too many layers of colors and suddenly you're looking for the image.

HOW DO YOU DEAL THEMATICALLY WITH THE BIG PICTURE OF DOING 30 OR 40 CUES?

At first, every score is a big puzzle and I have to know where my common links are in that puzzle. There's a start, a middle, and an end—I can't do the in-between stuff unless I know how the melodies are going to work in any situation. I want to know before I start that they can turn quirky, big, sad, melancholy, melodramatic, silly—whatever I'm going to be reaching for in that particular score. In those early improvisations, I'll be taking melodies and fragments of melodies, turning them inside out, and putting them through a rigorous testing to see what they're capable of.

AFTER YOU COME UP WITH YOUR MATERIAL, DO YOU WORK CHRONO-LOGICALLY?

In general, I like to work chronologically. However, I usually start working on two or three major scenes that won't be chronological at all. I like to go for the biggies first, and then having those blocked out, I know where my major themes are, how I'm gonna use them. Then I like to go back to the start, and go chronologically from the beginning to the end, if I can.

HOW MANY FILMS A YEAR DO YOU DO?

Recently, I've been doing four or five a year, but the first ten years I did two films a year because the other months I was touring and recording with Oingo Boingo. Everybody's got their own way of working and I admire people who can get up in the morning, do their day's work and then take off, and, you know, have a family or social life. But I can't do that very well when I'm composing. Composing becomes full-time, there's almost nothing else for me.

DO YOU SEQUENCE EVERYTHING?

When I first started, I was sequencing my ideas, playing them for directors, and then notating them—it was like double work! Even with MIDI take-down making my job a little easier, I still end up spending the first part of my day in organizational work; I'm working with my own performances, I'm working with samples. A lot of people don't realize that a lot of each score is actually me performing. All the percussion in almost all of my scores, all the synth work, and the percussion work is me. That's a lot of extra work because that part of it is neither getting transcribed, nor written down, nor replayed; it's going in the score exactly as I'm playing it. That means that I have to put in the time to tweak all the performances and get them to sound right. So I usually start writing late afternoon into evening, and I try to stop at around two in the morning. But my best hours are really six, seven at night until around two in the morning.

ONCE A ROCK 'N ROLLER ALWAYS A ROCK 'N ROLLER, RIGHT?

Yeah, right!

I HOPE YOU DON'T MIND MY ASKING, WHY DO YOU THINK PEOPLE CAME DOWN ON YOU SO HARD TOWARDS THE BEGINNING OF YOUR CAREER?

Well, there's a lot of jealousy and I totally understand it, by the way. You get somebody like me that comes from nowhere, and I made the mistake of saying in interviews early on that I was self-taught. In music, there's no such thing as self-taught.

It's always been a weird thing about music, unlike any of the other film arts. Because a director can be self-taught, a writer can be self-taught, but a composer can't be, and that's just the way people think. Some people are skeptical, but maintain an open mind. And some people are skeptical and get into this very vicious thing. I don't know what makes music different than the other parts of the process. If a writer who didn't go to film school decides to direct, and does something brilliant, they praise him. They don't sit there and go, "Oh god, he can't direct at all. Obviously he didn't go to film school." But musicians and composers tend to be more hard-core skeptics.

Now that I'm kind of like a veteran, sometimes I hear a new composer who comes out of pop music and I'm incredibly skeptical. I think they must keep a closet full of ghostwriters and stuff. So, I see myself doing the same thing that other people did to me, and I totally understand it. If I see somebody doing an orchestral score, and they came from a rock band or pop music, I don't believe it.

In my case, there was always the smoking gun that everybody was searching for, hoping to prove I wasn't really writing everything. And the thing that was most interesting was that the fingers never pointed at the one person who worked with me for all these years. People were always saying that so-and-so really wrote my stuff. Or that such-and such a person was ghosting all my cues. But of all the names that came up, no one ever mentioned the one person that has done the most, my orchestrator, Steve Bartek. And in the final analysis, I've written over 35 hours of film music, and only fifteen minutes of that was ever written by others when I was in a pinch—and they were always credited. People accused me of not knowing how to write music, but I have a four-foot high stack of sketches that I've done over the years.

ALL OF THIS MUST HAVE BEEN VERY HURTFUL TO YOU.

It was, but at a certain point I just said to myself, "This can't matter to me anymore." I realized I was imitated so much. At that time I did think it was ironic that I was so trashed, but I was also so imitated.

WHAT ADVICE DO YOU HAVE FOR YOUNG COMPOSERS?

Here are some contrary pieces of advice. If you want to be success-ful, learn to imitate. I think the entire industry right now revolves around plagiarism and imitation, and unless you're willing to pla-giarize you may find it difficult to proceed. On the other hand, if you want to be a good composer, or a real composer, learn to resist that tendency. That can be hard, and it can also mean you may not get certain kinds of jobs that you want.

But I could also say this: I think imitation is the easy way out, although it is very tempting, and very seductive. Once you go down that path, it's really hard to turn back. You may say you'll reverse yourself, but it's hard to.

Do your own work, work hard, and be original. I don't regret for a moment that I had to write 20 scores without any kind of help. That work was phenomenally hard for me, especially with being self-taught and writing relatively slowly. But, I think that if I didn't do that, I wouldn't have developed certain skills that I've devel-oped. So, at the risk of sounding like a Quaker or something, I think just the beauty of committing to the hard way out, or the harder road, is usually the best one, and the most rewarding.

Richard Gibbs

Starting his career as a keyboard player for such acts as Chaka Khan, Robert Palmer, and the rock band Oingo Boingo, Richard Gibbs has scored many feature films including *Dr. Dolittle, Fatal Instinct, Say Anything, 10 Things I Hate About You,* and *Natural Born Killers.* He earned a degree in composition from the Berklee College of Music before moving to Los Angeles where he played studio dates, in addition to touring. Gibbs has also scored many television movies and episodic television shows, and served as music director on *The Tracey Ullman Show,* and *Muppets Tonight.*

YOU HAD A CAREER AS A PLAYER BEFORE GETTING INTO FILM SCORING. WHAT WAS YOUR FOCUS?

Keyboards. I always refer to myself as a keyboard player because there are guys who are pianists who I could not pretend to keep up with. I really wanted to be a fusion player, and my heroes were Joe Zawinul and Jan Hammer. Programming and playing on synths was my thing. Plus, at one time, I was a pretty decent trombonist. I graduated from Berklee College of Music with a degree in classical composition, so I had a lot of bases covered.

WHERE ARE YOU FROM, ORIGINALLY?

Daytona Beach, Florida. I'm a surfer boy. That's why I moved out here to L.A. After I graduated from Berklee, I thought, "If I'm going to be a session musician and go try to find bands to hook up with, it's either New York or Los Angeles." And I surf, so it was L.A. It was just that simple. I didn't have any contacts or friends out here, either.

How did you get your first gigs?

When I got to L.A., I befriended this guy who turned out to be Chaka Khan's little brother, which led to a job as her musical director. The next step was rather bizarre, too. You know, my whole career has been one big serendipity. One day I was sitting in my living room, balancing my checkbook, and discovered I was flat broke. I was wondering what I was going to do about it, and, lo and behold, the phone rang. I answered and the guy on the other end was the musical director for Tom Jones who was looking for a keyboard player to go to Argentina for two weeks, and then go on a world tour. He had literally plucked my name out of a union directory, which, as you know, *never* happens!

Tom Jones was a very nice guy, but after the two weeks in Argentina, and two more in Vegas, I told the music director I simply couldn't play "What's New Pussycat" one more time. The other keyboardist on the gig gave me a number to call when I returned to L.A. It turned out to be Danny Elfman's number.

So that was Oingo Boingo?

Yes. Oingo Boingo preexisted my entrance to the band by probably a good ten years. Danny's older brother, Rick, started the band when they were in high school.

What attracted me to Boingo was that even though they were categorized as New Wave, a rather non-musician's medium in those days; they were extremely musical, energetic, and were trying and succeeding at doing different things, different styles. To me, doing an arrangement of "California Girls" in a blistering $15/8$ was fantastic.

WERE YOU INTERESTED IN FILM SCORING AT THIS TIME?

I had no plan for it, but it was a vague idea in the back of my mind. I had taken a class in film scoring at Berklee and figured, maybe I would do it when I turned 50. In the meantime, you know, hey, rock 'n' roll, girls, and all that fun!

I got into film scoring through session work. At the same time I was working with Oingo Boingo, I started doing a lot of session playing in town, primarily as a synth player, which was a pretty small category at the time. An engineer friend of mine called me and told me of a feature film from Tristar pictures called *Sweetheart's Dance*. The director was looking for someone who could translate old Elvis songs into score. So my friend arranged a meeting with the director, Robert Greenwald. The first words out of Robert's mouth was, "I don't really like to use a film composer." I said, "That's okay, I'm not a film composer." He hired me on the spot, and eventually, I talked him into letting me score a couple of scenes in addition to the adaptations. The end result was that I had screen credit on a major studio motion picture.

DID THINGS TAKE OFF FOR YOU THEN, IN TERMS OF FILM SCORING?

Not really. It took some time. In the meantime, I got a gig as music director on *The Tracey Ullman Show*. I ended up staying on that show for about three years. That was decent money and became my base of operations. And that show was the beginning of *The Simpsons*. *The Simpsons* started as a one-minute cartoon that would occasionally appear on *The Tracey Ullman Show*.

There was no music in *The Simpsons* at that time, except for every now and then, Matt Groening would want a little circus music, or something like source music. But the cartoon was so short, it didn't really call for me to score it. Eventually, it was spun off as its own series, and coincidentally, Danny Elfman was hired to write the theme. The producers asked me if I wanted to score the individual episodes, and they wanted to know if I could write in a similar style to Danny! They didn't even know that I had been in a band with Danny. So I did the first season of *The Simpsons*, and pretty much set up the template of the orchestra, and the sound of the show. They wanted me to come back and score some more, but by then I had been getting other offers to score movies because of *The Simpsons*. It was a big stepping stone for me. They ended up hiring Alf Clausen, who has done a great job since then.

WHAT WERE THE NEXT PROJECTS THAT CAME YOUR WAY?

At the same time as the beginning of *The Simpsons*, which was also my last year on *The Tracey Ullman Show*, I did a movie called *Say Anything*, directed by Cameron Crowe, and starring John Cusack. That was an interesting situation. They had already hired Ann Dudley to score it and apparently Cameron wanted to keep trying different things, and was asking Ann to rescore and rescore. She got fed up and literally hopped back on a plane to England. The music department at Fox came to me and asked me to help Cameron, who was monkeying around with the music. I tried a bunch of different little things, and Cameron liked what I was doing, so he asked me to look at a scene in which John Mahoney is giving Ione Skye a ring that once belonged to her mom. So we're in a recording studio, Cameron is out in the control room, and I'm sitting at a piano watching a TV monitor, and ad-libbing while I'm watching the scene for the first time. It's not very long, maybe a 30 or 40 second cue. I finish playing, and Cameron says, "Great." I asked him if he liked it, and he just said, "Great." And I said, "Well let me think about it while we're recording and I'll practice it some more." Cameron interjected and said, "No, you don't understand, we *recorded* that!" And that's what ended up in the film, my initial playing.

DID YOU SHARE THE SCREEN CREDIT?

Yeah. That was Cameron's call, so it was "Music by Richard Gibbs/Anne Dudley." I'd never even met Anne, to this day I haven't met her. So it's a little misleading when you look at it. I was using some of her themes and reworking them, in addition to my own writing.

WHAT IS YOUR COMPOSING PROCESS? DO YOU USE PENCIL AND PAPER, OR PLAY ALONG TO THE VIDEO?

A couple of things have happened to radically change my scoring approach. Not in terms of the notes that are written, but how they are written. I always used to write with pencil and paper; that's how I was taught. I would sit at the piano, use a clickbook and a metronome, and work out everything that way. I did everything that way up until two years ago when I was working with writer/director Charlie Peters for the second time. He had a movie called *Music from Another Room*, a small budget picture. Charlie wanted to hear every piece of music in advance of the recording sessions. All I had to sequence with was a primitive Akai MPC-60—it would take forever. Charlie would come over and listen to all the cues, but I was going crazy because after I sequenced it, I still had to sketch it out and give it to an orchestrator. So I was basically writing every cue twice. I finally bought a Mac G3 and hired an assistant to teach me the programs, including Digital Performer.

The next movie I did was *Dr. Dolittle*. This was the first movie I scored where I never held a pencil in my hand. I'd play every part into the computer, and I was nervous as a cat when I got up in front of the orchestra because I wasn't sure if what I had played into my synthesizer was going to come back out through the orchestra. It was a 95-piece orchestra, and it was the first Fox movie to be scored on their new scoring stage.

DO YOU LIKE TO SCORE TO THE SCRIPT?

To be honest, I'm not comfortable doing that. Personally speaking, I'm more of a reactive kind of composer. I'm very much a collaborator. I like to know exactly what I'm dealing with, in terms of picture. I like to have the emotional response to the movie to write to it. The lines may be in the script, but it's when the actors deliver them that I begin to feel the emotion and write the best music.

WHAT ARE SOME OF THE MEMORABLE COLLABORATIONS YOU HAVE HAD?

Working on *Fatal Instinct* with Carl Reiner was a wonderful experience. He was looking around at different composers that were available, and I went and gave an interview. I liked Carl right away; we just hit it off. I could tell we connected, and that I knew how to make him happy. And I could tell he knew it. At the time, I didn't have much of a résumé, but I just felt good walking out of the meeting, and I thought to myself, "I think I got that job."

In that film, we were lampooning so many different films, and I got to score some scenes in the style of Bernard Herrmann. It was hilarious to me. And the irony is that it sounded like I was twisting it and turning it, but I wasn't. I was scoring it as if I was Bernard Herrmann, as if the scene was straight. The comedy was all in the movie; I didn't have to touch on the comedy at all.

There is a postscript to the whole *Fatal Instinct* experience. One day, when we were dubbing the movie, I was hanging out having lunch with Carl. I had to ask him just for my own edification why he hired me. He said, "Well frankly, I hated your tape. I didn't like your music at all, and it was totally inappropriate to what I wanted. But your ideas were great, and I somehow thought it would be fun." And it was fun, it worked out great. We ended up going all over the map, musically. That was one of the more pleasurable experiences I've had.

I'd have to say 95 percent of the work I've done has been a blast. It's been a real pleasure for me. I've talked with a lot of composers who are very bitter, and they think that it's really hard, and people don't appreciate them. They've become tortured souls. Frankly, I don't get it. I'm of the school that thinks, "This is fantastic, I can't believe I'm getting paid to do this."

Elliot Goldenthal

Composer Elliot Goldenthal has created works for theater, orchestra, opera, and film. He has received Oscar nominations for his scores to *Michael Collins* and *Interview with a Vampire*. Some of his other well-known film scores are *A Time to Kill, Batman Forever, Heat, Alien 3, Drugstore Cowboy,* and *The Butcher Boy*. His concert work, *Fire Water Paper,* a commemoration of the 20th anniversary of the Vietnam War, has been performed with major symphony orchestras worldwide.

LET'S TALK ABOUT YOUR BACKGROUND AND HOW YOU GOT STARTED IN FILM SCORING.

My musical background is in composition. I got my bachelors and masters degrees at the Manhattan School of Music. I studied with John Corigliano and also unofficially studied with Aaron Copland. From 1978 until Aaron died, we were very close. We would sit together for hours on end, just playing through scores at the piano slowly, and he would look at my compositions. Although he wasn't my official teacher, he certainly spent months and months of time working with me, guiding me through stuff. But my principal teacher was John Corigliano; I studied with him every Wednesday for seven years.

WHAT WERE YOUR EARLY MUSICAL INTERESTS?

I've always been interested in all aspects of composing that include cinema. I remember as a teenager going to see great American and European movies and being really excited about the interrelationship between music and image, getting excited about the work of Prokofiev, Shostakovich, Bernard Herrmann, and Nino Rota, and really thinking of it as yet another medium in which to apply a musical craft. It became a passion of mine, along with theater. I really loved the interaction between acting or dance and music. I got involved working with theater, creating scores on the spot along with actors, doing experimental theater and dance, also composing incidental music for plays throughout the United States in theaters like the ART in Cambridge. I was working in several theaters around the country doing these kinds of things, and at the same time I was composing chamber music. And then I was doing more complicated types of theater, like musicals. I composed three musicals, two of which were performed at Lincoln Center and had extended runs, one of which continues to play throughout the world.

WHAT LED YOU TO YOUR FIRST FILMS?

My first films were back in the 1970s. They happened along with the other alternative kind of stuff back in New York. There were German producers and directors who worked with the Fassbinder school of film making. There was this film that I did with Andy Warhol, I think called *Blank Generation*, about the birth of the punk movement in New York in the seventies. I really had a good time with that score. I was working in film in those days, but chamber music and theater were pushing me in more compelling directions. So I just followed that direction until the late eighties.

SO WHAT HAPPENED THEN? WHAT WAS THE FIRST MAINSTREAM FILM YOU GOT INVOLVED IN?

Drugstore Cowboy, which happened concurrent to working on *Pet Sematary*. Those films were a direct result of Gus Van Sant hearing the scores of my earlier works. At the same time, I was also working on various symphonic works, one of which was for the 70th birthday celebration of Leonard Bernstein. I just felt really comfortable about that *Drugstore Cowboy* situation.

WITH ALL OF YOUR COMPOSITIONAL BACKGROUND AND ALL OF YOUR STUDIES, DO YOU STILL PUT PENCIL TO PAPER?

It depends on the cue. For example, if it's a type of thing where you know there's a theme, a big theme that's going to be used in over 50 types of scenes, then I prefer to be alone with a piano, and a pencil and paper, because I can generally have a feeling for the tone of how the theme is going to work throughout the movie. But with the advent of MIDI synthesis with video lock and all of that kind of thing, if I'm working on a scene that involves tremendous amount of synchronization—an action scene or a scene that you have to make a musical statement on the 21st frame—I find that the actual experience of working with the computer, the synthesizers, and the video all locked up is very, very similar to working with actors live in a studio. Very similar to my theatrical experience.

YOU MEAN THERE'S GIVE AND TAKE.

Yes, it's like I'm moving along with them at the same time. As opposed to pausing, reflecting, and going back to see if it works. The nature and the type of a theme, or the use of that theme, determines the way I like to work.

HOW DO YOU FIRST APPROACH WRITING THE MUSIC?

Well, first of all, let me preface this by saying that before I approach anything, I have a very strong concept of what I want to pull off, whether it works out or not. That might include limiting the choice of pitches or a very clear choice of orchestration. So I don't go into something and just start improvising, I find that if I do that, I just sort of waste my time. I stay away from the piano, away from the computer, away from the pencil. I think about the scene and I say, how can I achieve the dramatic effect that is necessary for the scene and have it still sound fresh? How can I make it sound like you haven't heard that before, you haven't lived that before? Sometimes the answer can be surprisingly simple. In *Alien 3*, for example, I used a solo piano to underline the scene with the little girl because I thought that having a piano way out in space would remind you of the most domestic of all instruments—it would remind you of home. Just things like that. That's a concept.

The other thing is that the study of orchestration is extremely important because it's not just the tunes, it's not just the melody; it's who plays it, what's the concept, what's the orchestral concept. And the sound, the development of electronics is all part of orchestration, of what that thing actually ends up sounding like.

HOW ABOUT A TIME TO KILL WHERE THE SCORE USED TEXTURES THAT WERE VERY DIFFERENT THAN THOSE IN YOUR OTHER WORK?

On *A Time to Kill* I used a lot of thick orchestral clusters that fit the sense of this agonizing racial struggle. But I also used instruments that were very rural, in a sense of folk music, such as harmonica, hammered dulcimer, and also penny whistle. I used those instruments in an unconventional way; they were accompanied with the type of clustery orchestral writing that one would associate with the Polish avant-garde.

WHOSE DECISION WAS IT TO USE THE GOSPEL SONG IN THE SCENE WHERE THE SAMUEL JACKSON CHARACTER GUNS DOWN THE TWO REDNECKS?

Yes, "Precious Lord." [Director] Joel Schumacher and I came up with that. That was three young girls called the Jones Sisters. They were about the same age as the girl that was raped. They were taped down in the Deep South, not in a studio. It was the sound you would hear if you went to a Sunday meeting and heard three girls get up and sing "Precious Lord." So I had this a capella three-girls situation. They were all 11 years old or so. And then I pitted it up against this heavy orchestral, clustery setting. It was almost as if the orchestra swallows up the a capella singing. This was something that was highly conceptualized even before the scene was shot.

WAS THAT WAS PART OF THE SCRIPT?

No, it wasn't part of the script; it was part of the conversation that I had with Joel on how to do the scene.

SO IN THIS CASE, YOU WERE INVOLVED IN THE FILM IN THE SCRIPT STAGE, WHICH I IMAGINE DOESN'T ALWAYS HAPPEN.

It has always been that way in my work with Joel. I would always come on the project in the script stage, or even while we were shooting. Then I'd go down to the set and there would be discussions. This does help me because it gives me a chance for my subconscious to think about concepts of how to approach something so it seems fresh.

WHAT ABOUT THE USE OF TEMP TRACKS?

For a young composer, or a new composer who doesn't have a strong enough background or backbone, it could be dangerous because they'll say, "The temp is working so well. I don't want to lose my job so I'll compose it just like the temp." But if you don't care about losing your job, and you're willing to go your own way as opposed to following something, you can come up with an original solution. There are fifty or sixty things that can work in a scene, so what you have to do is really be clear to the director about how much of this or that you think is right. You have to get intimate with the director so you don't make the mistake of just copying the temp track, which many directors would feel is ridiculous because they hired you to be creative.

WHAT'S YOUR ADVICE TO YOUNG PEOPLE COMING UP IN THIS CRAZY BUSINESS?

My advice is not to keep your head stuck in film. Open your horizons to what you really want to express in music. And no matter what it is, whether it's a rock background or whether it's chamber music, keep those avenues open. When anybody asks me how to develop their chops for movies, I say, do theater. I spent over 10 years doing theater before anything significant happened movie-wise. And that was like 100% preparation. In the situation with *Batman* or *Interview with a Vampire*, where it's the last minute, and you have three or four weeks to do the film, and you know that whatever you write any particular night, an entire orchestra is going to be there in a couple of days. It's going to be recorded and then 2 billion people are going to listen to it. You can't second-guess yourself, you can't backtrack, you can't be afraid. The way that I learned to overcome that fear was in theater, where you have to make those kinds of decisions and you have to be very, very, very clear. You go into rehearsal and it either works or it doesn't. But the theater world, it's sort of a Gold's Gym of dramatic composing.

Michael Gorfaine & Sam Schwartz

Michael Gorfaine and Sam Schwartz are two of the most well-known agents for film composers in Hollywood. The Gorfaine-Schwartz Agency, formed in 1983, represents people such as John Williams, James Horner, Michael Kamen, Elliot Goldenthal, and Ennio Morricone, among others.

HOW DID YOU GET STARTED AS AGENTS FOR FILM COMPOSERS?

SS: From about 1978 to 1982, Michael was the co-director of the West Coast office of ASCAP. In 1980, he hired me to begin a film and television division with the priority of building up the film-music repertoire. While we were at ASCAP, we became familiar with many composers and the process that they live through writing the music and getting work. One thing leads to another, and we decided to go off on our own.

MG: I have always loved films and film music, but I never focused on it until I worked at ASCAP. That is where I started meeting composers, and that is where I met Sam over 17 years ago. I enjoy working with these people. Across the board, film composers are just interesting, good people.

CAN YOU EXPLAIN THE ROLE OF THE AGENT AS IT RELATES TO YOUR WORK?

MG: The way we define it, there are many overlapping duties and roles that the agent performs. It's really a relationship between management and more traditional agenting.

First and foremost, we advise and counsel career direction, and look for opportunities in which our clients can fulfill their career goals. We peruse the film and television world for the jobs for our composers to compose their music. And we also advise our clients about lawyers and business managers with whom they are to work.

DO THE JOBS ALWAYS COME THROUGH YOU, OR DOES THE COMPOSER SOMETIMES GET THEM ON HIS OWN?

MG: Sometimes, if there was a preexisting relationship, a producer or director will approach a composer directly. When you've got people who have worked together and know each other, often that relationship has great communication in it, and they will talk directly to each other. This is a wonderful thing. However, eventually it will come through us so we can hammer out the details of the schedule, the fees—the whole deal.

SS: The way that this is normally operated is through protocol, through the agency. Normally, we sit down with the composer to find the potential creative opportunities, and plan the next move.

MG: It's an overall career-strategy approach that we take. It's not just building momentum, or making deals. It's our job to make sure that, at any point in time, we are manifesting the best possible opportunities for our clients, and advising the best next step. And certainly it's different in different times of an artist's career. In the beginning it about getting opportunities, period. Once you have the momentum it's about choosing properly. The funny thing is, it gets harder and harder once you get established. You want to make sure that the right choices are being made.

MANY COMPOSERS GET PEGGED AS DOING ONLY ONE STYLE OF MUSIC. HOW DO YOU BREAK THEM OUT OF THAT KIND OF PERCEPTION?

MG: I don't think any musician I know wants to do the same thing over and over again. No actor wants to play the same part over and over again. No director wants to make the same movie over and over again. The same thing holds true for composers. Any great composer can do a multiplicity of things. We know that. But they can become known for certain things and asked to do those things again and again. One of the things that we want to do is make sure that the people out there that will hire these composers know their multifaceted nature, and what they are able to do. We try to get in very early on projects—as early as the script stage when they are developing a project. We find out whether it's a music-driven project, like an animated musical with songs, or not. Most often it's not; most movies just need a good score. So we find out very early on what the musical requirements are. We get that information to the client we would like to see on the project, and we pitch that client to the project.

WHAT ABOUT PACKAGE DEALS? HOW DO YOU APPROACH THOSE?

SS: In the mid '80s, around the time of *Airwolf* and *Miami Vice*, we began this process called "packaging." This actually started with television films because of the fact that some of our clients, like Jan Hammer, had their own electronic studios where they could produce all the music. This was unique at that time. We felt that we could take the budgets that were being offered and have the composers just take all the money in exchange for doing all the production in their studios.

Now, twelve years later, almost all television music is done as a package. In the last three years, many of the motion picture projects are packages as well, even if the budgets are rather large. What this does is protect the producer from cost overruns, and it puts the responsibility to maintain a very specific budget on the shoulders of the composer.

MG: Yes. In addition, unless the client is really self-contained with his own facility and is set up to package, we veer away from that. If it's a big orchestral score, there is really little packaging. Especially when you are up against potential changes that almost always occur.

HOW DOES THAT GET HANDLED?

MG: We have a provision in our regular deals and in package deals that any rescoring is the responsibility of the producer's studio. We are very clear about that.

DO YOU SEE ANY DIFFICULTY IN THE BUSINESS FOR SOMEONE WHO IS A MINORITY OR WOMAN COMPOSER?

MG: Not that I am aware of. I think that opportunities are available, and we are not aware of any kind of difficulties. I can't tell you why there are not more women composers, I don't know why.

WHAT KIND OF THINGS ARE YOU LOOKING FOR IN AN UP-AND-COMING COMPOSER? WHAT'S THE COMPLETE PACKAGE?

MG: We are looking for real musical vision, real ability to marry music with images. Thankfully, there are a lot of wonderful musicians, writers, and composers out there. But it is a very special gift, this gift of being able to compose for film.

SS: There are so many talented musicians. But their musical gift is anchored by being film makers first, and their expression is made though music. The musical gift that is necessary to succeed today is to have a great traditional foundation combined with a sense of the abstract future. In other words, being able to express musical thought on computers and machines, on top of a foundation of a classical, traditional gift.

WHAT ARE THE THINGS YOUNG COMPOSERS SHOULD DO TO FURTHER THEIR CAREERS?

SS: In one word: anything. Student opportunities, student film opportunities, student television opportunities, commercials, even local commercials, whatever they can take. I would even suggest that they have their own computer operations going on. That they take videos of some of their favorite and most influential films, shut down the sound, and lay in their own music to show how they would approach a project. And having a CD demo of film music available is important.

But there is one thing that is even more important. In their professional milieu you know their musical gift is a given. What separates those who succeed from those who don't is their ability at the human relationships. It's the way they are perceived by others, and the way they handle meeting any number of people that they encounter—in particular, producers, directors, and studio people. There can't be a better piece of advice than to work on those basic human skills of communication. There are such gifted musicians out there that don't have the burgeoning and remarkable careers that they should at this stage in their lives, just as a result of this area being a complete, utter weakness.

MG: Film and television are collaborative mediums, and it's not one person, it's many people who make a movie or a television show. What Sam is saying is key because it is mainly about collaboration and communication. The composer sits with the director and spots a film, and they determine together where the music goes, and what it is supposed to do. The composer then goes off and uses his musical gift to create the score, but ultimately the score has to be married to the images. I keep repeating it, but it is so important: it is very much a collaboration on many levels.

WHAT DO YOU ENJOY ABOUT WORKING WITH FILM COMPOSERS?

MG: I find them to be great people. With different kinds of musical backgrounds, all of them got to where they are in slightly different ways. Because of the journeys they have taken, they are very responsible and interesting people. Films and television shows provide a wonderful canvas for composers. All that great music would never exist without the kind of inspiration the composers bring.

Harry Gregson-Williams

Born in England to a musical family, Harry Gregson-Williams earned a coveted spot at the Guildhall School of Music and Drama in London. He started his film career as an orchestrator and arranger for composer Stanley Myers and went on to compose his first scores for the veteran English director, Nicolas Roeg. Harry's initiation into Hollywood film scoring was then facilitated by his collaboration and friendship with Oscar-winning composer Hans Zimmer, and he went on to provide music for such films as *The Rock* (1996), *As Good as It Gets* (1997), *Armageddon* (1998), and *The Prince of Egypt* (1998).

Harry Gregson-Williams is now one of Hollywood's most sought after film composers, working on a variety of high-profile projects, both animated and live action. Over the last few years, Harry has scored some of the industry's biggest blockbusters, including *Chicken Run*, the *Shrek* trilogy, *Kingdom of Heaven*, *Gone Baby Gone*, *The Chronicles of Narnia*, *Prince Caspian*, *The Taking of Pelham 123*, *X-Men Origins: Wolverine*, and *Prince of Persia*.

COULD YOU TALK ABOUT YOUR MUSICAL BACKGROUND AND TRAINING?

Sure. I had a full-on musical education from the time I was very young. There is a particularly renowned choir in Cambridge, England that I was a part of, and I was sight-reading and learning music very early on so that it became second nature to me.

WAS FILM MUSIC ALWAYS AN INTEREST OF YOURS?

Actually, I had no particular interest in film music for many years, I never even noticed it. Except for my father having my brothers and I singing "Bare Necessities" from *The Jungle Book* when we were about six years of age. I never gave it too much thought until about twelve years ago.

SO WHAT HAPPENED TWELVE YEARS AGO?

I met Hans Zimmer. Right before that, I had collaborated with Richard Harvey, an excellent English composer, and another old-school English film composer named Stanley Myers. Coincidentally, Hans had apprenticed with Stanley a few years before me, and I snuck in behind him. Hans and I became friends very quickly, and he invited me—or rather, insisted, I come over—to the States. That was at the beginning of Media Ventures and it was small and intimate. I took over when Nick Glenni-Smith was taking off on his own.

HOW DID YOU GET YOUR FIRST FEATURE IN HOLLYWOOD? DID HANS RECOMMEND YOU FOR SOMETHING?

In my case, there were various things that happened quite quickly—moons that aligned for me to take the next step. I was at a birthday party for Hans and met Dan Ireland, who had been a producer and was making his directorial debut with a film called *Whole Wide World*. He desperately wanted Hans to score his first movie, but Hans was too busy. So we got to chatting, and eventually, it was agreed that if Hans more or less oversaw the operation and was there to pick me up if I fell over, then we would go ahead. Dan has become an amazing friend and collaborator since then.

I was also meeting other filmmakers through my work with Hans. And right around that time, John Powell showed up at Media Ventures from England, and we were asked to do *Antz* together, and that made a huge difference of course.

HOW WAS IT CO-WORKING WITH ANOTHER COMPOSER?

It worked out fine. I was very fortunate to be thrown into that position. I think with *Shrek*, our third collaboration a couple of years later, it was a more of a mature co-write.

LET'S TALK ABOUT GOING FROM BEING A PEN-AND-PAPER GUY TO USING ELECTRONICS. DID YOU HAVE EXPERIENCE WITH THAT STUFF?

I had none. I really had none, and it was a very steep learning curve. But I decided it was something I really wanted to do. I had a look at how Hans was manipulating sounds with all these machines—samplers and such—and I decided that was something I could really get into. You have to have an interest; otherwise, it would be tortuous. So I was, and still am to this day, fascinated and excited by the possibilities of using machines to make music. I hadn't really used a computer to make music before, so it was like a kid in the candy store, really. There's also nothing like learning on the job. To actually be on the film and be learning did not leave much room for error. It was all happening. It wasn't pretend; it wasn't rehearsal. So it brought the best out of me.

WHAT ABOUT YOUR PROCESS AS AN ORGANICALLY ORIENTED COMPOSER WORKING IN A COMPUTERIZED WORLD?

I don't look at it as a separate thing. It's all part of the same process. I'll often start at the piano with manuscript paper and pencil. And when I'm ready, I'll move over to my MIDI station with my preferred devices like Cubase, Pro Tools, and Ableton Live. I've got a stack of software and a stack of hardware. The process is to try to extract the music out of one's imagination—out of thin air—into something tangible.

HOW DO YOU FIND A COMMON VOCABULARY TO DISCUSS MUSIC WITH A
DIRECTOR WHO IS MOST LIKELY NOT A MUSICIAN?

That doesn't bother me at all. Andrew Adamson (*Shrek* and
Chronicles of Narnia) plays guitar and understands music, yet we
formed our own language that was not dependant on musical
lingo. Tony Scott has perhaps never played an instrument, but that
hasn't stopped us from finding a way of discussing music. You've
got to remember that the two filmmakers I mentioned are people
that I've spent hundreds of hours with in my studio. Tony likes to
learn each beat of the music and how it is synchronized to his picture. Other directors can be less hands on, and it can come back
around to bite you in the end. But Tony storyboards his films
meticulously and if he could, he would storyboard the music, I'd
imagine!

WOULD YOU EVER WRITE TO A STORYBOARD? OR DO YOU WAIT UNTIL YOU
GET A FINAL PRINT?

No, no, certainly not a final cut. There's no way to wait that long.
On the movie I just finished, *X-Men Origins: Wolverine*, if I had
waited till I got the final cut, I would probably have left myself one
day before the film had to be recorded and mixed. I actually don't
think I ever saw a final cut, and that's why I have a music editor
working with me.

WHAT WOULD BE A TYPICAL TIME LINE AFTER YOU START WRITING?

One really receives starter's orders when you receive any cut. Most
likely, I'll start when I get a director's cut. Then there could be
about ten to twelve weeks until the final dub.

TELL ME ABOUT THE ACTUAL START OF WRITING. MANY COMPOSERS HAVE SAID THAT THE WORST MOMENT IS AT THE BEGINNING, LOOKING AT A BLANK PIECE OF PAPER OR COMPUTER SCREEN.

Right at this moment I'm trying to set sail on *Prince of Persia*. I just got back from London where I was spotting the film with Mike Newell, the director. I know what is in his mind, as we talked concept in terms of what the music is trying to achieve. So I'm in that rather scary limbo before actually putting pen to paper—I'm literally just pacing around the room.

LET ME ASK YOU ABOUT KINGDOM OF HEAVEN. THERE ARE A LOT OF BATTLE SCENES, AND THE MUSIC FOR THOSE SEEMS TO PROGRESS FROM VERY NON-THREATENING, ALMOST ETHEREAL MUSIC TO MORE OF THE KIND OF BATTLE SCENE MUSIC ONE MIGHT EXPECT. THAT CONCEPT CAME OUT OF DISCUSSIONS WITH RIDLEY SCOTT?

Absolutely. The way he shaped the main siege of the battle of Jerusalem was kind of like distinct chapters, where the action would be broken up by nightfall and things like that. So rather than one continuous barrage of sound and music, that enabled me to pace myself. He had suggested that rather than the music driving things along, we find areas where the music was from the point of view of the essence of Jerusalem.

One also has to be careful with that kind of thing, because you are in danger of actually dragging the picture down, in terms of the pace. It could actually have a counter effect.

With Ridley's brother Tony Scott in *The Taking of Pelham 1,2,3*, there is a runaway train rocketing through the subway out of control. We discussed having some raging music that would go along side this. That was the first direction I took, and we both realized that rather than the music trying to keep up with the images, it would be better for the music to be more contrary to the images on screen and provide an emotional beat as opposed to attempt to push the pace.

*W*HAT IS YOUR SETUP REGARDING THE PEOPLE WORKING IN YOUR STUDIO?

Assistants are a necessity helping with all kinds of things: mock-ups, orchestration, music editing. There is not a composer at this level that doesn't work like that.

In fact, what goes around comes around. I bear in mind how I had the great fortune to be in the position I am now. Apart from my musical education, my apprenticeship here in Los Angeles was almost as perfect as it could have been due to Hans Zimmer. And I now have working for me a couple of people who are aspiring to do their own scores. That's part of what coming through this industry as film composer is about; it provides the opportunity to nurture the next batch. It works for everybody. In many circumstances one is pretty short of time, and without putting too much pressure or responsibility on a composing assistant, it is possible to give them the chance that they are looking for.

Photo: Jennifer Lewi

Mark Isham

Mark Isham has a diverse career as jazz artist and film composer. He has composed the scores for over 50 films, including *A River Runs Through It*, *Nell*, *Fly Away Home*, *Quiz Show*, and *Blade*. Beginning his professional career in the Bay Area, Isham played trumpet in the Oakland and San Francisco Symphony Orchestras. He has eight Grammy nominations for his work as a solo artist.

WHAT WAS YOUR MUSICAL BACKGROUND BEFORE YOU GOT INTO FILM SCORING?

When I was a kid growing up in the Bay Area, I wanted to be one of the cool guys in the back of the orchestra, so I picked the trumpet. But then, I think by early teenagerhood, I discovered more popular—not real "pop music"—but I discovered jazz. And I discovered it in two ways. Actually, Henry Mancini was probably the first commercial sound that really sparked my interest. It's only in very long distance hindsight that I realize that his music was for film, also. What was important at the time is that it was jazz-influenced music. That's what I found intriguing. And then, within a year or so, I discovered real jazz: Cannonball Adderly, Miles, and Monk. That was it. My life was over at that point—I was hooked— I was the jazz guy.

Then I discovered Morton Subotnick and the early stuff done with Moog and Buchla synthesizers. This was in the early '70s. That was the other seminal point for me; it defined the next ten to fifteen years of my own musical learning experience. I figured out pretty soon that the average college music department wasn't going to give me what I wanted to know. So I took it upon myself to study privately. I studied with some really excellent trumpet teachers. I even took some private composition lessons for a while from a guy who was sort of a rebel. We would dissect everything from a Herbie Hancock piano solo all the way to the Bartók string quartets.

HOW DID YOUR FIRST FILM-SCORING GIG HAPPEN?

By the end of the '70s, I was a fully eclectic guy with a pretty wide view of music, and a pretty good working knowledge of a lot of it. I was a good professional trumpet player for many years. I was based in San Francisco, and I played in bands that did all sorts of things. I supported myself, and started buying synthesizers when I had some extra money.

In 1982, a director had gotten his hands on a tape of some music that I had written with a friend of mine. It was a project that combined electronics and Chinese instruments. My friend was the Chinese instrument player, and I was the electronica guy. We didn't get that deal, but we made a number of tapes, and one of them was given by my friend to this director. He literally tracked me down and said, "Look, this is the sound I want for my movie." And that was *Never Cry Wolf*.

Understand that this hardly ever happens. I've never actually heard anyone else get their first film out of the blue like this. But to have someone who is totally unknown—I mean, I was not really successful yet making records. I was doing okay, but it wasn't like I had big-selling records or anything. I never set out to be a film composer. And I just happened to write music and someone heard it and said, "I want you to do it for a film." And all of a sudden I had another career.

HOW DID YOU HANDLE THAT FIRST PROJECT?

I had a lot of help. I had two great, experienced music editors to guide me through the process. I did the whole thing on a Prophet

5 with a little hand-held sequencer and multitrack tape. It took about four months to do 60 minutes of music. The idea of doing a film now with that kind of equipment sends shivers down my spine.

YOU HAVE AN EXTENSIVE ELECTRONIC SETUP NOW. DO YOU WRITE AT ALL TO PAPER, OR DO YOU RELY COMPLETELY ON YOUR KEYBOARDS AND SEQUENCER?

I'm still working off of the basic "thrown in the deep end" process of *Never Cry Wolf*, where this guy just said, "I want you to do it." So my basic compositional process at that time was that I would just come up with some ideas looking at the picture. The pictures themselves are always the inspiration.

And that's why I think a lot of us pump so much money back into the sampled sound world—so it's as good as it can be. I wasn't up to par in that regard a number of years back. The accepted level of quality in the demo world had gone quite a bit ahead of me, and I had not been paying attention. There have been a couple of composers in town who have spearheaded this. They use many, many, many samplers and many, many, many high-tech samples. I think it's actually a good thing. I had to rebudget things that year to get back in the game, but getting all that kind of gear has been real helpful for me. I see the difference it makes when it sounds so good that I get certain producers who come in and say, "Why are we spending money on an orchestra?" Yet I would never condone substituting samples for a real orchestra. But if the music is communicating to the extent where people are actually getting that little rush, getting that little tear in the eye even with a sample, then I know I've done it. I go to the scoring session and just have a great time because I'm not worrying whether or not I got the theme right.

DO YOU DO MOCK-UPS FOR EVERY CUE?

Absolutely. I try to mock-up the entire score if time permits. I hate going in front of the orchestra and having the director hear it for the first time. There may be some macho thing about that, and in the old days they had to do it that way. God bless them for surviving. But really, the greatest boon the electronic fake orchestra has given us is the ability to check it out. It gives a sense of what you're doing before any money is spent on musicians and a studio, and you find yourself in that $10,000-an-hour "I've got to fix it right now" scenario.

WHAT ABOUT TEMP TRACKS?

I think a well-done temp, along with a really excellent communication line with the director, is invaluable. Then I really understand when he says things like, "This is what we're learning here in this scene," and, "What I'd like to bring from that scene is another feeling."

I know there are certain composers who hate temp tracks. I understand that point of view. With certain directors temp tracks can be confining, because he will have made up his mind about the music, and unless you do something very similar to the temp, he's not going to be satisfied.

For *A River Runs Through It*, I only had three weeks to do the score. First, I heard a temp score and most of it was unmemorable. But there was one thing in it that validated exactly what I had been thinking. I was sitting there watching the work print, and about half-way through the film I was saying to myself, "I know what this needs. I know what I can do for this." And the last piece in the temp score was exactly that—a Celtic folk song. And I thought, "I'm right. I need to write five or six beautiful folk songs in the Celtic vibe, and choose one for the theme."

DO YOU FIND THAT BEING A JAZZ MUSICIAN INFLUENCES THE WAY YOU APPROACH WRITING FOR FILMS?

Yeah. I have a definite point of view. I mean, this is what composition means to me: Composition is actually being able to get down a great improvisation. It's the same act, as far as I'm concerned. You're making up music. You're creating something. The jazz world puts you in front of an audience, and you create something there with a few signposts that have been put up to guide you.

Composition is the same thing, except that you are allowed to go back and revise and improve and restructure. To me, the high-tech way of composing is great because I can just improvise scads of stuff, and then the music editor in me can come in and just say, "Well, let's rearrange. We've got to get to that point in the film sooner, so let's take those eight bars out." I'm improvising in the style of late Romantic orchestral music. And when I get a good improvisation, I can fine-tune it, and that becomes a composition.

DO YOU CONDUCT YOUR OWN STUFF?

No. First of all, I'm not a conductor. Second of all, I think it's inefficient. The sound in the room is one thing; the sound out of the speakers is usually something very different. And, if for no other reason, contractually I'm paid to write and produce the score. So it's really my responsibility to make sure it sounds right on tape. If I'm out there with the orchestra getting used to the sound of the room and tuning that up, I can come back in the control room and it can sound miles from what it should really sound like. Besides, the director's in there already listening, and already going "Oh god!" I would rather be there holding his hand and saying, "No, no. We're going to do this differently. Engineer, bring that down." So, my orchestrator conducts, because he's the guy that's decided exactly how the bassoons are going to handle that tricky thing there and how to crescendo the cellos. He's made all those decisions, so he should be the one out there handling the orchestral interpretation of that. He knows the score as a written thing much better than I do. I'm the one that has to make sure that the sound on tape is exactly right.

DO YOU ACCEPT PACKAGE DEALS?

I do, it's necessary these days. The important thing to remember is that everything is negotiable. You can negotiate for gross points. You can negotiate for album points. You can negotiate for publishing. You can negotiate for how many musicians you guarantee to employ. Every aspect of a package deal is negotiable. And make sure you do your homework, because if you miscalculate, and you agree contractually to supply 20 strings for 40 minutes of music, you better know what that's going to cost you. And you better do things like go to the director and say, "I will accept this on the terms that you sign off on everything that I play for you in demo form." Sometimes the director is sitting on the scoring stage and says, "What if this were faster?" Then you're looking at writing more music, changing your tempo, and somehow getting new music on the stand while the musicians are waiting for you. That could eat up your profit right there. So it's very crucial that you have a good line of communication with your director. Even if you can't get it in writing that they'll sign-off on the mock-ups, at least, man to man, get them to agree that this is a package deal, and you're going to try to help each other.

YOU SEEM TO FOCUS A LOT ON THE COMMUNICATION BETWEEN THE COMPOSER AND DIRECTOR.

I think more than 50 percent of the gig of the film composer is verbal communication. There are genius composers who couldn't survive in this business if their life depended on it. That is because they're not willing to work in a committee-type environment where you have to discuss, you have to duplicate someone else's point of view, and you have to be willing to create that point of view and somehow fit it in with your own. On the other hand, you can find people who are average composers who have a great ability to work in that environment who are very successful. It's the game. You are working in a group, and you're bringing a musical part to something that isn't all just music. You've got to be able to play in the group, to play in the game by the rules of the game.

Michael Kamen

Michael Kamen's film scores bring the pop, film, and classical music worlds closer together. He has also written several ballets and symphonic works. He is a song-writer and record producer who has worked with artists such as Sting, Eric Clapton, George Harrison, and Bryan Adams. His film credits include *Robin Hood, Prince of Thieves,* the *Lethal Weapon* series, *Don Juan de Marco, Brazil, Mr. Holland's Opus,* and the *Die Hard* series.

HOW DID YOU GET STARTED, MAKING THE JOURNEY FROM BEING AN OBOE STUDENT AT JUILLIARD TO A COMPOSER OF FILM SCORES?

Through a rock 'n roll band—that great archetypal, educational institution. I learned more and got more experience in the New York Rock and Roll Ensemble because it was our own. Because of the time and place we were in, we were, not surprisingly, asked to perform with orchestras. And because nobody else in the band wanted to do it, and I did want to do it, and I didn't know that I couldn't do it, I wrote the orchestra charts. It seemed easy at the time, something I could do. So I wrote bunches of charts for orchestra and found that I really liked it—those were for major orchestras, such as The Boston Pops with Arthur Fiedler.

DID YOU ALWAYS WANT TO COMPOSE FOR FILMS? WAS THAT A GOAL, OR WAS IT JUST SOMETHING THAT HAPPENED ALONG THE WAY?

I would have composed for an ice cream truck. I composed all the time, and I wanted to be a composer when I was a kid. I remember sitting in front of the piano one day when I was eight or nine and looking at all the busts of Beethoven, Schubert, Bach, and Mozart sitting there on the piano, and realizing with much disappointment, "They're all dead! Maybe it's not a job anymore. Maybe it's just one of those things that happened in the olden days, when the world was black and white." It occurred to me that I'd have to do something else; I couldn't be a composer because that job was no longer a job. Then suddenly, through a rock 'n' roll band, I wound up being a composer.

HOW DID YOU GET YOUR FIRST GIG ON A FILM?

The rock 'n' roll band was managed by a guy whose partner made *Dog Day Afternoon* and *Serpico*. He was a film producer named Marty Bregman, and I knew him because we shared offices. I was very visible in the office; I don't have a shy personality, and I suggested that he pick me to do a film score. He asked me to do a film called *The Next Man*. Then I did a film for another friend of mine, and the rock band also did some television films. One was called *Christina's World*, based on an Andrew Wyeth painting. It became easy for me to do these projects because I was able to continue doing what I loved to do: invent music every day.

IN THOSE EARLY FILMS, DID THEY WANT YOU AS A ROCK 'N' ROLL MUSICIAN OR AS A COMPOSER?

No, I was always a hybrid character—a classical musician that played rock 'n roll, or a rock 'n' roller who was also a classical musician, depending on which end of the street people met me. But it was clear that I was always in both worlds, and I've always brought that feeling into my work. I haven't seen those early films in a long time, but I remember I made a quite classical job out of it, and freely mixed classical music with a set of drums and a rock 'n roll spirit.

HAS YOUR COMPOSING PROCESS CHANGED MUCH OVER THE YEARS, ESPE-CIALLY WITH THE ADVENT OF NEW TECHNOLOGIES?

Well, technology is more of a memory device for me. In the old days when I used my brain completely to remember things, and pencils to write it down, I felt smarter, but I think everybody feels smarter when they're seventeen. I have an inbred mistrust of technology making the way simpler for us. I don't think it answers questions. I think it provides some solutions and I'm all for it now. I use it all the time. I'm definitely hooked. The difference between banging things out on a shabby piano and banging things out on a shabby Kurzweil is that the shabby Kurzweil remembers what I play.

IN TERMS OF SYNCHRONIZATION, JUST FROM HAVING BEEN AROUND A LITTLE BIT WHILE YOU'VE BEEN WORKING, IT SEEMS LIKE YOU'RE VERY INSTINCTUAL.

Yeah, it's instinctive. I have never depended on any of those devices like Auricle or whatever. They are systems that enable you to look at a piece of film and compute what the best click track would be. But I really hate math so much that I don't get myself involved. For years, I did try to get click tracks right, but inevitably I'd get them wrong, and I just punched my way out of that paper bag.

SO HOW DO YOU SYNCHRONIZE SOMETHING LIKE LETHAL WEAPON OR AN ACTION SEQUENCE THAT REQUIRES A LOT OF SYNCHRONIZATION? ARE YOU STILL JUST FEELING THOSE SPOTS?

Again, I do have an instinct for it, and I have to trust that instinct. That's one of the things you do as a composer: Trust your instincts, and have confidence in what it is you're saying. There are always ways to get it perfect, to refine it, and make sure that that big downbeat hits the explosion or misses the explosion, as the case may be. And certainly there are also music editors who can fix anything that needs fixing. But my job is to make music, and not equations.

WHAT ABOUT THE TIMES THAT YOU'VE CROSSED OVER FROM WRITING MORE CLASSICAL SCORES TO MORE ROCK 'N' ROLL THINGS? HOW DOES THE PROCESS WORK WITH ERIC CLAPTON, OR DAVID SANBORN?

It's the same thing. It's just relating to a musician in language that those musicians can understand, so I'm not confused or confusing. Eric is able to carry melody in his head and improvise better than any 15,000 people I know. Same with Sanborn. So when you're working with genius, you just allow them to be themselves. You don't try to constrict them or control them. Every once in a while you'll say, "I really *need* you to play guitar or sax on top of this." When you provide them with a track, they'll figure it out. If they don't figure it out, then you say, "Try this ..." and you can demonstrate and so forth.

I WOULD IMAGINE THAT YOUR EXPERIENCE IN BEING A ROCK 'N' ROLL MUSICIAN ASSISTS YOU IN THAT WHOLE PROCESS.

That's because I realize the real value in not being educated to death and not being overly regimented in the way you think. Rock 'n' roll is a great liberator in that there are no rules, and if there were you'd get rid of them. That's what it's about. That's why it was invented. I was really lucky to be around at that crucial period when it was being invented. It's been a little sad for me to see it go down such a predictable road, as it has done, and become a cash cow where the money is the all-important end product, and the music is secondary.

HAVE YOU EVER WRITTEN A SONG WHERE THE DIRECTOR SAYS TO YOU, "HERE'S A SCENE IN THE MOVIE IN WHICH WE NEED A SONG, NOT UNDERSCORE." HAVE YOU BEEN IN THAT SITUATION, WHERE YOU HAD TO COMPOSE A SONG THAT HAD REALLY DRAMATIC IMPACT?

No, unless it's a montage sequence, I don't think a song is very good news. You're trying to tell a story with action, colors, and characters and you don't need somebody singing in the background telling you what you're seeing. I don't actually agree with that, and very rarely do I think a song contributes positively in that way. There are some notable examples where it does work, however. The songs "Mona Lisa" and "Brazil" are deliberate attempts on the part of the director, not on the part of the composer, to be intrinsic motivations for the characters' actions. That's why we used them. It's not because we wanted a hit record.

Most often, songs in movies are there for commercial reasons. The great lesson of a lifetime was taught to me by Joel Silver, [producer of the *Die Hard* and *Lethal Weapon* series] when I said to him one day, "Joel, you have great taste and wisdom about art and culture. When are you going to make a great film and stop making this shit? " And he said, "I make shit. I buy art!" Movies are art as commerce, and to some people like Joel, that works very well. For me art is art, and commerce is commerce.

WHAT DO YOU THINK MAKES A GREAT SCORE? WHAT MAKES A SCORE STAND OUT IN YOUR MIND?

Melody. A great piece of music is qualified by its melody. There are great scores that are brilliant orchestrations or this and that, but they sound *like* other pieces of music, they're not great pieces of music. There's a difference. A great piece of music is like an invention. It's like a very rare jewel, or a beautiful vista. Even if you create a melody deliberately and say I want it to do this, or I want it to do that, as opposed to conceiving it instinctively, there still must be some degree of inspiration. There's no way on Earth that I could claim to really be in control of the melodies that I write. I'm just inventing stuff. It's a bit like fishing.

SO YOU WOULD NEVER SIT DOWN AND SAY, "I NEED A BITTERSWEET MELODY, SO I'M GOING TO GO UP A MINOR 6TH," OR SOMETHING LIKE THAT.

No, I don't really think of minor 6ths when I'm playing. But I do sit down and improvise a lot. In that sense, improvisation is really a starting point for an idea. I have some training, just enough to get me in trouble, but not enough to screw me up forever. I can recognize somehow what I've done, but I don't define it in musical terms. I never say, "This is serial technique," or "This is a 10th," or anything else. It just has a shape in my mind, and it's very difficult to describe what a shape is. It's blue, yet green. I wouldn't be a very good teacher in that regard, but I would be a very good teacher if I were just able to encourage people to express their own personality. That is what we do, that is the gift of music—being able to express a feeling and an attitude and a vibe confidently, and with some beauty. Believing it to be good enough to make beautiful things.

Do you organize yourself as far as themes are concerned? Do you put it all together at first, or do you just start and see where it takes you?

No, I never list things. However, the spotting process is a very crucial one; I often can see what the architecture of a score will be by talking about it with the director, or the producer, or whoever I'm spotting with. I learn more as I'm working on it, and sometimes I change my mind. But it's really the architecture of a score that you're talking about, and that is a very complicated, and yet quite simplistic design. Nobody goes to the theater to listen to the score. The score is assisting them in watching the film. The score is a component of the story and of the characters. So I don't want people to be sitting there going, "Wow, what a great ii IV V progression." That's not what I want, and I don't believe it's an important consideration in making music for films.

As far as themes are concerned, coming up with a theme, having several portions to that theme that you can assign to separate characters in the movie, and being able to bring the theme out with the character is important to me. But that's more mechanical to me than artistic. To say, "If Mel Gibson's on the screen I need the guitar, and if he's being angry and aggressive, I need a big orchestra behind it," that's a no-brainer.

What is your advice for the up-and-coming film students, in terms of getting started in the business?

Getting started in the business is always a dilemma because you can't advise people on getting lucky, and there is a great deal of luck. It's about the work that they do, and it's not about being in the right place or meeting the right people or going to the right party—though all of that can contribute to it. But there is no single thing I could say, other than make the best music you can, and be the best you can be at what it is you do, and what you do uniquely. There is a need for the individuality for each of us to rise to the surface, and for us to take our own work quite seriously. You should have fun while you're doing it. A really great musician doesn't convey their technical brilliance on stage. What they convey is how easy it seems to be playing this incredibly difficult stuff. The more relaxed you are as a human being and as a musician, the more effective your performance will be. This is far short of saying that if you want to work in film do this, do that, do the other thing. I'm afraid that kind of advice is not going to come from me. The kind of advice that I'm going to give you is to be yourself, find your own brand of music to make, and work hard. It's about the work, it's about the work, it's about the work. Your work will come to people's attention, and if you can produce more good work, you're onto something.

Mark Mancina

Mark Mancina composed scores for three of the top-grossing films of recent years: *Speed*, *Twister*, and *Con Air*. He won a Grammy for his work on *The Lion King*, and was music producer for its Broadway stage version. Additionally, Mancina has led an active career producing songs for such artists as Phil Collins and Elton John.

NOW THAT YOU'VE HAD SOME SUCCESS IN YOUR CAREER, DO YOU HEAR FILM SCORES DIFFERENTLY?

When I first came into film composing I used to be pretty critical of people's scores. I'd listen to some scores and go, "That guy's terrible," or, "This guy's brilliant." Now, I've changed my whole viewpoint. I feel that anyone who does this for a living—successfully completes a score, and goes on to his next score—has accomplished an incredible achievement because there's so much that goes on behind a movie score besides the music. Fielding the politics, the pressures, the emotions, and the wants and desires of some directors who think that they have something on screen that maybe they don't have—all those kinds of emotions are extremely challenging. So I have a huge respect for anybody that does this job. I think it's extremely difficult. In reality, sometimes the music is the *easiest* part, while everything else you have to deal with is really the hardest part of the job.

HAVE YOU EVER BEEN IN A SITUATION WHERE YOU REALLY DISAGREED WITH A DIRECTOR?

Oh yeah, every movie!

[LAUGHING] WHAT HAPPENED?

The majority of the time, we end up with a cue that the director likes better but that I think wasn't as good as my original cue. But that's from *my* perspective. The director probably would say that we ended up with a better piece of music. I would write a cue that I thought was the best that could be for that scene. Then the director comes in and says, "No, I had a completely different thing in mind for this." So where do you go? Who's right, who's wrong?

SO YOU DO MOCK-UPS FOR EVERY CUE?

It depends. I try not to because mock-ups really back you into a corner. But directors and producers are getting much more used to having things mocked up because they can hear what it sounds like before they hire the orchestra to play it.

HOW DID YOU GET STARTED IN FILM SCORING?

I started out as a classical player, as a classical guitarist. I went to school and studied composition—I went through that whole process. I also played in bands and did all kinds of different stuff—playing at night and paying the rent doing music.

When I was 22, a friend who was a cameraman called me and said he was doing a documentary for this guy that does these dog training documentaries; he does dog training, deer gutting, and marlin fishing—and he needs music for these shows. I said, "Absolutely." I had a little sequencer—a Roland—and a couple of keyboards. I put all this stuff in my car and I drove to this guy's production studio and set up. There was no sync or anything. Everything had to be written or clicked, and I had to just freewheel it. I wrote these documentaries, and, for way back then, they came out all right. I had a big orchestral sound in one of them and I wrote some songs, I was singing and playing all the instruments—this was all on an 8-track Fostex. I started to see the magic of putting music up against picture and running them at the same time. That's a whole school; I learned it by doing it. Nobody was there telling me, "That's really stupid what you're doing there." I learned it by doing it, and I did it for years. I really got a sense of what music does, what it can do, what it should and shouldn't do, and all those kind of things.

I did low-budget films and documentaries for nine years. Then Hans Zimmer heard something I did. He called me up and he said, "What part of Europe are you from?" And I said, "I'm not from Europe, I'm from Santa Monica." Then he said, "Well, your writing is really European and I would really love to work with you. Why don't you come down to my studio?" That day I went down to his studio. Trevor Horn was there, and Billy Idol was there, and they were doing this movie called *Days of Thunder*. I just dove right into it as an arranger, writer, and player.

Then *The Lion King* project was looming. Hans was doing the score, and he asked me to produce the songs, and be in charge of that. I said okay, and then dove into that without knowing that it would become the most successful animated motion picture ever made. At the same time I was working on that, I was doing films like *Monkey Trouble* and other little fun family films. While I was finishing up *The Lion King*, Jan De Bont came to me and said, "I want you to do my movie *Speed*, it's just a small movie." This is like a $30-million dollar movie. I told him I'd love to do it. They had me audition cues for them, though. Eventually I got the movie and those two movies—*The Lion King* and *Speed*—came out the same week, and everything just went crazy after that.

WHAT IS YOUR WRITING PROCESS NOW?

Basically what I've been doing now is playing a lot of the instruments myself while writing the cues and playing all the percussion. I collect instruments and any instruments I can get my hands on I'll learn and develop a part and write from that stand-point. Then I'll add the orchestra over the top of it. So, when I play a mock up, it's not really a mock up. What you're really hearing is all of the acoustic instruments that I've recorded, and vocals done myself. The orchestra is the only thing that's mocked up, to a point, or a piano track. Then we go in and record the orchestra and get rid of the synth stuff. So eventually, what you end up having is me playing a series of percussion instruments and a series of stringed instruments, then doing vocals, and then finally an orchestra play-ing. It becomes this hybrid. There is a certain randomness and air that is created when you play an acoustic instrument, and you cannot create it on a keyboard of any kind. I don't care how good your samples are.

HOW DO YOU HANDLE THE BUSINESS STUFF?

At the beginning, when I first start work on a film, I think about the music and what I want to do with it. But there is also a logistical side—a business side—to it. I came from being a producer on records, and an arranger, and that really helped me because part of writing a film score is producing a recording. And producing means being in charge of the entire outcome—the budgets and credits and everything. It can be extremely difficult for the studios to get all that together.

SO YOU'RE IN CONSTANT COMMUNICATION WITH A LOT OF OTHER PEOPLE?

You know, it would be wonderful to say that the composer has the final say on everything but that's not the truth. So many times, you'll hear a score and you'll say, "Man! I don't like that cue at all, how could he have written that?" And to be fair, it most likely wasn't the composer's doing. Who knows how it ended up there? Basically, when it all comes down, film composing is a service job, and there isn't a composer out there who would argue that. Everybody has to bend and learn to change things that they don't necessarily want to change because they're not the executive pro-ducer of the film, they're not the director of the film, they're only the composer. It's not the composer's film, it's the director's film. You always have to keep that in mind. And that can make it difficult because sometimes the composer really does know best!

David Newman

David Newman has scored over 55 feature films, including *Hoffa*, *Anastasia*, *Heathers*, *The Nutty Professor*, and *Matilda*. Coming from a Hollywood music family—brother Thomas Newman is also a film composer, and father Alfred Newman was the head of music at 20th Century Fox for many years—David Newman studied violin, and received a degree in conducting from USC.

YOU GREW UP IN A HOLLYWOOD MUSIC FAMILY. WAS THERE ALWAYS MUSIC AROUND AT YOUR HOUSE, OR WAS IT SOMETHING YOUR DAD WOULD LEAVE AT THE OFFICE?

My dad worked at home while we were growing up and there was a lot of music around. Music was a big part of the house, we always heard him banging away on the piano. We were also brought up very traditionally, studying music. My brother Tommy and I, we both grew up studying violin and piano from very young ages. We took theory, counterpoint, and orchestration at 11, 12, 13 years old. A traditional, sort of Germanic musical upbringing.

DID YOU REBEL AGAINST THAT?

No, no. I loved it. I always loved music. It was never a snotty or snooty or upper crust thing around my house. It was something my dad and his brother Lionel talked about with so much love. It wasn't just work for them. It was, in a sense, the only thing that they really talked about. They talked about music with love more than they talked about anything.

DID YOU ALWAYS WANT TO WRITE MUSIC FOR FILMS?

When I was young, I never wanted to write music for film. I didn't start writing until I was twenty-nine. I was studying conducting all through my twenties. I had gone to USC as a violin performance major; then, I got a masters there with Dan Lewis in conducting.

For a while after school, I was just doing studio work playing violin. There got to a point in my life when I wanted to change what I was doing. I wanted to be a conductor, but I wasn't doing what it would take to do that. I was just kind of floating around. I was playing violin, I was making a living and everything, but it wasn't satisfying. And film scoring was an option to me. I just decided to do it, and I made a demo, and went through this three or four year process to get going. It took me a really long time.

WHAT'S YOUR COMPOSING PROCESS NOW? ARE YOU SEQUENCING OR USING PENCIL AND PAPER?

For the past three or four years I've been sequencing. But I've done around 60 films, and about 40 of them I wrote directly with piano, and orchestrated at the same time. I never sketched because I was really sloppy. Sketching was really a hard thing for me to do because no one could ever read it.

SO WHAT IS THE PROCEDURE TODAY?

What I do is start to compose and orchestrate into the Erato software program. Then I have to mock-up up everything for the director. I use Logic Audio to sequence the stuff so people can hear it back. I've got several samplers and synthesizers, so I can get a really good sound here in my studio.

DO YOU PREFER TO WAIT FOR A FINISHED WORK PRINT OR DO YOU LIKE TO GET INVOLVED AT THE SCRIPT LEVEL?

I like to be involved early on, if possible. I have a really good relationship with Danny DeVito. I've done all the films he's directed since *Throw Momma from the Train*, and I generally get involved with those earlier on. In general, at that early stage of production, I find that it's better to be intellectually involved—not to start writing—because things tend to change so much. I find that the scripts are very much rough plans for what the movie is going to be. They very often don't pan out. To see the color, the imagery, and the visual sort of ambience of the whole thing is such a big part of conceiving the music that it is best to wait for the work print before writing. This is especially true today, where often the music that is wanted is just colors and tones—more textures than melodies.

WHAT WAS IT LIKE DOING THE UNDERSCORE FOR ANASTASIA?

I really liked *Anastasia*. I had a great time. I really liked Bluth and Goldman and it was really a fun thing to do. It was scored just like a traditional film. It wasn't quite finished when I got it; it was all animated but it wasn't colorized. So it was all there, a little hard to see, but not really any different from a regular work print.

DID YOU HAVE TO WORK WITH THE SONGWRITERS AT ALL, OR WERE YOU ON YOUR OWN?

I used all material from the songs because I thought that would be the right artistic choice for the movie. That's what my dad (Alfred Newman) would do with all those Rodgers and Hammerstein musicals like *Carousel* and *The King and I*. I really liked how he interwove the score right with the song, and then right out from the song back into the score. It's one of my favorite things. The seamlessness, taking of themes and developing them into other things, and making the movie seem really unified appeals to me a lot.

WHAT ARE SOME OF YOUR THOUGHTS AND EXPERIENCES ON WORKING WITH DIFFERENT DIRECTORS?

Some directors are really good to collaborate with, and some aren't. The ones that are good—you don't always know that they're good to begin with—tend to push you in a way that you end up with something better than you would have. My collaborations with DeVito have been really good and he pushed me to do different things. But more often than not, you find directors saying, "This scene doesn't work, let's put some music in it." Then it becomes non-collaborative. It can be okay, but you're not really adding anything, you're just getting from one place to another. Mostly they're looking for you to write a melody they really like.

WHAT DO YOU DO WHEN A DIRECTOR HEARS THE MOCK-UPS AND DOES-N'T LIKE THE DIRECTION YOU'VE GONE?

You just talk to them. Nobody's nasty! But if they say that it's definitely not right, that it just doesn't work, then you must talk to them and listen for clues to tell you what they mean by "doesn't work." They're usually not complicated. Most often, it's something like: It's too fast, or too slow; it's too dark, it's too light; I don't like this instrument, it sounds too sentimental, or it doesn't have enough emotion. It's more stuff like that.

WHAT HAPPENS WHEN YOU GET SOMEBODY WHO IS NOT A MUSICIAN, AND CAN'T MAKE THE LEAP FROM LISTENING TO A STANDARD MOCK-UP TO ENVISIONING HOW IT WILL SOUND WITH A REAL ORCHESTRA?

You have to explain to them. You have to educate them a little bit. It's surprising, the music is so much cleaner than it used to be. It often translates just fine. I don't find so much that directors are shocked when they hear the orchestra. That's the way it used to be—you'd play it on the piano, and when they heard the orchestra it was a complete shock. Now I find that it translates actually pretty well.

What's worse is the temp-music phenomenon, where they get so in love with the temp track. In fact, they might not even like the temp music, but they are so used to hearing it that anything else is completely jarring to them. That's more difficult to deal with, and they often won't admit it's the temp score because it's so unhip to say that. It means that their movie is just the same as everybody else's movie. But you learn to listen between the lines.

IT'S LIKE IN RECORD PRODUCTION WITH THE "ROUGH MIX SYNDROME." EVEN IF THERE ARE WRONG NOTES, THEY'VE HEARD THE ROUGH MIX SO MANY TIMES, THEY DON'T HEAR THEM ANYMORE.

Right. It's the same thing. It takes a really strong director to fight that. Most of them, even the strong ones, can't really fight that. With the temp scores they have so much at stake because that's what they use when they preview their movie. There's no scarier time. Because that's when the studio either signs off or doesn't. The scariest time for them is when they are testing their movie.

But as a composer, you have to deal with it. You can't ignore the temp track. Unless you have a really brave director.

ARE YOU CONTENT? DO YOU LIKE DOING WHAT YOU ARE DOING?

You know, I'm not the most calm, contented person in the world. But, composing to me is a relatively new thing. I really love music, and I really like where I am now. It doesn't mean I wouldn't like to do other things, but I really love writing music. I feel that the choice I made to switch from playing to writing was the right thing to do.

David Raksin

David Raksin has been active writing and teaching film music for over sixty years. His first major project was with Charlie Chaplin on *Modern Times*, and he also composed one of the most well-known songs of all time, "Laura," for the movie of the same title. He was one of the most innovative composers in Hollywood during the 1940s, '50s, and '60s; many composers today are still influenced by his scores, as well as his straight forward, honest, and enthusiastic approach to film scoring.

*YOU'VE BEEN INVOLVED IN THIS FIELD SINCE **1935**, FROM THE EARLIEST DAYS OF FILM SCORING ...*

No, no. Remember, there was music in films all the time. As a matter of fact, I remember when it was accompanied by a piano or an organ. Sometimes the organ players were incredibly brilliant.

Later they had orchestras. My father played in one in Philadelphia, and eventually became a conductor of music for silent films. So I was around this stuff from the time I was seven or eight years old. When sound films came in around 1926 things changed. Music became marginally more sophisticated, but not much. Remember there is a tradition around these things, and when one thing moves forward, it doesn't mean everything else does also. When Henry Ford invented the Model T, it didn't mean that horses stopped running around.

THE "ERAS" WE DESIGNATE FOR CLASSICAL MUSIC STYLES ARE LIKE THAT. WE TEND TO WANT TO PUT LINES OF DELINEATION AROUND SIGNIFICANT EVENTS, BUT IT DOESN'T ALWAYS WORK THAT WAY.

Absolutely. The point is that there were composers who carried over from the silent days, as would naturally be the case. They would be accustomed to standing in the pit and playing scores based upon pieces that were already written, which is what my father did. And they brought their own predilections for music, so there was a preponderance of European-derived music. It took a while for things to begin to look up. Eventually, guys like Max Steiner came in, and even though his was a European influence, he started to make some changes. For example, his score to *King Kong* was way ahead of its time. Then Waxman came in, and Korngold came in, and there were a number of other guys.

WHAT WERE THE SCHEDULES LIKE UNDER THE OLD STUDIO SYSTEM?

We did tremendous amounts of music. For instance, when I composed the score for *Forever Amber*, that had about 110 minutes of music—about 100 of those I composed myself. The rest was music of the story's time. Originally I had twelve weeks to do that, but they were messing around with the movie, and by the time they got finished doing that I had eight and a half weeks to do that tremendous amount of music. And I did it!

There were all kinds of crazy things. For instance, one time they were doing a picture called *The Goldwyn Follies*, and George Gershwin was the composer. Right in the middle of it he died, and they brought in Vernon Duke to complete the score. Vernon wrote the various songs, and he also wrote a ballet called *Undine* for the middle of the picture. When Gershwin died, the production had been effectively stopped; the sets were ready, the company was ready, but there was no music for George Balanchine, the choreographer, to work with. So I got a call that afternoon from Eddie Powell to meet him and Hugo Freidhofer at Zardi's Restaurant. After dinner, the three of us went into different rooms at the old

United Artists Studio, and overnight we orchestrated that ballet. That was some job. We got done at 3:00 a.m. and it was recorded later that morning.

HOW DID YOU BREAK IN TO WORKING AT THE STUDIOS?

Charlie Chaplin had made a movie called *Modern Times*. He was a violinist, and he had plenty of musical ideas, but he didn't really know how to develop them. So he always had a composer working with him, you know, a real composer.

HOW DID YOU WORK WITH HIM, DID HE PLAY AND YOU TRANSCRIBE?

No. He would have ideas, mostly fragments, and then we would discuss them. And he didn't always like that, so after a week and a half of that he fired me. I was brokenhearted and about to go home, when Alfred Newman [head of music at United Artists] said to me, "Don't go home. I've been looking at what you've been doing with his little tunes, and he'd be crazy to fire you." So I got a call from the head of Charlie's studio and he said, "We want to hire you back." I said, "No way, not unless I can have an understanding with him." And we came to that understanding. I told him that I wouldn't work for him if I was just going to be a yes man, and he accepted my terms. So I worked four and a half months on that. It is a co-composed score, and that's what started me off.

I had all kinds of offers after that. I had one from Steiner, who wanted me to be his assistant, but I didn't want to be anybody's assistant, so I turned it down, went back to New York, then went to Europe and worked on a show. Then I got various offers, so I came back.

WERE YOU CONTRACTED TO A SPECIFIC STUDIO?

Oh yes, I had several contracts. I was at Fox for quite a while from around 1937 to 1946 when I left. Before that, for about six months, I was under contract to Universal, but we really couldn't stand one another. I thought that their schlock way of doing things was absolutely indefensible. They were very glad to get rid of me, and I was very glad to get the hell out from under.

I also had a contract for a while at MGM, but that was only because I was broke and needed the money. MGM was a hellhole. It was a place where all the bad things said about Hollywood came close to being true. I think that whether it was conscious or not, they wore composers out by pitting the composers against their system.

I'D LIKE TO ASK YOU ABOUT THE SHIFT AWAY FROM THE EUROPEAN STYLE OF COMPOSING TO A MORE MODERN SOUND THAT INCLUDED INFLUENCES OF BARTÓK, STRAVINSKY, AND OTHERS. WHAT WAS YOUR EXPERIENCE OF THIS CHANGE OF STYLES AS IT WAS HAPPENING?

There were other people that influenced it greatly. Our country had a period where it was the world's leading and greatest source of great melodies. It was a time that began in the early twenties and continued into the middle fifties. That was the time of Jerome Kern, and Harold Arlen, and Richard Rodgers, and George Gershwin. There has never been such a time in the history of music anywhere, and I think it is the great glory of our country when that happened, because there has never been such a flowering anywhere else. So we were all influenced very much by these American composers, and we were also influenced by some of the Russian composers, such as Prokofiev, Shostakovich, Rachmaninoff, and people like that. They wrote a kind of music that deserves respect, and we loved it. We would have been idiots not to be affected by it.

And so generally, I am accused of being the guy that started the change going. I doubt very much that I am, but I was one of the very first to do things a completely different way. For instance, in 1936 or 1937 I was working at Universal, and there was a guy there named Lou Forbes, who was so fascinated with what I was doing that he told his brother Leo Forbstein, who was head of music at Warners. And Leo started to employ me there.

WHAT EXACTLY WERE YOU DOING THAT WAS SO DIFFERENT?

The nature of my music was very different. It had all kinds of other influences because I was a guy who loved the music of our time and I was also a jazz player.

I would go over to Warners on the weekends when I wasn't working at Universal, and I would only do chases and fights. I would never see the rest of the picture. One of those was a 58-second montage of boxing. Later, I actually reorchestrated that piece for Leopold Stokowski, who was working at Universal at that time, and he ended up doing it with the Philadelphia Orchestra a few months later. It was probably the first film piece played by a concert orchestra—a jazz piece in $5/4$.

WERE THERE PROBLEMS CONVINCING THE MORE CONSERVATIVE DIRECTORS AND PRODUCERS OF THE VALIDITY OF WHAT YOU WERE DOING?

I was very lucky in that when I was working at Warners, Leo Forbstein was fascinated by what I did. As a matter of fact, I finally got too fascinating for him. I wrote a piece where right in the middle of an *alla breve* meter, I had all these bars of $3/4$, and he couldn't conduct it. He asked me if I could, so I did.

WHEN DID YOU FIRST START TO USE ATONAL AND 12-TONE MUSIC?

I used twelve-tone rows here and there. I did a picture at MGM in 1949 or '50 called *The Man with a Cloak*, and the people at MGM utterly hated the score and wanted to throw it out. Johnny Green, the head of music at the studio, said, "Guys, you don't know what you're doing; this is an extraordinary score." It was also done for a crazy little orchestra. And they wouldn't listen. But all of a sudden, the producer of this film said, "There's something remarkable about this score," and they kept the music in, after a second preview.

Man with a Cloak had a 12-tone row, the first five notes of which spelled E-D-G-A-R. The R became D♭. I saw Johnny Green the next day and he said, "Gee that's a remarkable score, what's that crazy god-damned tune you've got there?" And I said, "Johnny, it's a 12-tone row." He was astonished, and wanted to know why I used a row. I told it was because in this picture you don't find out until the last 45 seconds or so that the hero, the man in the cloak, is really Edgar Allan Poe. So I thought I would start the main title with those five notes because I had the vision of Dore Schary, the head of MGM, coming out and saying, "Fire that son-of-a-bitch, he gave away the secret of the picture in the Main Title."

I had a great time doing the things I was doing. Sometimes I was motivated by jazz, sometimes by contemporary music. You would have to be deaf not to feel the enormous effect of the music of Stravinsky. For me, it was Stravinsky and Berg. So I wrote just the way I thought I should be writing. It was not unanimously accepted.

HOW DO YOU SEE THE EVOLUTION OF FILM-SCORING STYLES IN TERMS OF PRO-DUCERS, DIRECTORS, AND AUDIENCES ACCEPTING NEW SOUNDS?

The interesting thing about film music is that, as a composer, unless you have some idiot for a producer, which happens about two thirds of the time, you can do things that you could never do in a concert hall. There is a counter-validation between the screen and the music. If they heard it in a concert hall, the audience would run screaming, but when they hear it with a picture, the music and the image counter-validate one another. For example, if you have a really violent sequence and you write something that is really dissonant, they might not like to hear that as a piece of music. But they will accept it if it is the right music for a film sequence. That kind of thing opened up the world for a lot of people. So the first generation that was susceptible to films was prepared for newer music by the scores they heard in movie theaters.

AFTER THE SUCCESS OF LAURA, *WERE YOU PLAGUED BY PEOPLE WANT-ING YOU TO DO IT AGAIN?*

Oh yes, everybody wanted me to write another *Laura*, but I would say, "First you have to make me one."

WITHIN A DECADE AFTER LAURA, *TV HAD HIT FULL FORCE. HOW DID THIS AFFECT YOU PERSONALLY?*

There were times when I wasn't working anywhere else, and I was lucky to get television. I think I did my first television in 1950 on *Life with Father*. We all preferred film because it was much more civilized. I once described television as an industry where they manufacture debris. Television really is sad, although it employed the talents of some very, very good people. Many good composers did it, including Jerry Goldsmith, John Williams, and Johnny Green.

WHAT IS YOUR COMPOSING PROCESS, HOW DO YOU GENERATE IDEAS?

What I'm trying to do is to catch the spirit of a picture. And that means sometimes I go contrary to what's on the screen, and sometimes I go with what's on the screen. It's a matter of instinct. If your instincts are good, it's going to work for you.

Lolita Ritmanis

Composer and orchestrator Lolita Ritmanis has worked on more than thirty films and television shows. She has worked as arranger and orchestrator for Michael Kamen, Basil Poledouris, David Benoit, Shirley Walker, and Mark Snow on such projects as *Lethal Weapon 4, X-Files: The Movie,* and *Robin Hood, Prince of Thieves.* She has composed regularly for Warner Bros. animated series, *The New Batman and Superman Adventures,* as well as *Batman Beyond.* Her concert works include choral, solo, ensemble, and orchestral works that have been performed in cities around the world.

WHAT LED YOU TO FILM SCORING?

I grew up in Portland, and the first trip I took down here to Los Angeles was with my parents in my senior year of high school. I had a whole demo tape of songs, and I had stars in my eyes. I wanted the Hollywood experience. I ended up coming down here to go to a small school called The Grove School of Music where I studied jazz arranging and composition. I don't really even know if I ever made a conscious decision, I'm going to be a film composer. I knew I *was* a composer. All my life I was a composer. As a child, when I practiced the piano, I was making up my own little pieces when my mom wasn't looking. After the film-scoring program at Groves I studied composition and orchestration with Mauro Bruno. And I started to get jobs, some more glamorous than others, but to me they were all exciting.

Bruce Babcock gave me a shot at orchestrating a little bit for him on *Matlock*, and that was thrilling. I was also playing in a Top 40 band and working with a community choir. While I was doing all these other things, glad to be making a little bit of money, I got a job at the Warner Bros. music department Xeroxing violin parts. I was thrilled about that. The first day I had to be there, my boss, Joel Franklin, said, "Be here at 9:00 a.m." which is a late call for music library. I was outside the studio gate at about 7:00, with my briefcase and ready to go! From there I progressed to proofreading and orchestrating. All along the way, I had this demo tape I used whenever opportunity presented itself.

AS AN ORCHESTRATOR, WHAT IS IT LIKE WORKING WITH DIFFERENT COMPOSERS WHO HAVE VERY DIFFERENT WORKING STYLES? SOME GIVE YOU VERY COMPLETE SKETCHES, AND SOME ARE BARE-BONES.

It's very different in each individual situation. There are certainly composers that are incredibly gracious and grateful, and they acknowledge you, even at the scoring date. They might announce to the orchestra, "Oh so-and-so orchestrated this cue. Let's hear it for so-and-so." They sometimes acknowledge the soloists in the orchestra, and the good work of many people involved.

There are some orchestrators that tend to think that, because they have been given only melody and chords, they are writing the music. I'm not one of those. Whatever you're going to hum after hearing a particular cue, that's usually, hopefully, the composer's work. Every situation is different. There are many composers who don't really need an orchestrator—their sketches are absolutely complete. And some of the composers who run into the time crunch are also capable of doing very complete sketches. It is merely that the accelerated post-production schedules often do not leave time for detailed sketching.

I am only recently getting into the world of computers—MIDI files and notation programs. When I'm orchestrating from digital files, first I listen to a DAT that the composer provides, and get a feeling of the music. Then it's my job to translate it to make it work for the orchestra. And it's really exciting. I don't think that there is even one step in this whole journey that I've been on that I've really just been pulling out my hair, "Oh, how horrible this is." I've really enjoyed a lot of it, most of it, and I feel very fortunate.

DO YOU STILL USE PENCIL AND PAPER?

That's my favorite way to work. I can't imagine giving it up. It's so much faster for me. I can see the score right under my hands. If you've done it that way I don't know if you can ever completely switch to computers.

HAS DIGITAL TECHNOLOGY AFFECTED THE FINAL PRODUCT?

Yes, and with digital editing for picture, they can makes changes so close up to the last minute, you have to be ready for that, and be able to make changes at the scoring session. It's frustrating though, because many of us try to do things the right way, the proper way, sketch nicely, figure out accurate timings on either Auricle or Performer, and make things right. Not too late, not too early, just right. It can be frustrating when people make changes and your score gets all marked up. A cue gets completely changed around from what you originally thought it would be because the picture has been altered at the last minute.

IT SOUNDS LIKE YOU'VE COME TO A PLACE OF DETACHMENT ABOUT THE WORK THAT YOU DO, KNOWING THAT ANYTHING COULD HAPPEN TO IT.

On some of the really high-profile kind of pandemonium moments, you have to be detached. It's part of the job to apply yourself 100%, and let the chips fall where they may. Because if you get too worried about it, it's not going to do anyone any good. You are hired not only for your orchestration abilities, but for your professionalism in stressful situations.

IT MUST BE A REAL THRILL TO HEAR YOUR MUSIC, AS AN ORCHESTRATOR AND AS A COMPOSER, PLAYED BY SUCH INCREDIBLE MUSICIANS.

It is. I forget and sometimes I have to pinch myself and realize "Oh my goodness, this is amazing." These are the best players, and the best sight-readers, in the world. Absolutely the best sight-readers. The mistakes quotient is: there is hardly ever a mistake.

DO YOU ENJOY ORCHESTRATING?

Yes. And I do have to say that I'm not ready to give it up. There usually is a time for a composer where you have to say, "That's enough, I need to be the composer now." But you do say good-bye to quite a bit of income at that point. And I know several people who have done that.

IT'S HARD TO MAKE THE TRANSITION?

Yes, because there are only so many hours in the day. And if you're orchestrating on a feature for a couple weeks, that's full time. If you're under a deadline as a composer, that's full time. What to do? There are only twenty-four hours in a day.

There are people who will swear to you that if you're a TV composer you'll never get to do features. "Don't do this and don't do that." Well, it's hard because when a gig comes along and it's offered to you, and you have a chance to use your craft and your skills and do something other than waiting tables. And if it's in TV, why not?

DOES BEING A WOMAN IN THIS BUSINESS ENTER INTO THE EQUATION AT ALL?

I do know that, for me as a woman composer, sometimes there has been a request made, "We want a tape from a woman composer." That's been something that people say I should play up more. I should market myself because I'm a woman composer. I have yet to this day, to my face, been discriminated against because of that.

I think that ten years ago, fifteen years ago, there was much more a big deal made out of "Oh, so-and-so is a woman composer." So I do have to thank my predecessors for paving the way.

I think women sometimes get an edge because there are a lot of woman producers and directors out there. But it's still in this phase where some women directors and producers that have climbed up to a pretty high level don't want to be told they should use a woman composer. There's a little of this backlash. Once somebody recommended that I contact this particular woman composer, not Shirley Walker, and she was quite offended that this person said I should call her based on the fact that we're both women composers. She said something like, "What, why does he think I can do something for you just because I'm a woman?"

BUT THAT'S JUST A BACKLASH.

I don't even think about it that much. I think the bigger issue is your family life and how much time you dedicate to making your career happen versus living your life. I mean, at five o'clock, there's not a bell that rings and your career goes on hold. For me, family comes first.

DO YOU THINK THAT PROBLEMS EXIST IN A DIFFERENT DIMENSION FOR YOU AS A WOMAN THAN IT WOULD FOR MEN WITH FAMILIES?

It did more when my kids were babies. My children go to school now. It's a little different from when the kids were infants. I mean, who wants to take a breast pump to Warner Bros. for a session? And tell people you need to pump your milk during a ten-minute break. But I know session players who do it. It's part of life. There are things to consider. Marriage, having a healthy marriage has helped me a great deal. But it takes time. It takes maybe losing a gig here and there, or altering a plan to make it work. For example, during this last Christmas break I was orchestrating a television movie for David Benoit and the deadline kept getting moved. At first it was going to be right before Christmas, and everything would have been wrapped up nice and tidy so I could have my break. Well, it didn't happen that way. I took my Omnifax with me up to Portland to my parent's house. It was snowing the next day, and it was very surreal to be working where I grew up, and having this fax machine and a PowerBook with MIDI files. The kids are playing out in the snow, and Mom's in headphones trying to orchestrate some music and then fax it back to L.A. so it can get copied.

ARE YOU HAPPY WITH WHERE YOU ARE AT AS A COMPOSER?

A personal goal for me is to allow my voice to be heard, and to never stop learning and growing. I've had many great opportunities, and very few regrets. It is easy to sometimes disappear in the Hollywood film-music machine and to forget how wonderful it is to write music—just for the love of writing music.

As a composer it's important to let yourself write what comes to you, and write what inspires you. And not belittle that because people are telling you, "It has to be this way, it has to be that way. You should be doing this, or how can you do that?" You don't have to be what everybody tells you that you have to be. You choose much of your path, I believe.

This business is very exciting, and the people that discourage new composers or any composers that want to come out and give it a try, I think they're wrong. If you want to do it, you can do it. You just have to work really, really hard and be patient. And find little things along the way that will boost your spirits. There are plenty of little things out there, not just the big movies.

William Ross

William Ross is a composer whose work spans feature films, television, and the recording industry. He has composed music for films including *Tin Cup*, *My Fellow Americans*, *The Evening Star*, *The Little Rascals*, and the IMAX film *T-Rex*. His orchestration credits include *Forrest Gump*, *Contact*, *Mouse Hunt*, *The Bodyguard*, *Waiting to Exhale*, and *Father of the Bride*. He continues to work with a remarkable list of artists including Barbra Streisand, Celine Dion, Kenny G., David Foster, and Babyface.

HOW DID YOU DECIDE TO BECOME A FULL-TIME MUSICIAN AND ULTIMATELY A FILM COMPOSER?

I grew up studying piano, and I was fascinated by it, but I never had any notion that you could do that for a living. My parents were very blue-collar, and from the wrong side of the tracks. The notion of making a living at anything other than work—hard work—was ridiculous. My Mom wanted me to go to college, and my Dad wanted me to go into the Merchant Marines and be the captain of a ship. I decided to go to UCSB where I was pre-med— I always had a fascination with sciences. But there was so much that went on with my life at college—socially, intellectually, personally—trying to figure out, "Oh, wait a minute, now I'm away from home, what is life about, how do I orient myself in this world and make confident decisions for myself in the present and future?" I just kind of broke down. I got to the point where I couldn't go to the labs anymore. The smell of ether just nauseated me. Chemistry class … just the thought of it …

I was playing blues piano at fraternities and having fun with it. But I got to the point where I was so unable to determine what step I should take next, that I almost had a nervous breakdown. I came to the conclusion that I have to do today what I really enjoy doing. It sounds like a weird approach, but that's how I got out of it. I didn't look much further beyond "today." Then the next day was great, and I just built on that, one day at a time.

I spoke to a counselor at the school, and knew that there wasn't much future in being a blues piano player. Eventually I switched my major to Anthropology, which is what I got my degree in. So, I'm licensed to dig up your bones!

HOW DID YOU EDUCATE YOURSELF AND GO FROM BLUES PIANO PLAYER TO ORCHESTRATOR?

Just because of the way my mind works, I'm kind of an analytical guy; my way of studying was to get scores and look at them and break them apart. And there was an interesting thing I found. One of the things composers in European conservatories had to do in the past was to be able to write certain key pieces by memory. Like a piece from the *Art of the Fugue* or *The Well-Tempered Clavier*. Many composers mention this thing: that the act of writing it down somehow transformed them. Prokofiev, Ravel, and Mendelssohn all mention it in their writings. Something happens when you are actually forced to sit and write it down; the information comes in and is ordered in a way that you mentally have access to it. When you just buy the book and stick it on your shelf, you don't get the same familiarity with it.

I strongly believe that there is a lot of benefit in trying to understand what has come before, what makes something a masterpiece, what makes something valuable to so many people over a long period of time. I would study anything I could get my hands on. Ravel, Beethoven.

I would also take a piece and make myself write something in that style. Ravel talks about taking a great piece as a model being a legitimate way to improve your abilities and skills. Find great pieces, use them as models, and they will pull you up to their level.

How did you get your first orchestration jobs?

Allyn Ferguson got me my first job arranging and conducting for Raquel Welch, and I started getting credits writing charts. I did whatever I could to study film scores in my spare time. My first job orchestrating was for *Dynasty*, a job which came through a friend. Then I hooked up with Dennis McCarthy and started working on *MacGyver*. What a school that was! Dennis was terrific. He would let you take the ball and run with it and compose the cues, and he'd give you full writing credit. So then I had composition and orchestration credit.

I started to get a reputation as a guy who could get the job done and not create problems. The name of the game is to be a problem solver, not a problem creator. That is what a film composer is looking for. The composer wants to be able to say, "I've got so much on my mind, if I can just hand this to this guy and know it's going to work," that's what they're all looking for. There's this giant level of trust. If you get on that list of people that are easy to get along with, does the job, is not a jerk, and can deliver, then your name gets around.

What is the process for you as an orchestrator?

After I get the call, usually the first step is that a meeting is set up. The challenge is to understand the composer's working style, and to figure out how I'm going to fit into that. The composer may know exactly what they want and hand me a sketch where I'm just going to just transfer the notes onto a different sheet of paper and send it to the copyist. Or they may really need a lot of help because they don't have an orchestral background and that's what they've been asked to do. The first thing is to identify what the job really is. That is a big part of it.

Once you identify what the job is, you have to figure out if this job is for you. Are you comfortable doing it? Your pay thing has to work out. Usually when you first start out, you're so glad to be in the meeting and get the credit that the pay is kind of meaningless. My recommendation is to get that taken care of ahead of time. It took me a long time to learn this, but there is nothing wrong with talking about the money.

LET'S TALK ABOUT YOUR COMPOSING PROCESS. DO YOU WRITE TO PAPER, OR ARE YOU SEQUENCING?

That depends on the nature of the score. I relate best to paper. My set-up at home has a lot of different areas to it. My central core is the piano, a piece of paper, and a pencil. I like a period of time when I can sit and germinate ideas, and think about it in an unhurried fashion. Ideally, a week is paradise. Sometimes you get more, most of the time you get less, depending on the schedules.

Those ideas filter through in various ways. I could use a piano, or synthesizers. Auricle is also a great tool, whether it's click or free timing. It's a great way to get the streamers to film. I also have this Erato system, which is a computerized notation system.

WHAT ABOUT THE "MOVE TO L.A." ISSUE FOR YOUNG COMPOSERS?

That's a tough one, and one that I address with a lot of empathy. Most people are driven to this business out of love for music and film; they're not out to get rich, at least when they start. It's a hard thing to come out here, with the uncertainties of the business, to uproot yourself, to challenge yourself. To me, anyone who does that is a success no matter what happens. I say that with utmost sincerity. I've had people call me after years of being out here, they had kicked around the business, they did the best they could, and they were out of money. Or just fed up. And it broke my heart to hear them say they were leaving, they were calling to say goodbye.

I think we are in a business where you are a person first, and somewhere down the line you are a composer. But the top of the list for me is what kind of person you are, how you treat people, do you get along with people. That's got to be in place. So I approach it from the human point of view. That being said, the reality is that most of the people in the business are here in Los Angeles. So it's really an unanswerable question.

Marc Shaiman

AUTHOR'S NOTE: MOST OF THE COMPOSER BIOS FOR THIS BOOK WERE EDITED AND SHORTENED, BUT MARK'S OFFICIAL BIO IS SO DELIGHTFUL, WE DECIDED TO INCLUDE IT IN ITS ORIGINAL FORM.

Marc Shaiman very much enjoyed composing the music and cowriting the lyrics for *Hairspray* with Scott Wittman. For their score, the pair won the Tony, Grammy and Olivier Awards. Their next Broadway score was for *Martin Short—Fame Becomes Me*, for which they won absolutely nothing.

As a composer and arranger, Marc's film credits date back to the silents and include *When Harry Met Sally*, *Beaches*, *Misery*, *City Slickers*, *The Addams Family*, *A Few Good Men*, *Sister Act*, *Sleepless in Seattle*, *The First Wives Club*, *Patch Adams*, *The American President*, *George of the Jungle*, *South Park: Bigger, Longer & Uncut*, and *The Bucket List*. He has been nominated five times for an Oscar and lost every time.

As her music director and co-producer, Marc brought his long time partner Bette Midler the Grammy winning songs "The Wind Beneath My Wings" and "From a Distance," but it is their collaboration on her Emmy Award-winning performance for Johnny Carson's penultimate *Tonight Show* that will always remain a dream. He auditioned but was not chosen to play himself on her sitcom.

Besides the Carson moment, having recently co-written and appeared with both Nathan Lane and Billy Crystal for their respective musical bon voyages to Conan O'Brien and Jay Leno on both of their farewell shows, Marc recently became a figure of trivia, a one man walking *Jeopardy* question and most certainly the kiss of death to any talk show host who sees him approaching with a musical tribute under his arm.

Marc was Emmy nominated for writing on *Saturday Night Live* (the Sweeney Sisters) and an actual Emmy Award winner for co-writing Billy Crystal's medleys for *The Academy Awards*. His arrangements for Harry Connick Jr. were Grammy-nominated, as was the *Hairspray* soundtrack, and he has worked with many other artists, including Will Ferrell, Jack Black, Eric Clapton, Kristen Chenoweth, Jennifer Holiday, Jenifer Lewis, Patti LuPone, John Mayer, Barbra Streisand, Rob Thomas, Raquel Welch and, well, basically everyone in show biz.

Marc's Internet sensation, the "Webbie"-winning *PROP 8-The Musical*, had been viewed over four million times (@funnieordie.com) on, ironically, January 3rd, 2009, which was his and Scott Wittman's 30th Anniversary as a couple.

WHO ARE YOUR FILM SCORING AND SONGWRITING INFLUENCES? WHO ARE THE PEOPLE THAT YOU WOULD PUT ON YOUR CD PLAYER IF YOU WERE HANGING OUT?

All of them. I love everything. There's very few things that I've ever used the word "dislike" or "hate" for. It's all music and lyrics, and what's not to like? My first influences were Broadway musicals like *The Sound of Music* or *Oliver!* As I got older, I listened to everything: pop music, Motown, you name it.

THIS WAS GROWING UP IN NEW JERSEY? THEN WHAT HAPPENED?

The big revelation was when I started playing piano for community theater. Then my head really exploded with, "Oh my God, listen to these songs and feel those chords." And also, like, "Oh, listen to what those flutes are doing!" and "Why do those strings make me want to shiver?" (I later learned that was tremolo strings.) And you know, learning by those piano vocal scores that you get to do at a show in community theater, really getting to listen to the cast album and see what the trombones are doing and where the string lines are; that was my school. I'm jealous of people who get to go to Berklee and learn all that information. Oh my God, I can't think of anything more fantastic. But the grass is always greener, and everything worked out for me.

SO, YOU HAD NO STRICT FORMAL SCHOOL MUSIC TRAINING?

I had piano lessons as a kid. I was playing professionally at sixteen. I was given some Bette Midler records as a present after a junior high school variety show by the music teacher. And her records, and all this explosion of musical theater that I was being exposed to really filled my head. And then, the pop music of the day. I mean, I was just full of music. Then lucky breaks, one after another, that can't ever be duplicated by anyone else that still continue to amaze me.

AND THEN TO NEW YORK CITY?

The story is, I went to New York one day with a friend and ran into some other friends from New Jersey. I was just sixteen years old. It was in the afternoon in Greenwich Village, there was a bar right there on the corner, and we went in there because it was empty. I sat down to play at the piano because I was sixteen years old and always just wanted to play. The bartender was sweeping up, like out of an MGM movie, and he said, "Hey, kid! You're good!" He went next door where there was a comedy review rehearsing that needed a new piano player with a sense of humor. And they came in and said, "Can you play 'Together Wherever We Go' cheesy?" I said, "Oh, you mean like the way they do at a bar mitzvah?" They totally got that! And so we hit it off, and I would come and play for them and stay with them on the weekends,

AND THAT LED TO BETTE MIDLER?

These comedians lived across the hall from one of Bette Midler's backup singers, who were called the Harlettes. The Harlettes wanted to do their own act when they weren't on the road with Bette, and because I was a fanatic Bette Midler fan (I guess that's redundant!), lived across the hall, and was sixteen (or maybe at that point seventeen) and was not concerned about negotiating, I was cheap and I was there. So I became the Harlettes' musical director. And thank God, that act became a success on the cabaret circuit in New York, L.A., and San Francisco, because Bette then said, "Come back on the road with me, girls, and I'll let you open the show with your act." So, maybe just a little more than a year after moving to New York, I got to be opening for Bette.

Now the amazing thing is that my ultimate dream as a kid was to play for Bette and become her piano player, arranger, and then musical director, producer, and CD producer. When I was between thirteen and sixteen, I'd go to see her concerts and I would fanticize about running down the aisle and jumping on to the piano, pushing aside the piano player, and playing. She'd be sitting on the piano, looking at the audience, and go, "He's good!" and I would say, "Oh, Ms. Midler, I know every note of every arrangement of all your records."

So amazingly enough, just a short time later, I'm in a rehearsal hall here in L.A. getting ready to open for her with the Harlettes, and she decided to do a song that wasn't in her book. Really! The piano player didn't know it, and one of the Harlettes pointed to me! Bette said, "Do you know this song?" And I went, "Oh, Ms. Midler, I know every note of every arrangement of all your records." So there I was, actually living this dream I had had years ago. It all went forward from there.

So how did you get to films from there?

Well, a story I haven't shared much is that my first film-scoring moment actually ended in tatters. What happened was I went to help Bette one day when she was filming a movie called *Big Business*, and the script said she needed to yodel in front of a steel drum band on the street, and somehow they hadn't planned for it. There was no arrangement, there was no click track, there was no playback. They literally had hired a band that was an actual band on the street, and Bette was supposed to just show up and yodel over their song. So luckily she called me like on a Friday, she was like, "I gotta yodel, I have a cassette of what this band's going to be playing, help me figure this out." So I went on that Monday, had figured it out, and I kind of saved the day.

Suddenly I was hanging out on the movie set, and everyone seemed rather nice and accessible, and I just said, "How does someone audition to score a movie? I think I'd love to score movies!" And they laughed at me like, "Oh, you don't audition," but they were somehow charmed by my naïvité and were actually grateful for what I had done for them that one day, and so they actually *did* send me some scenes from the movie, and said, "Here, send us what you would write." So I did, and to my surprise I got hired to score this big-budget film based on what I had written, which was a very late 1950s to early 1960s business-gal-in-Manhattan kind of music. Once I got to L.A., it turned out they didn't want anything at all like what I auditioned with! They wanted something like *Beverly Hills Cop*. When they told me what it was they wanted, I said, "Guys, this isn't at all what you hired me on!" And their response was, "What you sent us proved you were talented, but we want something else here." So Jeffrey Katzenberg, the head of Disney, came to see the first test screening which had a temp score that only had a few minutes of my original music. All he could say was, "That's all the wrong music. Who's scoring this movie?" And they said, "Oh, it's this kid who never scored a movie before." So, he basically said, "No way!" Well, I pleaded and pleaded saying, "I agree, just let me have a chance to play him what I think it should be like." So a few days later, I got to go play him three different versions of three scenes at 6:30 in the morning, which was the only time he could slot me in. After that, they discussed it, and they brought me back in and he said, "Well, you're clearly talented with lots of ideas, but I need someone who has the experience to take charge."

But I still was working with Bette on *Beaches*, so I had to suck it up and still go and work with Bette for the same company, Touchstone. And I had the great good fortune to be the one who brought her the song "Wind Beneath My Wings," which was a milestone in her career—her first number one single, and it became her iconic song.

SO WHAT WERE YOUR FIRST FILM-SCORING SUCCESSES?

That came out of doing *Saturday Night Live*. There I was, working with Bette Midler in New York, writing musicals. None of them ever got the big break, but by writing a lot and getting a reputation for myself as a composer I became friends with one or two people at *SNL*. They started needing a piano player, as Paul Schaffer had moved on. So I would get these calls where they would say, "Hey, can you come in and help us with this or that?" And the year that Billy Crystal and Marty Short and Chris Guest were there, I started going up there a lot just to hang out with those three, and sit in a room and make up ridiculous funny songs. That led to my relationship with Billy Crystal and he asked me to go on the road with him. Even though he was a comedian. I would score some of his monologues, underscore fashion.

One day, while they were making *When Harry Met Sally*, Billy asked the director Rob Reiner, "What are you doing for music on this movie?" Rob said, "I need someone, I think I want to do standards." And Billy said, "Boy, have I got the guy! You know, Marc, you saw him play for my act, he's perfect." So I ended up doing that, and Bette's movie career also was taking off, and suddenly she was doing *Beaches* and she dragged me along happily to help choose the songs.

The first real score I did was *Misery*, also for Rob Reiner, who just trusted in me, and I suddenly had a film-score career that I never really had dreamt about. And then, thank God for Billy Crystal, he brought me into a meeting for *City Slickers* with the director Ron Underwood, and that worked out great. Then the producer Scott Rudin, who always has his ear to the ground, he was hearing about me, and he brought me into an *Addams Family* meeting. Suddenly I had a run of it for several years where almost every movie I did was a huge success—a crazy streak of luck.

I ALSO WANT TO ASK YOU ABOUT YOUR PROCESS WHEN YOU ARE WRITING. FIRST OF ALL, DO YOU LIKE TO SEE THE TEMP TRACK, OR WOULD YOU RATHER SEE THE MOVIE JUST RAW?

It's a double-edged sword. Sometimes it helps, sometimes it hurts. The temp track can allow you to have a conversation with the director that actually is musical instead of trying to verbalize abstract musical concepts. I sometimes go in and actually help with the temp score because, as I like to describe it, it's like a duel, and you're getting to choose your weapons. On *Misery*, I think he used mostly Jerry Goldsmith stuff for the temp, and I was like, "Oh my God, listen to this dense stuff… listen to those chords," It was so beyond what I thought I could do.

It was a school for me. There was no way I could imitate it and match it, but I could do my own version of, "Oh, I see that, if strings are doing this…," and I would go and try to create my own version of that. So on *Misery*, the temp score was a blessing, at first. On other projects, sometimes it gets really nit-picky, where the director wants you to mimic every single move, every note, every chord change in the temp track. That's where the temp track is a curse, not a blessing.

How MUCH PLANNING DO YOU DO THEMATICALLY?

In the beginning, I would write a thousand themes for the director, and that would be the first part of the process. He or she would come over, and we would sit and play those themes against scenes in the movie. And we would go through all of these themes and choose among them, and then I'd start writing. But the more and more I started doing it, and the more confident I was, I would just sort of really start scoring the movie. So as my career progressed, directors would come over, and I would have already mocked up or written piano versions of scenes with what I thought was the right thematic material. Then we could discuss and make changes from there.

I'M INTERESTED TO KNOW THE EVOLUTION OF HAIRSPRAY, IN TERMS OF WHERE YOUR INVOLVEMENT STARTED AND HOW IT ALL GOT GOING.

I was getting pretty burnt out, and just when I was ready for a break from film scoring, luckily, a woman named Margo Lion called me and said, "I've gotten the rights to John Waters' movie *Hairspray*, and I think that would be a great musical." Now, bizarrely enough, ten years earlier, Scott Rudin, who I had worked with before, had bought the rights to *Hairspray* but never pursued it. So when Margo called, ten years later, out of the blue, she barely finished the question, and I said "Yes. Yes. Yes." But she was only asking me to write music. And she said "Who would you want to write lyrics?" and I said "Me. Me and my partner Scott are very good lyricists, and I don't want to do it unless it's us." And from that phone call on, it was a fairytale, just being so well matched for the material that Scott and I could just write songs [snaps] like that! And the first four songs we wrote are still like the tent poles of the musical.

SO, YOU ALSO WRITE LYRICS?

I co-write or write the lyrics to everything I've ever worked on that has lyrics, and yet people just think of me as a strictly music person. And I guess if they see two names, most songwriting teams are a music person and a lyrics person. When I wrote *South Park*, it was the same thing. Music and lyrics, both of us, but on that one, people assume I wrote the music and Trey Parker wrote the lyrics, but it is absolutely not the case. Trey writes brilliant music. And I love lyric writing. We were a team. But lyric writing can be more fulfilling because the music is a gift that just kind of pours out of me.

SO WHAT WOULD HAPPEN, YOU WOULD WRITE THE SONGS, AND DEMO THEM WITH A SINGER, OR WOULD YOU DO A FULLY PRODUCED DEMO?

Yeah, I'm an overachiever perfectionist type, I don't see any line between arranging then orchestrating then composing. It's all one big ball of wax that helps put an emotion or story across. So my demos went full out, unless all I needed was the piano. By the time we finished writing the score, it was already orchestrated, and the demos were so produced that they really helped sell the show. We could send those CDs out, and it sounded like a cast album. As a matter of fact, the irony is, because you have to write for the pit band—a smaller group of musicians that have to be able to get through the show in one sitting—my demos were more fully orchestrated than the Broadway cast album or the Broadway version. It wasn't until the movie that I got to go back to my demos and really let any idea fly. So suddenly, on the movie, it was absolutely kid-in-a-candy-store time. It was just the greatest three months. Musically speaking, orchestrating the *Hairspray* movie was just a fantastic time.

WHAT WOULD BE A FAVORITE MOMENT OF YOURS?

The song "Welcome to the '60s." The scene was her trying to talk her mother into going to the clothes store, and Travolta's acting in the scene of being just kind of sad and not wanting to go, not knowing how to join her daughter with the joy that her daughter is trying to express in the song. So, I had this little puzzle, which was really fun to work out, which was, how can the strings play the mother and still give us a sense of melancholy? All the while, we are in the midst of this Motown sounding song, and then, little by little, those strings change as her mood changes. But I loved that challenge. And it's very subtle.

TELL ME ABOUT LIFE AS A GAY MAN IN LOS ANGELES IN THE ENTERTAINMENT WORLD.

I've been lucky enough to say that I have practically never been exposed to face-to-face bigotry about being a gay. Once, when I was teenager, one of my sister's friends wrote "fag" on a piece of music. I remember that. And then there's where I am today. Nothing in between that. I've been very lucky to live in that bubble of New York and Los Angeles and a community of people for whom it doesn't matter. I mean, straight or gay, it's all just normal. We don't even think about it. I'm happy to be gay! I mean, the things that seem to come with it, as much as it is cliché or a stereotype, a lot of it is true. Like the ability to find humor in all things, which is also a Jewish thing, I think (talk about stereotypes!). But, to find the beauty in things and to be able to create beautiful things or moving things, I wouldn't give it up for anything. So, if my being gay is, in any way, part of that molecular structure where all the other stuff comes from, I'd be happy to do it all over again.

SO HOW DOES THIS INFLUENCE YOUR MUSIC?

The way it does apply to music is the fact that the more in touch you are with yourself, the more you can express yourself freely. That has to do with accepting who you are and not be thinking about having to hide or even adjust who you are. Of course, you do have to adjust who you are, in the sense that you go to a meeting and you can't be the same person you are when you're out with your friends at night. But, it is important to never actually feel like you are, well, in the closet in any way—that there is any hiding who you are. How can you write music and be dishonest? You won't write good emotional music, which is what the movies call for.

WHAT ARE YOUR THOUGHTS ABOUT WHAT MUSIC AND BEING A MUSICIAN ARE REALLY ALL ABOUT?

Your question reminds me of something that I've been thinking about a lot. I've caught a lot of flak in the past few months, speaking out for gay rights. People have even accused me of hating God. My church happens to be music. To me, music is proof of God every second of my life. Who else could have created music? How could something like this exist without there being a God? And to me, the piano is my pulpit, or the blank page for lyrics is my sermon. And a singer, what could be more religious than hearing a singer—any human being—make a joyful noise? And then I get to write something for someone and get to hear it coming out of their mouth. They're all religious experiences, and I get to have that every day in my life.

Alan Silvestri

Alan Silvestri has provided a distinct melodic voice for many of Hollywood's most well-known films. Starting out as a guitar player, his first regular scoring gig was for the network television series, *CHiPs*. He received Oscar and Golden Globe nominations for his score to *Forrest Gump* and has scored over sixty films, including *Contact*, *Romancing the Stone*, *Who Framed Roger Rabbit?*, *The Bodyguard*, *Father of the Bride I* and *II*, *Practical Magic*, *The Parent Trap*, and the *Back to the Future* series.

HOW DID YOU GET STARTED WRITING FOR FILMS?

I had gone to Berklee, got a gig touring, and through a long series of chance events ended up in L.A. My first film happened because of a case of mistaken identity.

I was working with a lyricist as an arranger on a number of songs. He got called to do this film, *The Doberman Gang*, because the producers misread the credits (he was an academy-award nominated lyricist) and mistook him for a film composer. The lyricist in turn called me and asked if I was interested. I said yes, even though I knew nothing about film scoring. This was all happening really fast, and my meeting with the producers was the very next day. So I went out and bought Earl Hagen's book, *Scoring for Film*, and read it cover to cover that night. When I went to this meeting and we watched the film, I found that I had strong opinions about what the music should be. They liked my ideas, and I got the gig. I was a film composer!

My first big break came a few years later, when I came home one day and there was a message from a Harry Lojewski at MGM. So I called this man, a very nice guy, and I said, "What's up Mr. Lojewski?" He said, "Well, there's this show here at the studio, it's been around for a season, it showed promise, but we couldn't say that it did well and the people at the studio here want to take a different approach to it. They've hired a new staff, and they've asked me to find a young guy who can do the score for this show."

Now, this was in the middle of the disco craze, and I had rather long hair, I was about 28, I probably weighed about 120 lbs., I looked perfect. I looked perfect! I'm not some old establishment guy, or any of that; I'm a young guy who's a rhythm-section player.

It turns out that the show he was talking about was CHiPs. They really wanted to see if they could do a disco thing. So I wrote a score for that first episode of their second season—the one where they put Eric Estrada in a John Travolta suit and send him to the disco. Lo and behold, this show takes off almost immediately. I get a call from them that they want me to do the next three episodes, and this was like the end of the world to my wife Sandra and I because this is the closest thing to a steady job in show business that I've ever heard of. So that's how that all came about.

YOUR CONNECTION WITH ROBERT ZEMECKIS SEEMS TO BE VERY SPECIAL. HOW DID IT COME ABOUT?

Well, that's kind of interesting. I had done CHiPs for four years, and then it abruptly ended. I was out of work for almost a year, and was starting to go a little crazy. I did a couple of TV episodes for a show that the producers hated, and I started to wonder if I really was going to continue in this business.

In addition, I had a house, and a baby that literally had just arrived! Not only that, but when I got the news about them not caring for the music for the television show, my baby was in intensive care, and we were on the verge of losing her. I got the message while I was in the hospital, if that's not too dramatic for you.

So, after this year of nothing, I was thinking, "It can't get any worse than this." But I get a call one day about writing a piece of spec music for a new series at Warner Bros. I went to see the show, called *Blue Thunder*, and walked out of the theater realizing that I didn't even have a way to go about making a spec piece of music. I had a 2-track tape recorder. How could I even do this without spending a bunch of money? Money I didn't have. So the revelation was, if I'm going to try to make a go of this music thing, I need to find a way to show what I can do. At this point in the mid-'80s, things were just starting to happen in the electronic-music world.

My wife and I had a family meeting, and we decided that I should go out and buy the latest technology: a DX-7, which had only been out a few months and came with a Japanese manual, an 8-track tape recorder, and a Linn drum machine.

So now I've got these three pieces of gear, and one Friday afternoon the phone rings. It's Tom Carlin, who was the music editor on CHiPs. He says, "Al, would you be interested in doing something on spec?" I said, "Absolutely." He then says, "Okay, here's the deal. These guys have a movie. They've listened to a lot of tapes of people, and they still haven't found anything that they feel really works for them. If you'd be interested to try something, then let me introduce you to somebody. The director is a guy named Bob Zemeckis and the film is called *Romancing the Stone.*"

So Zemeckis told me about this one scene where they are running through the jungle and it's raining and they're trying to get away from the Federales. I got off the phone, I walked into my new studio. What I had staring in front of me was an 8-track machine, a Linn Drum machine, a DX-7. I'm not a piano player. I had no board to mix with, no work-print to see the film, and I had to bring them a tape the next morning!

I spent all night on this; I actually mixed it by making the RCA cables longer if I wanted a certain track softer. I didn't have to get up the next morning, because it *was* morning, and all I had to do is walk out to the car. I got to the studio and the first thing that happened was that Tom wanted to listen to the cassette, because he had recommended me, now he's on the line. Next thing I know, Bob Zemeckis marches in with his editor. The great coincidence in this story is that Bob and I were wearing the identical Calvin Klein sweater. It was kind of like an omen. It was the beginning of what I consider to be one of my great friendships.

DID THEY OFFER YOU THE GIG RIGHT THEN AND THERE?

No. Michael Douglas, who starred and produced the movie, called me that night. He asked me to send a demo reel. It's kind of interesting that when you're doing this job, you're selling your product, but you're also selling yourself. What counts the most is the impression that people have of you, the level of trust that they have in you, and everything else that goes with it.

The second I hung up the phone that night I realized that I had failed Marketing 101. Even though I felt incredibly empowered and confident that I could get work with my new gear to demo stuff, I was still going up against guys that had more impressive credit sheets and recording histories. I understood, at that point, that the phone call wasn't enough, what I needed to do was get into a room with Michael. That was my only hope.

I somehow got in touch with him, and told him I was going to be nearby Fox the next day and could drop the tape off, as opposed to sending it. He said, "Well, what time are you coming by Fox tomorrow." And I said, "Anytime you want!" Now, Michael is the kind of guy who appreciates somebody who's trying to extend himself for something that he really wants. He said "Okay Al, why don't you come to my office at 11 o'clock tomorrow." So that's what I did. I walked in and brought these tapes. Michael was incredibly gracious to me, and we had the meeting, but the most important thing was that I got to be in the room with him. Whether it was that afternoon or the following day, I don't remember, but the call came through, and I was hired by Michael Douglas to do *Romancing the Stone*.

LET'S TALK A BIT ABOUT SOME OF YOUR MORE RECENT WORK. THERE IS ONE SCENE IN FORREST GUMP *THAT IS INTRIGUING: WHEN YOUNG* FORREST *IS RUNNING FROM THE BAD KIDS WHO ARE THROWING ROCKS AT HIM, AND HIS LEG BRACES GO FLYING OFF.*

That is a really interesting cue from several perspectives. The start of that cue was a decision. Many people, including myself, may have started that cue when we first saw the bad boys, they may have started that cue when the rock hit Forrest's head, they may have started that cue after Jenny said, "Run." I didn't want to just jump in there with music. It deserved more than that. So, the question really was, What's this cue ultimately going to be about?" Well, that cue is ultimately about the celebration of someone who thought they had an infirmity, and to their surprise, they discovered that they didn't. When you consider what to do with the music on that level, all bets are off on the obvious stuff.

The cue basically comes in out of nowhere. He's already started to run, but that's okay because this isn't a running cue; this is a cue about the awakening of a realization in Forrest that something he thought was an infirmity, in fact, doesn't exist. Of course, we as an audience are seeing what's going on, we're seeing that this kid can move, we're seeing the braces come off, and we're way ahead of the game. We are getting all this, and were are smart folks. So, the music isn't about the audience seeing that this kid's gonna be able to run without braces; the music is about this kid discovering that he's already been running, and he doesn't need the braces. That's really the emotional release of this whole thing.

That's why the big musical moment has to be on the shot where he looks up with a smile that would just knock people down from coast to coast; this kid has just realized that he does not have this infirmity. That's when we start to celebrate. Boom, we blow the top off of it right then and there. Everything to that point has been a build-up to his awakening to that realization. Physically, then we cut back to the adult Forrest on the bench, and he says, "From that day on, if I was going somewhere, I was running!"

THERE'S A CUE IN CONTACT, WHEN SHE FIRST HEARS THE "SOUND," AND SHE ARRIVES IN THE LAB. AT THAT POINT, THE MUSIC FADES OUT TO SILENCE AND IT'S VERY EFFECTIVE.

That cue in the lab starts to wind down with the physical action. She arrives in the room after frantically driving back to the lab and running up the stairs. She's not running anymore, but the tension is still there. We're building to the moment where we first hear the signal in the lab. So, the music has been very active while she is driving and running, but gradually chills out when she returns to the room with her colleagues and all those computers.

SO YOU'RE TALKING ABOUT CONTRAST HERE.

Contrast, absolutely. That's one of the things that you have to understand about silence. Silence is like any other sense perception, whether it's sight, taste, touch, sound, or whatever it is. If those organs are being stimulated, they are less responsive to a more subtle stimulation. So this is a perfect example. If we are about to introduce a character, and in this case "the sound" is an authentic character, we don't want people's auditory sensibilities to shut down before the introduction.

WHAT ARE THE QUALITIES OF A GREAT FILM COMPOSER?

A film composer needs to understand that this is not music for its own sake, but it is music for a collaborative art. For me, a great film composer is always someone who not only has musical talent, but also a talent for telling a story with music. This is what makes film scoring a unique musical expression. It's all about how the composer can assist the telling of the story as well as write great music.

Mark Snow

Mark Snow is an eclectic composer who has become most well known for his music to the *X-Files* television series. His music for *X-Files* has been nominated for two Emmy's, which bring his total number of nominations—for both orchestral and electronic scores—to eight. Since moving to L.A. in 1974, Mark has scored over 70 television movies, as well as hundreds of weekly episodes for shows such as *Millennium, Hart to Hart,* and *Crazy Like a Fox.*

LET'S TALK A BIT LITTLE BIT ABOUT WHAT GOT YOU INTERESTED IN FILM SCORING.

I went to Juilliard where the oboe was my major instrument and the composing was just something off to the side. But I was very much interested in modern music—this is in the '60s in New York. I never thought about film music as being a good place for really out-there music; I thought it was all songs and schmaltzy love themes and stuff. Then I heard Jerry Goldsmith's *Planet of the Apes* score, which was 12-tone or avant-garde, and way out there for its time. That was really exciting to me and I thought, "Oh man, this is great, I want to do this." I loved that music and that was really the beginning of my interest in it.

SO HOW DID YOU MAKE THE LEAP FROM BEING A STUDENT AT A CONSERVATORY TO ENDING UP WRITING FOR FILM AND TV?

Well, my roommate in high school and Juilliard was Michael Kamen, and we put together this rock 'n roll band called the New York Rock and Roll Ensemble that played classical music and rock 'n roll. Not a group like Procol Harem, where they combined both styles—we'd play just straight classical and straight rock 'n roll. It was a big deal at the time.

I played drums and oboe in the band, and Michael played keyboard and oboe. We had five albums out. We stayed together for five years, never really had a hit record and weren't one of the big bands, but it was a fun five years. The important thing is that during that time, we all got to hear more about pop music and the music business, and I felt I had much more in me than just being a player. My wife's family was in the business; some of them still are. She suggested, "Why don't we go out to California, and they could introduce you to people, and you could do your thing out there?" So, I decided to take a chance. I had no job in California, nothing, maybe a thousand dollars. We took our two kids, piled into a car, and when we got to California her father helped us out a little bit. Six months after I got there, I got a job doing an episode of a TV series called *The Rookies*. That's where it started for me. I did another episode, and another one, and then I worked a lot for Aaron Spelling in the early days.

HOW DID YOU LEARN THE TECHNICAL STUFF?

Well, first of all, these were the days before anything electronic. No computers were ever happening then. This was click tracks, frames per minute, Moviolas—no videotape, and really detailed spotting notes. I was able to meet some other composers through some friends and they told me what was up with this stuff and how it's done. I remember my first scoring session. I made all the typical mistakes that newcomers do, where you write all these fragments. When you're starting off, you're so nervous about doing a good job that you think you have to catch all the action. So it sounds like a bad temp score where it's just these little fragments all over the place. That's what separates the men from the boys, when you can write a good piece of music that makes linear sense and also works with the picture.

So it took me a while to get that concept. I overwrote way too much and I was actually fired off a few jobs, which really made me think, What the hell am I doing wrong? I realized there are many, many more approaches than my limited ones at the time, and I started listening like crazy to other film composers and TV composers. That really opened my mind to try new things. I think that was a very important part of my development.

IT SOUNDS ALMOST LIKE YOU NEEDED TO GET FIRED OFF THOSE JOBS AND TAKE A LOOK AROUND.

Absolutely, that's right, because I was getting comfortable and complacent and people were telling me, "You're the greatest." And then one day some producer comes in, he hears it and says, "This sucks, we're getting someone else, you're out!" So, it was a really great learning experience and a good wake-up call.

HOW DO YOU RELATE WITH DIRECTORS AND PRODUCERS WHO ARE NOT MUSICALLY KNOWLEDGEABLE?

In the mid '80s the home studio thing was just starting up, and I bought a Synclavier. When that happened, it was a magical, wonderful learning experience for me because then people could come over and hear the score and make their comments. I learned so much from these people who know nothing about music. It didn't matter that they weren't musicians; they were talking about the drama and the emotional elements of the story. They would say, "Take this out, oh no that's fine, but take out the piano, or try it without the bass," and I would say to myself, "That won't work." Then I'd look at it again and say, "Oh my God, he's right, that's great!" So these people who came in and told me; "I don't know anything about music, but ..."—it never ticked me off. I always thought I could learn something from these guys.

SO, YOU REALLY LEARNED TO LISTEN TO OTHER PEOPLE EVEN IF INITIALLY YOU HAD A DIFFERENT POINT OF VIEW?

Yes. My personality in general is very cooperative and collaborative. I wasn't one with some huge ego who would tell people they were wrong, and it had to be my way. It was important for me to make the people feel comfortable, and that I would basically be doing what they wanted me to do. I might have gone a little over-board in that department when I was younger but it served me well at the time. The wonderful thing about what I'm doing now is that there is much more respect. They now ask me what I think, and often defer to that.

WHAT IS YOUR COMPOSING PROCESS?

With the *X-Files* and this *Millennium* show I do, I just sit here and basically improvise with the picture. These improvisations start to take shape, I start to add more instruments so it sounds less like an improvisation and more like a thought-out piece of music, but nothing is written down. I feel very comfortable with it, the results have been very good, it seems to get better all the time, and people dig it.

DO YOU START WITH A MUSICAL IDEA FOR EACH EPISODE THAT YOU FOLLOW THROUGH? DO YOU SCORE THE FIRST SCENE FIRST?

Most of the time, I actually score the last scene first because it seems to have the most music in it and the most stuff going on. It is usually a full piece with different themes and different rhythms and so on. Then I can pull that apart and go backwards and start at the beginning with smaller variations of that big piece. Usually, the last act of these things tends to be more active and more fleshed out dramatically, so then when you do that, it's easier to go backwards and pull things out

WHAT WAS THE CREATION OF THE X-FILES THEME LIKE?

With the *X-Files* theme, Chris Carter, who is very much of a con-trol guy, wanted input on this. He sent over a ton of CDs, a very eclectic group of CDs—rock 'n roll, Philip Glass, classical, jazz, rock—and told me exactly what he liked in each one.

So I did a first version that was okay, but looking back on it, I'd say this is was too predictable, nothing special, kind of loud and fast. Chris gave his feedback, and I tweaked it. So this happened two or three more times. He was very nice, but not quite satisfied, and I wasn't too happy with it either, so I finally said, "Listen, let me just try something on my own. Why don't you go away for a few days and let me see what I can come up with." That's when it started to happen. I put my hand on the keyboard, I had that Echoplex sound. It was there by accident and it sounded like a good accompaniment thing. I knew he didn't like harmony, I knew he liked very minimal sounding things, so I just put this bed, that accompaniment rhythm underneath. I had a melody and was searching for something really weird or interesting, or anti-thematic, whatever you want to call it. I tried every kind of voice imaginable, I tried woodwinds, saxes, guitars, and came upon this whistle thing for the melody, and it seemed just perfect.

DO YOU GET A LOT OF SATISFACTION OUT OF THIS KIND OF SHOW?

I do actually, because the shows are so great. *X-Files* has done so well, it's like doing a mini-movie, and no one tells me not to do anything, so I keep trying. I get a new sandbox, I try new stuff. I'll buy a CD of samples of crazy things, I try it. I got one the other day of nothing but gongs. All kinds of gongs, processed gongs, electronic gongs …

DO YOU HAVE ADVICE FOR YOUNG COMPOSERS JUST STARTING OUT?

The most important thing is a love for it, a fascination, a desire, a love and feel for music. It takes someone who is passionate about film music, who can go to a movie and hear how some music works with the picture and just think, Oh God, that is so cool, I wanna do it. That's the first thing. The second thing—if you have any relatives who know anyone—that's the next part. And if you don't have that, you just go to where the work is, and unfortunately, it's in ugly Hollywood. You knock on every door and you're merciless, you keep persevering like crazy and pray, and one out of ten guys who come to town make it. I don't know, maybe 1 out of 100. Maybe 1 out of 4. I don't know what the exact ratio is but it's not that promising, which is the reality. So just having the desire or being super-talented is not necessarily going to do it. It's having that, plus some good luck and some good breaks.

Richard Stone

Winner of five Emmy awards for his television music, Richard Stone is best known for his themes and background scores for Warner Bros. cartoons *Animaniacs, Pinky and the Brain,* and the *Sylvester and Tweety Mysteries.* After receiving a degree in music from the University of Indiana, he migrated to Los Angeles and worked as orchestrator and music editor for many film and television projects, including *Witness, Agnes of God, Ferris Bueller's Day Off,* and *Pretty in Pink.*

HOW DID YOU GET STARTED IN SCORING FOR ANIMATION?

I started out as a music editor, and learned on the way. I did some ghost writing and orchestrating at the same time as I was editing, and I gradually got my feet wet. Then around 1990, *Tiny Toons* was starting up. Bruce Broughton gave me a chance to score one of those, and I've been working exclusively at Warner Brothers ever since.

I became a supervising composer at Warner Bros., and *Tiny Toons* was eventually succeeded by *Animaniacs, Pinky and the Brain, Freakazoid,* and *The Sylvester and Tweety Mysteries.* Now we're doing a show called *Histeria.*

LET'S TALK ABOUT YOUR PROCESS FROM WHEN YOU FIRST RECEIVE THE SHOW RIGHT UP TO THE RECORDING SESSION.

It's like anything else. We still sit with the producer and have a spotting session. In our case, the music is wall-to-wall; it's not a case of where the music starts and stops, as it would be in a feature film or a live action television show. In our shows the music never stops. The question is always about musical style and what specific things we're going to hit, how loudly, and with what instrumentation. We might talk about which public domain tunes we will use.

The style we use is an extension of Carl Stalling's animation style that he started in the '30s and '40s. I've done a lot of research and study of his work. They have a lot of his scores at the USC archive where they keep old things from Warner Bros. So what we do is an outgrowth of his style that tries to stay in sync with as many things on screen as we can: characters walking across the screen with pizzicato celli and a bassoon, if a boulder falls on somebody it will have a piano glissando on it, the xylophone eye-blink, and all the rest of those clichés. We also try to do musical puns with folk songs—PD tunes that we can use. We quote from the classical literature all the time.

WHAT IS THE SCHEDULE LIKE ON THESE SHOWS?

We have about two weeks to write twenty minutes of music. I say "we" because I can't do this all myself; I supervise a team of composers. If everybody is healthy, each person can manage between two to four minutes per day. We all either work at home or in rented offices.

We get timing notes from the music editor via e-mail. Most of us use the *Cue* software for timing notes. We also use *Performer*. I will take timing notes written in *Cue*, and create a tempo map, which is a specific tempo and a bar layout with meter changes, if necessary. I then export that as a MIDI file and bring it back up in *Performer*. Then I watch it in sync to the video with an audible click-track so I can hear the dialogue and the click while I watch the scene. As I watch it, the music starts to appear in my head and I'll write it out on a six- to eight-line sketch that is very specific as to instrumentation. I write out every note, every voicing; it is an elaborate sketch. Then I'll fax that sketch to the orchestrator who will write out each individual part on a full score. He sends that to the copyist, and then we have the recording session.

How is this process different from the way Carl Stalling would have worked fifty years ago?

Aside from the technology and the fact that he had an office on the lot at Warner Bros. where he went every day, the musical process is not different at all. He sat at a piano. Most people don't know this, but he never saw the cartoon he was scoring. He scored from exposure sheets. These sheets laid out the action on paper. The director would decide, for instance, how fast a character was walking, and would have this very elaborate sheet saying, for example, "Daffy is walking across the street taking a step every eight frames." This information would be copied onto the exposure sheet giving Stalling a description of all the action and the frame measurements of all the action. That is what he wrote to.

In addition, all the tempos that he used were in even frames because they ran from an optical click loop, and if you look at his scores most of them will say 10-0, 8-0, 12-0, whatever.

When you have as many as thirty or forty hits in a thirty-second cue, how do you handle that, both musically and in terms of the click?

I often use a variable click. The art of writing for animation is in keeping the music musical, and still hitting the things that need to be hit without being choppy. I've found that sometimes in an effort to hit everything, people come out with something that is meaningless mush. Then it's not entertaining anymore. It becomes like musical sound-effects and that's what you don't want to do.

What you want to do is create a cue to be a piece of music with a beginning, a middle, and an end where every note means something. This will depend on the way things are animated. For instance, if a character gets hit on the head with twelve anvils one after another, they will usually be evenly spaced apart—each anvil hit will be 8, 10, 12 frames apart. You can take the rhythm of that and make it into a piece of music. That's a trick that you can use to make the music really live.

So, you are actually composing forward and backward from one pivotal moment?

Yes, that is one possibility. But you can also design your cues so that the start of your new cue is on the first anvil hit, for instance. This will make it even more in sync.

What is it like to be the supervising composer overseeing a whole team of people?

I have the advantage of being able to cast each segment according to each composer's strength. For instance, some composers handle adventure better than comedy. The disadvantage is that I have to take the responsibility for every cue, whether it works for the producer or not. But I have had the privilege of working with the best group of composers in the universe!

At the peak, when we had three or four different series going, we had five or six composers working steadily, as well as orchestrators. It's actually very similar to the old "studio system," where someone like Max Steiner would have an office at Warner Bros. right near the scoring stage, and next to him would be other composers and orchestrators. What we do today is the closest thing to that, including our wonderful orchestra, who, although they are not under contract as in the old days, are basically the same people week after week.

How does the music on some of the other cartoon shows today differ from what you do?

Well, for example, on *Superman* or *Batman*, they don't approach those shows as a comedic cartoon. That's why it works so well, it's very serious business. They choose what they are going to hit very carefully, much the way you would in scoring a feature. Similarly, the people that do the big Disney features, even the comedies, are not hitting eye-blinks. They are painting with a much broader brush.

WHAT ADVICE DO YOU HAVE FOR THE BEGINNING FILM COMPOSER?

My advice is familiar: compose, compose, compose! Have your music recorded whatever way possible. Score student films, plays, local commercial spots, anything. It also helps to befriend a working composer and try to arrange a situation where you're assisting him or her in some way. You can also learn a lot simply by hanging out at recording sessions.

Shirley Walker

Shirley Walker began her film music career as orchestrator, conductor, and synthesist on such films as *Apocalypse Now*, *Batman*, *Days of Thunder*, *A League of Their Own*, *Backdraft*, *The Black Stallion*, and *True Lies*. She has gone on to compose original music for films such as *Escape from L.A.*, *Turbulence*, and *Batman: Mask of the Phantasm*. Walker has written the scores to many television movies and series, including *Batman*, *Superman*, *China Beach*, and *Space: Above and Beyond*.

YOU BEGAN AS A CONCERT AND JAZZ PIANIST AND YOU HAVE A CLASSICAL MUSIC BACKGROUND. HOW DID YOU GET INVOLVED IN FILM COMPOSING?

My very first film experience was industrial scores. And it was fascinating to me. The whole concept of putting music to image was something I just lusted for. I certainly didn't know what I was doing. I didn't have any craft back then. I just had my raw ability as a person who could imagine and create. Because of my training, I knew how to work with other instruments. So I didn't have any problems of getting a recording session done.

DID THAT FIRST PROJECT GO SMOOTHLY?

It was just unbelievable that somebody was going to pay me money to record the music for the film. There was one problem, though. I didn't know it could help to play the music for him in advance of the session, and he didn't know to ask me anything about what it was going to sound like. And at first, the director just hated it. He didn't want to tell me at that time because we were friends and he had been coming regularly to my jazz-trio gig in Haight Ashbury. Then he listened to a cassette of the score for about a week, and he fell passionately in love with it—he just couldn't stop listening to it. He told me all of this way after the fact—how when he heard the way the music sounded he just couldn't imagine it working for the film. Then he finally saw it all put together, and just thought that it was wonderful.

WHAT WAS YOUR MUSICAL TRAINING?

My high-school band teacher had me writing for our jazz band. He also had me transcribing stuff. Count Basie arrangements. Oscar Peterson and Art Tatum solos. What wonderful training. Then I went to San Francisco State College for two years and studied classical composition and performance, but I was too shy for college! Of course, things have progressed since then, or I certainly couldn't be doing what I am doing now.

WHAT HAPPENED AFTER THAT FIRST INDUSTRIAL FILM?

I did some other projects like that, some jingles, and continued playing. My big break was doing some synthesizer stuff and orchestrating for the Francis Ford Coppola projects *Apocalypse Now* and *The Black Stallion*. Then there was a chain of events where one person led to another. On the Coppola projects I met Dan Carlin, Jr., who was conducting the orchestra for some of the stuff I had written. He introduced me to an agent, and I ended up on a TV series. I was very, very fortunate.

HOW DO YOU FEEL ABOUT SYNTHESIZERS TODAY?

If you want to work in the business today, you have to have some technology. There's no way around it unless you're way at the top of things and you just hire it.

I enjoy it now because I finally have gotten good enough with the sequencers and the recording technology to where I can create electronic music that has the same kind of emotional whole that I know how to get with a live orchestra. But I hated it until I got it to this point. At first, I was anti-technology. I resented the notion that I had acquired all these skills as a creative music being, and then here's this whole other thing that comes along that I don't know anything about. People who had those toys were making inroads on the turf that I was establishing myself on. So I had years and years of resenting technology. Now I'm more comfortable.

DO YOU ALWAYS DO MOCK-UPS?

That's such a fascinating area because every film production group that you work with has had different experiences with the mock-ups. For some people, I sit at the piano, I play and sing, and that's enough for them. Other people want to look at every single note. I play a fully-orchestrated sequence for them, and they go, "What's that thing that sounds like an organ, we're not going to have an organ here, are we?" Of course, it's just a synth string pad, and then you've got to talk them through the music.

Here is a good story: I was doing *Turbulence* with producer David Valdez. When we finally got to the scoring stage, on the first day he turned to me and said, "You know, whoever's been inventing those synthesizers should just be shot." And then he explained how scary it was for him to come out to my studio, listen to the mock-ups of the cues, and feel it was kind of okay, but he was not really sure. Then when he heard it with the orchestra, he was so relieved because it sounded as good as he had hoped it would.

When I've worked with someone a lot, they learn to trust me. They know what my dramatic instincts are and we have a vocabulary with each other. Once someone has a good experience with a composer, it's so much easier. It all comes back to the comfort and trust level in your relationship.

WHAT WAS IT LIKE WORKING WITH JOHN CARPENTER, A DIRECTOR WHO IS ALSO A MUSICIAN?

He's very knowledgeable about music in many styles, not just the one that he himself can play. When we did *Escape from L.A.*, he originally did the guitar and the synthesis. After the pressure of shooting and editing the film, it's a way for him of almost decompressing. He likes to get in and musically work with the film. So a lot of the cues were done at his home studio on his synthesizers, and then we redid them with the studio synth guys.

On *Memoirs of an Invisible Man*, it was going to be a total orchestral score. He is not totally comfortable or interested in working in that medium, so that was 100% mine.

WHAT IS YOUR PREFERENCE IN TERMS OF COMING ON THE PROJECT? DO YOU LIKE TO BE INVOLVED AT THE SCRIPT LEVEL?

I look forward to the time when I go in while they're shooting, and then write stuff based on the script. Working on some ideas with some themes as we go along. Some of the people that I've worked with really like that idea.

My favorite way to write for a film is when I get to watch something, and then without the picture, just sitting down and working with whatever emotion I take away from that experience. That becomes my raw material. In the Batman feature length cartoon, *Mask of the Phantasm*, I got to see some test footage from the animation houses—sequences that were not yet assembled into the final film. I just wrote thematic material for scenes I knew were going to take place.

DO YOU SKETCH AND ORCHESTRATE YOURSELF?

I don't transfer my orchestrations to the conductor's score. But when I'm writing, I'm putting everything in—all the dynamics, the phrasing, percussion—everything, it's all there. So I don't physically orchestrate myself, but my sketches are very complete.

WHAT IS IT LIKE SUPERVISING THE BATMAN *AND* SUPERMAN *CARTOONS?*

It has been an interesting process on the *Batman* show. From the beginning, I was establishing the musical style of the series. I wrote the first several shows myself just to get the whole thing up and going. I also wrote the themes for the major characters. So for the first number of years of *Batman*, any main theme was mine.

Ultimately all of the composers that are in the rotation now worked their way up from orchestrating on the shows I was writing. Then they got to write a few cues, then maybe a half of the show, and then finally I would give them a whole show of their own. So it's a great way to reward the people who really paid their dues. This season, we started doing *Batman* electronically, but I'm still involved with basically the same team. I like to go to the spotting, and I look at their show once they've got everything on its way. We go through every cue and make sure that there's not a misread somewhere, or something that I think could be handled in a different way. But the composers working for me now are excellent, and it is satisfying to see how they've all come along in their careers.

WHAT IS YOUR ADVICE FOR YOUNG COMPOSERS JUST STARTING OUT?

There's career success, and there's personal, human success. They aren't mutually exclusive, but parallel trains of thought that can both be happening in someone's life. If you focus on career success, you're going to keep your total concentration on, "How do I get myself hired?" You're going to find some way to associate with young film makers that you relate to artistically. You will always be out meeting people, going to film festivals, film schools; you get involved in everything they are doing, whether it's performance art, or theater, or films. You're not concerned so much about your skills; you look at each job as it comes up, and figure out how to do it.

For personal success, you may have some interest in developing your craft, and learning how to compose for film. Then you're going have an educational stream that comes into your life, and you're going to start your research. You're going to look at scores, listen to soundtracks, and note who's doing them. You're going to read everything that you can, and you're going to go to libraries or places where they have film scores. Then you'll be able to put together what you're seeing on a page with what you're hearing. You will develop an enormous respect for the traditions that have gotten the art to where it is today.

END NOTES

Chapter 1

—1.1. Smith, Steven C. *A Heart at Fire's Center*. Berkeley, CA: University of California Press, 1991. Page 122.

Chapter 2

—2.1. Prendergast, Roy M. *Film Music, A Neglected Art*. New York, NY: W.W. Norton & Co. 1977, 1992. Page 23.

Chapter 3

—3.1. Lumet, Sidney. *Making Movies*. New York, NY: Vintage Books, 1996. Page 171.

—3.2. Prendergast, 35.

—3.3. *USA Today*. 12/28/98.

—3.4. Prendergast, 30 to 31.

Chapter 5

—5.1. *Film Music* [Magazine].

—5.2. Prendergast, 122.

Chapter 8

—8.1. Seger, Linda, and Edward Jay Whetmore. *From Script to Screen*. New York, NY: Henry Holt and Company. 1994. Page 1.

—8.2. Seger, 64.

—8.3. Seger, 129.

—8.4. Seger, 129.

Chapter 9

—9.1. Seger, 138.

Chapter 16

—16.1. Baird, Stuart. *Film Music* [Magazine]. February, 1999. Page 37.

Chapter 18

—18.1. Thomas, Tony. *Music for the Movies*. South Brunswick, NJ: A.S. Barnes, 1973. Page 98.

Chapter 20

—20.1. *Boston Globe*, 2/21/99.

—20.2. *Boston Globe*, 2/21/99.

Chapter 21

—21.1. Campbell, Don. *The Mozart Effect*. New York, NY: Avon Books, 1997. Page 11.

Chapter 22

—22.1. Prendergast, 157.

—22.2. Prendergast, 157.

RESOURCES

U.S. Copyright Office, Register of Copyrights

Copyright Office
Library of Congress
Washington, DC 20559
Information: (202) 707-3000
www.copyright.gov

Performing Rights Societies

ASCAP

www.ascap.com
ASCAP (LA)
7920 Sunset Blvd. Suite 300
Los Angeles, CA 90046
(213) 883-1000
ASCAP (NY)
1 Lincoln Plaza
New York, NY 10023
(212) 621-6000
ASCAP (Nashville)
Two Music Square West
Nashville, TN
(615) 742-5000

BMI

www.bmi.com
BMI (LA)
8730 Sunset Blvd. 3rd floor
Los Angeles, CA 90069
(310) 659-9109
BMI (NY)
320 W. 57th Street
New York, NY 10019
(212) 586-2000
BMI (Nashville)
10 Music Square East
Nashville, TN 37203
(615) 291-6700

SESAC

www.sesac.com
SESAC (NY)
421 W. 54th Street
New York, NY 10019
(212) 586-3450
SESAC (Nashville)
55 Music Square East
Nashville, TN 37203
(615) 320-0055

Composer and Songwriter Organizations

Society of Composers and Lyricists (SCL)
400 South Beverly Drive Suite 214
Beverly Hills, CA 90212
(310) 281-2812
www.thescl.com
Film Music Network
(818) 771-7778 (LA)
(212) 592-3600 (NY)
www.filmmusic.net
Songwriters Guild of America (SGA)
6430 Sunset Blvd
Hollywood, CA 90028
(213) 462-1108
www.songwritersguild.com
Nashville Songwriters Association International (NSAI)
15 Music Square West
Nashville, TN 37203
(615) 256-3354
www.nashvillesongwriters.com

Publications

Film Music Magazine
114 N. Central Avenue
Glendale, CA 91202
(888) 678-6158
www.filmmusicmag.com

Education and College Programs in Film Scoring

Berklee College of Music (undergraduate degree program)
1140 Boylston Street
Boston, MA 12215
(617) 266-1400
www.berklee.edu
Berklee College of Music (Continuing Education Division)
www.berkleemusic.com
New York University (M.M. in Film Scoring)
Steinhardt.nyu.edu/music/scoring
USC (one year graduate program, certificate)
Graduate Studies Director
(213) 740-3211
www.uscmptu.com
North Carolina School of the Arts (Masters program)
School of Music
200 Waughtown Street
P.O. Box 12189
Winston-Salem, NC 27117-2189
(910) 770-3255
UCLA Extension (part-time film scoring courses)
(310) 825-9971
www.uclaextension.edu

Books

Angell, Dale. *Pro Tools for Film and Video*. Oxford: Focal Press, 2009.

Bell, David A. *Getting the Best Score for Your Film: A Filmmakers' Guide to Music Scoring*. First Edition. Beverly Hills: Silman-James Press, 1994.

Bellis, Richard. *The Emerging Film Composer: An Introduction to the People, Problems, and Psychology of the Film Music Business*. Charleston: BookSurge Publishing, 2007.

Farquharson, Michael. *Writer. Producer. Engineer: A Handbook for Creating Contemporary Commercial Music*. Boston: Berklee Press, 2007.

Hoffert, Paul. *Music for New Media*. Boston: Berklee Press, 2007.

Karlin, Fred. *On the Track: A Guide to Contemporary Film Scoring*. Second Edition. New York: Routledge, 2004.

Kompanek, Sonny. *From Score to Screen: Sequencers, Scores and Second Thoughts—The New Film Scoring Process*. New York: Music Sales Corporation, 2004.

Morgan, David. *Knowing the Score: Film Composers Talk About the Art, Craft, Blood, Sweat, and Tears of Writing for Cinema*. New York: Harper Paperbacks, 2000.

Nicholl, Matthew, and Richard Grudzinksi. *Music Notation: Preparing Scores and Parts*. Boston: Berklee Press, 2007.

Northam, Mark and Lisa Anne Miller. *Film and Television Composer's Resource Guide: The Complete Guide to Organizing and Building Your Business*. Milwaukee: Hal Leonard, 1998.

Pejrolo, Andrea and Richard DeRosa. *Acoustic and MIDI Orchestration for the Contemporary Composer*. First Edition. Oxford: Focal Press, 2007.

Prendergast, Roy M. *Film Music: A Neglected Art*. Second Edition. New York: W.W. Norton & Co., 1992.

Rona, Jeff. *The Reel World: Scoring for Pictures—Updated and Revised Edition*. Milwaukee: Hal Leonard, 2009.

Rose, Jay. *Producing Great Sound for Film and Video*. Third Edition. Oxford: Focal Press, 2008.

Web Sites

IMDB (Internet Movie Database)
www.imdb.com/
This is a database of everything about any film or TV show, and everyone who participated (all the credits).

Harry Fox Agency
www.harryfox.com/index.jsp
Mechanical licenses, royalty collection

TAXI
www.taxi.com/
A service that helps find opportunities to place your songs in a film. Record deals, publishing deal, film TV placement. There is a fee for this service.

PUMP AUDIO
www.pumpaudio.com/
An Internet "agent" for getting your music placed in films. Networks with filmmakers who need songs and background music.

KILLER TRACKS
www.killertracks.com/
A music library that pays for different kinds of music to be placed in films and TV.

ABOUT THE AUTHOR

Richard Davis is an educator, composer, orchestrator, record producer, performing musician, and author. His film credits include orchestrations and transcriptions for *Robin Hood, Prince of Thieves, The Last Boy Scout,* and *The Fall Guy*; original music for *Monsters, The Cyclist,* and others.

Photo: Mark Babushkin

He has performed with John Denver, Phylicia Rashad, Betty Buckley, Lulu, and Illinois Jacquet. Richard studied composition with Daniel Kessner and Aurelio de la Vega. He is currently an Associate Professor of Film Scoring at Berklee College of Music.

INDEX

E

M

CALIBAN REBORN

Renewal in Twentieth-Century Music

CALIBAN REBORN

Renewal in Twentieth-Century Music

WILFRID MELLERS

LONDON
VICTOR GOLLANCZ LTD
1968

Printed in Great Britain by
Lowe & Brydone (Printers) Ltd., London

"this Thing of darkenesse I
Acknowledge mine."

SHAKESPEARE: *The Tempest*

"In that earopean end meets Ind."

JAMES JOYCE: *Finnegans Wake*

"The artist is always engaged in writing a detailed
history of the future because he is the only person
aware of the nature of the present."

WYNDHAM LEWIS

Contents

Preface

This book is in no sense a comprehensive history of twentieth-century music. It seeks, however, to uncover the springs that have gone to create our music, and assumes that those elements which are most deeply revelatory are probably also the most "valuable." The argument, whatever its anthropological, psychological, philosophical and sociological implications, usually starts from fairly rigorous musical analysis, and some sections can hardly be fully intelligible without reference to the scores discussed. Music quotation, always a clumsy and unsatisfactory aid, seemed inappropriate to a book such as this; I have therefore indicated, where relevant, specified editions, and must hope that readers will make the effort to consult them.

A considerable proportion of the works discussed are theatre pieces, or anyway works involving extra-musical elements. This doesn't make the problem of writing about music, in musical terms, any the easier, but it does provide a frame of extra-musical, literary and dramatic reference which may make the argument less difficult to follow, especially for people who have no technical training in music. The choice of theatrical pieces hasn't, I think, involved any distortion of perspective: it's remarkable how much of the finest music of our time seeks to project its aural images into visual and kinetic terms, and this may be another manifestation of our music's derivation from late Wagner, and from *Tristan* in particular.

The germ of the book was a series of lectures which I gave for the Andrew Mellon Trust in the University of Pittsburgh, U.S.A., in 1960. The chapter on New Music in a New World draws on material already published in my book *Music in a New Found Land*,

and is used by kind permission of Barrie and Rockliff, the English publisher, and of Knopf, Inc., the American publisher. The section on Stravinsky's *Oedipus Rex* incorporates material originally published in a symposium on Stravinsky issued by the *Musical Quarterly* and subsequently as a book by W. W. Norton and Co.; acknowledgments are due both to quarterly and publisher. The section on Satie's *Parade* is a rewriting of material published in the Decca Book of Ballet; some of the paragraphs on Britten and Orff originally appeared, in a different form, in the *New Statesman* and the *Musical Times*.

I also owe a debt to many friends and students with whom I have discussed the ideas contained in the book: especially to my friend and pupil Malcolm Troup, from whom I've taken sundry tips that, when his research project is completed, will become part of what promises to be an important book on Messiaen.

W. M.

July, 1966
Department of Music, University of York

CALIBAN REBORN

Renewal in Twentieth-Century Music

I

Revelation and Incarnation:
The Legacy of the Past

There is today a widespread belief that music—and the civilization
of which music is a part—has reached some kind of crisis. We live,
we say, in an age of transition; and while every age is a transition
from one era to another, it is true that at some times we are more
aware than at others not only of the pace of, but also of the necessity for, change. The awareness of crisis is not, in music, peculiar
to our own times; we may point, as parallels, to the end of the
fourteenth and the beginning of the seventeenth centuries, and we
can learn something from considering in what ways our own crisis
resembles, and in what ways it differs from, these earlier crises.
There are, however, reasons for believing that the crisis in our own
time is more acute than similar crises in Europe's past, if only because the process of change—or our inability to deal psychologically
with so much physical change in so short a time—may literally lead
to our extinction. The purpose of this book is to consider in what,
if any, ways these changes represent a radical departure from
Western, European tradition, and if such a departure has occurred,
to ask how much or how little it means.

As Europeans, we are all heirs to the Renaissance, that singularly
European consciousness of Man's power and glory and, complementarily, of his pathos and frailty. For centuries we have been
brought up in the belief that man is, in Sir John Davies' phrase, "a
proud and yet a wretched thing," and we have considered art—the

creative manifestation of man's potentialities—both as an assertion
of our pride and as a confession of our wretchedness. Our art has
been concerned essentially with *expression* and with *communication*
by way of symbol-making: we have tried to record our responses to
the world (which includes other people), and we have wanted to
share our responses with our fellow men. In a sense, all our art has
been an assertion of our post-Renaissance pride, for it has implied
that other people care, or ought to care, about our experience. The
post-Renaissance conception of art is basically moral because it
assumes that art is concerned with moral responsibilities: to begin
with, our own, for we are what we "express," and secondarily, other
people's, because they are affected by our expression. This is not the
less true when artists have preached, or have pretended to preach, a
doctrine of moral irresponsibility, since to ask us to follow the whims
of our senses, rather than the demands of Reason or the Will, is still
an invitation to act in one way rather than another.

While this conception of art is our birthright and has gone to
make the world we live in, we have to realize that in the context of
history the notion is both newfangled and restricted. It is relevant
to only about the last five hundred years of Europe's history and to
the brief life span of her American baby. To this day another and
older view of music is prevalent in the East; and this view of
music—which we may refer to as Revelation, as opposed to the
post-Renaissance doctrine of Incarnation—has by far the longer, if
not (for us) the more rewarding, history. Between music as Revelation and music as Incarnation there is one basic technical distinction: music as magic, as contrasted with music as expression, lacks
the element of harmony. On the significance of this we shall comment later; for the moment we must inquire into music's nature at
its most primitive level. Music can exist—indeed existed for thousands of years—without harmony, but it can hardly exist apart from
its two prime constituents, rhythm and melody. If one puts rhythm
first, that is because rhythmic significance is possible without melody,
whereas melody, being a succession of pitches in time, inevitably
implies some kind of rhythmic organization.

What kind of organization is, however, the crucial point. The basic melodic "shapes" are inherent in acoustical facts and in the structure of the human vocal organs. In the music of all primitive cultures, however widely separated in time and place, the natural norm of progression is by the intervals of fifth and fourth, by the *step* which is defined by the difference between fifth and fourth, and by the pentatonic minor third; we find these melodic formulae recurrent in all musically "monodic" cultures, sophisticated and unsophisticated alike. The effect of these melodies will, however, be conditioned by their structure, which in turn is conditioned by two different conceptions of rhythm, one of which we may describe as *corporeal,* the other as *spiritual.* As the term suggests, corporeal rhythm comes from bodily movement: from physical gestures in time, associated with work or play. It thus tends to be *accentual;* the regularity of the stresses measures off Time without necessarily having any relationship to melody. Indeed, accentual rhythm tends to curb melody by reducing it to a short, repeated pattern (in very primitive societies often a mere two-note figure, the pathogenic yell of the falling fourth). The effect of this Time-measuring thus tends to be incantatory and hypnotic. In becoming habituated to Time's beat we cease to be conscious of it, and this unconsciousness of our earth and Time-bound condition is precisely the magic effect that primitive man sought through his music. We can still hear this, today, in a Tahitian drum-accompanied chant, or in the Beatles' beat. The other kind of rhythm, which we have called spiritual, arrives at a similar effect by the opposite means. Whereas corporeal rhythm is accentual, spiritual rhythm is numerical, having the minimal relationship to bodily movement. It thus tends to be subtle and complex in its organization; to suggest, indeed, a self-generative spontaneity that counteracts any sense of periodicity or beat. Whereas corporeal rhythm is divisive or multiplicative (four as a multiple of two two's, two as a division of four), spiritual rhythm is additive (two plus one, plus three, plus five, etc.), and therefore tends to have no regular metre and no strong accents. In effect it is liberative and, therefore, ecstasy-inducing. We shall see later why spiritual rhythm, unlike corporeal rhythm, can flourish only in a monodic music, and can survive only with difficulty, if at all, in a music that is harmonically conceived.

In the music of primitive cultures—and this is true too of the music of children, who are at a primitive stage of evolution—the rhythm is usually corporeal and the music is never self-expression but rather a communal act of work or play which may have magical as well as social significance. But the more developed, the richer a culture becomes—which may or may not mean that it becomes more sophisticated—the more the corporeal rhythm will involve within itself elements of spiritual rhythm. Additive rhythms, often of extreme complexity, may exist over and above the fundamental corporeal rhythm, as in much African music; at a further stage (for instance, in classical Indian music) these complex additive rhythms will be combined with subtle melismatic distortions of pitch in the basically pentatonic patterns of the melody. There is a heterophony of both line and rhythm, whereby the music seems simultaneously rooted to the earth and an escape from it. It is interesting that a similar compromise occurs in European folk music, even in societies whose art-music is unambiguously post-Renaissance in concept. It is, of course, especially noticeable in European cultures that veer towards the East (for instance, the Magyar music that was so richly explored by Bartók), and is a spontaneous part of the folk music of the American Negro, and therefore implicitly of jazz.

As the ancient civilizations grew more complex and less primitive, there was a tendency for corporeal rhythm to be absorbed, or even "sublimated," into spiritual rhythm. This did not affect music alone. East Asian poetry, for instance—that of China, Japan and Mongolia —has no qualitative accents, only quantitative or numerical proportions. Even the dancing has little physical drive. There's a basic two or four pulse which creates an equilibrium—one, two, one, two. But this pulse is so immensely slow that it cannot be apprehended as a beat, and within it the movements of hands, arms and body are infinitely subtle, a manifestation of Being rather than of Becoming, and so beyond temporality. Similarly, the music that accompanies the dancing measures Time in percussive gong tones so slow that they cannot be experienced as metre, while the melodic variations on the basic pentatonic patterns are usually additive in rhythm. This applies even to the music of the Chinese and Japanese theatre which, if it is an imitation of human action, is action viewed *sub specie aeternitatis,* to which "development" is extraneous.

In classical Indian music this "spirituality" reaches perhaps its highest point. When the Indian vina player takes up his instrument it is not to "put over" his own personality. The drone, which is eternity, independent and oblivious of our joys or distresses, hums continuously, the music of the spheres. Against it, the player will begin to mull over the raga appropriate to the hour and place. The raga is in no sense the player's invention. It is neither a theme nor a scale, but rather a *series,* an arrangement of pitch relationships which is usually pentatonic at base, though it may introduce chromatic or microtonal intensifications. Almost certainly, the raga's remote origins were in folk song, in the recurrent melodic formulae which the voice employs to "get going," as we can see from the evolution of British or any other folk music. In time, however, these formulae were imbued by centuries of tradition with specific ritualistic or religious associations, which were further sophisticated by the technical refinements of highly skilled virtuosi. Thus the raga became a technical esotericism, and also the Word of God, who has a different word for various times of the day and seasons of the year.

While the vina player tries out the raga appropriate to the time and place, the percussion or tabla player will tentatively explore the tala or rhythmic pattern which is ritualistically relevant. While the tala usually embraces the physical energy of the body, it tends to be an additive pattern, often of considerable complexity; it will increasingly be swept into the melodic player's ecstasy as the "composition" begins. To compose, indeed, is to improvise, with a wealth of microtonal inflection and with the utmost subtlety of rhythmic nuance, on patterns which are preordained. String player and drummer mutually stimulate one another, and it's almost true to say that the composer-player's talent or genius is manifest in inverse proportion to his terrestrial passions, for the better composer he is,

B

the more sensitive to human agony or mirth, the more his improvisation will float and soar, the more his complexities of rhythm will defy the metrical pulse of Time. The fact that he employs pitch distortion—which brings with it a high quota of nervous dissonance —is part of the effect. The anguish and the physical tension of our earthly lives are present (as they are more crudely in the "dirt" of scat singing and jazz horn-playing), and both the distonation and the nasal quality of vocal production are considered to be erotic. Yet the function of the music is precisely to release this tension when the vina player, emulating vocal technique in playing closer and closer to the bridge, achieves his ultimate ecstasy, and his melodic, nonharmonic, nonmetrical music takes flight, liberating both himself and his listener-participants from Time and the Will. It's interesting that jazzmen still use the word "flight" to describe their wilder arabesques; and although these arabesques are cumulative, the sense of progression is irrelevant to them, as it is to those of the Indian vina player. Theoretically, a vina player's (or a jazzman's) inprovisation could go on all day and all night and, to Western ears, sometimes seems to do so, however much we may admire (in both the literal and the colloquial sense) the moments of ecstasy. How irrelevant our temporal and harmonic concepts are to oriental music is indicated by the fact that Indian folk singers can still be heard singing the same tune at and in different times simultaneously, and that Japanese Buddhist monks will sing the same chant in any time and at any pitch (often twenty or more at once) convenient to their voices. In neither case is there any intention to depart from monodic principles, let alone to sing in formal canon or in twenty-part homophony.

It is obvious that to such music the Western theory of communication is not pertinent. There is no audience to be communicated with, for composer-performer and listeners (who will become directly involved in the performer's ecstasy) are participants in a rite. The composer's duty is not to express but to reveal; what he reveals is the Reality within the God-given raga and tala. Such revelation is, however, a human activity, and we may see the "corporeal" and the "spiritual" music as manifestations of complementary aspects of man's nature. Music built upon corporeal rhythm is concerned with man as a social being, engaged in communal activity; music built upon spiritual rhythm deals with Man alone—not with his awareness of his own consciousness, but with his relationship to God. In corporeal music man loses his consciousness of personal identity in equating his lot with that of his fellow beings; in spiritual music he loses this consciousness in discovering, or seeking to discover, the will of God. Some interrelation between the two would seem to be essential for human growth. One reason why the culture of classical Greece has been so important in the history of the human race may be because it came closer than most Eastern cultures to achieving such a dual relationship.

We do not know a great deal about the music of Greek antiquity, but we do know that its melismatic arabesques and additive rhythms were, unlike those of classical Indian music, associated with words. This inevitably entailed more direct "human" references; and we may suspect that corporeal rhythm played a predominant part in the Dionysiac aspects of Greek drama. A Greek tragedy—and for that matter a Greek comedy too—was fundamentally a religious rite; its music seems to have been monodic; and the Greek modes were like ragas in that they had magical properties that were supposed directly to influence human conduct. At the same time it is clear that Greek drama was passionately "humanistic" in a way that a Japanese Noh play was not; and it seems probable that Greek dancing was less static, more accentually percussive, than Indian dance. The balance between the Dionysiac and the Apollonian which the Greeks sought for as an ideal is in one sense an equilibrium between the corporeal and the spiritual. It also, however, brings in another concept which was not to be thoroughly explored, or re-explored, until the Renaissance: for the Apollonian idea involves the subjection of passion by reason, as well as its sublimation into spiritual ecstasy.

This being so, one might have expected that the Greeks, proceeding from the monodic concept, would have gone on to "discover" harmony. Indeed, Pythagorean science *had* discovered it, and was to become the basis of harmonic theory thousands of years later.

Pythagoras, in relating the mathematical laws of Harmonic Proportion to a developed cosmology, had indicated how music could "keep unsteady Nature to her law," as Milton put it; emotional *ekstasis* could be reconciled with the intellectual worship of number, and the claims of body, spirit and intellect be mutually satisfied. What prevented the Greeks from finally achieving this synthesis was in part the qualities to which they owed their greatness. Pre-Socratic Greece was still mainly an oral, nonliterate culture, intuitive, irrational, built on the all-embracing love of the earth goddess, Demeter; its passionate, religious, mystical matriarchy (closer to medieval than to post-Renaissance Europe) remained at war with, and was too powerful to be absorbed by, its new, empirical, rationalistic patriarchy. This *potestas*—this patriarchal authority—was taken over by Roman civilization; in Greece the unity of Pythagorean science split into Platonism and Aristotelianism, and the Dark Ages deliberately separated "spirit" from the physical world. Plato, obsessed with the perfection of circular form, turned his back on reason; Aristotle, cultivating reason, removed it completely from cosmology; and Ptolemy could say that since we can know nothing of the behaviour of heavenly bodies precisely because they are heavenly, it is our duty to teach the doctrine of their circular behaviour regardless of what may once have been known as scientific fact. Christianity, arising out of the ruin of the ancient world, battened on this separation of spirit from flesh, of belief from reason. St. Augustine counteracted his *omnis natura, in quantum natura, bonum est* with the doctrine of predestination and with the theory that intellectual knowledge was no less a seduction than submission to the flesh. So the Dark Ages reinterpreted cosmology, using the theory of the Chain of Being in a way that has much in common with oriental religions, seeking a ritual protection against sin, guilt and anguish. (See Arthur Koestler, *The Sleepwalkers.*)

Something of this evasion remained when, during the heyday of the Middle Ages, Aristotle was rediscovered and Reason reinstated, as against the Platonic shadow. For Reason was relevant only to man's theological nature, and to his social nature in so far as he lived in a theocratic universe; the wonderful flowering of spirit and, indeed, of humanity must not disturb the status quo or infect a walled-in universe with the blight of mutability—which is still feared, as late as Edmund Spenser. This is why medieval man was so reluctant to investigate the facts of musical harmony, which were part of his theoretical legacy from the ancient world. More than a thousand years later, he still stubbornly turned his back on the implications of Greek theory. It was to take him another two hundred years to admit to the evidence of his ears—and nerves, senses and body. His intellect submitted last.

So the compositional principles inherent in European music before the Renaissance are not radically distinct from those of Oriental music. The music of the Byzantine church may be in direct descent from Greek monody and certainly absorbed elements from oriental cantillation by way of the music of the Jewish synagogue. In Gregorian monody the core of the music is the modal (and basically pentatonic) pattern which, being almost as "natural" as breathing or the heartbeat, becomes (like a raga) a source of creativity. To compose is to extend, embellish, intensify the formula with rich melismata, freely additive in rhythm, culminating in the sequences and tropes which were an ecstatic act of praise. The link with the East is, as we have seen, direct; the composer is always anonymous, and he always starts from the traditional musical "doctrine" of his Church. He does not, like the Indian vina player, re-create the doctrine with each performance; but the traditional forms of the tropes must have been arrived at through a process of improvisatory experiment, and were certainly modified in repetition. The still unresolved arguments as to the correct rhythmic interpretation of plainchant perhaps testify to the fact that the music looks forward as well as back; but we can hardly doubt that the rhythmic conception was in origin numerical, and that if recurrent rhythmic patterns exist, they are not aggressively metrical or Time-dominated. The monks' intention, in singing their chant, must have been very close to the intention of the Indian vina player: by dedication to the Word—his Christianized raga—the plainchanter aimed to liberate the spirit, allowing the melodies to flow, unaccompanied, mainly by step and by pentatonic minor thirds, overriding metrical time and the pull of harmonic tension. He sought freedom from the self through the revelation of the divine; and the nasal quality of his vocal production, reinforced by the church's vaulted echoes, would have had unmistakably Eastern affiliations.

But while medieval performance would certainly have incorporated more "dirt" (in the jazz sense) than do modern attempts to revive or preserve ecclesiastical tradition, it's probably true that Christian chant *denied* more aspects of experience before its sublimatory process could begin. The plainchanter's melismatic tropes and "jubilations," though wilder than anything we're likely to hear in contemporary liturgical performance, were almost certainly less wild than those of his Byzantine and Jewish, let alone his specifically Oriental, forebears; the Christian has become a shade more self-conscious in his yearning for sublimation. This is one way of saying that the Renaissance was latent in Christianity; and in musical terms the change has something to do with the growing importance of words. For while the words in plainchant are impersonal, being *the* Word in a hermetic language different from the normal means of communication, it is significant that European monody preserved its contact with the most "human" of all instruments, the voice; whereas oriental monody, having derived its basic formulae from the voice's spontaneous activity, achieved its highest manifestations in instrumental form.

We can better understand the significance of the affiliation between medieval monody and words if we turn from the doctrinal music of the Church to the secular monody of the Middle Ages— the songs of the troubadours. The nature of the melodic lines in troubadour music is hardly distinguishable from plainchant, for they proceed by step and pentatonic minor thirds, introduce melismatic extensions which are comparable with oriental cantillation, and may even have been directly influenced by Arabian and Moorish music during the Crusades. The correct rhythmic interpretation of troubadour song, even more than of plainchant, is still a matter of scholarly dispute, but it seems highly probable that troubadour singers, being originally their own poets, would have employed flexible additive rhythms derived from their words, and

that if the theory of rhythmic proportion is appropriate we should
see this not as an aggressive assertion of accentual dance metre, but
as a more rudimentary form of the Indian tala. The literary themes
of troubadour song centre, significantly, on the *sublimation* of terrestrial passion. The Apollonian-Dionysiac relationship of the Greeks
is given, in a Christian context, a changed emphasis. The troubadour's Beloved is outside marriage, because marriage is a terrestrial
institution; but whether she is the Dark Goddess of Gnosticism or
the Virgin Mary or (which is more probable) both at the same
time, she is unattainable. Being such, she provokes—especially in
the northern, Germanic development of troubadour music—a death
wish, inducing an element of melancholy and frustration within the
melodies' ecstasy. The essence of plainsong melody is that it seems,
in its winging continuity, eternal, whereas the most characteristic
and beautiful troubadour melodies counteract their air-borne flow
with an obsessive reiteration of falling fourths and fifths. This
feature is associated with what may be the tunes' more regularly
periodic lilt. In any case the troubadour singer does not invite us to
participate in a ritual, as the plainsong cantor does, or as does the
Indian vina player, who induces ecstasy (unless, being untalented,
he invokes merely boredom). The troubadour singer tells us of his
desire and of his sorrow, both unappeased and unappeasable.
Though he sings of an eternal longing, for mankind as much as for
himself, the Renaissance is already implicit in him. In his melancholy, he says that although the mother of God was a virgin, he
cannot but be battered and bruised by his *awareness* of the flesh.
Already a dualism is latent: which in musical terms was to lead to
the end of the monophonic principle—and of the belief in music as
a revelation of the ultimate unity.

The great oriental religions had, of course, always admitted to the
eternal dualities of light-dark, hot-cold, self–not self, even the moral
issues of good and evil. At the same time they made the evasion of
the implications of duality the very heart of their philosophy and
ritual: fulfilment could never be through conflict, only through the
relinquishing of the Many in the One. Similarly primitive peoples and
the members of oriental cultures must have been aware of the simul-

taneous sounding of tones, without being either philosophically or
psychologically interested in exploiting this dualism. Harmony is of its
nature a dualistic phenomenon, since it involves two or more tones
of different vibration rate, in varying degrees of tension one with
another. We know that the troubadours had instruments with which
to accompany their monody. We don't know what they did with
them, but suspect that they for the most part used instruments merely
to double the vocal line, maybe with melismatic embroideries, or to
play quasi-oriental drones, or melodic ritornelli between the stanzas.
Yet it also seems possible that they—unlike musicians of oriental
cultures—may occasionally and fortuitously have explored the effect
of simultaneously sounding tones: for they represented a Christian
civilization, and Christianity is the one great religion based on *consciousness* of duality. Its God became Man, and in so doing encouraged man to think of his earthly life as drama—a conflict between
good and evil. It's probable that Christianity became the dominant
creed, surviving through the humanism of the Renaissance and the
age of the baroque, precisely because it stressed the fact of human
guilt and the possibility of redemption. The Christian symbol, the
Cross, is itself a duality, as opposed to the circular eternity symbols
of oriental religions.* Even though Christians believed that we live
here and now in a vale of tears, they thought that what happened to
us in the vale was supremely important, since it affected our chance
of future bliss. The idea of life as a pilgrimage itself implies that
Time is of consequence, whereas to religions centred on eternity
it is irrelevant. This is why the harmonic revolution in European
music is inseparable from a revolution in the temporal concept.

One can observe the beginning of this change in the medieval
theory of rhythmic proportion itself. Like the Indian talas, the
rhythmic "modes" in troubadour song and in medieval music

---

* Cf. Owen Barfield, *Saving the Appearances:* "The oriental conception of
time was essentially cyclic. The picture was of eternal repetition rather than of
beginning, progress, and end, and the path of the individual soul to the bosom
of eternity was a backward path of extrication from the wheels of desire in
which it had allowed itself to become involved. To reach, or to resume, the
supreme identity with Brahma, with the Eternal, was the object and its achievement was a matter which lay directly between the individual and the Eternal.

generally had doctrinal and ritualistic significance; the association of "perfect" rhythm (which is triple) with the Trinity dates back at least as far as Philippe de Vitry. Superficially, moreover, this looks like an additive rhythm, two plus one, which is what one would expect of a mystically inclined society. But triple rhythms are also rooted in a fact of nature, for they are the rhythms of breathing (in-hold-out), and thus may have a more direct association with the rhythm of the human voice, and a more immediate relationship to "feeling," than the immeasurably slow duple rhythm of the East. Perhaps it is not an accident that triple rhythms continue to be associated with "human" fulfilment, through the Renaissance and the age of the baroque. Certainly during the Middle Ages the triple additive rhythm is, compared with the Indian talas, so simple that it could also function accentually and corporeally. This *may* have happened in some troubadour monody; it indubitably happened when, in polyphonic music, the triple rhythm had to be to some degree accentual if the performers were to keep together.

The troubadours were not aware of the equivocation at the heart of their music, nor were the creators of harmony aware that they had arrived at a revolutionary principle. Harmony evolved in Europe as a consequence of two accidents that must have occurred in primitive cultures and in the great oriental civilizations also, the difference being that the European Christian was fascinated by the implications of these accidents, whereas the primitive and oriental musicians were not. If one takes part in community singing among untrained voices, one soon becomes aware that, while everyone thinks he or she is singing at the same pitch, some singers adapt the tune to a pitch convenient to their voices; they sing a fifth above or a fourth below the main body of voices without realizing (for the hold of the absolute consonances is so strong) that they are not singing at the same pitch. This is an unconscious example of *organum,* which probably began fortuitously in the medieval Church, but was then deliberately exploited because the sound was awe-inspiring and superhuman, especially when reinforced by the Gothic cathedral's echo. Once the duplication of the voices at different pitches had been admitted, it was only a matter of time before the parts would sometimes move—at first by accident, then by design—in contrary instead of parallel motion. The sound of seconds, thirds and other intervals more sophisticated than fourths and fifths would thus become familiar, and a compositional principle based on the alternation of harmonic tensions would be feasible, if not immediately necessary.

Another accident that occurs in primitive mass singing reinforces this awareness of harmony. The singers, intending to sing the same tune simultaneously, may not succeed; their "wrong notes" will disturb the melodic unison and provide examples of fortuitous harmonization. At first the effects will be chaotic and arbitrary. Before long, however, such heterophonic effects will be used to artistic purpose, and the more skilful singers will be encouraged to embroider melismatic embellishments around the simple form of the melody as sung by the main group. Medieval polyphony sprang from an interaction of these two principles of organum and of melismatic heterophony. Both elements were intended to be an enrichment of traditional monody; neither was meant to be a denial of the monodic principle. Nor was it a denial, at least for a matter of two hundred years. In the polyphony of Perotin the additive triple rhythm often functions corporeally, since a basic 3/8 pulse becomes two bars of 6/8 or four of 12/8 with a pronounced, even dance-like, lilt. But this accentual feeling has, as yet, no harmonic manifestations. The only "real" harmonies are fifths and fourths, passing dissonances being the accidental result of the melismatic elaborations; and the immensely long instrumental notes of the plainsong cantus firmus become the Word, the Rock, upon which the ecstatic melodies proliferate—an effect directly comparable with that of the eternity-drone in Indian music. Despite Perotin's relatively earthly, triple-rhythmed lilt, he dissolves our corporeal energies into spiritual levitation; the whirling of pentatonic figurations around the fundaments of octave, fifth and fourth creates an aural phenomenon close to the tintinabulation of bells. The occasional fortuitous dissonance, evoking unexpected partials, would emphasize this, letting in the "dirt" like the pitch distortion in Indian music: so that although Perotin apparently writes harmonized part-music, its behaviour is hardly more harmonic (in the modern sense) than is monophonic oriental chant.

This remains true even as late as Guillaume de Machaut, at the end of the Middle Ages. In rhythms and structure the additive principle still remains dominant. There is a close analogy between the structure of a Machaut motet and that of a Gothic cathedral. The main structure of the cathedral is a feat of mathematical engineering, to which the individual craftsmen add their contributions. Similarly, the medieval motet is built on the rock of the plainsong cantus firmus, the other parts being added separately, each as an independent entity, beautiful in itself, if more beautiful in relationship to the whole. Machaut's famous *Messe de Nostre Dame* is likewise constructed as musical architecture, on linear and metrical-mathematical principles, and his more recognizably melodic form of the cantus firmus—the Word from which the melodic material is derived—has a clear affinity with the "preordained" oriental raga. Similarly the technique of isochronous rhythm—a metrical pattern which remains constant for a given part, though the pitch relationships change—is comparable with the oriental tala, especially since the rhythmic patterns are complex and numerical, and often have doctrinal as well as musical significance. From the harmonic point of view there is more movement and more "density" in Machaut's four-part than in Perotin's three-part texture; nonetheless, the dissonant clashes produced by contrary motion are still not harmony in the post-Renaissance (structural and dramatic) sense. One may compare their effect to that of the gargoyles in a Gothic cathedral. In Machaut's day one entered the church and listened to the music as it was sung and played, as an act of worship. One sought to lose consciousness of personal identity, and while the savage dissonances that intermittently assailed one's ears and the gargoyles that unexpectedly leered down from the walls reminded one of sin and mortality and the nameless horrors that make us human, one no longer needed to fear them. One could forget the gargoyles on the wall and within the mind and senses, as the eyes and soul were swept heavenward by the building's air-borne architecture. Similarly, Machaut's fierce dissonances would be absorbed in the splendour of sonority, the unalterable grandeur of the mathematical proportions, the godlike reiteration of the absolute consonances of fourth and fifth, the ritual tolling of bells and gongs.

It is inevitably difficult for us to respond to this music in a way that is appropriate. For all its sophistication, it has also a Byzantine glory and a quality that is primitively wild and terrifying. Perhaps it has an element of desperation, too: an intuitive awareness that the end of a world is at hand. In the Middle Ages both gargoyles and the creatures of beauty—saints, angels, Mother and Child— that adorn the cathedral are distractions that may be sublimated into the architectural whole. In Machaut's day, however, the process of sublimation had become much more difficult: the gargoyles are more savagely potent, the things of beauty more alluring. There may be a direct manifestation of this desperation in what has been called the restiveness of the late Gothic motet. The desire to impose the ultimate unity on the most intractable experience reaches extravagant lengths. Different texts will be set simultaneously, often in different languages, and although they are usually doctrinally related, the music seems to emphasize rather than to disguise their disparities. The isochronous rhythmic patterns grow so complex that there is no parallel to them until some music of the mid-twentieth century. The patterns are often broken or fragmented by the hoquet or hiccup; even words and syllables are disintegrated, so that their human meaning is unintelligible. Rhythmic contrariety between the parts is carried to fantastic lengths, so that one hardly knows whether the concourse is held together by science, by doctrine or by black magic rather than white. Corporeal rhythm has virtually disappeared; so has the ecstasy induced by spiritual rhythm. Such music is a grotesque perturbation of nature and the end of a world. A new world, and a new principle of order, must grow from an acceptance of human nature—gargoyles and mothers and saints— on its own terms.

This first happened, not unnaturally, in Italy, where late Gothic composers devoted less attention to the rituals of the Church than to the celebration of the world in hunting scenes and nature pieces which were usually a background to sexual love. Here the rhythmic

excitations of late Gothic style could find a more spontaneous out-
let, and could begin to be combined with triadic harmony of the
type which was to lead to harmonic revolution. It was, however, a
long time—about a hundred years after Machaut's death—before
the implications of the harmonic revolution were fully manifest.
Even a very late medieval piece, such as Dunstable's celebrated
Veni Sancte Spiritus, seems to us to go on "too long," by which
judgement we imply the (for us) traditional dichotomy between
form and content. The judgement is strictly irrelevant, for although
Dunstable was in one sense a man of the Renaissance, his approach
to composition remained medieval. He was not concerned with his
own response, which had to seek incarnation in Time. He was concerned to create an atmosphere in which, through the medium of his
music, an act of revelation could occur. He did not know when, or
even if, it would happen, but he did his best to provide the musical
circumstances in which it might. Just as an Indian vina player would
perform for hours or even, with a few necessary intermissions, all
day, while his audience or "participants" came and went, so the
ritual music in a medieval cathedral would continue for hours,
while the congregation fluctuated.

So the concept of order in Dunstable's *Veni Sancte Spiritus* is
unambiguously medieval, linear and mathematical. The plainsong
cantus firmus is repeated three times in notational values that decrease "doctrinally" by a third (a musical synonym for the Trinity);
the rhythmic structure is isochronous; and there are three doctrinally
related texts sung simultaneously. The Christian version of the raga
and tala are still present, and the rhythm of the individual lines is
still numerical, freely flowing, nonmetrical, dissolving away the sense
of temporal progression. The Renaissance element in the music consists in the sensuousness of the triadic harmony, which is mellifluous,
even tender, compared with Machaut's Byzantine starkness. But
although this sensuousness entails an awareness of the flesh, it does not
bring the devil with it. The harmony is not so far from the passive
sensuality of the early Renaissance style known as fauxbourdon,
wherein the chains of 6:3 triads, floating directionless without a
before or after, hypnotize us in sensory delight, like a cat lying on its

back, purring in the sun. Dunstable's harmony remains independent of the controlling will, and therefore of temporal progression and of dramatic significance. Nonetheless, that the harmonic principle was admitted meant that sooner or later its implications had to be recognized; and we can almost date a moment in history when this happens. In one of his last compositions—a four-part Ave Regina which he asked to have sung at his deathbed—Guillaume Dufay incorporated an appeal to God to have mercy on His dying Dufay; and this unmedieval intrusion of the personal (we may compare the portraits of the artist or the donor that find their way into Renaissance paintings) provokes too a "modern" harmonic technique. Up to this point the four-voiced music has absorbed its triadic sensuousness into the continuous flow of melody. With the words "miserere tui labentis Dufay," however, the liquid major triad sonorities are abruptly contradicted by a *minor* third; and the dramatic effect of this is inseparable from the fact that it implies opposition, and therefore dualism, rather than monism. Moreover, the effect is inconceivable except in relation to Time. Because it is a shock, we are conscious of *when it happens;* momentarily, the music no longer carries us outside Time but makes us aware that the sands of Time—our time, for we are dying—are running out.

Of course it would not be true to say that "expressive" dissonance had not been used in music before: even in Machaut's Mass the reference to the Crucifixion would seem to have prompted an abnormally virulent coruscation of dissonances. But it might be true to say that *dramatic* dissonance, dependent on the Time sense, had not previously been employed in this way; and that in this passage is implicit the essence of late-Renaissance, sixteenth-century musical technique. In Dufay's music the principle of monism, of oneness, is still present in the survival of cantus firmus technique, and in the imitative principle whereby each part, flowing spontaneously as an act of worship, follows its predecessor. But the music is no longer, like plainsong, an act of worship only; its poly- rather than monophonic principle makes it a social as well as a religious act, and the harmonic order (based on the triad) which the parts now seek is a humanly imposed togetherness. Monody, we have seen, is a matter between man and God. Polyphony may start from the man-God relationship, but inevitably involves social relationships also, since several men attempt to create order out of their separateness, and must modify their separateness accordingly. Then, finally, the dissonant *contrast* in Dufay's setting of the word "miserere" presents us with the element of separateness itself. As soon as we centre our experience upon our human identities, in Time, we have to admit that these identities are various and conflicting. The oneness of God is eternal and unalterable, but the oneness that man seeks in his social institutions is fallible, because it must be dependent on the vagaries of individual passion. It is interesting that in medieval polyphony strict imitation was hardly an imperative necessity as an aid to unity between man and God. Once the modern harmonic principle has been admitted, however, polyphonic composers (notably those of the first Netherland school) develop a fanatical obsession with canonic imitation, as a bastion against the terror of duality which their harmony unconsciously expressed. As we shall see, their contrapuntal devices, offsetting the harmonic disintegration of vocal modality, exactly parallel Schoenberg's serial processes, offsetting the harmonic disintegration of diatonic tonality.

Moreover, this harmonic revolution is inseparable from a rhythmic revolution, for as soon as man becomes conscious of his personal identity he can no longer—as could primitive man—achieve a social identity that seems independent of Time. In music, the principle of harmonic order cannot exist without alternations of tension and relaxation such as are not present, to anything like a comparable degree, in a purely monophonic music; and alternation implies progression, a beginning, a middle and an end. Similarly, the concept of the suspended dissonance—the sigh of sorrow, the cry of pain—is inconceivable except in reference to a strong and a weak beat on which the dissonance is prepared and resolved. This is why harmony must imply multiplicative and divisive, not additive, rhythm. Corporeal rhythm has to become at least as important as spiritual rhythm, and to enter into a new relationship with it. We may hope to preserve the integrity of the spirit, but having experienced "the pain of consciousness" we can never again be oblivious of the ticking of Time's clock. The sixteenth century was the great age of clockmaking; all over Europe the tintinabulations of Time's clock now chimed against the tolling bells of worship. Nor is this surprising; for the more *conscious* we are of our humanity, the more sensitive we become to our mortality, which terminates human endeavour.

Sixteenth-century musical technique, then, achieves an equilibrium between vocal melody, dance rhythm and harmonic tension: these elements approximating to the aspects of music as worship, as social function and as personal expression. The balance between these forces is what matters, and sixteenth-century musical theory (significantly owing much to Greek theory) insisted that the health of music depends on the proper interaction of its constituent elements, just as did the health of the body politic. It was not an accident that dance rhythm became, during the Renaissance, a constructive principle in its own right. People have always danced; but in medieval music the dance intrudes into "serious" music (which was usually liturgical) as a science or magic of numbers rather than as physical and sensual impulse, and we have seen that in this respect the Middle Ages have something in common with oriental cultures. In the sixteenth century, however, dance became a constructive principle in its own right, closely related to harmonic order: and almost a substitute for a religious principle. The order of human institutions as manifested in the ritual of the dance ought to be a simulacrum of the divine order. This is why the Civil Music and the Divine Music had to be complementary, which (as we have seen) they strictly were in terms of musical technique. The "divine" freedom of vocal polyphony (spiritual rhythm) was now in part ordered by the "human" principle of dance movement and of harmonic solidarity. Conversely, the human order of dance music and of madrigalian homophony (corporeal rhythm) never completely lost contact with the divine order of vocal counterpoint.

The truly revolutionary element in sixteenth-century technique was, however, the third element: that of harmonic tension, as a manifestation of personal passion. The realities of passion could hardly be evaded in an art based on a humanly oriented society; yet the preoccupation with dissonance was always liable—as was evident even as early as Dufay's "miserere"—to threaten the dance-dominated social order. Renaissance men believed that it was precisely as a resolver of the dichotomy between the Many and the One that the traditional, divine associations of music could be most important. This may explain the almost obsessive influence exerted by the Orphean myth during the sixteenth century. The new music —*musica humana*—could express the realities of man's passion. But the process of self-discovery ought also to be a revelation of man's divine origin; *musica humana* ought also to put man in touch with the other music, *musica mundana,* the music of the spheres. So Man-Orpheus may become, through the joy and the suffering his music represents, a thing of wonder who may move the gods to pity and succour him. In so far as this happens, man -becomes himself godlike. Though his music is still a ritual act, it is now not so much an act of revelation as an act of incarnation. This is what Monteverdi's *Orfeo*—the first artistically significant opera—is about.

Throughout Shakespeare's plays music is valued as a manifestation of human passion, as when Mariana at the Moated Grange uses the boy's song as a means of assuaging her frustrated passion. But the point lies in the assuagement: the *musica humana* puts her in touch with the *musica mundana,* which helps her to go on living. Similarly, Lear's "restoration" music is passion music in every sense: a string fancy which starts from human passion yet dissolves its (harmonic) suffering in the benediction of quasi-vocal polyphony. The act of incarnation may lead to revelation: the Flesh become Word, and the Word Flesh. Like sixteenth-century technique itself, this was an equivocation which, in spite or because of its richness, could not be long maintained. Shakespeare and Byrd could have occurred only at this time, when an extraordinarily potent apprehension of human sensuality and mortality could be reconciled with an awareness of divine grace. Yet some such equivocation remained an ideal even when Europe had abandoned the equivocation and come down heavily on the side of the flesh: and this may be why, during the seventeenth century, a pronounced elegiac tone enters our thinking about music. Milton's *At a Solemn Musick* is a magnificent example of this, here in England. He opens by referring to Voice and Verse as a "blest pair of *Sirens,* pledges of Heav'ns joy," who are "sphear-born," harmonious and divine. While he is almost certainly thinking of the Verse as being in part the Word, as in plainsong, the traditional doctrinal music of the Church (if not *his* church), he nonetheless presents the "wedding" as an Orphic experience. Voice and Verse will employ their "mixt power" in order to pierce "dead things with inbreath'd sense." Their force will be affective, in the baroque sense; a creativity that directly influences human behaviour. Then, however, the elegiac flavour of Milton's poem becomes dominant, for when the "high-rais'd phantasie" is created out of death it proves to be not an incarnation of life-as-it-is, but a vision of life as it once was and ought—in Milton's view—to be again. Music ought to evoke that "undisturbed Song of pure concent," such as is sung in heaven, and was sung on earth in our prelapsarian state. We have to be reminded of the music of the spheres in order that:

> . . . we on Earth with undiscording voice
> May rightly answer that melodious noise;
> As once we did, till disproportion'd sin
> Jarr'd against natures chime, and with harsh din
> Broke the fair musick that all creatures made
> To their great Lord, whose love their motion sway'd
> In perfect Diapason, whilst they stood
> In first obedience, and their state of good.

What Milton is asking for in his "perfect Diapason"—the oneness of the octave between Man and God—is a return to the old monody and to medieval organum. But of course he couldn't admit to that, and wouldn't, in his heart, have wanted to; for he knew that the "pain of consciousness" or—in theological terms—the consequences of the Fall cannot be evaded by wishful thinking. So he ends with a prophecy:

> O may we soon again renew that Song,
> And keep in tune with Heav'n, till God ere long

To his celestial consort us unite,
To live with him, and sing in endles morn of light.

The lingering, protracted rhythm of the final line reinforces the
wistfulness inherent in the passage, and the wistfulness remains,
whether we think of the lines in personal terms (we will be fulfilled
only when we are dead), or whether we think of them as a prophecy
about the destiny of the human race. The whole of Milton's work
proves that he knew that, if ever the prophecy were fulfilled, it
could not be in the form of a return to the past, since innocence
once lost is lost for ever.

Milton's image of light is employed in a then obsolete, almost
medieval sense. The essence of the "pierced" technique in Gothic
architecture—or of the art of medieval illumination, or even of the
texture of Gothic polyphony—was that it let light *through,* being
an act of revelation: whereas men of the post-Renaissance world
were interested in shedding light *on* the variety of the visible and
tactile universe. The discovery of visual perspective, which directly
parallels the discovery of harmonic depth in music, began as a desire
for verisimilitude, a literal imitation of the external world. Soon it
became inseparably related to the need for information; interlocking together, "An exactly repeatable pictorial statement, a logical
grammar for the representation of space relationship in pictorial
statements, and the concepts of relativity and continuity revolutionized both the descriptive sciences and the mathematics on which
the science of physics rests."* For medieval man neither space nor
time was homogeneous, and medieval painters often repeated a
single figure many times in the same picture, since they were interested in the connected meanings of various possible relationships
rather than in the logic of geometric optics. On the other hand, the
geometric space invented in classical antiquity and rediscovered at
the Renaissance could be cut and parcelled up in any direction; and
this is connected with a Rabelais's desire to *conquer* the world of
gigantically inflated physical appetites, with the "hypnotic immoder-
ate thirst after humane learning" referred to by Donne, with the

* William Ivins, *Prints and Visual Communication.*

more trivial itemizing of the Renaissance (as represented by Jonson's Sir Politick Would-Be) and in general with the splintering of social activity and of the private life of the senses into specialized segments. Marshall McLuhan has suggested that in *King Lear* Shakespeare offers us something like a medieval sermon-exemplum "to display the madness and misery of the new Renaissance life of action," the "frenzy to discover a new over-all interplay of forces."

The musical parallel to these disintegrative and reintegrative forces was, we have seen, the phenomenon of harmony. Harmony is of its nature a duality, since it involves more than one tone in shifting vibration ratios, which in turn produce alternating degrees of tension. Sixteenth-century theory and practice had managed to preserve an equilibrium between the human and the divine; but it was inevitable that in time the "pain of consciousness"—which in music involves the awareness of harmonic contrariety—should destroy the old order. This is evident by the early seventeenth century, when disruptive dissonance has enfeebled both vocal modality and polyphonic unity, and when Monteverdi's Orphean opera has given a mythological parallel to what was already implicit in his madrigals. The new order that was emerging negates Milton's view of the purpose of art as revelation, and it is not an accident that this second great revolution in musical history exactly complements the final acceptance of the Copernican system, which was unequivocal by about 1600. For as long as the earth was considered to be the centre of a divinely appointed universe, the relationship between Man and Divinity could remain intimate. When once, however, the First Cause was shifted from the periphery of the universe into the physical body of the sun, from which all things derived life, man's relationship to God became too complex to be apprehensible. It seemed easier, as well as more logical, to dismiss God as a mystical entity; to concentrate instead on man's ability, through his intellect, to explain away the mathematical processes of nature (seeing God as geometry) and at the same time to rejoice in man's power to appreciate, understand, and therefore control his sensual passions. During the course of the seventeenth century we can observe how man attempted, in his art forms, to discover means of ordering the human passions which Renaissance consciousness had released. If any extra-human sanction was given to them, it was usually by analogy with the mathematical or scientific "laws" of the natural world—the gravitational pulls of Newtonian physics. The important point, however, is the manner in which natural law is used as an analogy for human, social institutions, so that the world power of the God-King comes to take the place of the divine power of God.

This is evident in Dryden's St. Cecilian odes, which, written only about forty years later than Milton's *At a Solemn Musick,* are as "modern" as Milton's poem was outmoded. He begins by relating music not to the divine order, but to the mechanical view of Nature:

> From Harmony, from Heav'nly Harmony
> This Universal Frame began:
> When Nature underneath a heap
> Of jarring Atoms lay,
> And could not heave her Head,
> The tuneful Voice was heard from high:
> "Arise, ye more than dead."
> Then cold, and hot, and moist, and dry,
> In order to their stations leap,
> And Musick's pow'r obey.

The "force" may be called heavenly in that it is the First Cause, but once the jarring atoms have cohered to create the Newtonian universe, music's power is to be valued only for its human effects. These are twofold. Music's order is a social analogy, for the disruptive tensions of harmony must bow to the public ceremonial of the dance and to the scheme of tonality which was closely related to divisive dance rhythm—just as the individual must be subservient to the state. But music's function is Orphic too, and a properly ordered Whole leads to the fullest expression of the Parts. Thus music is to be valued for its direct effect on human conduct. The trumpet's loud clangour excites us to arms, the double double beat of the thundering drum makes us yet more bellicose, the warbling flute renders us more amorous, and so on. Indeed, the universal order is dedicated only to the fulfillment of man's sensual nature. Though "from Heav'nly Harmony/This Universal Frame began," it runs through "all the compass of the Notes" in order that the Diapason may "close full in Man." Milton deplores the loss of the "perfect Diapason," the octave that was man's oneness with God; for Dryden, the octave is synonymous with Man himself, who is thus the apex of creation. Through the enjoyment of his senses, the command of his reason, and his power over Nature, man has taken God's place. This is the fulfilment of the Renaissance's sensual-material ostentation, which had in turn been made possible only by the economic development of a mercantile society. The Renaissance had, indeed, directly symbolized the deification of man in the ceremony of the King's Two Bodies—his real, mortal body which was carried, at his funeral, to its last resting place and to dusty disintegration; and his garishly coloured effigy, made of relatively durable *material,* which represented his "eternal" divinity as a terrestrial institution.

It is not therefore surprising that the divine or mystical aspects of music, associated with St. Cecilia and with the organ, are mentioned in Dryden's poem only perfunctorily, among the other affective attributes of music: having a beatific vision is one among the many varieties of experience, like making love or enjoying a good dinner. Orpheus, Dryden says, could transport savages, and even trees, into a state of ecstasy; complementarily, Cecilia can make angels mistake earth for heaven. This was precisely what men of the heroic world wished to do: to believe so potently in man's glory that they could imagine that paradise on earth was feasible. Dryden's longer St. Cecilian ode, *Alexander's Feast,* explicitly presents the God-King of classical antiquity as symbol of Modern Man. He has his lovely Thais by his side, "like a blooming Eastern Bride," and—with the help of the music of Timotheus, here equated with Orpheus—he fulfills his sensuality, as well as his sexuality, exhibiting his heroic stature by loving more, drinking more, fighting more, weeping more than any ordinary mortal. Significantly, it was during the sixteenth and cumulatively the seventeenth century that sex became supremely important in European culture. In primitive musics the complexities of percussive rhythm transform the erotic in our natures into something approaching religious ecstasy; even in classical Indian music the erotic is still manifest in the drumming, though it is an encouragement rather than an embarrassment to the "spiritual" proliferation of melody. Only in Christian chant and polyphony does there develop a dichotomy between sexual and spiritual impulse, related to the dualism of harmony; only in baroque art does this dichotomy become a primary impetus to creation. In a humanistically oriented world we are *aware of* sex (the basic human instinct from which, indeed, life starts) as a fundamental human division and conflict; yet we may find in it a substitute for religious experience, in the sense that duality may seem to be momentarily obliterated in a Time-denying act of physical union.

So in Dryden's poem music is synonymous with the fulfilment of the sensual appetites. Through it, Alexander's ears may be (in appropriately sexual metaphor) ravished, after which he—human though he is—"Assumes the God,/Affects to Nod," and even "seems to shake the spheares." Once more, Cecilia is brought in only at the end, somewhat apologetically. She shares the crown with Timotheus (equated with Orpheus), because he "rais'd a mortal to the skies;/She drew an angel down." We are left in no doubt that Timotheus's achievement is considered more impressive. If there is a kind of stupidity in this assumption, there is also tremendous courage. This comes out in the epilogic stanza to the earlier St. Cecilian ode:

> As from the pow'r of Sacred Lays
> The Spheres began to move,
> And sung the great Creator's praise
> To all the bless'd above;
> So, when the last and dreadful hour
> This crumbling Pageant shall devour,
> The TRUMPET shall be heard on high,
> The Dead shall live, the Living die,
> And Musick shall untune the Sky.

So at the end the Trumpet no longer excites to vainglorious expressions of a power that is in the last resort self-love; becoming the last trump, it tells us that we are snuffed out like a candle. Music inverts its traditional function, as John Hollander has pointed out; instead of reminding us of the divine purpose, it "untunes" heaven itself. Mundane music, in the modern sense, has defeated *musica mundana*.

This inversion precisely complements the latter end of the ancient world. Greek civilization merged into Roman civilization, and that into the Dark Ages, because its mysticism could not ultimately absorb the implications of rationality, literacy and technology; complementarily, at the turn into the eighteenth century Europe's materialism rejected spirit. Either way, Reason is divorced from Belief, and the Pythagorean harmony relinquished. In the light of this we can understand why all baroque music, from Monteverdi to Handel, is a celebration of man's humanity and at the same time a paradox. It attempts to impose the unity of (corporeal) dance rhythm on the chaos of man's harmonic passions; and the additive rhythm of speech inflection, now represented not by liturgical chant but by operatic recitative, gets progressively less significant musically, as the dance-dominated aria grows stronger. But a humanly imposed order can never be finally satisfying, because man, not being in fact god, is both fallible and mortal. This is what all the great operatic myths of the period are "about"; in the old sense of the term there is no spiritual music in the baroque era, no music conceived as an act of revelation. All the greatest music of the seventeenth century *yearns* for the lost unity: this is why Monteverdi's and Purcell's ariosi are poised so poignantly between corporeal and spiritual rhythm; why Purcell was obsessed, even more than men of the sixteenth century had been, with the dualistic pain of false relation; and why the elegiac flavour of Purcell's finest music comes from an intuitive recognition of the conflict between the new and the old values, exactly parallel to that expressed in Milton's poem. Similarly, if Bach is, for us, the greatest of all "religious" composers that is because his music reconciles the greatest awareness of a spiritual order (not unrelated to Pythagorean number symbolism) with the maximum awareness of "the pain of consciousness": the most "perfect" development of contrapuntal science and linear growth (often overriding, even contradicting, the metrical pulse) with the highest density of harmonic tension.

Bach, in achieving so sublime a fusion of the divisive and the additive, the corporeal and the spiritual, is of course exceptional in his period. Yet paradox is inherent in the central convention of the classical baroque; for while the *aria da capo* is a static, non-developing form which "gets nowhere," since the recapitulation is identical with the exposition except for the additional ornamentation, the mere fact that there is a "middle section" admits to the possibility of dualism. The middle section may habitually serve an architectural rather than a dramatic function, but it was not there by chance, and being there, must inevitably be used, sooner or later, for contrast rather than balance. The central theme of heroic opera is the failure of heroism: the ultimate impossibility of man's "assuming the god." So man gave up the attempt. Admitting to a duality between the Self and the World, he came to see that this duality concerned every man; not merely our leaders, who are fallible as we are, but every one of us, in so far as we are human. A humanistic philosophy must lead to what we now call democracy; for if one submits to no law except that which is man-made, the question will soon be asked, Why *that* man (Louis XIV or whomever) rather than another, rather than *me?* If everyone wants to be his own master, he becomes responsible for his own destiny, and he must understand his own nature before he can hope to influence other people.

So there is a change, within the conventions of art, from an "objective" to a more "subjective" approach. *Opera seria,* in the heroic age, was objective in that it was an imitation of men in action. Their behaviour was, of course, inseparable from the imaginative life of the man who created them, but it was a projection of that inner life, having direct reference to the behaviour of the public that participated in it. When music lost its public significance as a ritual of humanism, it became "public" only in the sense of being entertainment; much rococo music was the relatively plain man's music of social persiflage, an agreeable noise to eat or chatter to. The imaginative meanings of music turned inwards; and the central

convention of the age of democracy—the sonata—became, in the
hands of Haydn, Mozart and particularly Beethoven, a subjective
expression of a dualism within the mind. For Beethoven, the
gargoyles within cannot be sublimated in a ritual act, as they were
in the Gothic cathedral, nor can they be brushed aside, as they
sometimes were in the anti-masques of heroic opera. The battle has
to be fought out and the victory won within the "Becoming" which
is Beethoven's sonatas and symphonies. Beethoven's triumph of the
will is humanism's supreme achievement, and in triumphing Beethoven destroys the barrier between the "inner" and the "outer"
life. Ego-assertion could hardly go further than Beethoven carries
it in his middle period works, in which the desire to reconcile the
"separateness" of harmonic contrariety with the "togetherness" of
corporeal rhythm attains a violence that is not far from frenzy.
Yet at the height of this frenzy Beethoven spoke of his art to
Bettina Brentano in the following terms: *

This is harmony, this is expressed in my symphonies in which the
confluence of many-sided forms surges along in one bed to its destination. In them, one can feel that something eternal, infinite, never
wholly comprehensible, is contained in every product of the human
spirit, and although my works always give me a sense of having succeeded, I feel an insatiable hunger to recommence like a child—even
though the last work seemed to have been exhausted with the last
beat of the kettle-drum which inculcated my joy and my musical con-
victions upon the audience. (Speak to Goethe about this, tell him to
listen to my symphonies, for then he will admit that music is the only
entrance to the higher world of knowledge which, though it embraces
me, a man cannot grasp.) A rhythm of the spirit is needed in order
to grasp the essence of music: for music grants us presentiments,
inspiration of celestial sciences, and that part of it which the mind
grasps through the senses is the embodiment of mental cognition. Although minds live on it, as we live on air, it is still a different thing
to be able to grasp it intellectually. Yet the more the soul takes its

* Translated by Michael Hamburger in *Beethoven: Letters, Journals and
Conversations* (London, 1951). Bettina Brentano is usually considered a roman-
tically unreliable authority; this conversation sounds convincing, however—certainly more Beethovenian than Bettinian.

sensuous nourishment from music, the more prepared does the mind grow for a happy understanding with it. Yet few ever attain this stage; for just as thousands marry for love and love is never manifested in these thousands, although they all practice the craft of love, so thousands have intercourse with music and never see it manifested. Like all the arts, music is founded upon the exalted symbols of the moral sense: all true invention is a moral progress. To submit to these inscrutable laws, and by means of these laws to tame and guide one's own mind, so that the manifestations of art may pour out: this is the isolating principle of art. To be dissolved in its manifestations, this is our dedication to the divine which calmly exercises its power over the raging of the untamed elements and so lends to the imagination its highest effectiveness. So always art represents the divine, and the relationship of men towards art is religion: what we obtain from art comes from God, is divine inspiration which appoints an aim for human faculties, which aim we can attain.

We do not know what it is that grants us knowledge. The grain of seed, tightly sealed as it is, needs the damp, electric warm soil in order to sprout, to think, to express itself. Music is the electric soil in which the spirit thinks, lives and invents. Philosophy is a striking of music's electric spirit; its indigence, which desires to found everything upon a single principle, is relieved by music. Although the spirit has no power over that which it creates through music, it is yet joyful in the act of creation. Thus every genuine product of art is independent, more powerful than the artist himself, and returns to the divine when achieved, connected with men only in as much as it bears witness to the divine of which they are the medium. Music relates the spirit to harmony. An isolated thought yet feels related to all things that are of the mind: likewise every thought in music is intimately, indivisibly related to the whole of harmony, which is oneness. All that is electrical stimulates the mind to musical, flowing, surging creation. I am electrical by nature.

Is it not extraordinary that Beethoven who, in the ego-dominated, Time-obsessed finale of the *Seventh Symphony*, created music which would seem to be the polar opposite to oriental monody or Christian plainchant, should thus express belief in the pre-Renaissance doctrine of music as revelation? He stresses music's humanistic efficacy: it "tames and guides" the passions and in so doing establishes our moral identities. But it does this, not through an assertion of the Will, but through submission. In so far as this submission is to God as absolute, it might seem that Beethoven is merely denying Europe's history and his own transcendent contributions to it. But he is not saying that for him art could or should be pure monism, like plainchant; he is rather saying that if, like the oriental or medieval monodist, he must perform an act of sublimation he, as a post-Renaissance man, can do this only by accepting the senses' terrors and the mind's contradictions as part of the pattern of the whole. This, indeed, is what he came to do in his "third period" works; and in this respect his account of his art is both Jungian and Freudian, while his use of the term "electrical" anticipates some very recent theories about the nature of the human mind. There is something awe-inspiring in the fact that Beethoven, employing a key word of his time that was then but obscurely understood, should prophetically have hinted at truths we are just beginning to apprehend. For him the monism of monody would have been "indigent," like philosophy. His sublimation is born of the pain of consciousness, as is manifest in the techniques of the music of his last years.

The dualities that began to appear in European music at the Renaissance—those between harmony and counterpoint, subject and countersubject, polyphony and homophony, tonic and dominant, content and form, and so on—prove to be musical synonyms for wider and deeper dichotomies between thought and feeling, extroversion and introversion, individual and state, art and science. The separation of the functions—what Blake called "the spectre of the Reasoning Power in Man . . . separated from Imagination and enclosing itself as in steel"—can reduce us to submission to Macbeth's "Tomorrow and tomorrow and tomorrow"; and in so far as Cartesian separation—"single vision and Newton's sleep"—may turn knowledge into a mere mode of sequence, nothing can assure us of one instant's being continued into another. Descartes called this the terror of failure in Time. We have seen that it dominates, or threatens to dominate, Beethoven's *Seventh Symphony:* but it proved to be a prelude to works wherein divisions are healed through a return to springs of the unconscious life. Perhaps it is not altogether fanciful to hold, with Marshall McLuhan, that some such intuitive search for a new-old organic "wholeness" may (to pick up Beethoven's own analogy) in fact have hastened the discovery of electromagnetic waves. In any case, no later artist could be oblivious of Beethoven's confrontation of modern man's predicament. Wagner may have been wrong in regarding himself as Beethoven's direct successor, and we would not immediately think of him as a religious composer in the sense that Beethoven was in his last years. Nonetheless, Wagner too had to roll back all aspects of experience into the unconscious, obliterating traditional distinctions between the outer and the inner life, and his life's work also culminated in a mystical act. *Tristan und Isolde* is the end of a phase in human consciousness which began with the Renaissance; it is also, we are often told, the beginning of modern music. We shall therefore start our inquiry into the nature of the twentieth-century revolution, if that is what it is, with a consideration of some aspects of *Tristan,* and of certain works of Schoenberg, regarded as sequels to the Wagnerian cycle.

II

Eros and Agape: A Theme
in Wagner, Schoenberg and Webern

Wagner was an opera composer, not a composer of instrumental sonatas; yet for him opera had become, by the last years of his life, no longer a public or a social event. Indeed, he spent much of his life attacking conventional opera—which had been in origin and history a social ritual of humanism—as a sham, while advocating his own form of music-drama that had many of the characteristics of a religion. Bayreuth was the temple for the worshippers to congregate in; what they celebrated was the projection of Wagner's own inner life as a "modern myth." It is significant that Wagner, representing humanism's ultimate climacteric, should have deified the ego in its most fundamental impulse, that of sex. Whereas Beethoven, in his last works, appeased the anguish of sonata-conflict in the oneness of fugue and the continuity of song-variation, Wagner started, more primitively, from the most fundamental reality known to him: the surge of harmonic tensions which was his own erotic life. From them he derived, in his later work, a polyphonic-harmonic texture which became a cosmos. There is some evidence to suggest that Wagner was aware of what we would call both the Freudian and the Jungian implications of his operas; certainly he thought of himself as "standing for" humanity (as Christ had once done!), and could say, with sublime self-confidence, that the building of Bayreuth was the fulfilment of the destiny which he had planned for himself and humanity.

34

It is well known that *Tristan und Isolde* is in one sense a dramatization of the situation existing in Wagner's life at the time, in the triangular relationship between himself and Otto and Mathilde Wesendonck. More significant, however, is the fact that in this most directly autobiographical of his works, Wagner should have chosen to re-create the Tristan legend; for of all the great medieval stories, that of Tristan most potently expresses man's awareness of Eros, a simultaneous longing for the senses' fulfilment and for their extinction. At the end of the cycle that began with the Renaissance, Wagner takes up this theme and imbues it, in his fervid, passion-laden chromatic harmony, with five hundred years' burden of consciousness, sensuality, frustrated aspiration, and guilt: with the awareness that we have seen to be latent in troubadour song, though it could not then be expressed. The opera begins with a marvellous musical image for this burden of sensuality, aspiration, and guilt: for the notorious "Tristan chords" consist of interlocked perfect and imperfect fourths. Now in the Middle Ages the perfect fourth and its inversion, the perfect fifth, had been the musical synonym for God, the Absolute Consonance according to Pythagorean science, whereas the imperfect fourth or fifth—the tritone— was the Devil ("Si contra fa diabolus est"). The genesis of the opera is thus the most fundamental dualism, which since the Fall is inherent in sexuality itself; in this sense the four and a half hours of the opera are a protracted attempt at an orgasm which would resolve the dichotomy between spirit and flesh. This is implicit in the nature of the Wagnerian sequence, which is a musical symbol for the interdependence of life-instinct and death-instinct. The rising sixth and falling chromatic scale with which the Prelude opens is repeated sequentially over and over again. It urges the music forward, especially since the sequences usually rise; yet at the same time each sequence is also a cessation, a failure, in so far as it falls back to the point it started from, to try again. From the anguish of the rising-falling phrase, the repeated sequences, the drooping appoggiaturas and the tense dissonance, proliferate the themes and motives of the entire, gigantic score in what Wagner positively, if wistfully, called "endless melody." Only at the very end is the frustrated aspiration resolved.

Most significant is the manner of this resolution. From the literary-dramatic aspect, Wagner's adaptation of the Tristan myth is designed to show in three stages (or acts) how the only fulfilment is that of personal passion; how this cannot be achieved except by separation from the conditions of the material world (society, civilization, domestic loyalties); and finally, how it cannot be achieved within Time at all. And in a sense, as Mr. Joseph Kerman has ably demonstrated, the end is implicit in the beginning. In the first act it is the fact that the lovers believe that they have accidentally drunken Death (the love-potion) that releases their passion and frees them from conventional restraints. The second act shows that failure to live out their love in the world; and the climax, when Melot stabs Tristan, or rather Tristan wounds himself on Melot's sword, is the consequence of the inner conflict generated by the attempt at compromise. It creates what we would call nervous breakdown, and it is from his state of near-paralysis that Tristan hears, at the beginning of Act III, the Shepherd's pipe, which (as represented by cor anglais) sounds like an infinitely forlorn, broken, instable vision of Paradise lost. At what may be the beginning of the end of the harmonic cycle in European music, Tristan—or Wagner—hears, emerging out of the deepest, darkest, weariest permutation of the Tristan chords and motive, *a continuously monophonic, unaccompanied line*. Moreover, the nature of this unaccompanied melody is profoundly interesting: for it is a *linear* version of the perfect and imperfect fourths and fifths of the Tristan chords themselves. It starts from the perfect fifth, which is God, but then crumbles into imperfect fifths and fourths, wandering chromatically in long, nonmetrical convolutions, seeking but only intermittently finding again the fifth's perfection. Both the fluid, noncorporeal rhythm and the chromatically intensified melismata have an oriental flavour, and invoke the spirit of troubadour monody, though the innate melancholy of troubadour music is, of course, deepened by centuries of harmonic "consciousness."

Once Tristan has heard, however faintly, the Shepherd's monody, the process of regeneration may begin, not merely for him, but for post-Renaissance man. In this last act of *Tristan* Wagner does what had long been latent in his operatic technique, for the action is traumatic and, with the possible exception of the arrival of Mark, takes place entirely within Tristan's mind. As Kerman has pointed out, it deals with what one can accurately term Freudian regeneration. The reminiscence of monodic innocence induces Tristan, from near-death, to yearn for "day," but the resurgence of harmonic passion produces in him only agony, for the pain of living is too much to be borne. So he curses Day, which is life; and his ecstasy of anticipation, when Kurwenal leads him to expect Isolde's coming, subsides in another enormous frustrated cadence. At this point the monodic piping is the *empty* sea: the unknown and the unconscious, to which Tristan must surrender. It is this surrender which is effected in Tristan's immense monologue, which this time is distantly accompanied by the piping: so that although the process of curse and relapse is repeated, it is also changed. Now the piping leads Tristan away from amnesia towards an acceptance of his and our pain. He re-experiences the events of his traumatic past: not merely the events of the opera, but also those of his childhood and even the life and death of his father and mother. The gigantic recapitulation of the events of the first act is both a musical and an experiential resolution: an act of understanding and, indeed, of revelation. So the last curse becomes the purgation of his own guilt; it was *I myself* who brewed the potion, and man is responsible only to himself. But this ultimate climax to humanism is also an admission of humanism's inadequacy, for the revelation is also an initiation. Isolde at last comes, Tristan revives in a state beyond Day or curse or yearning, and the Shepherd pipes his "new tune," from which the chromatic anguish has been purged away, so that it is innocently diatonic, even pentatonic.

Seventeenth-century humanism, we saw, had thought of the sexual act as a dying, which seemed to negate Time. Now the admission is overt; the only escape from duality is in death itself, and Tristan dies to the merging of the Love and Death themes, which are now one. The ultimate beatitude is left to Isolde, as the orches-

c

tra at very long last resolves the tritonal tension of the Tristan chords into a luminous B major triad, infinitely sustained—infinitely in the sense that whenever the chord fades to silence must seem too soon. By this time the lovers are no longer separate beings. They are the male and female principle within Wagner himself, and within us all; and Wagner gives to the female the heavenly gift of intuition. At the end, Isolde is pure *anima,* into which *animus* is both absorbed and absolved.

Like Beethoven's last piano sonatas and quartets, Wagner's *Tristan* thus expresses the end and the inversion of humanism. The distinction between them lies in the fact that Beethoven entered his paradise in the sublime melodic proliferations of the arietta of Opus 111, whereas Wagner, performing a mystical act in dissolving time, consciousness and sexuality, does not completely achieve this lyrical consummation. The Shepherd's pentatonic "new tune" is notably inferior to his original melody, which was still tremulous with chromatic yearning, whereas the new tune of Beethoven's arietta might be called the fulfilment of his life's work. But it is given to few to enter paradise, which may be why Beethoven's last works had no direct successors, while Wagner's last works were the beginning of modern music. The greatness of *Tristan* is that although it tells us that perfect love can be realized only in nirvana, it affirms and reaffirms the nobility of man's aspiration. This too is the burden of the subjective mythological cycle of *The Ring.* By the time we reach *Die Götterdämmerung* the Dark Forest is unequivocally the Artist-Hero's mind, and although Brünnhilde is still the white dove, the troubadour's Eternal Beloved to be won or lost, the dark and light forces that fight for her are inextricably mingled, being aspects of one consciousness. This is why Hagen has such uncanny potency, and why Siegfried becomes his own betrayer. There can be no simple social answer to so cataclysmic an upheaval, no canalizing of harmonic tension by jolly fugato, or by the public conventions of aria or dance. All these external symbols of the things that make humanism workable have vanished; there *is* no fugato, no aria, no dance, only the surge of the symphonic texture which must work out the motives' musical and experiential destiny

—and has been doing so, not merely (as in *Tristan*) over four and a half hours, but through four enormous operas. One may feel claustrophobia—and rebellion—in submitting so utterly and for so long to Wagner's consciousness, yet one has no choice in the matter. And what makes one finally submit is that *The Ring's* ego-assertion has the "terrifying honesty" of great art. For Wagner's gods are men, or Man as he might be if all men could be Wagner; yet the cycle concludes with the man-god's twilight. Man relinquishes his attempt to be totally responsible for his destiny; Valhalla perishes in the purgatorial fire and—like the Wagnerian sequence itself—returns to its source, being renewed in the waters of the unconscious.

This return to the springs of consciousness—almost to pre-consciousness—has bearing on the distinction between *Tristan* and Wagner's last opera, *Parsifal,* which is also *Tristan's* imaginative complement. For the dark brother—the Hagen figure—is virtually banished, or reduced, in Klingsor, to impotence: while the heroic ego—the Siegfried figure—is transformed into Parsifal's pity for "the wound of the world." This could not have happened without a Christian heritage, but is not necessarily a Christian theme: what happens is that the burden of consciousness—the agony of yearning that had made Tristan and Isolde quintessentially human—is released, along with the fevered chromaticism; and in the vastly slow exfolitation of harmonic polyphony time (as Gurnemanz put it to Parsifal) is one with space. In a sense one might say that the immense slowness of the harmonic pulse of *Parsifal* is Wagner's most "prophetic" achievement—more so than the chromaticism of *Tristan.* It's a renunciation of the basic principle of opera which, having begun as the central expression of European humanism, had always been concerned' with the dominance of the will. Parsifal uncovers the path through the Dark Forest: which Debussy and Schoenberg, and ultimately Boulez, had to take.

After Wagner, submission to the dark forest or to the waters of the unconscious becomes an obsessive theme. It may, of course, be negative, a search for oblivion. In the music of Delius, for instance, the burden of the passion-laden, Wagnerian appoggiatura is again too great to be borne, and the ego longs to lose itself in "innocent" penta-

tonic arabesque and in the eternal nonhumanity of sea and hills. Out
of the tension of chromatic harmony flows a new kind of harmonically born polyphony which, especially in the choric vocal writing,
wings and sings. Yet the contrast between the chromaticism of the
harmony and the pentatonic tendency of the melody produces, in
Delius's most characteristic music,the pronouncedly nostalgic flavour
which differentiates it from Wagner: it longs for a lost Eden, not
for a Paradise regained. This is obvious if one considers Delius's
opera *A Village Romeo and Juliet* as a sequel to Wagner's *Tristan
und Isolde*. The theme is the same, for the opera deals with the
impossibility of achieving an identity between Word and Flesh,
between spirit and body, in the conditions of the temporal world.
The difference is that the lovers are young; we first meet them as
children, and they remain childlike, at the dawn of consciousness,
when they grow up to sing their love-music. What destroys them is
a sordid squabble over material possessions; love and property,
which are the conditions of this life, cannot mix. But their answer
to this situation is not, like that of Tristan and Isolde, to try to grow
up; it is rather to wish they were children again, preconscious.
This probably explains the ambiguous effect of the Dark Stranger
who helps them to escape from the conditions of mortality. He leads
them into the water gardens, which are Paradise Gardens, and into
the company of the gypsies who are oblivious of the trammels of
social convention, and directly in rapport with Nature. But the
Dark Stranger is also a Fiddler, like the Devil, and the gypsies are
Circe-like characters who seem in some ways sinister and minatory.
The wordless choral music they sing in the Paradise Gardens is
miraculously beautiful, inducing a pantheistic merging of ego-
dominated passion into Nature, as does the wordless chorus in
"A Song of the High Hills." But the young lovers' surrender is a
surrender, not an act of triumph; they do not transcend, in making
their own, the dark turmoil of passion which the Fiddler presumably
is. Because the Eden of their childhood cannot be recovered they
voluntarily surrender consciousness, slowly sinking their boat, allowing the waters to envelop them. The end of the opera is not a
rebirth, or even a potential rebirth, from the waters, but a slow

dissolution and relinquishment. This is why the orchestral summation, in "The Walk to the Paradise Garden," is miraculously poignant but consistently elegiac.

The village Romeo and Juliet surrender life because they cannot leave their childhood behind; Tristan re-experiences his childhood in order that he may live and die. The interdependence of love and death which both *Tristan* and *Götterdämmerung* sing of suggests how any composer looking to the future—not, like Delius, to the past—from the heights or depths of the Wagnerian crisis, had to seek a renewal of life within the psyche itself. We can observe the beginnings of this in one of Schoenberg's earliest works, the string sextet *Verklärte Nacht*, which was later transformed into a work for string orchestra. Although this piece is purely instrumental, it is a one-act, symphonically "subjective" opera on a theme closely related to *Tristan*. The poem by Richard Dehmel, which is translated into music, describes the walk of two lovers through the Dark Forest. She bears within her another man's child, possibly that of the husband she doesn't love; and the child is the burden of man's guilt. Walking through the darkness, and speaking with growing agitation of their awareness that their love must involve pain, they come upon a clearing in the forest which is "transfigured" by moonlight. Here they make love, and in the act of love the burden of guilt is assuaged, so that the child can be accepted as their own. This again is a regeneration myth, which has direct consequences in the music. To begin with, the texture is Tristanesque, though even riper and more sumptuous in its chromaticism, and the dialogue between high and low strings, representing the woman and the man, makes the operatic affiliations manifest. As the texture grows more harmonically agitated, however, so it grows more polyphonic; the Wagnerian sequences flow into a winging ecstasy, the "transfiguring" quality being in the whirling continuity of the lyricism and in the asymmetry of the melodic proliferations. In this sense *Verklärte Nacht* is a *positive* sequel to *Tristan*, as *A Village Romeo and Juliet* was not.

Despite the freedom of the polyphony, *Verklärte Nacht* contains no technical feature that is in itself revolutionary. Its conception of tonality is traditional: the D minor in which it opens is associated by Schoenberg, as by Beethoven, with the strife that is life's essence, while the D major in which it closes is a key of resolution; the moment of transfiguration is traditionally represented by an excursion into the high "sharpness" of F sharp. Nonetheless the linear independence of the music tends increasingly to override the Wagnerian sequences. And the more "air-borne" the polyphony becomes, the more the texture veers toward the ambiguous acceptance of chromaticism which, when once it is *unequivocally* accepted, will release us from the earth-pull of harmonic tension. This release comes in Schoenberg's "free" atonal period, and specifically in *Erwartung,* a work in which the literary theme is almost identical with that of *Verklärte Nacht.* The earlier piece was a "subjective" drama which takes place entirely in instrumental terms; in *Erwartung* the drama is, in a sense, theatrically objectified, but the implications of *Tristan* and *The Ring* are fulfilled, since there is now only one character, within whose mind the action takes place. Again, a woman is wandering, this time alone, through "the blind mazes of this tangled wood." She is possessed by a sexual passion of Tristanesque violence. Waiting to meet her lover in the wood, she knows at the same time that he will not come, that he has deserted her for a ghostly, white-armed other love who is probably, psychoanalytically speaking, his mother.

The climax comes when she stumbles upon his murdered body. It is not clear who murdered him; she refers, confusedly, to the other woman and to an indeterminate "they." But it is unclear because, of course, the action has no existence outside her own mind. She enters the dark wood of the unconscious, and the first stages of her wandering are a mingling of her memories and inchoate desires. Her discovery of the body is her recognition of loss, and complementarily of guilt and renunciation. From here on the unconscious takes over completely; text and music become hallucinatory, and "free" atonality is the musical synonym for this subconscious expressionism. Yet the pattern established by *Tristan* and *Verklärte Nacht* is continued, for submission to the unconscious brings release from terror; the piece ends with a "transfigured" vision of her lover, wherein passion is absolved, hatred forgotten. The absolution is also subjective. The point lies in her mind's and senses' aspiration; we don't know whether her love ever was or could be fulfilled in the conditions of temporality.

So the subjective fulfillment happens only in the music: which is why the text that Marie Pappenheim devised from Schoenberg's own suggestions is content to allow the music to re-create the fluctuations of the unconscious life; and is also why *Erwartung,* even more than *Tristan,* is a symphonic opera in which the drama takes place in the orchestra. The vocal line carries Wagnerian speech-song to a further point of melodic disintegration, as it follows the vagaries of the half-thinking, half-feeling mind; yet we have only to consider the first words the woman sings to see how the speech-rhythm, floating on the unconscious, has begun to counteract the earth-bound tug of metre and of harmonic symmetry. This fluctuating "additive" rhythm can be intimately related to the intense expressiveness of the orchestral texture which, in creating the atmosphere of the Dark Forest, creates too the realities of the imaginative life about which the woman is murmuring or crying in self-communion. For this reason the parlando line of the voice is not separate from the orchestral fabric. We find that, although the score contains a minimum of organization or repetition (since it is intended to express the gradual disintegration of mind and senses), the most dramatically crucial phrases which the woman sings are also those which attain greatest significance in the orchestral texture, and which recur not in exact recapitulation, but in evolutionary permutation. The phrase wherein, early in the opera, the woman says that if she cries out perhaps her lover will hear her, is echoed in the self-involved, undulating phrase wherein she admits he hasn't come. Alternating seconds and thirds are the basis of the extraordinary orchestral passage in which she panics, thinking she is pursued by black things of the woods, while the "cry" phrase reappears in anguished and modified inversion when she finds, or thinks she finds, her lover dead. This leads to the wonderful passage where she re-imagines her meetings with her lover in the walled garden (which, being a garden, and walled, is safe, compared with the forest's wildness). Here it is the luminosity of the orchestral texture that creates something like affirmation out of apparent dislocation, and this affirmative quality is never again lost, not even when she seems to be giving way to jealousy and nightmare. The climax of absolution comes when she asks "hast du sie sehr geliebt?" but can then add that he is not to blame. Perhaps one could almost say that during the course of the opera's "stream of consciousness" she learns that the tree trunk she had stumbled over (which let loose her nightmare) and the trunk of the murdered lover which she later discovers are the same. They are her own guilt, and she knows, like Tristan, that it was "I myself who brewed the potion." Then, with self-knowledge, the guilt can be lifted and, as morning glimmers through the blackness, she can have a vision in which she imagines she sees her lover, alive. The opera ends with her ineffably moving cry of longing, "Oh, bist du da? Ich suchte"; and the sensory life of the orchestral texture dissolves away in contrary motion chromatics.

It is difficult to know what to call this if it is not, as well as a moment of vision, an act of faith; and Schoenberg's music has demonstrated how the glimmer of faith is to be attained only by the relinquishment of consciousness, of corporeal rhythm, of thematic definition and of harmonic volition. The inner drama fades out in the flood of the unconscious, and in the final pages the orchestra transforms the Dark Forest into a water image. This dissolution into the gurgling waters harks back to the end of *The Ring* and of *A Village Romeo and Juliet* and looks forward to the waters that engulf Berg's Wozzeck, while his little child plays ball, as innocent of death as he is of whatever life has in store for him. It would be an exaggeration to say that this tremulously disembodied orchestral texture is a "positive" end, as compared with Delius's death-tending lament. It would, however, be true to say that the fluctuating, linear texture and radiant sonority of the Schoenberg and Berg passages contain at least the potentiality of a new birth. This mystical interpretation of the release from consciousness acquires explicit form at the end of *Die Jacobsleiter,* the gigantic oratorio that was to be the consummation of Schoenberg's "free" phase, though it remained (significantly) unfinished. The ladder of the title is the link between dying mortality and some kind of reincarnation, and the final passages of the score describe a woman on her deathbed who, having experienced the transition from life to death, floats upward, disembodied. The speaking voice becomes a wordless singing voice, winging over a dissolving orchestral texture that was to be distributed throughout the hall on loudspeakers, in a manner that we would now call stereophonic. Like the visionary moment in *Erwartung*, this transfiguration scene is not elegiac in feeling; and was, of course, a beginning as well as an end in compositional techniques, for the air-borne cantilena strikingly anticipates the melismatic vocal writing of Boulez.

This is clear if one considers *Pierrot Lunaire*, now generally accepted as one of the key works in twentieth-century music, as a successor to *Erwartung* and to Schoenberg's free atonal period in general. We are now a stage further away from Wagnerian heroism; the Hero has become a clown, the Pierrot-figure as symbol of Modern Man, and the rich sensory life of symphonic texture has given way to a chamber music idiom, usually thinly scored. The lyricism of the declamatory line has almost gone, too, for this Pierrot's song-speech, though freely notated as to pitch and duration, is now closer to speech than to song. Yet at the same time the Pierrot is a reincarnation of Tristan and of the Woman from *Erwartung;* though more broken and pathetic, he still yearns for love and the dream's fulfilment, and in nightmare imagines that he as lover has murdered the beloved. *Because* the voice can no longer sing, finding lyrical release, the instruments must seek the maximum of intensity from the minimum of physical force, so *Pierrot Lunaire* is a sequel to the Woman's cry of "Ich suchte," and if, in one sense, it is a piece about disillusion, it is also a search for Belief.

Since *Pierrot Lunaire* is in this sense a further twitch to the death-throes of humanism, we aren't surprised to discover that, within its humanistic "expressionism," it contains elements that might be described as ritualistic or even magical. The poems are grouped in three sets of seven, both magic numbers; and for the rest of his life

c*

Schoenberg was to be haunted by number symbolism. It's as though he had to seek some cosmological certainty (mythical as much as mathematical) to offset his obsession with the flux; and this "mythology," like *Erwartung's* moment of vision, is discovered *through* submission to the unconscious. Similarly, the contrapuntal ingenuities that begin to appear as a substitute for orthodox harmonic and tonal criteria led inevitably to the serial principle. Even in the amorphous stream of *Erwartung* there is a hint of this, in that Schoenberg associates an ostinato figure with the *path* the Woman must take through the forest's obscurity. The ostinato is the Way, and so is the Row, when Schoenberg has arrived at his fully fledged serial principle, for even more than the Wagnerian leitmotif it fulfils some of the functions of an Indian raga in that both the melodic and the harmonic aspects of the composition are derived from it. It is the source of the composition's life, the element within which the creator's talent *must* manifest itself: in which sense the Row becomes, as Valen said it was, the Word of God, the certainty beyond the flux.

We can trace the transition to serialism within the sequence of *Pierrot Lunaire.* The first group of seven poems is formally the freest, the most *Erwartung*-like. If the Woman in *Erwartung* is Isolde in nervous disintegration, Pierrot is the Artist—indeed, Schoenberg himself—weary and sick with insatiable love-longing. Columbine, the woman and mate, cannot satisfy his yearning; he cannot laugh it away in the Dandy's frivolity; the romanticized love-dream turns into drops of blood on the lips of a consumptive; he cannot find religious sanction in offering his verses to the Madonna. It is significant that this first cycle ends with its seventh number, a poem wherein Pierrot is ill unto death with his unappeasable longing; that the music of this latter-day Tristan should be scored for speaking-singing voice with solo flute; and that the melismatic character of the flute line should be even more oriental in feeling than is the Shepherd's pipe in *Tristan,* largely because it is, in its chromaticism, further removed from harmonic implications. It is this monodic song—in which the "decadent" irony of the text becomes a means of achieving detachment from Self—that leads into the second cycle, wherein Pierrot descends into the Night of the unconscious and, in his broken and pitiful fashion, faces up to the images of guilt, crime and punishment, as Tristan and the Woman had had to. The wings of giant moths obscure the light of the sun; Pierrot sees himself as grave-robber, as blasphemer, as the murderer of love; and in the last song of the cycle imagines himself crucified for his guilt, the crucifiers being the Crowd or the World, his guilt being his verses. This set of pieces begins with a passacaglia wherein the rigidity of the ostinato saves Pierrot from madness as he is submerged in Night; elaborate contrapuntal devices are used, with similar intention, in all the songs of the group, and the solo flute monody returns at the emotional climax to the entire work— the instrumental interlude that links Pierrot's moon-vision to his crucifixion in the fourteenth song.

In this work the implicit equation between the Artist as Scapegoat and Christ is not taken up, for the third group of songs seeks for release from the agony of consciousness in fantasy: nostalgic reminiscences of the old Italian Comedy, dadaistic nonsense, and dreams of a fairy-world where guilt wouldn't matter. Naturally enough, the pieces are much freer; there are no embryonic serial pieces, except for "Moonspot," which, in its canonic complexities, seems almost parodistic—intentionally, for in it the spot (of guilt) which Pierrot tries to rub off his black jacket turns out to be moonshine. We can see here why *Pierrot* is so crucial a work in the history of twentieth-century music: the two complementary yet contradictory responses to the "crisis of humanism" are both implicit in it. Man could throw off consciousness as completely as is humanly possible, retreating to the Absurd, accepting the absurdity of life as itself a positive; or he could attempt to achieve a new integration of the splintered personality which could only be, at this stage in the checkered history of Europe, in some sense "religious." In the latter part of his career Schoenberg, like Freud, chose the second of these alternatives, and became a religious prophet. Both men were Jews, born about the same time, in the same city; both, in their life-work, started from the primary human urge of sexuality; both faced up to a hiatus in the flow of creative vitality that man's dedication to self had led him into. Freud sought to reintegrate the dislocated fragments of the personality; Schoenberg sought a linear and polyphonic (and later serial) integration of the chromatically splintered mind and senses.

The Jews, Owen Barfield has suggested (in *Saving the Appearances*), were a necessary link between the Ancient World and the flowering of Christianity—just as Jewish liturgical chant was an essential transition between oriental and Greek monody and the plainchants of western Europe. As against the oriental conception of Time as cyclic, the Semitic way was a progress forward through history, and it was a way "shared, indeed, by the individual but trodden by the nation as a whole." Only after the Greeks had "polarized creation into consciousness on the one side and phenomena, or appearances, on the other, was memory made possible, and it is through memory that man acquires his self-consciousness. The position of the Jews in history is comparable with the position occupied by memory in the composition of the individual man." Paradoxically Schoenberg, ultimate composer of the European consciousness of self, is also a composer of history, retracing the racial memory. In his earlier years he—identified with the Woman of *Erwartung* and with the lunar Pierrot—seeks to heal the breach between flesh and spirit created by post-Renaissance man's obsession with materiality; in his later work he attempts more radically to obliterate the mind's divisions, absorbing the Wagnerian yearning of his early music into a "mystical" resolution comparable with that of late Beethoven. His string trio and third and fourth quartets are the same kind of music as Beethoven's last quartets, with the important difference that Schoenberg's music fails to enter Beethoven's paradise; and like Beethoven, Schoenberg knew that if nameless terrors exist below the level of our consciousness, "God's kingdom is in ourselves" also. It is significant that, in the unfinished opera-oratorio *Moses and Aaron*, he saw this personal vision specifically within the context of the history of his race. This consummatory work stands in the same relationship to Schoenberg's serial period as the (also unfinished) *Die Jacobsleiter* stands to his free chromatic phase. The crisis within the inner life is now seen as an historical crisis also; in both, musical technique and philosophical statement are identical.

Like Freud, Schoenberg associates himself with Moses, as the revealer of the Spirit; yet he is also Aaron, the (necessary) mediator between God and the World, the instrument through which spirit might be made flesh. Though the human situation with which the opera deals is basic to the human predicament at any time and place, it has a painful pertinence to us today since, living at a time dedicated to materiality, we are acutely aware that any attempt at incarnation seems in some degree to sully spiritual revelation. Schoenberg demonstrates this, in his opera, in a characteristically uncompromising form, for all the "materials" of musical tradition become for him a partial betrayal. Thus he associates his most richly developed harmonic textures—his heritage from post-Renaissance Europe—with the World, and makes Aaron an operatic tenor, whose arioso often employs the row in harmonic contexts, with a prevalence of "sensuous" major and minor sixths. Similarly, the most powerfully "human" music in the score—the only music dominated by corporeal rhythms—is the "Dance Around the Golden Calf," which concerns man's ultimate degradation through his submission of the Idea to the Image. The horrid, lurching motor rhythms—the raucous, squealing orchestration, the realistically heterophonic polyphony—are images of chaos: "in the destructive element immerse." As a result, Schoenberg's erotic rite is not a positive impulse; if vigorously earthy, it is also sadistic, and the broken fragments of line and motive and rhythm are, at the height of the frenzy, disintegrative.

Yet in a sense this negative impulse is potentially also positive. Although Moses, in the biblical story, breaks the tables of the Law in anger at the people's idolatry, that idolatry is not wholly evil. The Golden Calf was also a Mithraic fertility symbol; in scattering his ashes upon the waters and then forcing the people to drink, Moses appealed directly to the dark forces which the Law would seem to deny. While this is never explicit in Schoenberg's music, one might say that in breaking up the animal rhythm of the body, the music yearns, in ecstatic inarticulateness, for transcendence. This is most notable in the unfrenzied, beautiful music sung to the Calf by the Old Men and the Invalid Women. Similarly, Aaron— who might be God's messenger—sometimes sings music which reminds us not of the row's material and sensual permutations, but of its divine origins, as he does, for instance, when he first "floated rather than walked" towards the people. The row itself—the Idea as against the multiple Images created from it—is here quite explicitly God: the alpha and omega of both the physical and spiritual universe, the ultimate unity of musical space in which, as Schoenberg himself said, there is no up or down, no right or left, no backward or forward, and no longer any tension, only suspension. The vertical form of the row which opens the opera on *wordless* voices has become, doctrinally, the Law, magically dividing the twelve semitones into four trinities of perfect and imperfect fourths (the Tristan chords) and of minor thirds and augmented fifths, producing chords which have the minimum of harmonic implication for the tonally trained ear. Similarly, the first horizontal statement of the row is a mirror structure with retrograde inversion—the serpent eating its own tail. The row, being God's eternity and infinity, could release us, as Moses *speaks* the Idea of the spirit's delivery, from consciousness and guilt. Yet the more Aaron the mediator *sings,* and the more he engages in musical and dramatic action, the more the melodic and harmonic properties of music become identified with the falling away from God, which culminates in the nervous and corporeal frenzy of the "Dance Around the Golden Calf." Aaron is perpetual change, and change, being of its nature mortal and ungodly, must involve corruption. This theme was implicit in Schoenberg's work as early as *Erwartung,* wherein the same neutral god-chords occur at the moment when the Woman has her transitory vision of peace and the Lover and Beloved become one in the safety of the Walled Garden, before the ultimate disintegration of mind and senses. Perhaps the end of *Erwartung* was the point at which Schoenberg relinquished the (Wagnerian) belief or hope—still latent in *Verklärte Nacht*—that the body's consummation might be also the spirit's grace.

Certainly it would seem that music, which for Schoenberg was essentially a search after Spirit, became in effect the Spirit's denial, completing Dryden's prophecy in "untuning the sky." Moses can only speak the Idea; Aaron in singing of it betrays it, while the people's vacillation, their lost state, is manifest musically in the fact that they exist in a no man's land between speech and song. The union of spirituality and corporeality—and therefore the spirit's fulfilment—cannot be achieved: so although Schoenberg's *text* for *Moses and Aaron* ends with the prophecy "In the wasteland you shall be invincible and shall achieve the goal: union with God," the last phrase that he actually set was "O Word that I lack,"* after which Moses sinks to the ground in despair. The orchestra's tritonal tensions coalesce in a unisonal F sharp on violins that swells to fortissimo, but then fades into silence; we are left with this momentary vision of the eternal unity, which neither Moses nor we can compass. It is difficult to imagine how the opera could have been completed since when, in the text of Act III, Moses reasserts the Idea, Aaron, though freed from the chains in which his denial of the Law had cast him, is liberated only to die. That Schoenberg, dually identified with Moses and Aaron, "fails" to lead his people into the Promised Land does not imply an artistic failure. On the contrary, one might say that it is because he experiences the spirit's revelation and the desire for its incarnation, yet cannot finally realize it, that the myth inherent in his life's work, and in *Moses and Aaron* specifically, is so immediately and deeply relevant to us. He wrote his most philosophically religious work at the time when he had temporarily renounced Judaism, because he had to face up to the crisis of humanism irrespective of any orthodoxy, inherited creed or *a priori* assumption. Like his Pierrot Lunaire, he became our scapegoat, purging our guilt in the fury of the Golden Calf episode, which is why we find the music so nervously, as well as physically, disturbing. Yet although Schoenberg does not himself achieve the new revelation and is in that sense an end to

* Schoenberg uses the terms Idea and Image as more or less synonymous with the Christian concept of the Word and the Flesh. His "Wort" is almost the opposite of St. John's Word that was in the beginning, for it is the means through which the Idea might be made manifest.

centuries of European humanism, it is clear that in reaching the
ultimate inversion of humanism that was presaged in *Tristan,*
Schoenberg's music could imply, for future generations, a fresh start.
Harmonically based, even melodically founded, European music
has proved to be a frustration of Spirit; and if Schoenberg did not
himself ultimately explore the denial of the harmonic concept that
is inherent in his musical synonym for God, Webern was to attempt
precisely that, within the premises of serialism. The Jewish race,
springing from the orient, made possible Christian humanism, which
explodes in *Tristan* and *Parsifal;* Schoenberg, as Wagner's successor,
reinstates Jewish consciousness and the duality of spirit and flesh;
then his successors seek the supreme identity with the Brahma,
wherein duality is meaningless.

For although Webern was a pupil of Schoenberg it would be
true to say that from his earliest composing years his approach was
in part non-Schoenbergian. Thus Schoenberg, who ultimately (as
we saw) "inverted" European musical history, nonetheless started
from the Beethovian and Brahmsian notion of music as Becoming:
which notion we do not find even in Webern's opus 1, the
Passacaglia for orchestra. Despite its obvious derivation from late
Wagner, this work recreates Wagner in terms of Bach. Being a passacaglia, it is essentially a monothematic piece, on a D minor theme,
including almost all the chromatic semitones, so that it is an anticipatory series. The technique throughout is that of monistic variation,
the second motive being a crab or backward inversion of the first.
The result is that, even in this opus 1, form is for Webern—much
more consistently than for Berg or Schoenberg—the antithesis of
development. It is interesting that if the *Passacaglia* reminds us of
any then contemporary music it is of Mahler. Polyglot Vienna, at
the end of the nineteenth century, saw the twilight of Western
civilization, from the disintegration of which must come a rebirth
within the psyche. Schoenberg, we have seen, was obsessed with the
Wagnerian "subjective" crisis, with disintegration and reintegration
within the ego itself. Mahler, though a fanatically self-revelatory
composer, saw the self within the framework of civilization, and for
him the symphony was a cosmos; he was concerned, both tragically

and ironically, with the totality of the ego's experience, within a social context. Thus his last completed work, *Das Lied von der Erde,* is an elegy both on the Lost Self and on the world the self is lost in, and it is not an accident that the last movement should be a *farewell* both to the World and to Western consciousness. This is not a consequence of the fact that Mahler chose to set Chinese poems; on the contrary, he selected Chinese poems because he was concerned with this experience. The harmonic pulse of the music slows almost to immobility; the reverberation of percussion is separated by immense silences; the orchestration becomes luminous, linear, soloistic, as melismatic arabesques flower around ostinato notes and pedal points. These arabesques, predating Messiaen by thirty years, remind us both of oriental cantillation and of bird song, while the final chord, a Debussyan added sixth, is also a verticalization of the pentatonic scale.

The weeping appoggiaturas of the final pages of Mahler's *Das Lied* imply that the surrender of harmonic consciousness is reluctant; we weep for the self unfulfilled and the world lost, and can find in Mahler—an Austrian Roman Catholic Jew—a musical synonym for our own alienation and uprootedness. Webern's *Passacaglia* is almost exactly contemporary with Mahler's work, and resembles it in its luminous scoring, its rhythmic fluidity (largely created by triplet figurations sometimes stated, sometimes only implied, against a duple pulse), and in its use of silence. It differs from Mahler's *Das Lied,* however, because its stringent contrapuntal organization banishes lamenting nostalgia. In so far as it has a valedictory flavour it is more Brahms-like than Mahlerian. On the whole, however, we may relate it to the forward-looking, soloistic chamber-music polyphony of Mahler's work rather than to Mahler's regressive characteristics. We can already see why it was to be Webern, rather than Schoenberg, who was to create the new world of the spirit from which avant-garde music was to spring.

This brings us to the significant fact that Webern's early music is related to Debussy's revolution no less directly than to Schoenberg's. The *Five Pieces,* opus 5, for string quartet have obvious affinities with the tiny pieces of Schoenberg's "free" period, and like them relinquish sequence, repetition, architectural balance and dramatic argument. Yet they resemble the most Debussyan aspect of Schoenberg's earlier music, as exemplified by the piano pieces of opus 19, in each of which a "moment of sensation" is distilled, often from a single chord or interval. The fourth of Webern's five pieces carries this technique to a still more rarefied exquisiteness. Melody is a broken sigh, haloed by pedal notes and ostinati in harmonics. Despite its fragmentation, the music acquires a tender passivity more comparable with Debussy than with Schoenberg's nervous intensity; already it induces a characteristically Webernian calm.

This "seismographic," Debussyan quality is still more evident in the *Six Pieces* for orchestra, opus 6, which are the "Farewell" of Mahler's *Das Lied von der Erde* re-created not in epic terms but in terms of an exquisitely nervous inner life. It is interesting that even the comparatively extended, superficially agitated pieces, such as No. 2, use very short if pliant melodic phrases, repeated in obsessive rhythmic patterns, while the orchestral texture splinters into "points" of orchestral colour, with single tones being repeated in complex numerical metres, like a tala. It's as though the melodic phrases are a last twitter of Western consciousness, which is dissolving into an oriental contemplation; and the use of the word "twitter" reminds us of Paul Klee's twittering machine and of the profound affinity there is between the minutely calligraphic art of painter and composer. Both Webern and Klee had deep roots in the past; yet if Webern would hardly have said, with Klee, that he wanted to be "as though new born, knowing nothing about Europe, nothing, knowing no pictures (or music or poems), entirely without impulses, almost in an original state," we can see that it is precisely some such liberation from the past that the young have found in him. The marvellous fourth piece from opus 6—composed as long ago as 1909—is in some ways closer to certain aspects of avant-garde music even than Webern's later work. It is in effect scored for two orchestras. One, immensely slow and almost pulseless, is an oriental orchestra of tolling gongs, bells and drums; the other, alternating sustained, gong-like ostinato chords on woodwind and thudding, funereal bumps on muted trombones and tuba with jittery, broken melodic phrases, rises to a kind of stifled scream: at which point Western consciousness expires, leaving the oriental percussion band alone.

The short, slow pieces (Nos. 3, 5 and 6) all use tiny, infinitely expressive melodic phrases which whimper into silence over ostinato chords on muted brass, or static ostinato figures on harp, celesta or string harmonics. Here it is not merely the individual chord, as in Debussy, which has become an end in itself; the isolated sound or tone-colour has become an event, without antecedence or consequence. This tendency is still more marked in the *Five Pieces* of opus 10 (1913). Even briefer than the pieces of opus 6, these "moments of sensation" are now scored for very small forces, light and airy in sonority. The extraordinary third piece, with its quivery ostinato on mandoline and guitar, has no harmonic movement at all; the sound is startlingly suggestive of Japanese koto music.

The spontaneous affinity between Webern and the oriental and medieval mind in part explains why, when he began to write serial music, he tended to employ the row in a spirit different from Schoenberg's. For Schoenberg, the row was a refuge from chaos; the pressure of harmonic and tonal tension was so extreme that it had to be released into linearity. Webern, though highly wrought in nerves and senses, could live in and on his nerves in relative passivity; the explosive figurations that intermittently erupt in his music do not ultimately affect its radiance, nor even its serenity. This may be precisely what the music is "about": the music effects the catharsis of hypernervosity, in the same way as does Klee's meticulous, child-like, yet complex, quasi-oriental calligraphy. Webern can do this because, although rooted in humanist tradition, he was by nature a mystic: which is what Schoenberg frustratedly sought to be. This may mean that Webern is, for us, the more limited composer, but it also helps us to understand the curiously timeless perfection that his works achieve, almost from his earliest years.

It is interesting that when Webern scores the Ricercare from Bach's *Musical Offering* he makes it sound more medieval than baroque, for the presentation of the theme in "Klangfarben" style emphasizes its structure as a collocation of cells or tiny units and tends to deny the sense of growth. Webern makes the Ricercare not so much a religious piece in a social context—an equation between the human and the divine like most of Bach's music—but rather a still more hermetic version of the "abstract" rite of Bach's *Art of Fugue*. It's a religious piece, in that it seeks a haven of quiet within the mind: not a public affirmation of faith, but a private meditation wherein the contrapuntal unity is the oneness of God. Webern's own serial, especially canonic, processes are thus related philosophically as well as musically to the medieval aspects of Bach's art. Medieval contrapuntal unity is relevant to Webern's art, whereas Bach's "humanistic" ordering of harmonic tensions is not. Even in his most ostensibly Bachian work—the *Passacaglia,* opus 1 —the contrapuntal process whereby the second motive is a backward inversion of the first is medieval, and in his serial works he has an instinctive partiality for the circular structure that is reflected, mirror-wise, into eternity. The rows he favours are not only more remote from tonal implications than Schoenberg's, they are also more mathematically ordered. For Schoenberg, the row was derived from the themes, a crystallization of melodic utterances; for Webern the row is a preordained structure within which, and only within which, creation may exist. In this sense, "what we establish is the law," as Webern has put it, and what is established (the row) is for Webern synonymous with what used to be called inspiration. Similarly, quoting Goethe, Webern has said that everything arbitrary or illusory must fall away: "here is necessity, here is God." So if the row is an abstraction, "the highest reality," it is also a revelation; and "a primal blessing shall come to bestow greater blessings."

The eternity-serpent dominates the form of many of Webern's later works; the *Piano Variations,* opus 27, gives us the row-theme accompanied by itself backwards and inverted and, in the process, divests piano sonority of most of its traditional sensual appurtenances. The persistent major sevenths and minor ninths no longer have any effect of harmonic tension, but become a tinkling of bells surrounding melodic phrases that still have great expressivity, but are brief, broken, disembodied. If there is an oriental connotation in this, the music no longer has the directly sensuous appeal of the more Debussyan early works; corporeality has almost completely dissolved into spirit. The first movement of the *Symphony,* opus 21, for instance, has much in common with the techniques, and even the sonorities, of the late Gothic motet. The piece is in two symmetrical halves, both repeated, in double canon by inversion. While the material is, of course, chromatic not modal, the fragmentation of theme and motive, the "emptiness" of the texture, the dislocation of rhythms and the discontinuity of scoring all have their parallels in late Gothic technique. Then it was as though the preordained order of the cantus firmus and of the isochronous rhythms just held together the disintegrating fragments of a civilization, so that the music's seemingly suprapersonal order was at once austere and desperate. Here in Webern's *Symphony,* at the end maybe of the humanist phase of European civilization, Viennese (in particular Mahlerian) sensuality and pathos are reaching back to an order similarly preordained, and the more needed because European consciousness has travelled so far. And Webern succeeds—for himself, at least, and for us as participants in his private rite: for the final effect of this broken texture—in which "expressive" melody is fragmented into little sighs of two notes, or even into isolated single notes whose continuation is merely implied in silence—can validly be described as "ruhig." We can understand this more clearly if we consider the *Symphony* in relation to the sequence of vocal cantatas that were Webern's *opera ultima,* all of which have mystical texts, usually by Hildegard Jone.

Das Augenlicht, opus 26, being scored for four-part chorus with a chamber orchestra, reminds us that Webern was in fact a scholar in the field of late Gothic music, especially the motets of Matteo da Perusia. But his scholarly interest is a result, not a cause, of his creative instinct, for he too sought a quasi-mathematical, suprapersonal order from a texture (and experience) that was chaotically disintegrated. What was implicit in the *Symphony* is here explicit: the initial vocal entries in canon by inversion, the isolated sonorities of the individual notes in the instrumental parts, the silences within the triplet figurations that are often only latent, even the super-

human treatment of the human voice—all these have direct counterparts in the doctrinal or magical order and the hoqueting (or
hiccuping) styles of late Gothic music. Moreover, the words of the
text specifically concern "the light of the eye": how "one man's
vision" may become miraculous, when light is born from the soul's
retreat to the "sea's bed." The moment of vision becomes a moment
of broken homophony; then the harmonic flesh finally disintegrates
in the exquisite coda when the eyes open "und es macht ihn gut."

The mingling of Christian mysticism with pantheism which we
find here is characteristic of all Webern's work, and may be responsible for the *affirmative* effect of many of his most abstract
and—it would seem—nervously jittery compositions. The *Concerto*
for nine instruments, opus 24, is a case in point. The piece has been
much analyzed because its "machinery" is comparatively easy to
describe. Thus it is based on the most symmetrical and mathematically ordered of all Webern's rows. What has not been pointed
out, however, is that Webern's use of the row-material is part of an
experiential process and that this—not the mere fact that serial-
contrapuntal ingenuities exist—makes the piece good music. The
segments of the row are initially hurled at us in a hierarchy of
speeds. The rhythmic dislocations grow gradually more pronounced
until the movement ends with a stretching out of the segments both
in pitch and in rhythm (crotchet triplets against quaver triplets
which often override the bar lines), followed by a brief coda stating
all the segments in separation, and ending with a triplet hiccup
across the beat. The total effect of this movement is thus highly
nervous, like a cat on hot bricks.

By contrast, the second movement is almost completely immobile.
The 2/4 movement is regular throughout, though it is complicated
by the fact that some instruments move from strong to weak beat,
whereas others move from weak to strong. This two-way pendulum
creates a subtle sense of suspension and equilibrium. This is com-
plemented by the fact that the harmonic texture keeps consistently
to the alternation of thirds and major sevenths (chromatic semitones inverted) which is implicit in the row. Even more than in the
Piano Variations, therefore, the dissonant harmony is deprived of

its traditional tension; the dissolution of the melodic line, over the piano's pendulum, thus achieves, in this case, an oriental rather than medieval calm. Moreover, this immobility influences the nervosity typical of the first movement, for while the last movement is very quick and explosive, its canonic order is Gothic, and immediately apprehensible to the ear as well as the eye. Though the concept of development in the classical sense is irrelevant to Webern's work, it is true to say that there is an experiential process, if not progress, in this piece: because of our entry into the slow movement's timeless heaven we can reassert a kind of corporeal rhythm, and when that in its turn becomes broken and disrupted, we can find in the process a kind of gaiety, even hilarity, for the hoquets at the end of the movement remind us of a jazz break: nor is the comparison facetious, since the jazz break seeks ecstasy from the beat's destruction. If this movement is comedy, it is high comedy which tunes with Webern's mysticism and reminds us that he still has the essential humanity without which sublimation becomes meaningless.

Discovering in abstraction "the highest reality," Webern in a limited sense succeeded where Schoenberg, in *Moses and Aaron,* had failed. As a human testament, Schoenberg's failure may be more significant than Webern's success, but it was the apparently consummatory nature of Webern's achievement that led to his becoming a seminal figure, whose music in part precipitated the new world of the avant garde. Webern's abstraction was not, however, the only possible extension from Schoenberg. Other composers were to follow through the implications of that haunted and haunting flute monody from *Pierrot Lunaire,* and of the surrealistic tendencies of the songs in the third cycle. This surrealism could be and was allied to certain features of the music of Claude Debussy, that other great seminal figure whose revolution is in some ways even more radical than that of Schoenberg. In the technique of Schoenberg we have observed the disintegration of the burden of harmonic passion inherent in the Wagnerian sequence, its attempted sublimation, and its ultimate frustration, until it finds a kind of release in the abstraction of Webern, Schoenberg's disciple. Now in Debussy's music Wagnerian sensual passion is still (harmonically) evident; but although it is not sublimated it has ceased to be a burden, for it is accepted with oriental passivity. Thus, while Debussy created in *Pelléas et Mélisande* an operatic myth closely related to both *Tristan* and *Parsifal,* he neither sought nor desired any mystical release from passion, for unlike Schoenberg he was concerned with what happens to passion when the Will is not frustrated, but extinct. This is why *Pelléas* is a key work of our time, the ramifications of which extend beyond music into the theatre, poetry, the novel and the visual arts.

III

The Dark Forest: Debussy's *Pelléas et Mélisande* as a Parable of Relinquishment

In Wagner's *Tristan und Isolde* the identity between love and death is the beginning of the end of humanism. For Wagner, it is a triumphant end, for though Tristan has to die, he dies in the belief that his consuming passion is the universe. That was a heroic achievement. More naturally, the twilight of humanism led to a pessimistic view of human destiny; this is evident both in Maeterlinck's play of *Pelléas et Mélisande* and in Debussy's almost verbatim setting of it. For though the theme is the same as that of *Tristan,* the treatment of it could hardly be more different. Wagner wrote the libretto of *Tristan* himself, directing it towards the music which, in its continuous flow, is his own inner life. The music is the shaping reality, which achieves its triumph even as it seems to be driven by forces outside the Self—by Time and by Fate (what happens to us). Debussy, on the other hand, sets the play as a play, allowing the music the minimum of energy as a shaping force. Technically, his approach returns to Monteverdi's conception of opera as a play in music, making allowance for the fact that Monteverdi expected heroic actors to declaim, whereas Maeterlinck's language and Debussy's setting of it—coming at the end of the cycle of European humanism—dethrone the Hero and are naturalistic in expression. This is a logical extension of Wagnerian technique, for Wagner's song-speech would have been naturalistic if he and his characters had not been supermen.

If we compare Debussy and Schoenberg as successors to Wagner, we see that, for Schoenberg, retreat to the unconscious had to lead to a mystical vision, a renewal of the religious instinct, however thwarted. For Debussy, however, the state of will-lessness becomes a good in itself. This distinction is evident in the orchestral texture of *Erwartung* and of *Pelléas et Mélisande*. Both Schoenberg and Debussy start from Wagner's orchestral sensuality, both achieve from it an exquisite refinement that does not cease to be sensual. Yet the "expressionist" concentration of Schoenberg's harmony is created from a texture that is increasingly linear and, in that sense, harmonically disintegrative. The "air" which he thus lets into the Wagnerian cocoon gives to the texture the typical radiance on which we commented, and this sonority is inseparable from the work's approach toward a metaphysical vision. If Schoenberg frees the Wagnerian leitmotives still further into linearity, Debussy does the opposite, for although the texture is softer and more delicate than Wagner's, it is still more pervasively enveloping. It feels like a release because the Wagnerian desire egoistically to shape the themes and mould the sonority has gone; we live and move—insofar as we move at all—within the mists of the unknown that surrounds us. In a sense the sonority is the All, to which, however intense our passions, we can do no more than react seismographically.

This is evident in every aspect of the technique. Thus, whereas Wagner's "endless melody," though repeatedly frustrated, is always sequentially pressing onward, seeking the ultimate resolution of the Tristan chords' tension in the Shepherd's monodic piping and the melodic consummation of the "Liebestod," Debussy's leitmotives tend to be isolated from one another, even to be restricted to separate scenes, and although they change, they do not grow. Complementarily, his sensuously undulating harmonies, his Wagnerian chromatics, differ from Wagner's in that they do not even seek to progress. They oscillate around fixed nodal points; thus, the harmonic sensuality is paradoxically unrelated to *corporeal* energy, and the *spiritual,* numerical rhythm of the vocal line (which is closer to plainsong than to operatic recitative) floats, directionless, on the sensual harmonies. The static nature of the harmony, combined with the melismatic, usually pentatonic, arabesques into which the melodic lines flower, often gives Debussy's music an oriental flavour, which derives not from the superficial fact that he heard Javanese music at the Paris Exhibition, but from his intuitive need to counteract "the pain of consciousness" with an oriental passivity. In Wagner, the inner life tries to take control, to become the universe, and in Schoenberg the spirit seeks, if it does not find, ecstasy through the unconscious. In Debussy, retreat to the inner life becomes a surrender to destiny. We are lost, will-less, in the dark wood, and to accept this as the essential human condition is the only wisdom we can hope for. It doesn't matter that God as creator or as preserver is absent. Instead of God, there are feelings, sensations, and whatever causes sensations. Accepting the flux, human consciousness is reduced to existence without duration. There is only the present moment, no causation and no consequence; the revolution in Debussy's world lies in the fact that this condition no longer induces terror.

The profound difference between this surrender and that in Delius's *A Village Romeo and Juliet* is that in Delius the sense of Wagnerian harmonic progression still implies the will to desire, however frustrated it may be, and still involves memory of happiness past. Debussy, more radically, seeks to release consciousness from both memory and desire; this is why his opera is so disturbing and has had so deep an effect on the history of our time. We can see this in Maeterlinck's treatment of the myth itself. The story of *Pelléas* is very close to that of *Tristan,* with one crucial distinction. The climax of *Tristan,* we saw, was the hero's immense soliloquy, his traumatic Delirium, wherein he admitted that the responsibility for drinking the potion was his alone; thus *he* is Fate, and the recognition is both his death and his triumph. *Pelléas* reverses this. Golaud—the only character who attempts to take action about anything—is the villain, though a sympathetic villain because he is a part of us, as King Mark is a part of Tristan. For the young lovers the only happiness consists in submission, and since they do not even know what they are submitting to, submission becomes at the end identified with inanition.

Since Debussy seeks freedom from memory and desire, *Pelléas et Mélisande* takes place in a timeless antiquity which is also an eternal present, and in a *selva oscura* which is also the subconscious and the world of dream. The first sounds we hear are those of a slow, march-like theme, built on a rising fifth, which in the Middle Ages was God, but now is Destiny, taking precedence over all. Imposed on it is Golaud's theme, which would imply action in its syncopated rhythm, yet revolves on itself, unable to break away from its obsessive anchor D, and then peters out over neutral whole-tone chords which are an ellipsis of two Tristanesque tritones, no longer attempting resolution. Mélisande's theme first appears over a pedal note, in whole-tone harp arpeggios; incapable of growth, her tune is pentatonically innocent and drifts, rudderless, on the whole-tone flow. Golaud finds her, weeping, by a well: the source of spiritual life from which everyone is cut off. He tells her that he was out hunting, but his prey—a wounded boar—escaped. Since we learn later that he was in fact on his way to make an important marriage, for reasons of state, we may suspect that this boar was phallic, and that even Golaud, the man of action, acts to no end. Lost in the Dark Forest through Experience which he cannot understand, he lights on Mélisande, who is no less lost through her Innocence. She runs away from him in pentatonic scurrying and says she will throw herself into the well if he attempts to touch her. She would return to "spirit" because she fears the contagion of the world, by which, she tells us in a quivering of pentatonic thirds, she has been irremediably "hurt." The hurt, apparently, explains why she has lost the Golden Crown that an anonymous "he" had given her, as she is later to lose Golaud's ring, and any hope of sensual fulfilment. Most significantly, when Golaud, as potential man of action, offers to recover the crown for her from the water, she won't hear of it, but breaks into hysterical protest. She doesn't want to be "whole," and this in part explains the extraordinarily potent effect of the "innocence" of Debussy's recitative.

It is interesting that in this initial scene the vocal lines don't change in character as the exchanges between Golaud and Mélisande become more passionate. The harmony grows more distraught, the orchestral texture suggests a suppressed agitation by cross-rhythms, but floating in whole-tone sequences the music acquires no harmonic momentum, and the vocal lines, murmuring in speech-inflected, pentatonic incantation, are powerless to direct the incipient flood of passion. Despite the incessant chromatic oscillations, the only real modulation in this scene is the shift to a whole-tone pentatonic F sharp when Golaud at last tells Mélisande his name, and she, faced with the fact of human identity, becomes immediately conscious of mortality, and remarks that his hair is greying. Over an obsessive syncopated rhythm he tells her that they can't stay in the wood for ever, his "hunting call" theme linking him with both destiny and the possibility of action. Despite his clarified, A-flat-majorish lyrical expansion, she says she will do *nothing*. Passive again, however, she finally agrees to go with him if he will promise not to touch her.

The next scene takes place six months later. Mélisande, her innocence presumably submitting passively to his experience, has married Golaud, and it is significant that we are aware of this temporary triumph of Golaud's activity over Mélisande's passivity in the orchestral interlude *between* the scenes. We hear of the situation from a letter which Golaud has written to his half brother Pelléas, and which Geneviève, his mother, is reading to King Arkel, his grandfather. She reads, in pentatonic incantation, like someone telling an old tale, with an occasional intrusion of a diminished fourth (on the word "sanglote," for instance) reminding us of the vibrant reality of passion, even if we are directionless. Golaud confesses, in the letter, that he found Mélisande in the Dark Forest when they were both lost, and that he knows no more about her now than he did when they married. He fears that Arkel will not approve of the marriage, and asks Pelléas to light a lantern on the tower that overlooks the sea if all is well. If he sees no light, he will sail away and never return home; even the man of action, apparently, is craven.

When Geneviève has finished the letter, the orchestra sighs a Tristanesque phrase built on a rising fifth and drooping appoggiatura which takes the place of what Arkel cannot bring himself to utter. The phrase appears in various forms, always nondeveloping, while Arkel says that he doesn't like the marriage and had hoped that Golaud would have effected his marriage of social convenience, especially since his father and acting king is sick, and probably dying. Nonetheless, Arkel never battles against fate; what must be, will be, and there may be a pattern in destiny which we cannot perceive. Arkel's theme, rising up a fourth and then descending, is faintly liturgical, without Golaud's whole-tone vacillations, for he is the closest Debussy's world can come to quasi-divine sanctions. Not surprisingly, the theme is related to the Fate motive, both in its contours and in the regularity with which it is repeated. Though fateful, it is not sinister, but tenderly compassionate.

Arkel, if wise, is significantly almost blind: in so far as we see truly, we cannot see much. Pelléas, who now enters, is the grandson of Arkel and the son of Geneviève by the Dying King, whereas Golaud is Geneviève's son by a previous husband, long dead. Pelléas's youthfulness is thus contrasted with the "grey-haired" experience of his half brother, and he sings music which has a simple animation, if not energy; his life-enhancing qualities are associated with a characteristically eager, syncopated rhythm, and with the "sharp" key of E. But his music, too, is obsessed with ostinato figures and with oscillations between two tonally neutral chords, so that it never "gets anywhere" harmonically. The first thing he tells us is that he has been summoned to visit a dying friend—which may be a premonition of his own death. Arkel persuades him not to leave, since his king and father is dying also, and the scene ends when they hang the lantern on the tower, to light home Golaud and Mélisande. The simplest pentatonic version of the Mélisande theme provides a reticent, if subtle, extension to fluttering harp arpeggios and bell noises. In the interlude the music takes over, becoming—as it does in *Tristan* and in *Verklärte Nacht*—the life of the psyche. Here the ostinati and harmonic "nodes" turn into a more Tristan-like chromaticism, and although the music never promises anything like Tristan's final affirmation that comes *from* frustration, the energy and yearning are the more desperate for being caged in two-bar periods. The interlude brings Golaud and Mélisande over the unknown sea; and although she and Pelléas haven't yet met, their love and their fate are, in the interlude, already preordained.

In the next scene Mélisande, having arrived at the castle, is talking with Geneviève about the gloom of the forest which surrounds the castle. They are all in darkness, blind. She wanders to the seashore through an opening in the forest in order that she may seek some light. But the sea itself is shrouded: a tempest is raging far out, and undulating ninth chords combine with a distant, ghostly sailors' chorus to suggest the flux of the natural, and perhaps supernatural, world. Pelléas comes to look for her, and together they think they see, through the mist, lights that might be a guide. But these lights are all dubiety, as was, perhaps, the lantern that had summoned her and Golaud home. Hints of the high, sharp love-keys of E and F sharp dissolve in vaporous tremolando ninths, and in echoes of Golaud's hunting theme. The orchestra's storm stops when Pelléas tries to take Mélisande's hand to lead her back to the castle. But she cannot touch him, she says, for her arms are full of flowers. The miraculous lyrical effloresence of the phrase, as opposed to the speech-norm of the recitative, gives incarnation to the words, and is the beginning of their love. But it fades to silence in a mingling of the sea-mist music with the love song, with added sixths echoing around an F-sharp-major triad.

If Golaud is the Flesh and the Will and Mélisande Spirit, Pelléas is perhaps potentially their union, and therefore what each needs. The next scene certainly suggests that the fulfilment of sexual love could be the spirit's renewal, for it takes place in a park, by a fountain. To luminous E-major-based music, but with no harmonic movement, Pelléas speaks to Mélisande of the fountain's miraculous properties. It used to be called "Blindman's Well" because it cured blindness; but it does so no longer, and Arkel himself is nearly blind. The "religious" note is suggested by hymnic distonic concords, the failure of spirit by undulating chromatics. Softly, tenderly, the young people begin to indulge in love play and Mélisande tries, but fails, to touch the water with her life-fearing hands, though her long hair can just reach it. Pelléas tells her of how Golaud had found her by a fountain, just as he has; reminiscences of Golaud's music induce agitation in her and she drops Golaud's ring, with which she had been playing, into the water. She has lost the life fulfilment Golaud might have been, if she had ever found it. The water noises, as the ripples settle down, are all whole-tone uncertainty, and the Golaud theme takes over in the next orchestral interlude, which is the longest thus far, and the most Wagnerian in intensity, though it is still in part immobilized by pedal notes.

The dark realities of passion are now released in music that is not the less disturbing for being irresolute. Golaud is telling Mélisande how he had an accident while riding; at the stroke of twelve (when Mélisande dropped the ring), his horse stumbled, and the water splashing of the previous scene is the stumble. He felt as though the woods were closing in on his body. Mélisande sobs in her "hurt" pentatonic thirds, but denies that her misery has anything to do with Pelléas; it's just that the castle is so old and dark, and everyone is dying. She cannot accept the fact that action is inevitably subject to decay, just as, when she and Golaud first met, she had been frightened by his greying hair. Golaud, taking her hand to comfort her (though he says he could *crush* it), notices that her ring is missing. This takes us immediately into the world of action; his agitated questioning in cross-rhythm is at first almost entirely unaccompanied, but grows increasingly fervent, harmonically, though it is still without direction since the harmonic patterns are nondeveloping ostinati. Mélisande pretends that she lost her ring in a cave by the sea (with patent Freudian implications), and Golaud insists that she go at once to look for it, taking Pelléas with her if she's scared! To an acute harmonic tension, Golaud says that Pelléas will do anything she asks, won't he? and Mélisande goes out crying how unhappy she is, to the same falling thirds as had expressed the first efflorescence of love.

So Pelléas and Mélisande descend together to the sea's depths and to the womb. The interlude mingles Pelléas's yearning motive with the fountain's pentatonic innocence, but dissolves both in undulating chromatic sea noises as they enter the cave. When they are in darkness—in the obscurity of a modal C-sharp minor which is the *relative* of Pelléas's daylight E major—we know that they had no choice but to make their dark pilgrimage, pointless though it seems, since they both knew that the ring is not and never was in the cave. As they go further in, the music modulates vaguely, and Pelléas tells her not to be afraid, for they will stop when they can no longer see any light from the sea. Then, in the depths, Mélisande gives a yell as a sudden shaft of moonlight reveals three (once more highly Freudian) white-haired paupers, starving remnants of famine in the land. The whining, medieval parallel fifths on the orchestra, unharmonically related, are a striking musical image for the withering of life both within the psyche and in the external world. How closely the inner and outer life are connected is indicated by the tentative reappearance of Golaud's music of action; Mélisande's love becomes nightmare because it cannot be realized in action, while the external world starves because it cannot embrace love. One could almost say that this opera is directly "about" the sundering of body and spirit and the consequent death of both.

So the lovers' descent into the waters and the cavern of the womb only *seems* to lead to love's consummation. They know they have to make the descent, and the reason is not the footling one that Pelléas gives (the necessity for Mélisande to be able to describe the cave to Golaud). Yet they explore the cave like children, almost as a self-scarifying game. This is probably why Mélisande is so terrified by the beggars revealed by the transfiguring moon; she can't stand the light of illumination, yet can't accept the dark in lieu of the light of day. Pelléas says he'll take her back before the light from the sea has totally vanished, and that maybe "nous reviendrons un autre jour" —the child's habitual "tomorrow." With the sundering of flesh from spirit and the decay of volition, the love scene that opens the third act, though complementary to the love nocturne in the second act of *Tristan,* becomes a consummation in dream, not reality. The image of Mélisande isolated in her tower emphasizes this. She croons to herself a folk-like incantation about her yellow hair, based on the oscillating thirds of her "hurt" motive and accompanied by orchestral night noises. The lyricism is beautiful and heart-easing; yet its ballad-like simplicity makes her seem a little girl, or a fairy princess, rather than a woman. This chant is in a Dorian E minor,

D

complementing Pelléas's E major, and its monodic innocence brings in the opera's only reference to Christian sanctions. Perhaps this further emphasizes the division between spirit and flesh, for when Pelléas comes in to tell her (as he does at intervals throughout the play) that he must leave tomorrow, Mélisande can't decide whether she's glad or sorry. She cries "No, no"; but though she leans towards him from her tower, she cannot touch him with her hands—just as, leaning over the well, she had been unable to bathe her hands in the water. Her hair, however, cascading down the tower, does just reach him as he climbs towards her, in the same way as her hair had dabbled in the well-water which her hands could not contact. Enveloped in the whirl of her hair, Pelléas finds a kind of rapture. That the rapture is qualified is suggested by the fact that Mélisande is startled by an object in the darkness which she thinks may be a Rose (of sexual fulfilment?), though Pelléas, not altogether surprisingly, doubts whether it is a rose at all. Thus Pelléas's music in this love scene grows increasingly extended and lyrical; it is almost possible to speak of a climax when the music modulates from Pelléas's E major to F sharp, the key of heightened consciousness, here enharmonically noted as G flat. Yet the flatness, in this most beautiful music, seems to make a difference, since the tender lyricism does not achieve a mating of spirit and flesh. The music representing Mélisande's cascading hair is significantly related to her "hurt" minor thirds, and at the climax of his passion she utters another yell and complains that he is causing her pain. The love theme sounds more tenuously as doves fly round them in the gloom. The modal C-sharp minor which is reality, as compared with the bliss of E-major heaven—is interrupted by footsteps and, to a hushed, expectant rhythm, Golaud enters. As his hunting theme sounds distantly he (self-protectively) calls the lovers silly children, and leads Pelléas away. The interlude mingles Golaud's theme with Pelléas's yearning, and is suspended, unresolved, around the transfiguring key of F sharp.

Now it is the turn of Pelléas and Golaud to descend to the depths, and we begin to understand how the opera is concerned with a life failure in all the marvellously "realized" central characters. Mélisande's innocence could not accept Golaud's experience and because of this failure she cannot be renewed by Pelléas's love: she cannot find the Rose for the Thorn. But if Mélisande's spirit has never found a body, Golaud's "corporeal" experience has lost touch with spirit; so he can find no answer to his crisis of jealousy—whether or not it be justified—except madness and despair. He descends with Pelléas into the vaults of the castle, where the water isn't even living like the sea, but is stagnant, with the stench of death. In a sense, he seems to be playing a kind of game, as did Pelléas and Mélisande in their descent to the sea cavern; and his grimmer game seems to be the consequence of the separation of his will from love, for he deliberately frightens Pelléas by flickering his lantern. This must be why his descent—like that of Mélisande—only *seems* to be a prelude to a moment of illumination and forgiveness.

As they return to the light, the cascading whole-tone arpeggios on harp become "air from the sea," and the breezes mingle with the smell of freshly watered roses and the sound of bells in a pentatonic F sharp. Children are bathing in the sea, and there, too, is Mélisande, with Geneviève. Musically this is, and is meant to be, a miraculous moment. Dramatically, however, it is tragic irony, for after Golaud has remarked that he knows all about Pelléas and Mélisande but recognizes that it's only child's play, he himself exploits the child-innocent motive to sinister purpose. Golaud cross-questions Yniold, his little son by his first marriage: is Mélisande often with Pelléas? What do they talk of, what do they do? Golaud's music is all speech inflection, with no song left; Yniold's answers are in the simplest pentatonicism, like a nursery incantation. Significantly, Golaud's questions are accompanied by the whole-tone "vaults" music, the revelation of the horror beneath the surface of the mind, until at the climax of this nagging the vault motive turns into a febrile version of Mélisande's "hurt" thirds, and he painfully crushes Yniold's arm, as he had longed to crush Mélisande's hand. Experience, by itself, seems as inadequate as Innocence, for Golaud breaks down and says he is a *blind man,* stumbling across the sea floor, searching for his *lost gold* (his ring, and Mélisande's hair).

The contrast between the innocence of Yniold's pentatonic nursery music (rather Moussorgskian in flavour) and Golaud's frenzy grows more acute as his questioning continues. The climax comes when he sets the boy to spy on the lovers through a little window. Yniold says they're doing nothing, just standing, looking; he must get down or he'll scream. Golaud's frenzy is expressed in short, self-revolving phrases in whole-tones; he again hurts Yniold as he tugs him down from the window and the act ends brusquely, with unisonal tutti on the "hurt" motive inverted—in a Phrygian E minor, as opposed to Pelléas's E-major paradise.

The "positive" elements in the fourth act are thus again in part tragic irony. Pelléas, returning to his static E major, makes an assignation to meet Mélisande, before he finally leaves, by Blindman's Well. It is not clear why he is leaving: whether in response to Golaud's warnings, or to succour his dying friend, or from an incapacity to face the consequences of passion or, most probably, from a mixture of all these motives. The water ripples of the fountain figure, which dominate this scene, have in any case acquired a certain suppressed agitation, because love seems of its nature to involve pain: Pelléas hurts Mélisande in loving her, Mélisande hurts Golaud, and Golaud hurts Yniold, perhaps as a scapegoat. The inescapability of pain and death is recognized in the crucial scene in the opera when Arkel, in the heightened sharpness of B major, speaks to Mélisande of the new life she has brought to the castle through her youth, beauty and innocence. Because of this, he says, the Dying King seems to be recovering: but he is not so much hinting at a rebirth as saying that only the apprehension of beauty can make it possible for us to bear the fact of death. So his passively fateful theme is exquisitely intertwined with the love theme, high up, in E major, and the fatefulness is stronger than the love. His song of affirmation, being still anchored by pedal points, has no real movement; and movement is life. So gradually the love theme changes into the theme of Golaud, who appears with blood on his brow. He speaks brusquely to Mélisande, as the E-major lyricism ceases. More peasants have been inconveniently dying of starvation around the castle, he testily remarks; then he turns to the death within himself, taunting her about her innocent eyes, growing increasingly hysterical in obsessive repeated notes and neurotic wholetone scurryings. Now it is he who says that Mélisande must not touch *him,* for he cannot bear the contagion of flesh. He, too, cannot take her hands, but only her long, gold hair, which he seizes ferociously, hauling her up and down, forcing her to her knees: the lid is off the libido, indeed. When Arkel comes back he regains control, but we are left with Mélisande's broken "Je ne suis pas heureuse," and with the sighing appoggiaturas that comment on Arkel's statement that, if he were God, he would have pity on human suffering. As a mere human, albeit a king, he can feel for human beings, but do nothing. He is more fortunate than Golaud, Pelléas and Mélisande only because he is very old, and to that degree habituated to suffering.

The next scene is introduced simply to demonstrate this inescapability of destiny. The man is father to the child, the child is father to the man; little Yniold, the next generation, is trying to move a great stone, behind which he has lost his *golden ball,* as Golaud had lost his golden ring (his arm isn't long enough to reach it, as Mélisande's hand couldn't touch the water, and Pelléas couldn't stretch up to her in her tower). A flock of sheep pass by, crying. The unseen shepherd, asked where they are going and why they're crying, says they're not going to the stable, that's certain. He and they disappear into the mist. This scene, outside the action, is musically the most continuous in the opera. Rhythmic continuity and simple lyricism, like nursery songs, can live in the preconscious world of childhood, but, depending on incantatory repetition, they cannot develop. The point seems to be that as we grow up we lose even this lyrical self-sufficiency. We disintegrate into fragments, like the flock of sheep, at once one and many, fading into the mist. The scene peters out in a drooping minim figure, an inversion of the original nursery motive.

It is at this point that Pelléas enters and admits that he has been playing "like a child," knowing no more than the sheep what he was doing nor where he was going. He must go away, like a *blind man* leaving a house that is burning down, not because he would not love if he could, but because he doesn't know what is reality and what illusion; significantly, he says he cannot remember what Mélisande looks like. When she arrives for their assignation, they attain a moment of utter stillness and speechlessness which is the closest they come to illumination. But the very slow, lyrical expansion of the music after the castle gates have shut them out merges the love theme, the water motive and Golaud's hunting theme with the bare fifths of fate. From the "heightened" stillness of F-sharp major the music moves into an almost Wagnerian climax, though with very brief, panting phrases. This is the lovers' only real physical contact, apart from Pelléas's playing with Mélisande's hair; and (Parsifal-like) his confession of love is also a renunciation—he must go *because* he loves her, which, as we have seen, is only part of the truth. For all his dubiety, they touch F-sharp major again, just before Golaud, chasing them, slays Pelléas, and Mélisande scuttles off into the dark ("je n'ai pas de courage"). The end is abrupt, in F minor, after the F-sharp-major climax and the whirling chromatics.

So Mélisande has failed to grow from her innocence to experience, to give her Spirit a bodily consummation; Golaud has failed to renew his experience in her innocence, so that his Flesh turns destructive and sadistic; and Pelléas, the half brother and the lover who might have grown to love and life, is slain by their failure, which is inseparable from his own. We don't know what happened outside the castle gates, before the frenzied Golaud's approach; but if the lovers' passion is finally consummated in their last moment of F-sharp-major illumination, when Pelléas speaks of hearing Mélisande's voice float over the sea, in spring, the consummation is in no sense a triumph. More probably, their love is not consummated, and the moment of revelation is a dream of what might have been. In any case, the murder of Pelléas does not lead to his mystical union with the beloved. She, wounded in the affray when Pelléas is killed, dies not of her wound but because the pulse of life, with the failure of love, gradually slows to inanition. The last act opens at her deathbed, with a tremulous, frail, chromatically altered version of the Mélisande theme which sounds through the act like a knell. Interestingly enough, this theme—with implicit false relations and whole tone ambiguities wherein the A flats sometimes "stand for" G sharp—is very similar to the ostinato theme that dominates the neutral "waste-land" finale of Vaughan Williams's *Sixth Symphony*. Both the chromatic alterations and the regular, pulseless repetition give it a raga-like oriental quality. Passion, having been consistently destructive, is spent. Golaud, penitent, admits that they were innocent, he guilty, as fragments of his theme wander disconsolately in the bass, and the whole-tone fountain motive quivers on top. Mélisande, accompanied by diatonic concords, asks for the window to be opened, so that she may watch the sun setting on the sea. Arkel asks if Golaud may speak to her; she says Yes, there is nothing to forgive. The knell undulates chromatically as everyone leaves except Golaud. The orchestra stops and he asks her a question: did she and Pelléas love one another? he has to know. She says Yes, to which he replies that she doesn't understand. He means did he love her bodily; she must tell him the truth, for she is going to die and cannot die on a lie. So despite his repentance, the horror returns, and the fateful, obsessive-rhythmed seventh chords turn into whole-tone hysteria again. It seems we can never undo the consequences of our mistakes. She whimpers "la vérité . . ." and relapses into unconsciousness. So he, and we, never know "la vérité" and this, it would seem, is the essence of the human condition. There is neither a physical nor a metaphysical consummation, only an intense capacity to feel, and an oriental passivity in the acceptance of the unknowable mysteries of birth and death, and of the fact of human suffering.

So to speak of failure, in this twilight of humanism, is perhaps hardly relevant. We are all, like Mélisande, deluded by our innocence and, like Golaud, corrupted by our experience; and so, like Pelléas, we never fully realize our love, because we cannot recognize it, or distinguish truth from falsehood. And the end of the opera tells us that this is a perennial human destiny. Arkel prevents Golaud from attempting to waken the unconscious Mélisande and the servants enter in ritualistic procession, to pray as Mélisande dies, while the knell slows to immobility, continually returning to Pelléas's

E, but with an oppressed, flattened, Phrygian feeling. She tries to hold her newborn baby (presumably Golaud's), but is too weak to do so. Arkel utters an exquisite benediction on suffering humanity and, in the final words of the opera, says "C'est au tour de la pauvre petite." The babe is born, and life will go on, but the next generation will weep the same tears anew. We hear those tears as the music peters out in fragments of the fountain's whole tones and the Mélisande love theme. In the last few bars the cycle starts again, for the simplest, most innocently pentatonic version of Mélisande's theme has re-emerged from the chromaticized knell, while the sighing appoggiaturas of the fountain scene have become the *lacrimae rerum*. The static, moveless tonality is C-sharp major, the highest, sharpest point of illumination in the opera. Perhaps it is not fortuitous that this key is the major form of the minor key which had been "reality," relative of Pelléas's paradisal E major. The concept is profoundly oriental: only through shedding the not-self can the Reality beyond our earthly passions be apprehensible.

Yet if the revelation is at hand for the dead Mélisande, what we are left with is Arkel's quietly compassionate fortitude; if the bell tolling has a ritualistic flavour, it is a ceremonial elegy on humanism. *Pelléas et Mélisande,* the quintessence of Debussyan technique and of the Debussyan theme, is one of the supreme seminal works of the twentieth century because both its passion and its relinquishment are uncompromising. It offers no heroic apotheosis (like Wagner), no metaphysical hope (like Schoenberg), no refuge in nostalgia (like Delius); but it does leave us purged, and for that reason ready to go on living. It can do this because of the intensity of its awareness of human passion, however purposeless that passion may seem. Because its apprehension of the "moment of sensation" is so exquisite, we rejoice in, rather than deplore, the fact that these moments have no before or after of which we can have certain knowledge. This is why *Pelléas et Mélisande,* offering what would seem to be a gloomy view of human destiny, is not in the least a depressing work, any more than are the moments of sensation which the impressionist painters discovered in their seismographic response to the visible world. These painters anarchically inverted traditional "architectural" values, made backgrounds foregrounds, allowed sitters to look outside and beyond the composition's frame, and accepted the disorder of the flux of appearances with the apparent passivity of the camera. Yet in both the painting of Monet and Degas (to choose one painter concerned mainly with the natural world and one concerned mainly with people) and in the music of Debussy the *acceptance* of Nature's disorder becomes itself a kind of order. Both find *light* within the mist of uncertainty, and something like happiness from their humility before the natural world and from their admission of human limitation. This may be why *Pelléas et Mélisande* has more to offer than its numerous progeny, which include existentialist drama, the Theatre of the Absurd, and much of the music of avant-garde which we shall be discussing later in this book.

IV

The Ego and Things, and the Return
to Magic: A Theme in Satie,
Stravinsky and Orff

A direct link between Debussy's moment of sensation—his compassionate purposelessness—and the surrealistic cult of the irrational
was provided, contemporaneously, in the music of Debussy's friend,
Erik Satie. *Tristan* and *Parsifal* had brought humanism full circle,
achieving religious ecstasy from the identification of Love and
Death; *Pelléas et Mélisande,* dealing with the same theme, had replaced religious ecstasy with a tender fortitude. But what was the
artist to do if he wasn't, like Wagner, heroic or bumptious enough
to offer his inner life as a symbol of the future destiny of man, nor
yet, like Debussy, courageous enough to accept the impermanence
of his senses as the only truth, the only order, apprehensible to him?
If he was not religious but was uncompromisingly honest, committed
to the world in which he found himself, he had no choice but
humbly to accept the world of appearances. He must try neither to
dominate through the assertion of personality, nor to submit passively to sensation, and if human experience failed him, he must seek
the logic of geometry.

In the first phase of his career—which was contemporary with
Pelléas—Satie sought to reintegrate the disintegrated materials of
tradition by juxtaposing fragments of melody and chord successions
in patterns unrelated to orthodox ideas of "development." The

harmonies in his Rose-Croix works are Wagnerian and Debussyan, but they differ from Wagner's harmonies in that they neither achieve nor seek any climax, and from Debussy's in that their "purposeless" oscillations accompany melodic lines that are clearly defined and exquisitely shaped. These melodic phrases are derived from plain-song, not because of its mystical associations, but because plainsong is linear, nonharmonic, impersonal and ritualistic. Satie's *Messe des Pauvres,* and all his early Rose-Croix works and piano dances, are thus "poor men's masses" in a strict and oddly touching sense. The chaste, hypnotically repeated, often pentatonic melodic phrases suggest liturgical ritual, while the wandering, rootless harmonies suggest a sensuous humanism that is lost and disembodied. The verbal irony that Satie sometimes introduced into his written directions is self-protective, and this remains true when, in the second phase of his career, he related his melodic pattern-making not to liturgical chant, but to the clichés of popular music. Since this music was communal and mechanistic, Satie found in it a musical "myth" appropriate to the antimystical world he lived in. No less than plain-song, popular music was, for Satie, impersonal and nonsubjective. So there is no *volte-face* between his first phase and his second, nor between that and his third phase wherein (especially in *Socrate* and the piano *Nocturnes*) he relinquished irony and went as far as is humanly possible—and perhaps a bit further—towards losing the personality in the pattern. In all his music, the juxtaposition of unrelated melodic and harmonic conventions induces a sense of incongruity which, like the crazy logic of *Alice in Wonderland,* is the more telling because it is self-consistent. Satie's music is child-like only in the sense that it is unusually direct, independent of the accumulations of sentiment. It moves towards the liberation of the post-Renaissance Ego from memory and desire; it is not surprising, therefore, that Satie and Debussy are among the few relatively "orthodox" composers admired by John Cage and the more advanced avant-garde.

It is obvious that Satie's attempt to reintegrate with geometric logic the splintered fragments of the past has something in common with the cubist painter's search for a geometric order beneath the broken fragments of the visible world. In addition, Satie's art was always closely associated with the ballet. In its sixteenth- and seventeenth-century origins, ballet had been a ritual of humanism, a symbolic manifestation of the belief, or wishful thought, that man could create paradise on earth. As the paradoxes inherent in humanism became more obtrusive, however, ballet either grew up into opera, which was concerned with musical and dramatic conflict and with the realities that make paradise humanly unattainable, or it became a dream-art dealing (as do Tchaikovsky's fairy-tale ballets) with the fulfilment of personal frustrations in a voiceless, timeless world of mime. Tchaikovsky's ballets are "romantic" in the sense that their world of exquisite lucidity and grace is directly related to the chaos of his own neuroses. But the "order" of balletic movement could easily become opposed to romantic introspection: a self-conscious and sophisticated ritual, as a twentieth-century ritual is bound to be. This, as we shall see, is why ballet became the favoured medium of the most representative twentieth-century composer, Stravinsky; and it is also why Satie's first full-length ballet, *Parade* —created by the Diaghilev Company in 1916, to a book by Jean Cocteau, choreography by Massine, and costumes by Picasso—is a key work of our time.

Parade is a ritual which is also a dream; that is, it has no relationship to a belief or to a community, only to the images which our subconscious throws up in sleep. The action takes place in a Fair, or rather at the parade just outside the Fair, for in our spiritual isolation we are spectators at, not participators in, the dream that is life. The human beings are the circus performers, but what they do, or are made to do, bears only an illusory relationship to the dreams by which they live, which would seem to be dreams within a dream. The performers thus have the melancholy of Picasso's harlequins; even their desires are disembodied, and all that is, or seems to be, "real" is the things, the objects, among which the human comedy is enacted. Cocteau symbolizes this by making the Managers, who direct the Fair, cubist abstractions—mechanical combinations of geometric forms disguised as human (or divine) beings. The curious poignancy of the conception comes from its denial both of humanism and of theocracy. The performers' humanity lies in their dreams, but they can become "real" only through accepting things, or the world of appearances. The tragedy within the comedy is that the public (which is also the spectators in the theatre, you and I) remains equally indifferent to the performers and to the Managers. They have neither human aspiration nor respect for divine authority; and perhaps they have lost aspiration because they can't be expected to show respect for gods who have become crazy engines, pushing the performers around in purposeless activity.

All the performers can do is to walk their respective tightropes as delicately as possible (while the managers crack their whips), keeping themselves going by little miracles of poise and balance. These little miracles are inherent in the music. It is the most cubist of Satie's compositions, in that each single movement, and the sequence of movements as a whole, is built on a mirror structure. Within this objective self-sufficiency are the most eccentric alliances, the most surprising contrasts of emotion. Though the music is divested of subjective intensity, a perturbing experience results from the manner in which the simplest fragments of melody and harmony are recombined in patterns that seem independent of time. These patterns are delineated by the scrupulously clean orchestration; although the ballet is scored for large forces, the instruments are treated like a chamber ensemble, and in this sense the geometric lucidity of Satie's score is a tenuously frail, yet resilient, riposte to the orchestral haze of the Debussyan unconscious. Indeed, Satie's score originally included several aural manifestations of the "real" world. Though the parts for typewriter, spinning top, revolver, sirens and tumblers, etc., were not all used in performance, they were more than the product of an unfunny dadaism. They were literally noises which, like Picasso's "objects," were to be transformed into something rich and strange.

Parade opens with an orchestral chorale, scored for brass and low strings. The effect of this is not merely, if at all, ironic. The Fair has been pitched close to a church; and humanity needs, if it forlornly cannot find, a ritual of belief. So the fugal, quasi-liturgical

"Prélude du rideau rouge" reminds us of Satie's "poor men's masses," and appropriately introduces the dream ritual of the action. After the suave but harmonically directionless ecclesiastical polyphony of this introduction we are surprised when the cubist abstraction of the French Manager appears, but the irony is pointed. The chorale has induced a "religious" mood, which the Manager appears to contradict, but doesn't, because he is the best approach we can make to a god figure.

The French Manager's theme has, indeed, already been anticipated, in solemn augmentation, in the opening chorale. Now he dances with mechanical rigidity. His tune, revolving around itself in an ambiguous rhythm that conflicts with a $3:8$ ostinato swaying between E and B, suggests relentless bustle, a pointlessly ant-like energy. The theme is stated four times in various and more remorselessly nagging permutations and in increasingly harsh scoring. Its continual revolutions around an unchanging "node" and its hypnotic rhythm give it a somewhat Eastern flavour, despite its aggressiveness. So there is a natural transition when the Manager's fourth statement brings in the first of the Fairground characters—a Chinese Juggler. His Chinese get-up is clearly a disguise, behind which lurks the sad smile of a Picasso or Beckett clown. Nonetheless, there is a genuinely Chinese quality, psychologically and philosophically speaking, in the nondeveloping passivity of his music. A tender delicacy, quite different from the Manager's obsessive momentum, typifies his theme. It is introduced by two flutes in swaying fifths, over a pedal F sharp on horn, like the oriental drone of eternity. The phrases are all pentatonic, the glint and clink of the ostinato patterns recognizably "Chinese" in sonority, and as he juggles with an egg, spits fire, burns his fingers and tries to put out the flames, we realize that his juggling has the pathos of human fallibility. He doesn't deal too well with the egg of birth or with the Promethean fire; Man as Hero has become the Chinese Juggler, who *just* keeps going, as well as he can. His pathos is objictified in the tenderness of a fragmentary little phrase, played first on solo horn, then on flute, that floats into the equilibrium of his nondeveloping ostinati. This tune tries to establish the serenity of the major triad, but the texture of the music gradually disintegrates until nothing is left but silence. The French Manager (thinking, no doubt, of financial loss) stamps his disgust at the public's indifference to the Juggler's display. The various fragments of the Juggler's music are played rapidly in reverse order (a musical synonym for purposelessness, for everything returns to its original form), and the Second Manager, who has been listening sympathetically to the First Manager's complaints, begins to bellow, through a megaphone, the praises of the second act.

The Second Manager is a cubist abstraction of the New World, symbolized in skyscraper forms and cowboy boots. His act is an American girl dancer, who goes through a series of actions in bewilderingly rapid sequence. She mounts a racehorse, rides a bicycle, quivers like the pictures on a cinema screen, imitates Charlie Chaplin, chases a thief with a revolver, dances a ragtime, is shipwrecked, and so on. In this hectic existence she lives her cinematic dream, the unreality of which is suggested by three distinct musical processes: the shimmering bitonal ostinato to which she first appears; the descending major thirds in her first tune, which create a whole-tone ambiguity; and the persistent syncopation which disrupts metrical regularity. The ostinato figures and whole-tone sequences tell us that her myth of fevered activity, hardly less than the Juggler's egg-balancing and fire-eating, is activity to no end. The nostalgia within her gaiety becomes patent in her ragtime dance, marked "triste." Though the static ostinati characteristic of the Juggler's music have disappeared in favour of a more sustained melody and a singing bass line, the tune has an almost chorale-like gravity; the melancholy of its symmetrical contours is enhanced by the accompanying brass chords.

Again the music disintegrates into silence. The two managers express their rage at the public's indifference in a dance *without music,* and there is a rapid recapitulation of the American girl's tunes in reverse order. The Third Manager enters: not a cubist abstraction, this time, but a dummy Negro riding a horse of unusual sagacity and aplomb. The horse—not the Negro—introduces the third act, a pair of acrobats. The young man and girl dance a fast waltz, the mechanical rhythm being picked out by xylophone. Their acrobatics are in cross-rhythm against the waltz, and the pentatonic nature of their tune and the regularity of their ostinato pattern relate them to the orientalism of the Juggler. The tenderness of their phrases contrasts with the angularity of the rhythm; they walk their tightrope precariously, hopefully emulating the flight of birds. The personnel of *Parade*—jugglers, bicycling dancers, acrobats—strikingly anticipate the unheroes of Samuel Beckett for whom (as Marshall McLuhan has pointed out) the bicycle is "the prime symbol of the Cartesian mind in its acrobatic relation of mind and body in precarious imbalance. . . . The acrobat acts as a specialist, using only a limited segment of his faculties. The clown is the integral man who mimes the acrobat in an elaborate drama of incompetence. Beckett sees the bicycle as the sign and symbol of specialist futility in the present electronic age, when we must all interact and react, using all our faculties at once."

But if Satie's acrobat lovers are (unlike the birds) the victims of fate, so apparently are the managers who seem to be controlling them. This identity of the drivers and the driven—anticipatory of the relationship between Pozzo and Lucky in *Waiting for Godot*—is musically manifest when Satie introduces an aggressive pedal on a low E, the Manager's original ostinato note. Played on an organ 32-foot stop, this causes a horrifying reverberation, over which sound rigid patterns of pentatonic fourths and sevenths. This leads once more to a recapitulation of the acrobats' material in reverse order, and so again to silence.

The organ pedal, as the voice of God, or the First Cause, scares everyone, the Managers included. The managers return *with* the various performers, and dance to a fierce orchestral tutti wherein their original "obsessive" theme is punctuated by siren blasts on the drone note, reminding us of the organ reverberation. The Chinaman, the American girl and the Acrobats leave the theatre in tremulous tearfulness at the audience's lack of appreciation. The managers and the horse dance themselves into a state of collapse in their efforts to explain that the real show is still to take place inside the booth. There is an extraordinary, minatory venom in the contrast between the nagging of the Managers' self-enclosed theme and the hubbub of the tutti. The ballet ends on this note of tragic misunderstanding. The audience refuses to realize that it has seen only the "trailer" to the show, not the show itself, and the curtain falls to a telescoped version of the original fugal exposition.

In *Parade* both the spiritual rhythm and the corporeal rhythm have submitted to geometry, and the pathos of Satie's circus performers consists in the passive inarticulateness with which they keep going, even though there seems to be no point in it beyond the geometry of the abstract patterns they make. But although they are inarticulate, they don't totally surrender their humanity in accepting a mechanistic, post-Cartesian world which would equate them with inanimate things. If in one sense a denial of life, they are also a point from which new growth may begin.

"Je suis venu au monde très jeune," Satie said, "dans un temps très vieux." The probity and the intrinsic beauty of his compositions are his only necessary justification: which cannot finally be separated from those quasi-philosophical gestures which have made him a John the Baptist to the mid-twentieth-century avant-garde. In his *musique d'ameublement* he invented the pre-juke box Musak which is anti-art in that it is not meant to be listened to; while in remarking that "this work is utterly incomprehensible, even to me," or that "experience is one of the forms of paralysis," he came close to the complete acceptance of purposelessness as a *principle,* which is typical of Cage and Beckett. Like them, he combines provocation with boredom (his *Vexations* is an eighty-second piece which is to be played 840 times!); like them, he knew that "boredom is mysterious and profound." Even in the purely musical aspects of his work, however, Satie negates European history. Although his basic fragmented materials are all—except possibly in the early *Gnossiennes*—Western, his static approach to the time sense and the syllabic rhythmic structure of his later music, especially *Socrate,* have much in common with the numerical rhythms of John Cage; and how deep this orientalism runs is suggested by the tiny piano pieces called *Sports et Divertissements,* written in 1914. Seldom more than two or three lines long, they are copied in coloured inks in Satie's exquisite musical hand, accompanied by a verbal commentary, which is meant to be looked at, not recited; they must be almost unique in European art in depending, like Japanese haiku, simultaneously on music, poetry and calligraphy.

Gertrude Stein—who greatly admired Satie, and whose linguistic patterns have affinities with Satie's sound patterns—perceived how the cult of the object or "thing" leads to the rediscovery of the child, and how that is linked to the rediscovery of primitive instinct and of non-Western cultures. Speaking of two greater artists, Stravinsky and Picasso, who are closely related both to Satie and to herself, she said:

And then it came to me it is perfectly simple, the Russian and Spaniard are Oriental, and there is the same mixture. Scratch a Russian and you find a Tartar. Scratch a Spaniard and you find a Saracen. And all this is very important with what I have been saying about the peaceful Oriental penetration into European culture or rather the tendency for this generation that is for the twentieth century to be no longer European perhaps because Europe is finished.*

We have discussed the sense in which, in the music of Schoenberg and Debussy, "Europe is finished," and have commented on Schoenberg's frustrated search for a renewal of spirit. Complementary to Schoenberg's attempt, however, man had to seek the body's renewal, and this search too involved a turning away from "Europe." This is evident in the "Russian" works with which Stravinsky—the third, central, key figure in twentieth-century music—opened his long career.

It is instructive to compare Stravinsky's ballet *Petrouchka*, also written for Diaghilev, with Satie's *Parade*. That there is something in common between the two works is obvious, for the circus performers in *Parade* are puppet-like and (in Picasso's decor and costumes) have some relationship to commedia dell'arte characters, while Stravinsky's characters are ostensibly puppets and Petrouchka himself is a Russian fairy-tale version of Pierrot. Just as the circus performers in *Parade* are controlled, or seem to be controlled, by

* Gertrude Stein, *Everybody's Autobiography* (London: 1938).

the managers, so the puppets in *Petrouchka* are activated by a Showman, significantly also titled the Charlatan, whose role as synthetic god figure is suggested by his portrait painted on a back-cloth; wearing sumptuous apparel, he squats on a cloud, like a baroque *deus ex machina*. There are also many technical features in common between the two ballets, for *Petrouchka,* like *Parade,* depends on very short melodic phrases incantatorily repeated in geometric patterns, on recurrent ostinati, on nondeveloping oscilla-tions between chords and on surprising juxtapositions of mood (reflecting the multifarious bustle of the Fair). The difference be-tween the two works—which is no less remarkable than the simi-larity—derives from the Russian origins of Stravinsky's music, which gives it a corporeal energy that Satie's music does not have. This means that its "documentary" significance is less uncompro-mising than Satie's work, while its human potentiality is higher. But it isn't, in this piece, much more than potentiality. Whether or not Stravinsky was aware of this, we may see *Petrouchka* as a parable of the sickness of our century, from an awareness of which all Stravinsky's later work developed.

Thus the Russian peasant world, in which the Fair takes place in *Petrouchka,* is a real world, whereas *Parade* takes place in a no man's land *outside* the Fair. Yet Petrouchka-Pierrot—who is Modern Man no less than Schoenberg's Pierrot Lunaire, Debussy's Pierrot *fâché avec la lune,* or Picasso's harlequins—is, as puppet and artist, shut out from this world, and the parable concerns his struggle towards a Western, unpeasant-like "consciousness." His story is a comic, Chaplinesque tragedy: he loves the ballerina, Columbine, who is the sophisticated Western world in decay (she dances to a Russianized permutation of a Lanner waltz that came from Vienna, the melting pot of Europe), and he is destroyed by a Moor, who is the primitive and bestial roots of our natures, whose music is both savage and sumptuous, orgiastic and oriental. The Ballerina's civilization and the Moor's animality ought to be com-plementary virtues, but she is a heartless chit of a girl and he is a stupid oaf who falls down to worship a coconut; so when their two tunes are played together as they dance, the effect is of grim farce.

That this breakdown, this dislocation between Nature and Nurture, is peculiarly a product of twentieth-century stresses is suggested in the last act. A peasant enters driving a dancing bear on a chain, to a hurdy-gurdy tune that revolves obsessively round itself; the bear is related to Petrouchka's struggle to aspire from puppetdom to consciousness. A Rich Man distributes banknotes indiscriminately to the crowd who, if ostensibly human, seem to be no less automatic in their movements than the Moor and the Ballerina, and much more so than Petrouchka. A rout of Masquers comes in accompanied by Devil, Goat (lust), and Pig (greed and stupidity), emphasizing the theme of Appearance and Reality. The Devil, his theme leaping through sevenths and ninths on the brass, excites the crowd to savage, nonhuman hysteria. It is at this point that cries are heard from the puppet theatre and Petrouchka rushes out pursued by the Moor, who kills him because he had attempted to rescue the Ballerina from the Blackamoor's ravishment. The crowd, despite its exuberance, is hardly more aware of suffering, or of any kind of feeling, than is the audience in *Parade*. *Petrouchka* is, however, slightly less pessimistic than *Parade*, because after the crowd has slowly dispersed to accordion harmonies that run down like a melancholy clock, the puppet-Pierrot is not, after all, finally deflated. The sawdust seems to be pouring out of him; as the Charlatan points out, he was only a puppet, so his murder is of no consequence. Yet the puppet-artist turns out to be more "real" than the crowd, just as the cubist abstractions in *Parade* were more real than the audience. It seems that he has a soul. His ghost appears above the little theatre-within-a-theatre, jeering at the Showman, who nervously drops the body and scuttles off, to a snarl of bitonal trumpets based on the F-sharp major–C-major tritonal tension that had originally expressed Petrouchka's—and the artist's —separation from an insensate world. This whimpering flicker of "consciousness" suggests how, for Stravinsky, *Petrouchka* was a starting point, not an end. The first stage in his pilgrimage towards the puppet's regeneration into man was to begin *ab ovo:* to learn to accept the Blackamoor's bestiality as in itself potentially a virtue.

This happens in the series of pseudoprimitive works that succeeds *Petrouchka*.

Thus Stravinsky's *The Rite of Spring* is both a fertility ritual and a sacrificial act, like Schoenberg's "Dance Around the Golden Calf." Unlike Schoenberg's work, however, it exists as an end in itself, not as a negation of something else, and this is true even though it contains within itself both a destructive and a reconstructive principle. Superficially, its primitivism may seem to be destructive, associated with the sadistic violence that was ravaging Europe in the first of the World Wars. But it is also constructive, in so far as it returns to the roots of human experience, suggesting that if consciousness has led civilization to this pass, we'd do well to be rid of it, at least temporarily. The instinctual experience of primitive peoples, who surrendered their egoism in a communal act, was at least genuine, without emotional prevarication. *The Rite of Spring* attempts to re-enter, to re-create, a primitive ritual of death and creation. Of course, it cannot do so; if we experience the ballet in a theatre we know that we are not in fact taking part in a ritual murder, but are only being self-consciously unself-conscious, deliberately liberating the libido. This may be good for us, and was certainly a necessary step for Stravinsky. Using the stylized gestures of ballet mime and the sophisticated paraphernalia of an enormous symphony orchestra, he explored one of the sources of strength which he, as a Russian, possessed, and which modern, "Western" man had surrendered. It was not something about which Western man could be indifferent, though he might, as the scenes at the notorious first performance testify, be scared to the point of hysteria. At this date we can see, or rather hear, how the "destructive" sadism of *The Rite of Spring* leads inevitably into its spring-like renewal. Though still immensely exciting, it is no longer frightening, as Schoenberg's "Dance" is and, in the context of the opera as a whole, always will and should be.

We can also see now that although the music of Stravinsky's rite is violent, whereas Debussy's music is usually nonviolent, the two are closely related both technically and "philosophically." Both use short, hypnotic melodic phrases, often pentatonic, in incantatory repetition, and both employ a static harmonic texture which, involving oscillations between chords and recurrent ostinati, produces an effect more oriental than occidental. Stravinsky's rhythms are corporeally energetic, whereas Debussy's are passive or nonexistent; yet since these rhythms are hypnotically repetitive, they, too, tend to destroy the temporal sense and on occasion to break into complex, additive, ecstasy-inducing metres comparable with those found in real primitive music. Moreover, Stravinsky, in using the orchestra as a gigantic percussion instrument that deprives the individual instruments of melodic and harmonic identity, creates an effect comparable with Debussy's atmospheric "cocoon" of sound. This is true of the rowdily orgiastic passages as well as of the nocturnal interludes, such as the strange and marvellous piece that introduces the dance of the adolescent girls. Stravinsky's use of incremental rondo form in the final "Sacrificial Dance" is also related both to the incantatory repetition of primitive music and to the nondeveloping processes of Debussy.

The Rite of Spring is a "sport" in Stravinsky's career which could be done once only. Its release, both of violence and of potency, profoundly influenced his later work however, and through that, the whole of Western music. The transition is effected in *The Wedding*, which Stravinsky sets not in a primeval past, but in a Russian peasant world that, although immensely ancient in its traditions, probably still existed when the work was composed. (It is interesting that although all the tunes sound folk-like, there is only one authentic folk tune in the score, and that is a modern factory song.) This means that the life ritual has a more immediate reality than it had in *The Rite,* especially since we no longer have ritual murders, but do have weddings, which are at once a personal act, a social act, and a ritual of creation. Stravinsky intended this dual relationship to past and present to be manifest in the performance; the dancers were to use stylized forms of genuine peasant rituals, but the musicians were to be visible on the stage, in modern evening dress. This would suggest that, although "true," the ritual was also a masquerade in which we are involved, but only vicariously. This wasn't in fact done in performance, though a somewhat similar effect was achieved by making the dance movements in part geometrical and architectural, with stylized black and white costumes and decor. For us uprooted creatures the "cubist" abstraction of *Parade* is unavoidable, for we are to some degree *abstracted* from experience. Here, however, in the dance ceremony, is an ideal of emotional and physical spontaneity which is still real, and which we can share to some degree, because we still know something, however little, about falling in love, and desire or lust, and family ties, and fear and parting. The realism of *The Wedding* extends to the scoring. Stravinsky abandons the gigantic symphony orchestra of *The Rite,* which is inescapably associated with European "concert" music, in favour of a percussion band wherein four pianos emulate the sounds of genuine peasant bands (he had originally intended to use "local" instruments, such as the cymbalon). Moreover, he introduces voices, singing, speaking and shouting in pentatonic phrases which are close to the origins of song in speech or yell. Words and human voices bring in "reality," as they do in the operas of Tchaikovsky, as compared with the silent mime of his ballets. However, Stravinsky places his singers in the orchestra, so that the reality of the experience is deliberately separated from the miming of it by the dancers.

The musical technique carries that of *The Rite of Spring* to a more extreme point. The post-Renaissance element of "personal" expression is almost completely denied, for there is no melody except brief ostinato utterances, no harmony, and virtually no modulation. The music depends entirely on the "melodic tonality" of incantatory phrases oscillating around a nodal point; on hypnotic patterns of rhythm, beginning corporeally, but becoming "additive" at points of maximum excitement; and on percussive dissonance. This latter element is sophisticated by the use of unresolved appoggiaturas, which emphasize the barbarism while giving it an edge of hysteria which may be modern rather than primitive. Bartók uses a similar technique in the percussive works of his "middle" period.

Whereas *The Rite* is entirely pagan, *The Wedding* fuses pagan

with Christian ritual, as does the Russian peasant society in which
it happens. This more "modern" feature is reflected in the fact
that the wedding is both a communal celebration and fertility rite,
and also something that concerns a specific pair of human creatures.
They have solo parts, while the chorus represent the community.
This duality is established in the first scene, the "Benediction of
the Bride." The people, dressing her hair, sing in fierce, unflinching
ostinati, oscillating around the node E. She has the same notes but
in transposed octaves, so that she utters a cry of personal pain.
This is both physical (for they are tugging her hair) and nervous
(for she is scared of the unknown). They try to console her, in a
more lyrical phrase, hypnotically repeated. This phrase is in the
other pentatonic scale on E, with an A-ish feeling, accompanied by
less harsh percussion noises, rather like a Balinese gamelan. These
noises continue while they describe the garden of Love where the
nightingale sings, but ostinato dissonances obtrude percussively into
the pentatonicism, in contrary motion polytonal triads, because her
lover's approach will wake her up. Repeated E's rise almost to
hysteria and carry us back to the "tressing" motive. She sings a
lovely, lyrical pentatonic phrase about her blue ribbon, while they
continue their sadistic ululations, imitating her tune (perhaps
parodistically) on occasion. She ends in wistfulness, her phrase
declining as she says the ribbon is blue, like her eyes.

This benediction, in which all the tunes are based on the pentatonic minor third and major second, has been mainly pagan. The
second tableau, the "Benediction of the Bridegroom," is specifically
Christian, though the technique is unchanged. We begin with male
voices intoning metrically repeated notes, with no hint of the
pentatonic lyricism, around a new nodal point, C. The parents are
here to some degree characterized, or perhaps caricatured, for they
are not presented, as the lovers are, as potential human consciousness. They sing folk-like incantations, with oriental-sounding chro-
maticisms, to convey their anguish at the thought that "another will
love them." But the chorus community brushes aside this personal
feeling in asking for the benediction of the saints on the marriage,
in quick, rhythmic intonation. The Bridegroom himself asks for his

parents' blessing and the general benediction becomes orgiastic over a double ostinato. The next tableau performs the same function for the Bride, whose parents are also characterized, as she leaves home to regular rhythmic ostinati, and to the lyrical A-ish version of the nondeveloping pentatonic tune. Polytonal triads in contrary motion work up the excitement as everyone goes out; the two mothers indulge together in a little chromatic whimper of self-pity, mincing and wheezing around the nodal point A.

The final tableau is the marriage feast, scored for double chorus (the two families) with all the percussion in action. Although still built around nodal ostinati, the music now employs a number of different nodes simultaneously, so that the bustle is increased. Sundry village characters look in on the festivities, interrupting from various parts of the chorus. The lovers are brought together by the two families and instructed about their domestic duties. Suddenly the racket stops and the girl sings solo, "I was far away on a great sea": a more expansive lyrical tune built on rising fourths. The chorus embraces the fourths in a rocking lullaby, comparing the lovers to Leda and the Swan. This introduces the "moment of love" and the bed-warming; the chorus, beginning tenderly with pentatonic patterns around the node E, grows gradually fiercer and more sharply dissonant, returning to its social role as the japes and bawdy jokes increase outside the bedroom door. The song becomes half speech here, for everyone is tipsy. But when the lover has gone in to his love, the clatter-chatter stops, and he sings the only continuous cantilena in the work. This is a sublimation of the melodic ideas of the whole piece, still pentatonic but flowing and growing, both a personal and a social fulfilment. It is unaccompanied except for static gong and bell noises around B—the *dominant* of the original node E. So this love song is, like the Song of Songs, at once sensual and religious; love makes the fragments of physical energy and sensation grow into song, which is a monodic outpouring of Spirit. The relationship between song and speech in Schoenberg's *Moses and Aaron* is thus reversed. The bells and gongs get slower and slower until we're left with the moment of love's consummation in the silence of the night, and the physical consummation is a

revelation of Spirit. This miraculous freeing of song from the burden
of Self, this obliteration of Time, is a deeply moving musical
synonym for re-creation; if it seems to be a denial of the Western
world, this denial was essential for Stravinsky if, in his later work,
the Christian religious consciousness was to be reborn.

Nor is it entirely just to say that this re-created primitivism,
this liberation of the corporeal into the spiritual, is *merely* a stage
which Stravinsky himself passed through. For it has had repercus-
sions in other and later composers and, as we shall see, ultimately
links up with the other "retreat from Europe" that began, not as a
reassertion, but as a denial of corporeality. Even before this fusion
is effected we can observe, in the music of Carl Orff, an example
of the survival value of Stravinskian primitivism. We may think, and
would be justified in thinking, that Orff is a small composer compared with Stravinsky. But if he has concentrated only on one aspect
of Stravinsky's work and hasn't "grown to consciousness" with the
European-Russian, it is not true to say that he has left Stravinsky's
primitive phase exactly where he found it, that he has done nothing,
in thirty years of music creation, except repeat what Stravinsky had
already done better. Though we have often been encouraged to
think of *Carmina Burana*—the work with which Orff made his
name—as a poor man's *Les Noces,* the analogy has no more than
limited validity. It is obvious that Orff's work is restricted in rhythmic and textural invention compared with Stravinsky's masterpiece;
it should be equally obvious that Orff's work has certain assets which
are outside Stravinsky's range. Quite simply, what Orff has is "the
gift to be simple," as the old Shaker song puts it: a gift of memo-
rably haunting tunefulness, exemplified, for instance, in the soprano
solos from the Court of Love movement; and those who think such
tunefulness is easy should try it. The medieval Latin and Middle
German texts are pre-Renaissance, halfway between Christian "consciousness" and a direct, immediate ("pagan") acceptance of life in
and for the senses. While some vestiges of traditional harmonic practice remain, this music, flowering from the dawn of Europe, expresses
itself mainly through rhythmic excitation and through melodies that
are in essence physical gestures: there is no dichotomy between

thought and process, and emotion becomes the body's action, which is meant—as in all Orff's works—to be physically projected on a stage. So this music, with its beguiling tunefulness and the patterned symmetry of its rhythms, is a ritual related to the innocence of real folk music, to the street songs and runes of childhood itself, and to contemporary pop, which has at its heart an adolescent yearning for release from self-consciousness. Certainly *Carmina Burana* may have some historical significance as a genuine halfway house between concert music and pop. Like the tunes and rhythms of the Beatles, its banality is sometimes inspired; and this may be salutary, even though it doesn't invalidate the adult experience of greater composers.

Stravinsky's primitivism is merely one tensely ambiguous aspect of his response to the contemporary scene; with Orff we really are born again into childhood. That this return might be a new start in a different sense from Stravinsky's recreation of the past is suggested by a comparison of Stravinsky's *Wedding* with Orff's *Trionfo di Afrodite* of 1950. Both pieces describe a nuptial ceremony; but Orff's wedding carries on where Stravinsky's leaves off, in that the elements of corporeal rhythm and of melismatic monodic lyricism are now equally weighted. Orff's piece, like Stravinsky's, is a "concerto scenico" for solo voices representing the lovers and for chorus representing the people. It is accompanied by an orchestra in which normal forces are used abnormally, reinforced by a very large percussion battery. The music is meant to flow into action, mimed by dancers on a stage. It is significant that the texts, taken from Catullus, Sappho and Euripedes, and sung in the original Greek and Latin, have none of the Christian associations from which Stravinsky's return to European consciousness was to spring; they are a restatement of elemental pagan truths which Orff believes to be eternal. Though the essence of the music is sensual and corporeal, Orff is justified in saying that in his ritual of marriage and fertility "the timely element disappears" and "spiritual power" is generated from physical action. This is manifest, naturally, in the technique of the music itself. The structure of the seven sections of the work is dramatically comparable with that of Stravinsky's *The Wedding;* we begin with a "Song of the Maidens and Youth to the Evening Star," while awaiting the Bride and Bridegroom, and proceed to a wedding procession, a meeting of the Bride and Bridegroom, an invocation and "Hymn to Hymen," and to nuptial games and songs before the lovers are led into the Wedding Chamber. We don't, however, have to wait for the ultimate consummation and the epilogic appearance of Aphrodite for the translation of corporeality into spirit, for the two elements are in equipoise throughout. Thus, the percussive ostinati are simpler than in Stravinsky, even when excitement is enhanced by cross-rhythms. As a result, the rhythmic patterns can carry simple melodic phrases which, though still incantatory and hypnotic, are more lyrical than Stravinsky's, and in that sense more fulfilled in their innocence. Similarly, the ostinati of diatonic harmonies are more consonant, less exacerbated by unresolved percussive dissonances than Stravinsky's, while the more varied colours of the orchestra, used ritualistically rather than atmospherically, attain a glowing incandescence. Choirs of brass and woodwind, interspersed with the homophonic vocal choirs, give the percussive noises of bells, gongs, pianos and drums a simple melodic and harmonic identity, whereas in Stravinsky percussive attributes communicate themselves to the melodic and harmonic instruments. So, even in the opening movement, the metrically chanted incantations to Hymen can be interrupted by solo voice invocations to the Evening Star, wherein all physical movement, and even the most rudimentary harmony, stop, and the voices sing whirling melismata over a static drone. In these stepwise-moving, "spiritually" rhythmed melismata, from which temporal accents have vanished, the pentatonic love song such as concludes Stravinsky's *The Wedding* flowers and burgeons. And in the beautiful third movement, when the Bride and Bridegroom meet, we have an extended section of music which is entirely lyrical cantilena over a drone. This music is certainly more oriental than occidental in technique and feeling, while carrying conviction within this twentieth-century work. Thus the finale— the consummation of the marriage itself—does not (like the conclusion of Stravinsky's piece) carry us into a *different,* more spiritual world; rather, it consummates the identity of flesh and spirit of which we are already aware, just as, in real primitive ritual, erotic orgy would lead without break into religious ceremonial, and *vice versa*.

It is significant that the "Song before the Wedding Chamber" is the most *songful* of all the incantatory chants, though it still has a hypnotic pattern and an undeviating metrical pulse. Beginning quietly and tenderly, it rises to orgiastic fervour, and leads into the scene in the Wedding Chamber when the Bride and Bridegroom make love in entirely nonharmonic, nonmetrical melismatic lyricism, monodically unaccompanied, or with the simplest sustained drone. Their pentatonicism turns into rising chromatics as they twine together in sensuous parallel thirds, and the melismata of their ultimate love cries is the music most completely liberated from metrical Time and from the earth pull of harmony. So the final invocation of Aphrodite is an inevitable sequel to the physical consummation, which musically as well as dramatically had been presaged in the third scene when the Bride and Bridegroom had been awakened, by the lyre's music, to the spiritual reality of their love.

One can easily say—and it is true—that the music of this *Trionfo di Afrodite* is extraordinarily simple, even childish, to have been created in the mid-twentieth century. Yet if the music convinces, its simplicity is its strength, and its childishness a positive virtue. It links up with the music Orff has composed especially for children, because he believes that any renewal within modern civilization must grow from the young, who alone preserve some notion of the instinctive celebration that art once was. Orff's *Trionfo* may be an odd piece to have been written in our time. Nonetheless, the fact that it *has* been written is important, and although it's unlikely that many composers will either want or be able to compose similar music, it reminds us of certain positive values that will have to be preserved, or reborn, in any vital music of the future. It is a *positive* answer to Schoenberg's "Dance Around the Golden Calf," and the fact that Schoenberg's dance is a greater as well as more complex piece of music does not alter the fact that some such answer was necessary. That Orff's primitivism is not merely regressive is indicated if we consider him in relation to Olivier Messiaen who, as one of the shapers of the "New Music," learned much from both the serial and the Debussyan revolution.

V

The Circle Renewed: The "New Music" from Messiaen to Berio

We have seen that Schoenberg's tussle with the flesh, beginning with the Tristanesque *Verklärte Nacht,* led to a desperate search for a rebirth of spirit, and that Debussy sought a renewal of the spiritual simply by accepting the sensory moment as an end in itself. No less pagan in outlook, Orff and the early Stravinsky were composers whose rediscovery of corporeality led to a recreation of the irrational, the magically intuitive, which (in Stravinsky's case at least) was to lead to a renewal within Christian consciousness itself. Olivier Messiaen, on the other hand, was born within Christian tradition, while being no less passionate, sensuous and even paganly erotic in sensibility than Debussy, his compatriot and forebear. Of its nature his music is far more highly charged, harmonically, than that of the ritualists Orff and Stravinsky. In this sense it is more nervously personal, less communal; yet even in his earliest, most sensuous works it was evident that his harmonically centred music could tend toward ritual, in that he carried the isolation of the sensory moment from before and after to a still more extreme point than did Debussy. Indeed, the more highly charged are the artist's sensations, the greater is the need to be released from the grip of the Will. So the movement of the chromatic chords in a piece like *Le Banquet Céleste* is so slow as to be almost stationary, and the chords are so submerged in a plethora of "added notes" as to be without tonal identity; similarly, the relationships between the chords are as dis-

turbingly without harmonic *direction* as are the comparable passages in the Rose-Croix pieces of Erik Satie. The later, immense
piano work *Vingt Regards sur l'Enfant Jésus* is a series of "looks"
in that each movement is virtually without movement, being built
on an alternation of two or three chords, an ostinato, a pedal note
and a reiterated figuration. This, again, is a vast expansion of the
static technique explored in tiny works by Satie, and implicit in the
"spatial" aspects of Debussy's music. Since such music evades the
concept of beginning, middle and end, the European time-sense is
no longer relevant to it. This is why Messiaen's works last, chronometrically speaking, so long. There is no reason why they—any more
than a Gothic motet or the improvisation of an Indian vina player
—should ever stop.

The combination of these spatial and ritualistic techniques with
such sumptuous and nervously titillating harmony suggests that
Messiaen's music started from a desire to sublimate his eroticism
comparable to that of another fervent Roman Catholic, César
Franck (who was also an organist, at times drunk with the sensory
power that the organ, being a one-man band, may give to the
player). Messiaen's sublimatory mysticism would seem, however,
to be the more authentic, for it has specific musical consequences.
Thus, whereas Franck's chromatic harmonies, trying to grow, re-
volve narcissistically around themselves, Messiaen's harmonies,
making no pretense of growth, can proliferate (like Debussy's) into
melodic arabesques related to medieval cantillation. The cult of
Mariolatry in Messiaen's music may be directly related to the
Mariolatry of the original troubadours, for whom the Eternal Beloved was at once the Virgin Mary and an earth goddess. We remember that for the Gnostics Jesus was conceived of a Holy Spirit
(which was female in Hebrew) moving "on the face of the waters,"
and that the name of the mother in whom he was made flesh originally meant "of the sea." So the Virgin Mary cannot have been so
far removed from Aphrodite, "the Wise One of the Sea," from
whom descended Eleusis the Divine Child—after whom the
Eleusinian Mysteries were named. The "return to the waters of the
unconscious" is thus implicit in Messiaen's Christianity, and it is

not surprising that, in intuitively rediscovering the remote mythological roots of his religion, he should metamorphose Christian chastity into fecundity, in a whirl of ornament both linear and harmonic. This may also be why, in later works, medieval Christian features merge into a conception that is ritualistic in a more general sense, and the neomedieval techniques become inseparable from oriental processes. Not only does Messiaen employ Eastern melismatic devices, he also uses Indian ragas and talas both in pure and in modified form. Sometimes the chord formations may be a vertical statement of a traditional or invented raga; sometimes the themes may be a horizontal version of the "mystic chords," a procedure close to that of Scriabin, a still more esoteric musical theosophist who, depriving sensual harmonies of momentum, aimed to create a Mystery, performed in a hemispherical temple in India, which would induce in the participants a "supreme final ecstasy," after which the physical plane of consciousness would dissolve away and a world cataclysm begin.

Belonging to an orthodox church, Messiaen is less atomically literal, but it is significant that the work that sums up the first phase of his career should have been written in 1940 (in a prison camp), a year in which a catacylsm was indeed unleashed. The *Quatuor pour la fin du temps* for clarinet, violin, cello and piano relates this factual experience to the Apocalypse. Seven movements parallel the days of creation and the Day of Rest, while an eighth movement transports us to Eternity. The beautiful first movement, "Liturgie de Cristal," consists of bird twitters at dawn, in "le silence harmonieux du ciel," floating over a repeated metrical pattern or tala on the piano. The piano's chords are deprived of their Western sense of progression, while the bird song, in its numerical rhythm, is related to Eastern monody. This links Messiaen's Catholic mysticism to his pantheism, his awareness of Nature as an "other," a nonhuman reality. From this point of view there are affinities between his music and the Stravinsky of *The Rite of Spring,* as well as the obvious analogy with Debussy. In "Liturgie de Cristal" the birds are both Nature's voice and God's, and therefore are also man's desire for a heaven beyond consciousness. The destruction of

Time and consciousness is then prophesied by the Angel of the Apocalypse, who announces the consummation of the divine mystery. This movement is violent but nondeveloping: it releases the "bird" of the spirit who, in the next movement, sings alone, from the abyss of Time, in an unaccompanied clarinet arabesque. Monody and Spirit are here explicitly identified, and the arabesque technique is a fulfilment of the oriental implications of the flute solo in *Pierrot Lunaire,* for it employs not only raga and tala series and floating, additive rhythms, but also pitch distortions such as could not occur in a Western context. This liberation of the bird voice cannot be an end for Messiaen, however, for he has, after all, Europe's past behind him. This may be suggested by the brief, scherzo-like movement that follows, which seems to oppose the bird voice to the terrestrial, even trivial, circumstances of our everyday lives; the dancing, simple-textured, relatively diatonic music combines charm and grace with a faintly comic pathos. If this is our frail humanity, it leads us to the specifically Christian element of the work: the humanity that God assumed for our sake. The next movement is a cantilena for solo cello, representing Christ as the Word, accompanied by pulsing piano chords in an isochronous rhythmic pattern. Though this pattern is preordained, and in that sense medieval and possibly oriental too, the chords themselves are richly chromatic and in that sense humanistic. The long, floating cello melody flows over, and grows out of, the harmonic tensions. Identifying Christ with us, the music tells us that our sensuality, pain and mortality can find lyrical assuagement through Christ, as the notes of the melody become increasingly sustained, the pulse of Time slower and slower.

It is only after Christ's Incarnation that the Seven Trumpets of the Apocalypse can ring out. They, of course, are entirely monodic, because the divine voice (whether represented by Nature's birds or by God Himself) cannot admit the intrusion of "human" harmony. They also sound in a preordained metre, rotating in an eternal circle; here, conventional European instruments are made to create an extraordinary, gong-like, brazen sonority. When the Angel of the Apocalypse effects Time's destruction in the seventh move-

ment, Word and Flesh become one; melismatic arabesque is absorbed into, and grows out of, a ripely sensuous piano harmony and,
at times, a jazzily orgiastic and corporeal rhythm. The coda movement for violin and piano returns to earth—unlike Schoenberg's
Moses and Aaron—to take us into heaven. Representing Christ as
Man, it complements the cello solo that, representing Christ as
Word, had concluded the first part of the work. Significantly, it is
the fact of Incarnation that brings us our heavenly vision. The
"endless" line of the solo violin floats higher and higher until, with
oriental melismata, it fades away, "paradisiaque," into the stellar
spaces, while the piano pulsates, with senses suspended, on high
(Debussyan) chords of the added sixth. Here, as in the much
simpler music of Orff, eroticism is a gateway to mysticism.

From Messiaen's later works the "humanism" inherent in the
rich texture of the *Quatuor* has, for the most part, disappeared. The
chords become increasingly percussive in effect, without harmonic
meaning in the Western sense; complementarily, the organization
depends increasingly on a kind of magical-oriental serialism. If the
Christian element in these pieces is less patent, their nonhuman,
pagan "magic" is no less erotic in impulse. One of the most remarkable of these works that introduce Messiaen's third phase is
the *Cinq Rechants* for twelve unaccompanied voices, written in
1948, and specifically described as a "chant d'amour." In this work
the division between sacred and profane has ceased to exist. As
Messiaen has himself pointed out, the work has two musical sources:
the Harawi, a love song from the pagan folklore of Peru and
Ecuador; and the Alba, or medieval dawn song, which warns the
lovers of the approaching day. The text, by Messiaen himself, is
partly in surrealistic French and partly in an invented, pseudo-
Hindu language that dissolves "meaning" into purely musical
sound images: these sometimes become bird or insect or animal
noises. References to Tristan and Isolde, Vivian and Merlin,
Orpheus and other legendary lovers occur alongside contemporary
references (for instance to the flying lovers in the paintings of Marc
Chagall). Although the movement of the note values is almost
consistently rapid, thereby suggesting "the dramatic brevity of life,"

the forms are all nonevolutionary and the harmonies, in so far as they exist, nonprogressive. The Beloved stands beyond Time, "ses yeux voyagent dans le passé, dans l'avenir," and the same neutral tritone symbolizes the before and the after, of which we can have no certain knowledge.

If the structures have no relationship to Western tonal development, they have close connections with oriental serial permutation and with medieval variation techniques; the title *Rechants* is borrowed from the French Renaissance composer Claude le Jeune, who experimented in numerical rhythms derived from verbal inflection. After a free, monodic invocation in the invented language, the first Rechant introduces the panoply of legendary lovers, either monodically, in wildly whirling leaps controlled by the Deci Tala pattern of 2 plus 2 plus 3/16 alternating with 2/8, or in brutal, somewhat Stravinskian homophony. Interspersing reiterations and permutations of these brief motives are more extended, lyrical couplets in two- or three-part polyphony. The texture and rhythmic patterns are here medieval, though the sound doesn't lose its tender, post-Renaissance voluptuousness, partly because of the recurrent thirds in the texture, partly because of caressing grace notes comparable with those of oriental monody. It is interesting that the words of this section describe the crystal bubble in which Hieronymus Bosch enclosed his lovers. Medievally biased, Bosch saw the encroachment of Renaissance will as a nightmare; Messiaen, at the twilight of the Renaissance, relinquishes the tonal perspective analogous to the visual perspective that Bosch had just become aware of, and once more dissolves antecedence and sequence in discontinuous space.

Each of the five Rechants is constructed on this same principle: an introductory invocation; the Rechant (which is the ritornello or refrain of troubadour music), alternating with Couplets; and a coda which returns to the original invocation and sometimes includes motives from the Rechant and Couplets also. There is no climax within the individual movements, though one might possibly say that the central (third) Rechant forms an apex to the whole work. It begins, not with strict monody, but with undulating tritonal cantilena accompanied by wordless, sensuously static chords and attains, from this sensuality, the highest degree of magical or "doctrinal" impersonality, since the three verses are in nonreversible rhythm, developed by augmentation and then by diminution of the central values. "The left and right values remain invariably symmetrical. In the third verse the effect is maintained and intensified by a long crescendo, which unfurls like a veil of sound in twelve-part canon, culminates in a collective cry, and falls back to a soft, supple, and tender coda." There is a direct affinity between this cry and the yell of consummated passion in Orff's *Afrodite,* and it may be significant that in the later Rechants tritonal figurations become increasingly prevalent in the melodic lines themselves. Indeed, the basic theme of the fourth Rechant is the *si contra fa* that used to be the Devil, and the ululation of the Couplets is all tritonal organum. The tritones from which Tristan yearned to be released seem to have become, monodically, a positive; the Flesh has become the Word. In this sense Messiaen can claim to have created, in the triptych of works of which *Cinq Rechants* is the last, a song of love and death which is a positive continuation of the Wagnerian cycle; Tristan no longer needs to die in order to achieve the metamorphosis of Flesh into Spirit. Debussy, in depriving Wagnerian harmony of the need for resolution, had shown the way to the apotheosis of the flesh; Messiaen completes the process by transforming harmonic tension into monodic line.

It would be difficult to imagine a more complete reversal of the will domination of post-Renaissance Europe than the gigantic *Turangalîla Symphony*—the second member of the triptych of love and death that concludes Messiaen's middle period. In this work the corybantic fast movements are significantly allied to the new-old primitivism of jazz both in the hypnotic repetitiveness of their riffs and breaks and in the blatantly scored juiciness of their harmony. They seem as eternally long, as Time-obliterating, as the slow movements which evoke the sensual heaven of a garden of love wherein the birds (represented by a gamelan orchestra of piano, vibraphone, xylophone and celesta) ecstatically twitter, both tonally and rhythmically independent of the almost stationary string homophony.

Such a pantheistic attempt to create a musical cosmos embracing man, God and the natural world increasingly dominates Messiaen's later works, such as *Le Reveil des Oiseaux* for piano and orchestra. In 1953 this work inaugurated the series of compositions based on the scrupulous imitation of the songs of birds. The writing here, as in the *Cinq Rechants,* tends to be monophonic in principle, even when the strings are divided in thirty-two parts! And the fascinating sonorities are an ultimate expression of Debussy's desire to "reproduce what I hear . . . the mysterious accord that exists between Nature and the human imagination." Of the quality of Messiaen's imagination —which creates out of the imitation of Nature—there can be no doubt; even so, there are times, especially in the immense and apparently interminable *Catalogues d'Oiseaux* for piano solo, when one finds oneself wondering whether Messiaen hasn't carried "l'atrophie du Moi" a bit too far. Maybe birds are angel voices that have something we have lost; nonetheless one can't completely follow Debussy in saying that there is more to be gained by watching the sun rise than by listening to the *Pastoral Symphony,* for sunrises, like birds, have never lost something that Beethoven had, because they never had it to lose. However post-Renaissance man may have misused his knowledge and his power, he certainly hasn't toiled through centuries of "the pain of consciousness" to end up listening to the birds —while squatting on an oriental midden.

Such subversive grumblings as one has permitted oneself, however, have been negated in the event. Even the most passive of Messiaen's bird pieces is justified, if not intrinsically, at least in the light of his development. In *Oiseaux Exotiques* for piano and wind instruments (1955) he had already indicated how the recording of natural phenomena might be used to creative and visionary ends. Despite its debt to the birds, this music makes a new sound which, if it reminds us of any other music, suggests affinities with some of the polyrhythmic work of Ives. This fact alone would seem to indicate that Messiaen's abnegation of the will is not necessarily a denial of his humanity; and it prepared the way for the great *Chronochromie* of 1960, a work for large orchestra which is one of those rare pieces that make history. It would seem to complete Messiaen's "magical" retreat from humanism, for the structure is based not on human awareness of progression in time, but on rhythmic proportions inherent in Nature, at once preordained and permutatory, like crystal formation and snow flakes. In a music wherein "Nature is the supreme resource—an inexhaustible treasure-house of sounds, colours, forms and rhythms, and the unequalled model for total development and perpetual variation" (as Messiaen has put it), the ticking of the clock is no longer relevant, and the melodic material, derived from the imitation of specific (and specified) birds, has no more need of thematic growth than have the bird carollers themselves. The astonishing dawn chorus for a plethora of solo strings becomes a climax only in the sense that it attains the maximum of heterophonic freedom. Hermes was a winged messenger, Papageno a feathered child of Nature, and Messiaen's birds are angelic presences who can be free of humanly imposed restraints—such as tonality, "accepted" musical timbre, and so on. They are a manifestation of the flux and perhaps of the female principle, as are the waterfall images which also appear in this work.

The return to Nature "in and for herself," as a release from human complexity, has a long heritage in the music of our time. Perhaps it begins with the bird that sings to Siegfried from the dark forest; certainly it is evident in Debussy's *Nuages* and in the marvellous night pieces of Bartók, with their onomatopoeic representations of chittering birds and barking frogs. In all these, however, Nature's otherness is seen, or rather heard, in opposition to the human: the broken cor anglais phrase that wanders through Debussy's clouds suggests man's littleness against the vast sky, while the middle section of the slow movement of Bartók's *Music for strings, celesta and percussion* juxtaposes man's melodic-harmonic endeavour against the timeless continuum of the (preconscious) sounds of the natural world. Apart from the Parisian-American Edgard Varèse (whom we shall discuss later), Messiaen is the first composer who seeks to reassert man's validity not in conflict with, but as part of, the principles—if not the "laws"—of Nature. He, more than any other single composer of our time, represents modern man's weariness with a literate, will-dominated, patriarchal culture, and his desire to rediscover a matriarchal culture that worships the White Goddess and accepts the Terrible Mothers. It is not an accident that Messiaen's formal sequence of "Anacrusis," "Accent" and "Desinence" parallels the lunar calendar, nor that the processes of rhythmic and intervallic metamorphosis which he began to explore in the *Etudes de modes rhythmiques* of 1949 have direct affinities with the transmutation techniques of the old alchemists, both medieval and Arabian. Indeed, the fact that alchemy has again become a respectable subject is part of our age's rediscovery of the irrational, our consciousness of the unconscious. In a profound sense Messiaen is a musical alchemist, for he is concerned with the nature of Matter (in this case sound-matter) in itself; with the possibility of *changing* matter not through man's will, but by way of an understanding of its laws; and with the ultimate possibility of man himself being reborn through achieving identity with the multiplicity of matter, so that the All becomes the One. A re-cognition of magic and of the chthonic forces that surround us may, of course, release only evil, as it did in Hitler's Germany. But it may also release unsuspected positive powers, in so far as an understanding of natural process may become identical with a fulfilment of the self. In a very real sense Messiaen, in his music, loses the self in order that he may find it, which must be why the man who suffers and rejoices is instantly recognizable in the idiom of the mind that creates. It is pertinent to note that the strophic and antistrophic structure of *Chronochromie* is analogous to the chorus of an ancient Greek tragedy. Certainly, having listened to the piece, we feel that the springs of our humanity have been not relinquished but renewed. Without denying his Christian heritage, Messiaen has attempted to heal the breach that Christianity has committed us to, by reasserting the spiritual validity of the sexual impulse, and rediscovering the identity of the Creator with Created Nature.

So far we have traced the two strands that, becoming intertwined, gave impetus to the "New Music." Webern, harking back to Schoenberg, dissolves beat and pulse, and disintegrates harmony into line, recreating a serialism that has affiliations with the Law of the Gothic motet (which was the twilight of the Middle Ages), and reaching out intuitively toward conceptions more typical of oriental than of occidental cultures. Debussy, the complementary figure, dissolves his Wagnerian harmonic sensuality into quasi-Eastern arabesque; his successor Messiaen seeks to heal the breach between Creator and Created by a fusion of Christian with Buddhist and, indeed, pagan pantheism. If Schoenberg inverted European history (in so far as in *Moses* the Idea is inexpressible, and cannot become manifest in created nature), Webern and Messiaen between them look towards a new—and also a very old—conception of music as Revelation rather than as Incarnation. Today Pierre Boulez, now the Old Master of the avant-garde, consciously rejects those elements in their work which relate to the immediate past. *Schoenberg est mort;* but Webern isn't, any more than is Messiaen or Debussy. The new-old, pre-Renaissance, non-Western elements in Debussy, Webern and Messiaen are his initial impulse. These are reinforced by certain neoprimitive rhythmic conceptions from Stravinsky (especially *The Rite of Spring*), and by certain melodic and textural elements suggested by Schoenberg's *Pierrot Lunaire,* which Boulez admits to be one of the seminal masterpieces of our time.

Of recent years Boulez has deservedly won fame as a conductor; his performances of the music referred to in the previous paragraph are profoundly revealing in reference to his own composition. For instance, his playing of the Webern *Symphony* is, strictly speaking, a revelation; what it reveals is the continuity of lyrical line beneath the apparent fragmentation. The song sings in a metaphysical heaven, infinitely far off; yet, supported by a structure of fine steel, sing it does, infinitely tender. That it sings, that its structure is aurally intelligible, this is the work's greatness, and it makes most of the music that has been influenced by it seem banal. Complementarily, when Boulez plays Debussy's *Images* his precision of rhythm and meticulous delineation of texture enhance, rather than restrict, spontaneity; he "swings" the music and, as in the best jazz, swing metamophoses harmonic corporeality into spiritual grace. Even in performing *La Mer* Boulez plays down the heroic, "symphonic" element and hands back the music's passionate vagaries to the wind and waves. The dominant ego is at a discount, as it is in his performance of Messiaen's *Oiseaux Exotiques;* the precision of the stresses within the complex texture makes the music sound as though it were *playing itself,* relinquishing the will, like *Nuages,* yet richer and stronger because there is so much more to be relinquished. Having once heard *La Mer* this way, which is surely Debussy's, we never want to hear it again with the customary rhetorical gestures.

Most revealing of all, however, is Boulez's performance of Debussy's last orchestral score, *Jeux,* where the physical energy and painful nostalgia that are still latent beneath the surface of Debussy's marine and Iberian evocations finally evaporate. The ballet concerns a tennis party, and tennis, as we recall from Shakespeare, is a sexy game. But it takes place at twilight and is love play without conclusion. Opening with tritonal whole-tone oscillations that are Tristan's imperfect fourths freed from even the yearning for resolution, the score becomes a flickering within the subconscious. Little, broken, Tristanesque sighs wail on the strings, only to dissipate into coruscating figurations of threes against fours against fives. Mood, tonality and tempo are in flux, by the acceptance of which we are released from memory and desire. So this sombre comedy is a musical anticipation of the Theatre of the Absurd, just as *Pelléas* had been the first existential opera. No single work is closer to the heart of Boulez's own music, as is immediately evident in the volatile fancy of one of his earliest works, the *Sonatine* for flute and piano.

How this Debussyan heritage merges into that of Webern is revealed in another early work of Boulez, the cantata *Le Soleil des Eaux,* composed in his twenty-second year. The second of the two movements, in which René Char's poem speaks directly of man's betrayal of Nature, tells us that man's hanky-panky with the natural world will result only in his physical annihilation unless he finds self-annihilation in submission to the will of God. The technique is Webernian, but more violent; the savage rhythmic and harmonic contrarieties seek a law beyond the self, a serial principle analogous to the cantus firmus technique of late Gothic music and to the Indian

raga and tala. The first movement, however, is more positive, less
harried by the Law, more Debussyan in technique. The poem cele-
brates a lizard's will-less passivity on a rock; he's at once above and
beyond, yet envious of, a goldfinch, aggressively involved in love and
life and the war between man and nature. Here the disintegration of
harmonic tension into points of sonority releases lyricism. The long
passages of unaccompanied monody acquire, despite their nervosity,
something of the levitating ecstasy of oriental cantillation; even the
wide leaps and the fragmentation become air-borne, so that the
denial of civilization is a positive act. It is already evident that the
spirituality of Boulez's music springs from a sublimation, not a
denial, of the body's joy.

In *Le Soleil des Eaux* the two movements still exemplify the
unresolved tension between the Webernian and the Debussyan (and
Messiaenic) heritage. A complete fusion of the two concepts is
effected in Boulez's first mature work, *Le Marteau sans Maître*. This
work, too, has a surrealistic text by René Char, releasing the mind
from consciousness, yet asking too what happens when control of
the "hammer" is voluntarily abandoned. What makes *Le Marteau*
a historically important work is the manner in which Boulez uncompromisingly faces up to the latent implications of Debussy's and
Webern's music: implications which may at first seem to be technical, but which cannot be merely that. Thus, if *Le Marteau* is
immediately recognizable as a "new noise" (which occurs infrequently in musical history), it is because the texture is even airier,
more floating, more disembodied than that of Webern. The instruments—alto flute, viola, vibraphone and guitar, with a large battery
of exotic percussion—are all light in timbre and air-borne, as is the
sonority of the Gothic motet. Added to this, the rhythmic disintegration is far more extreme even than in Webern. The implied triplet
figurations of Webern become in Boulez fives, sevens, nines and
what-else, and these irregular units often have to be played in the
time of some other unit, so that each player is working to a different
silent pulse which he must feel as best he may. The result of this
airy fragmentation, so far as the listener is concerned, is that he
becomes hardly aware of pulse or of harmonic density. The terms

consonance and dissonance have ceased to have much relevance;
what one is aware of is the interplay of timbres and sonorities, in
which the actual pitch (and therefore "tonality") is less important
than its quality and character—high, low, piercing, soft, long,
short, etc. This is the more so because of the fantastically rapid
speed of the music. Boulez's typical fast movement goes at about
208 to the minute, whereas Webern's average fast speed is about
160–170. Paradoxically, this makes the feeling of Boulez's music
slower, not faster, for the less ability the ear has to distinguish alternations of tension, the more static will be the total effect. This is
manifest in Messiaen's bird pieces also, and of course the effect is
intentional; in becoming stratospheric, we no longer desire conscious
direction.

The serial processes in Boulez, as Robert Craft has shown, are
related to this increase in the speed of the figuration, and they
further decrease the sense of temporal progression. Webern's fragmentation had meant that the interval rather than the note sequence
became the unity and the silences between the intervals could be a
part of the latent theme. In Boulez the four forms of the serially
ordered twelve semitones are always interval rather than note
transpositions. One remembers the intervals but not the relationship
of the pitches; that everything is now serialized—dynamics, frequency, articulations and timbre—tends further to reduce the
supremacy of pitch. The fact that everything moves in serial sequence means that everything is constantly varied; yet the change
is a kaleidoscope, the eternal circle of Buddhist philosophy, for if
all is change, change itself is meaningless. The effect of this music,
as distinct from the analysis of its technical process, is to create an
awareness of the *flux* of reality, in which is included "nature" and
the nerves, while at the same time releasing us from the flux into
"space" and eternity. Thus its oriental affiliations, like those of
Debussy, Webern and Messiaen, are as much philosophical as
musical. Because of, rather than in spite of, its complexity and restlessness, the music, if adequately performed, should induce—in
Charles Ives's wonderful phrase—"a kind of furious calm." Even
more than Webern's music, it is antidramatic, rendering the horrors

of the text irrelevant. The preordained conditions within which the ecstatic shimmer of sound occurs create magic, in some ways similar to that created by a Balinese gamelan orchestra, which has a comparable sonority and equally rapid figuration within an almost immobile basic pulse. Though we may not know—as we presumably do, if we are born within the culture, when listening to Balinese music—precisely what the magic signifies, we are nonetheless aware that it has the faculty of release.

Despite this "flux-like" character, *Le Marteau sans Maître* is constructed on a cyclical (not progressive) form that owes much to Messiaen's rondo structures. The first vocal movement is preceded by two instrumental movements: an air-borne chitter of sound scored for flute, vibraphone, guitar and viola, in four sections with strongly marked fermata; and the first commentary on the "Bourreaux de Solitude," which is in effect a flute solo accompanied by percussion, every note being serially organized in dynamics as well as pitch and rhythm. The wide-flung flute line achieves a disembodied ecstasy which is both reinforced and controlled by the fantastically complex tala of the percussion instruments. A wildly disintegrative middle section or trio is scored for xylorimba, pizzicato viola and two bongos, and is followed by a return to the flute's song in telescoped form. The first vocal number, "L'Artisanat Furieux" is a duo for alto voice and flute, in which the relationship to the flute solo movement from *Pierrot Lunaire* is no less obvious than the oriental affiliations of the melismatic style. Despite the enormous leaps and "difficult" intervals, the rhythms float delicately, almost tenderly. All the nervosity comes from the blood-thirsty words. In the marvellous setting of the phrase, *"je rêve la tête sur la pointe de mon couteau le Perou,"* fear and terror are dissipated in the act of creation, as they are in Schoenberg's Pierrot, who is also the murderer of love.

The second commentary on the "Bourreaux de Solitude" is highly nervous and jittery, with elaborate hoqueting comparable with that in some of Stravinsky's recent music. The horror within the mind emerges, to be assuaged in the fantastic, freely soaring lyricism of the second vocal movement, "Bel Edifice et Pressentiments," in which the voice is intertwined with an equally melismatic flute and viola. In the "Bourreaux de Solitude" movement itself the texture is more open, the tala pattern of the maracas more aurally intelligible; this may be why the music sounds convincing as the pivotal point of the eternal circle. The last three movements effect the return. "Après L'Artisanat Furieux" is an interlude related to the first movement, also in four sections separated by four fermata; the third commentary on "Bourreaux de Solitude" is a second "double" related to the first commentary, but comparatively slow. It leads to the double of "Bel Edifice et Pressentiments," which has a brief introduction recalling (without literal repetition) earlier movements. Various phrases built on the augmented fourth fulfil a refrain-like function, and for the first time there is direct recapitulation, or rather flashbacks thrown up on the flux. The music to the words "je rêve la tête" is identical with that in the third movement, only backward, with the guitar playing the first part of the vocal phrase. "J'écoute marcher" also quotes in modified form the *marcheur* passage from the sixth movement, an effect the more striking because it occurs in a music which habitually avoids both recognizable repetition and architectural symmetry. Such reminiscences of the past occur, however, only because the past has ceased to matter, for this movement completes the final sundering of consciousness and of temporality. The *Pierrot Lunaire*-like creepy noises drift into the refrains of the voice, and this lyrical apotheosis is consummated when the flute returns for the coda, accompanied by gongs and interspersed with long silences. The effect is very similar to Japanese temple music; lines no less agile, nervous and twittery than the calligraphy of Paul Klee (whom Boulez, like Webern, greatly admires) fade into reverberations that become slower and slower, calmer and calmer, until they vanish into silence.

We are left unsure whether what is revealed is indeed God's will or merely an emptiness that is better than agony. One's first reaction is to be wary of Western music that attempts to evade progression so completely. But if *Le Marteau sans Maître* seems a fascinating but abortive experience that overstays its welcome, the reason may be not because it goes too far, but because it doesn't go far enough.

Similarly, if we find the *Second Piano Sonata* baffling—except in so far as the slow coda seems beautiful on the analogy of the madman who hammered his head because it was so nice when he stopped— the reason may be that we can't help listening to it traditionally, looking for and missing affiliations with Viennese chromaticism. Boulez himself is said to have referred to it as his Beethovenian sonata, an opinion we can accept only with the eye, and still more the ear, of faith. When, however, he completely finds himself, in *Pli selon Pli,* his largest work to date, he no longer arouses expectations which he can't fulfil. Perhaps because of this he proves that his apparent evasion of human responsibilities may be no such thing.

Two things are immediately obvious about Boulez's prodigious musicianship as revealed in this work. One is the originality and sensuous precision of his aural imagination, which rivals that of Debussy; the other is the sensitivity of his command of vocal line which, with its melismatic grace notes, is now no less nervously agile, yet still more radiantly lyrical, than that of Webern. Boulez's choice of Mallarmé's poems is itself significant, for Mallarmé's "concentric universe" creates an eternal present in which "all is always now" and there can be no historic past or future. It is true that the fluttery tenderness of Boulez's setting roots us in the ex- perience we have lived through, in so far as, during the early stages, the leaping convolutions imply a harmonic density comparable with that of Webern. Gradually, however, we're levitated skyward by the quasi-oriental arabesques, over a variety of celestial-sounding ostinati, until in the second "Improvisation" any preordained serial control is no longer necessary. Abstract supernatural law gives way to the truth of the subconscious mind. The voice becomes purely monodic, floating rhythmless, in unmeasured notation, without harmonic implication, over shimmering drones and reverberating gongs. Yet at this point, when we're most freed from time and space, the clattering hurly-burly of nature comes back in the wild music that Boulez scores for his gamelan orchestra of xylophones, harps, celesta, vibraphone, piano and multitudinous bells, gradually reinforced by normal orchestral instruments playing in quasi- improvisatory heterophony. There's something reminiscent of Varèse's use of the sonorities of the natural world in this movement, as there is in Messiaen's comparable hubbub in *Oiseaux Exotiques*. But whereas Varèse and Messiaen positively evoke the animate world, we experience Boulez's cacophony of nature as an opposite pole to the hermetic calm induced by the vocal monody. Though there's nothing personal, ego-dominated, about the racket (which Boulez conducts chronometrically, as he does the still passages), the effect is to carry us back to the exacerbated bark from which the work had started.

So whereas Beethoven grows through each work progressively more involved in tonal and motivic conflict, seeking ultimate resolution, Boulez begins at a high point of harmonic and rhythmic contrariety, which dissolves in increasingly monodic, nonmetrical, nonharmonic cantillation. He abnegates reason and consciousness to enter nirvana; then the cycle starts again. The title of *Pli selon Pli* presumably refers to the experiential as well as the technical process. So the music isn't a withdrawal into a Japanese temple in order to evade our perplexities; rather, it's a contemporary disassociation from our perplexities in order that we may understand what they are. This may be why Boulez's apparently eccentric work seems so relevant to us, and its hour and a half duration not a moment too long. It's difficult to know how to estimate "greatness" in works that have no beginning, middle and end. But whatever the future has in store for us, and however equivocal this work's position between East and West, we may hazard a guess that it will establish itself as a crucial masterpiece of our time, as Debussy's *Jeux* and Webern's *Symphony* were of theirs.

Boulez was trained as a mathematician and the preordained serialism of musically abstract works such as the *Structures* for two pianos go about as far as humanly operated instruments can hope to go in building musical forms from mathematical proportions— from the laws, such as the vector section, which underlie the cosmos. We can appreciate the logic of this denial of the personal in an increasingly scientific world, and such structures presumably affect our response to the total experience on repeated hearing, even though they cannot be aurally intelligible in an art that exists in time. In a sense one could say that this submission to mathematical process is a culmination of post-Renaissance's man's desire to play God; he becomes the lawgiver, or at least the law-revealer, so that his abnegation of the self is also a final arrogance. Boulez's later career, however, suggests that he's aware of this dubiety of intention. Whether or not the mathematical laws of the cosmos are God's will, it's an inescapable fact that human beings cannot interpret them infallibly, and in the relationship *between* God and man something other than mathematical principle is involved. This is why Boulez has, in part, retreated from "preordained" serialism to some kind of indeterminacy—to a reliance not on mathematical law, nor on the human will, but on the most primitive springs of our nature. There's some evidence to suggest that this is true not merely of *Pli selon Pli* (which employs the human voice even though Mallarmé's words are intentionally devoid of specific "meaning"), but also of his recent, purely instrumental works, which would seem to be organized on mathematico-scientific principles. The *Third Piano Sonata,* still in progress, includes indeterminate elements, and the *Doubles* for orchestra are in three sections which represent a transition from order to flu... The first section, "Figure," is geometrically precise; the second section, "Doubles," effects mutations of the original mathematical proportions, giving at least the illusion of greater freedom; while the last section, "Prism," refracts and splinters the patterns to create a heterophonic hurly-burly strikingly similar to the "cacophony of Nature" in *Pli selon Pli.* It is interesting that this retreat from the Law should be echoed even by the most fanatically doctrinaire of post-Webernian composers, Karlheinz Stockhausen.

He, too, was trained as a mathematical engineer, and found his starting point in a creative misunderstanding of Webern's most difficult and rigidly serial works, opus 14–20. For Stockhausen the "circular" rather than "progressive" implications of Webern's serialism outweigh the expressivity at which Webern still aimed. Works such as the *Kontrapunkte* of 1952 (which are contemporary with Boulez's *Structures* and *Polyphonie X*) go even further than Boulez in total serialization, for "each note is fixed in the time span of the whole musical structure by a conjunction of coordinates

which determine its pitch, dynamic, duration and mode of attack."
Stockhausen next extended these techniques to what he calls "group
forms." In a piece such as *Gruppen* for three orchestras, the indi-
vidually determined notes are "constellated" into groups (played on
the three orchestras), which are in themselves predetermined, but
flexible in the relation of one group to another. Thus the individual
elements are a microstructure within the macrocosm of the groups.
That comparable techniques had been used many years ago by
Charles Ives (without the predetermined elements) points to the
fact that Stockhausen's release from the "will" implies a simultaneous appeal to mathematics and to the unconscious; the determined and the indeterminate elements will, for him, be complementary.

Zeitmasse for five woodwind, though written for conventional
resources, effects a more radical metamorphosis of traditional notions of music than any superficially comparable work of Boulez.
"Beat" disappears even more completely, and with it any sense of
man's corporeal nature, his heartbeat and physical gestures. Though
the title means time measurement, the music concerns time's negation. The serial organization of the rhythms is based on extremely
short time values which organize the music into numerical patterns,
like the talas of oriental music, only incredibly more rapid and more
complicated. Occasionally these patterns may exist over a pulse
evident in one part, since if we lost all sense of pulse we wouldn't
be aware of what was being relinquished. Against this latent pulse,
we feel the loss of beat as exactly parallel to the loss of pitch that
occurs when the patterns, in their flickering complexity, shade over
from notable pitch to microtonal inflection and to noise. This is
strictly comparable with what happens in oriental monody, or in the
improvised roulades of a Charlie Parker, Sonny Rollins or John
Coltrane, except that they, as jazz musicians, start from a frank
admission of a corporeal beat, which the solo line divides into
fantastically rapid numerical rhythms, usually involving an Eastern
distortion of pitch.

It follows that Stockhausen's music, even more than Boulez's,
denies traditional harmonic centrality. Indeed, he abandons tonal

notation, using only the sharp sign; and because rather than in spite of the serialization of pitch, rhythm and dynamics seeks an ever greater differentiation between the parts. This is achievable because the parts are less (if at all) concerned about their vertical relationships. In this again Stockhausen resembles Webern in more extreme form, while both may be related to the late Gothic motet, wherein the strangest disparities of text, melody and rhythm were precariously held together by the doctrinal magic of cantus firmus series and of isochronous rhythm. In *Zeitmasse* the ultimate disintegration is just, but only just, suspended. Each instrument has its own preordained time scheme. Sometimes one part may have an implied beat which the others must think against in elaborately numerical rhythms, but the "goal" of the work is the complete disappearance of beat: a condition wherein each part has a distinct metronomic indication as starting point, from which it may accelerate or retard independently of the others. Such unmeasured identity is an ultimate form of the "restlessness" of the Gothic motet. Interestingly, Stockhausen's most typical direction is "as fast as possible," which in aural effect is indistinguishable from his other frequent direction, "as slow as possible," for with the disappearance of pulse goes any sense of movement from or towards. Again, there may be a parallel in the later work of a jazz saxophonist like John Coltrane.

The freeing of music from beat is thus an attempt to escape the limitations of merely human potentiality. This is why this kind of music had to lead to electronic realization, for electronic instruments can perform perfectly rhythms and pitches of which human beings, however skilled, are but dubiously capable. The world of sound is a continuum, as Busoni said many years ago, and the world of our traditional music is but a fraction of a fraction of one diffracted ray from that Sun music which "fills the heavenly Vault with Harmony." This reference to the music of the spheres reminds us how medieval, or non-Western, the implicit philosophy is. Music is becoming Revelation rather than Incarnation again; the substitution of the mathematician's order for the artist's, however, prompts questions which we hardly needed to ask in considering Boulez's *Pli selon Pli*. The medieval composer was at once artist and mathematician; so is the twentieth-century electronic composer. Both are medicine men, promulgating a Mystery. The difference is that although everyone in the Middle Ages knew that God worked in a mysterious way, they had no doubt that his Church was relevant to their everyday lives, whereas the twentieth-century scientist in his laboratory is a mystery man in a somewhat different sense. We regard him with awe, but we can't profess to understand the relevance of his pronouncements to our lives, except in so far as we know that it is within his power to destroy us. This may be why most electronic music doesn't sound like the revelation of a Faith, but rather like creepy space noises for a science-fiction film. And it is a fiction, however scientific; though it fills us with a sense of the unknown, it hardly leaves us feeling that we have conquered space, either without the mind or within it.

Nor have we, of course. We are only beginning to learn what the qualities and potentialities of a new medium are; it is still the com-position, the creation of the musical order, that will give life to the order of engineer and acoustician. It is interesting that although Stockhausen has constructed works according to the most rigid principles of mathematical engineering, he has sometimes (we are told by other scientists) got his mathematics wrong! The Law is illusory; but the value of the composition may lie precisely in the illusion, which is an admission of human fallibility. In Stockhausen's *Kontakte,* for instance, the contacts are between purely electronic sounds, between sounds of metal, wood and skin, and between processed natural noises. The essence of the work is that it is an interplay between mathematical law and the flux of nature; the scale of electronically produced timbres "mediates between" the familiar tones and noises, and "facilitates transformation of sound from each one of these categories into every other one, and mutations of sound into completely new, previously unknown, sound events." While we cannot apply to this music the normal criteria by which we value traditional music, we can see that the criteria we apply to *Zeitmasse* are not irrelevant to it. The patterns may be metrically more complex, the infinite gamut of pitches more widely investigated, the ultimate tempo still more orientally immobile;

nonetheless, human identity still struggles within the spaceship.

That this music is a beginning, however, is important in more than a technical sense. We have referred to the fact that both Webern and Boulez, hypersophisticated artists though they are, were concerned with being "new born," in Paul Klee's sense. Similarly, it is probably not an accident that the piece of electronic music that makes most imaginative sense to us, at least among the works produced in old Europe, should be Stockhausen's *Gesang der Jünglinge,* which is specifically concerned with the theme of childhood and youth. The texture is made up of children's voices, speaking and singing snatches of street songs and nursery tunes; of processed abstractions from vowel sounds and consonants (a human language phonetically transmuted to mathematics); and of pure electronic sounds in which there is no intrusion of the human at all. Thus the piece deals with embryonic human life within the mathematical laws of the cosmos. Human language is literally disintegrated into its component noises—an ultimate form of the process that was manifest, in the twilight of the Middle Ages, in the late Gothic motet. The nonhuman appears to be inimical, destroying the possibility of communication; nonetheless, when apprehensible human words do emerge they prove to be an act of praise, sung by the Man in the Fiery Furnace, from the Book of Daniel. The fiery furnace may be hell, and is certainly our postatomic world; yet, though the gibbers and twitters get faster and fiercer while the children's cries (scattered stereophonically on five loudspeakers in different parts of the hall) grow fainter and more forlorn, the voices are not finally obliterated. Indeed, the disintegration of human language into phonetics and its identity with "abstract" mathematics become a way of reaffirming the human and a potential new life. From its awareness of disintegration, the music praises God; its rebirth is a religious act.

At the time he composed *Gesang der Jünglinge* Stockhausen was formally a Roman Catholic. Though he has since renounced the Church, he remains a mystical composer in the sense that he follows Messiaen in wishing "alchemically" to transmute the material of sound. Indeed, in his case the transmutation analogy is literal, for unlike Messiaen he employs electronic techniques to change the quality of sound matter itself. (In *Microphony No. 1,* for instance, two players stroke, tickle and hit an enormous Chinese tam-tam while two other performers transmute the reverberations by the application of contact microphones.) Since alchemy is in part a rediscovery of the irrational which is inherent in Nature, it is not surprising that in all his later works Stockhausen has tended to emphasize the variable and indeterminate elements in his music at the expense of the predetermined elements. Some of the *Klavier-stücken,* or the *Refrain* for three performers, employ sound fragments of which the order, and to some extent the character, is determined by the performer. The concept of progression, of beginning, middle and end, which we have seen to be largely irrelevant to Boulez's music, is here entirely meaningless; the form of *Klavierstück X,* for instance, is described by Stockhausen as the *augenblick* —the instantaneous glance of the eye, in which every "event" is coexistent with every other. There is a direct parallel here with primitive visual art, as well as music; the art of the Eskimos, for instance, is a multidirectional and nontemporal filling-up of space which can be seen equally well from any direction, so that our notion of a "right side up" only excites their mirth.

It would seem that most of Stockhausen's later music implies at least a partial return from the duality of the Christian Cross and from Montaigne's depiction of "passage rather than Being" to the circular processes of the East and of primitive cultures. The key work in Stockhausen's later career is specifically entitled *Zyklus.* In the score of this extended work for one percussion player "sixteen pages of notation have been spiral-bound to one another," Stockhausen says, "side by side"; there is no beginning and no end. "The player may start on whichever page he pleases, but he must then play a cycle in the given succession. During the performance the player stands in the centre of a circle of percussion instruments and turns, from one playing position to another, once round his own axis, clockwise or counterclockwise, depending on the direction in which he has chosen to read. Areas combining dots and groups of notes and symbols vary from one another through differences in the number of possible combinations; they mediate continuously, in their composed succession, between the entirely unequivocal and the extremely ambiguous. The structure with the greatest indeterminateness, the most ambiguous form, is shaped in such a way that it comes to be almost indistinguishable from the immediately following, most firmly fixed structure. Thus one experiences a temporal circle in which one has the impression of moving constantly in the direction towards ever-increasing ambiguousness (clockwise) or certainty (counterclockwise), although at the critical point at which the extremes touch, the one imperceptibly turns into the other. The purpose is to close the open form through the circle, to realize the static state within the dynamic, the aimless within the aimed, and not to exclude or destroy one aspect or another, not to seek a synthesis in a third state, but rather to attempt to eliminate the dualism and to mediate between the seemingly incompatible, the utterly different."

This may seem a tall order for one percussion player; yet the work is powerful enough, at least as interpreted by the phenomenal Christoph Caskel, to stand as a *locus classicus* of musical-philosophical principle. "To eliminate the dualism" has certainly been the impulse behind all Stockhausen's recent music, and the traditional post-Renaissance dichotomies between sound and noise, content and form, composer and performer, performer and audience are in a state of flux, if not finally broken down. It's no longer a question of the artist in relationship "to" society, for if the artist is the creator, the maker of order, yet as he makes his world, so simultaneously is he made by it. Stockhausen's immense, seventy-five-minute *Momente* is a case in point, summing up his creative career up to this stage (1965), and employing his group forms, collective forms, variable forms and multiple forms in powerfully convincing relationship.

The work is in fact scored for "natural," not electronic, vocal and instrumental resources, but these are of astonishing variety: soprano solo, four choirs and thirteen wind and percussion instruments (including two electronic organs). The piece opens with desultory clapping by the choirs, interspersed with random "Bravo's"

and "Pfui's"—expressions of approval and disapproval. As the
music unfolds we hear a main text (mostly allocated to the soprano
solo) which is biblical, but taken not from the Book of Daniel this
time, but from that great paean to eroticism, the Song of Songs.
This text (which should be sung in the language native to the
audience) and the wide-spun lyricism of the solo line are again an
affirmation; they are surrounded by other fragmentary texts in
several real languages and one invented (nonsense) language,
spoken, yelled and screamed, sometimes disintegrated phonetically
into syllables that are "pure sound" (as in *Gesang der Jünglinge*),
but sometimes retaining intelligibility. Whatever the nature of the
texts, which the composer picked at random from his reading during
the period of composition, the point would seem to lie in the crucial
aphorism of William Blake: "He who kisses the Joy as it flies/
Lives in Eternity's sunrise." To live in the moment is to obliterate
Time and defy contrarieties, and the work consists of "moments"
precisely because we are *involved in* an aural universe, in which
there is no dramatic sequence, and no division between the objective
reality of the external world and our subjective response to it. The
relevance of such a conception to the world we're beginning to live
in is obvious. Instant speeds are abolishing time and space and, in
Marshall McLuhan's words, the "mechanical principle of analysis
in series has come to an end"; any number of different acts can
be simultaneously synchronized on magnetic tape.

More than any other European composer of our time, Stockhausen is engaged in writing the history of the future because, as
Wyndham Lewis put it, he is more aware than most of us of the
nature of the present. It's hardly surprising that the immediacy of
such awareness should be, in *Momente,* of such lacerating sonorous
intensity as to approach hysteria. Yet the hysteria isn't the composer's but is rather what the world—our "human predicament"
in the present—does to us; the composer's function may be precisely to *compose* us, to help us to accept, and therefore to sing our
love song from, the violence that surrounds us. Moreover, although
sounds of the external world—laughter, sighs, whispers, croaks,
wails—occur in what appears to be the random sequence one might

experience them on the street or in the underground, yet at the same time these sounds and noises are shaped by the mind of the artist. Fortuitous clapping may become a notated rhythmic pattern; the heterophonic and statistically rhythmed first section will be balanced against a largely homophonic middle section, and that against the third section's fusion of heterophony and polyphony in more traditionally notated metres. The recurrent magnificent refrains for chorus and brass remind us that traditional notions of the human imagination and even of will are not entirely discounted in Stockhausen's new, "momentary" universe of sound. This music may be profoundly appropriate to our embryonic society founded on electronic technology. In the strict sense this is a synthetic music for our synthetic culture, for it brings together and alchemically synthesizes as many aspects as possible of experience and of sound matter, embracing elements of non-Western and primitive music, as well as noise which is not strictly notatable.

We shall see later that only in America (in the sequence of Ives, Varèse, John Cage and Earle Brown) can one find a comparably radical development. But if Stockhausen is by far the most forward-looking of European composers, his attempt to eradicate dualism has had an effect even on music which accepts more traditionally humanist premises as a starting point. Luigi Nono, for instance, began from a vivid apprehension of humanism's failure; if human cruelty and injustice, under the shadow of the mushroom cloud, is as it is, then one has to seek a law that isn't humanly arbitrary. So his acceptance of rigid serial principles, in every aspect of composition in his earlier works, was related to his acceptance of Communist dialectic: but for the Law, both music and society might collapse in hysteria. Though *Polifonica-Monodia-Ritmica* of 1951 is on every level among the strictest of serial compositions, it achieves, by way of the tenuity of its texture, a relaxed passivity that sounds (especially in the second and third movements) almost Japanese, with an additive rhythmic series of drums and gongs. However, Nono soon abandoned this unequivocal reliance on an external law in discovering, as Boulez and Stockhausen did contemporaneously, that rebirth can happen only within the psyche. The technical developments of his music, such as his partial relinquishment of pitch and harmony in favour of the *campo sonoro* or sound field, are a manifestation of this spiritual change. Thus, the first three movements of *Il Canto sospeso* are in the post-Webernian, pointilliste manner, serially organized, with elaborate, tala-like rhythmic permutations; the lack of metrical pulse, the *latent* lyricism, the rarefied sonority extend, without radically modifying, Webern's principles. In the fourth movement, however, Nono introduces a semitonic note cluster on strings, long sustained, with individual notes picked out in sequence by wind instruments. Interval and harmony are no longer the point: the cluster is a "density" (in Varèse's sense) covering from two to twelve semitones, interlocking in different dynamics and durations. In *Canciones a Guiomar* the process is extended to quarter-tone clusters, and also to unnotatable pitches, since the instruments are mainly percussive with complex overtone resonances, like Japanese temple gongs. For Nono the orchestra is no longer a polyphonic-harmonic medium. Brass, woodwind and strings are separate consorts, and the percussion group is a separate band with its own dynamic and pitch relationships. Several works are scored for voices with percussion; the tender *Liebeslied* of 1954 is for chorus with harp, vibraphone, bells, timpani and cymbals, while the *Cori di Didone* of 1958 employs chorus in thirty-two parts with eight suspended cymbals and four gongs of different sizes, the tone-clusters revolving around the numbers 9, 7, 5, 3.

The gradual elimination of harmony instruments from Nono's music reflects a spiritual as well as technical change. The instrumental texture is disintegrating into "noise," but the noise is a background to words (usually of urgently contemporary implication). Although these words are syllabically fragmented as they are in Stockhausen or in the Gothic motet, the point is nonetheless that the voice sings them. In *Il Canto sospeso* the human voices echo, against the reverberating percussion, not merely from the Nazi prison camp wherein the letters were written, but from an immense, empty cavern—which becomes a womb, in which life may lyrically begin again. Vocal monody is thus the essence of Nono's music, as it is of Boulez's *Pli selon Pli,* and we can understand why he said that for the contemporary composer the central problem is how to write a melodic line. Nono's music has an Italianate lyrical fluidity, and if the lyricism seems pitifully broken, the isolated notes of what would be a continuous line echoing into emptiness, he nonetheless makes us feel that these fragments are shored against our ruin. Perhaps against his intention, his music has become a religious, even a mystical, act. Rebirth within the psyche is the only point we may grow from, in an atomized world; no political panacea can provide a solution.

Another Italian composer of Nono's generation, Luciano Berio, having less direct affiliation with an authority outside the self (whether it be the Roman Church or the Communist Party), has accepted this *ab ovo*ism more readily, without equivocation. This is evident in an abstract instrumental work, using electronic resources, such as *Différences* (1958–60). The differences in question are between "live," humanly operated instruments (flute, clarinet, harp, viola and cello) and tapes of the same instruments modified by electrical-acoustical techniques. The cello, recorded directly on a central loudspeaker, acts as liaison between the human and the nonhuman. In describing the music as "a modern music in the spirit of the commedia dell'arte," Henri Pousseur neatly indicates the music's combination of improvisatory spontaneity with a near-ironic detachment. The work's "aural illusion" is typical—some might say symptomatic—of our time, in that it discredits "reality." The experience is Absurd, in the theatrical sense; if its exploration of the electronic renewal of material and form is in one sense a renewal of our (not merely musical) consciousness as Berio says it is, in another sense it is a liberation from what Boulez called "robotism."

Certainly it is not an accident that Berio's most justly celebrated work, *Circles,* should directly involve theatrical elements, and should be a setting of poems by E. E. Cummings, the aboriginal

New World poet of the Now and Is, who sought for the springs of
life in dreams, in coition and in a preconscious abnegation of the
Will. Predetermined elements exist in it insofar as the five movements set three poems in a circular ABCBA structure. But this is
the "existential" dimension of the piece; it is a serpent eating its own
tail because it's an "Is" without precedence or consequence. This
allows scope for the unconsciousness of improvisation and favours
indeterminacy of pitch from both the singing-speaking-yelling
voice and from the mainly percussive instrumental ensemble. Thus,
like Varèse's early *Offrandes,* the work is a logical extension of
Debussyan impressionism, rather than of Webernian serialism (a
relationship still more obvious in the lovely, radiantly airy settings
of poems from Joyce's *Chamber Music,* which date from 1953).
Certainly Berio has found, for *Circles,* his ideal text, for Cummings's
poems are the sensory moment as an end in itself. Sing-speak the
poems as Cummings's typography indicates and they become music
in which "any relevant action is theatrical." If you're as marvellously natural a musician as Berio, and as superbly vital a singing
actress as Cathy Berberian, the work is as good as made for you.
Essentially a music of beginnings, *Circles* is a blessedly simple, even
simple-minded, piece. The miraculous conclusion—or rather in-
conclusion, for the voice floats as though reborn from the murmuring mists and the "chime and symphony of Nature"—does what
had to be done. We should be grateful for it, even though man,
having gone through so much, can hardly be forever content to
live childishly in an eternal present, and even though Berio himself
may never take the next step that will reawaken consciousness and
the tragic sense.

Like *Momente* and much of Stockhausen's recent music, Berio's
Circles creates and involves one in a world; in its way it, too, is a
piece of musical "theatre," and we may note also that Nono has
given a ritualistic or dramatic projection to most of his recent works.
Again, the barriers are broken, and among the barriers shattered is
that between the Old World and the New. Both Stockhausen and
Berio spend much of their time in the United States, and *Circles,*

which carries the swing against the Renaissance about as far as a
European could hope to take it, is a setting of an American poet.
In the next chapter we must discuss the American avant-garde,
whose impingement upon Europe we have already had occasion to
notice.

VI

The New Music in a New World:
Parallel Lines in Jazz and Pop

It has been difficult for European composers, with so much past behind them, to release themselves from "the pain of consciousness." But we have in this book traced how it gradually happened, in considering how Schoenberg is Wagner's successor, and Webern, Schoenberg's, how Messiaen follows Debussy, and how Webern and Messiaen effect the transition to Boulez and Berio. In all of them there is a partial retreat from the West, and an affiliation with techniques and philosophies having contact with pre-Renaissance Europe and, still more, with oriental cultures. But the transition has been hard, and is still uneasy, whereas the American retreat from the West has been more empirically spontaneous. This is natural enough, both because America has less consciousness of the past, and also because her polyglot culture, Janus-like, faces East as well as West. Even in the central figures of the American scene one finds elements that are in part a denial of the West: consider the final movements of Ives's *Concord Sonata* and of the *Piano Sonata* of Copland, both the creation of great American humanists. So it isn't surprising that avant-garde tendencies should have been manifest in American music as far back as the years of the First World War, nor that they should have more to do with Debussyan empiricism than with Webernian serialism. One of the key works in the early history of "progressive" music in America is the extraordinary *Piano Sonata* that Charles Griffes wrote in 1917, the last year of his short life. This employs static Debussyan harmonies and Scriabinesque "raga" formations to generate, from Eastern techniques, a peculiarly Western frenzy. Sophisticated though the idiom is, this music of the asphalt jungle could have been created only in America. Still more typical is a phenomenon like Henry Cowell, who is what Debussy might have been, shorn of most of his genius, and brought up in the streets of San Francisco and on farms in the Midwest, by parents who believed that children, like plants, should be left to grow.

Cowell was familiar with Chinese theatre music, Japanese children's street songs and American fiddle music before he knew anything about Brahms or Beethoven. He played the fiddle by ear at the age of five, and began his composing career at the age of eight, not so far behind Mozart. He composed empirically, experimenting with the noises he could extract from an upright piano. Debussy's moment of sensation becomes, with him, the (American) Moment of Sensation, with a capital M and S. But although the composition in the piano pieces Cowell produced during his teens is rudimentary, their sound sensation remains invigorating after forty-odd years. In a piece called *The Banshee*, a piano's strings become a harp capable of an infinite gamut of pitches; the experiment has become the experience. This is the work of an aboriginal, the American Boy in the Woods, who didn't lose his innocence when, grown up, he acquired some academic know-how. Cowell's vastly prolific later output is not very good music, and he's a figure of historical rather than of intrinsic interest. Nonetheless, we can see from his youthful piano pieces why he has become a father figure to the American avant-garde, and it's this quality of ab-originality that sometimes makes American avant-garde music more congenial than its European counterpart.

Certainly the quality is present in the major figure of the older generation, Edgard Varèse, who was (significantly) born in Paris, and became an American citizen in 1916. He called the first work to which he owns *Amérique*, because it was a New World of sound. But if one listens to his *Offrandes*, written in 1921, one can hear how this new world—like that of his friend, colleague and contemporary, Charles Griffes—is related to the world of Debussy. Varèse has told us that, as a young man, he admired Debussy above all composers "for his economy of means and clarity, and the intensity he achieved through them, balancing with almost mathematical equilibrium timbres against rhythms and textures, like a fantastic chemist." The chemical metaphor is significant, and links up with Varèse's complementary admiration for Satie, who wrote "some rather remarkable music, such as the Kyrie from his *Messe des Pauvres*, a music which always reminds me of Dante's *Inferno*, and strikes me as a kind of pre-electronic music." Varèse thus saw Debussy and Satie as a starting point for his own experiments, since if one liberates the chord from antecedence and consequence, the logical step is to proceed to the liberation of the individual sound. This is not just a technical procedure; it is also a new (and at the same time very old) musical philosophy. Varèse must be the earliest composer to reject the Renaissance conception of art as expression and communication; music he composed during the twenties anticipates by thirty years some of the discoveries of the mid-twentieth-century avant-garde. Bypassing twelve-tone serialism (which he regards as a musical "hardening of the arteries" because of its dedication to notated, equal-tempered pitch), he makes manifest the prophecies of Busoni in his *Entwurf einer Neuen Aesthetick der Tonkunst:* he is at once a magical composer like Messiaen and a scientific composer like Stockhausen, demonstrating that the two types are in fact complementary in that they effect a revelation, rather than an incarnation, of natural law. Dedekind said of mathematicians: "We are a divine race, and possess the power to create." To live in a scientific-mathematical universe is inevitably to lose consciousness of self; and it is significant that Varèse, who had some scientific training and as a youth considered the possibility of becoming a mathematical engineer, should, in naming one of his works *Arcana,* specifically relate the revelation of natural order to the activities of the alchemists.

So it is not surprising that Varèse's highly sophisticated music should be also primitive (and often oriental), in the sense that it does not involve harmony, but rather consists of nondeveloping patterns and clusters of noises of varying timbre and tension. These interact in a manner that Varèse has compared, in detailed if inaccurate analogy, to rock-formation and crystal mutation:

I was not influenced by composers as much as by natural objects and physical phenomena. As a child, I was tremendously impressed by the qualities and character of the granite I found in Burgundy. . . . And I used to watch the old stone-cutters, marvelling at the precision with which they worked. They didn't use cement, and every stone had to fit and balance with every other. . . .

This conception of music as sound-architecture survives when the development of electronic resources finally gave Varèse an opportunity to "realize" his theories. Whether through indirect human agency or electronics, composition for Varèse is "process":

I am fascinated by the fact that through electronic means one can generate a sound instantaneously . . . you aren't programming something musical, something to be done, but using it directly, which gives an entirely different dimension to musical space and projection. For instance in the use of an oscillator, it is not a question of working against it or taming it, but using it directly without, of course, letting it use you. The same pertains to mixing and filtering. To me, working with electronics is composing with living sounds, paradoxical though that may appear.*

Nothing could be further from the mathematically determined electronic music of composers such as Milton Babbitt. Of Babbitt, Varèse has said:

He wants to exercise maximum control over certain materials, as if he were *above* them. But I want to be *in* the material, part of the acoustical vibration, so to speak. Babbitt composes his materials first and then gives it to the synthesizer, while I want to generate something directly by electronic means. In other words, I think of musical space as open rather than bounded, which is why I speak of projection in the sense that I want simply to project a sound, a musical thought, to initiate it, and then let it take its own course.

Nonetheless, Varèse's music does not take the ultimate step to

* From an interview reprinted in *Composer.*

completely open forms and improvisation. In one sense his music is more closely rooted in traditional concepts than is the recent music of Messiaen and Boulez, let alone Stockhausen, for it still implies some kind of dichotomy between Nature and the Self. The structure of a comparatively recent work such as *Deserts* (1953) may seem to be independent of the will's volition, but the controlling force is still the human imagination. It achieves a powerful image of man's isolation, while enabling him to come to terms with the alien universe in which he exists. The music explores the deserts of wind, of sand and sea and rock, of the city street and of those vaster deserts within the human mind. Normal orchestral wind instruments interact with electronically processed natural sounds (of wind, sea, street and factory), while a large percussion band serves as liaison between the human and the nonhuman world. The humanly operated "noise" of the percussion doesn't seem to save the human from being threatened by the nonhuman in a series of cumulatively increasing tensions, and the end of the work, in which the noise fades into the eternal silence, is grim rather than assuaging. Nonetheless, there is grandeur, as well as excitement, in Varèse's attempt to emulate, through human means, the processes of Nature. If the music is frightening, because it admits that the human ego has lost touch with natural order, it is also unafraid, because the admission helps us to live again.

Maybe only God can make a tree, but Man at least can make sounds behave like crystals; in this sense, there is a powerful affirmation behind Varèse's bringing together of the aural disparities of the natural world. Whereas Ives, who in some of his music attempted something comparable, was content to be humanly amorphous, Varèse sought the scientist's precision, which could not ultimately be achieved because an artist, being human, is humanly fallible. In this respect, Varèse has more in common with a visual artist like Jackson Pollack than with Ives, or with any earlier musician; both Varèse and Pollack seek to *reveal* the (basically mathematical?) order inherent in the natural world. This is the artist's new social justification, if justification is necessary, as Harry Partch, another senior "progressive," seems to think it is. Like

F

Cowell, and unlike Varèse, whose background is both sophisticated and European, Partch is an American aboriginal, brought up in the parched and parching wastes of Arizona and New Mexico. From his earliest years he rejected the paraphernalia of harmonized music, rediscovered the justly intoned monody and the rhythms of primitive and oriental cultures, and designed his own instruments, which are tuned to a forty-three-tone-to-the-octave scale, and are capable of fairly extensive monophonic, if not harmonic, tonal organization. But this turn to the East is as instinctive, as nonwillful, as that of Varèse. We may see this if we compare Varèse's *Deserts* with Partch's *Windsong,* which was written as an accompaniment to a cinematic version of the Apollo and Daphne story, and which deals specifically with the metamorphosis, indeed the loss, of human identity in the contemplation of the immense solitudes of (American) Nature, of the nonhuman world. Varèse's score sometimes reminds us of the distonated screech of Japanese gagaku music, while Partch's score reminds us of the infinitely slow, microtonal wail of Japanese koto music; yet in both cases the affinity comes not from imitation, but from the attempt to create musical images for emptiness, space and nontemporality.

Normally, however, Partch is a magic composer who, like Carl Orff in Europe, relates music directly to theatrical action; both want to renew a moribund society by rediscovering the instinctual springs of life. Partch thinks the proper function of music is that which it fulfilled in classical Greek drama. His own "musicals" may be considered as an American version of the still vital popular tradition of the Japanese kabuki theatre, aiming at a renewal of modern life by incantation, by "spiritual" monody and by "corporeal" rhythm. In *The Bewitched,* described as a "Dance-Satyr," four lost Musicians consult an aged Seer, seeking a remedy for the ills of the modern world, and learn that they already possess, in being true to the moment, the only truth that is humanly apprehensible: "Truth is a sandflea; another moment must find its own flea." So the Musicians are also Clowns, divine fools, and outsiders, bums, hobos—like Partch himself, who for eight years lived by riding the rails. When social satire and musical parody dissolve into what Partch calls slapstick, the resulting dadaism links contemporary nonvalues to values so old that they seem eternal. Human beings who microtonally yell, moan, shout, wail, guffaw or grunt in jazzy abandon or hysteria may become indistinguishable from hooting owls, barking foxes and the wild cats of the woods. But in returning, below consciousness, to Nature, they may rediscover their true selves. In the prelude to scenes 8 to 10, the wailing pentatonic chant evokes an age-old quietude that is nonetheless full of longing. Significantly, it is based on a cantillation of the Cahuilla Indians—aboriginal Americans who live in the emptiness of the Californian deserts. This weird chant, sounding the more disturbing against the wavering ostinati of Partch's forty-three-tone reed organs, reminds us simultaneously of what home means, and of what it means to be homeless.

In Partch's theatre works jazz appears, usually parodistically. But jazz isn't only a negative force; it's also part of our intuitive rediscovery of our passional life. It has had so pervasive an influence because, starting as the outcry of a dispossessed race, it came to stand simultaneously for the protest of man alienated from Nature, and as a reminder of the corporeal vigour that modern man has surrendered. So it isn't surprising that jazz, in America, has undergone a development parallel to that in the music we have discussed. Ornette Coleman is a jazz saxophonist who, during the formative years of his career, couldn't read musical notation, though he has since taken lessons with Gunther Schuller. Thus his "composition" was inevitably spontaneous, like that of primitive oral cultures. In a piece such as *Lonely Woman* there is, of course, a corporeal beat such as is alien to the music of Varèse, if not Partch, but against the implicit beat the drumming is of almost oriental complexity, numerical and additive rather than divisive. Moreover, there is no harmony instrument, and the minimum of harmonic implication. The solo voices, overriding the beat with Charlie Parker–like freedom, collide in dissonant heterophony, and the lines are not only of extreme rhythmic flexibility, they are also fragmented, disrupted by silence. Despite the sophistication, the effect is disturbingly primitive, like a more distraught and nervous version of the field holler, wherein the Negro cried out his isolation to the empty fields.

In his most recent work Ornette Coleman—in part stimulated no doubt by the phenomenally virtuosic and beautiful string bass playing (both bowed and plucked) of David Izenzon—has developed the oriental aspects of his art in a positive direction: in no sense could one use the word primitive about as haunting and magical a performance as their *Dawn*. It is also worth noting that a white jazz clarinettist, Jimmy Giuffre, has—on a somewhat lower level of musical invention—taken the ultimate step in dispensing with "beat" altogether, creating a true improvised monody in complex numerical rhythms, again with effects of pitch distortion (achieved by split reeds and overblowing) that have affinities with Asiatic techniques. These strange nocturnal bird and animal, as well as human, noises link up with Varèse and Partch; with the sound, if not the philosophy, of electronic music; and with both the technique and the philosophy of the music of John Cage.

For Cage's music, no less than the jazz surrealism of the later Ornette Coleman and Jimmy Giuffre, is a descent below consciousness and an abnegation of the Will. The parallel between Partch and Cage's early music is also close, for both discarded harmony and returned to music as incantation, conceived monophonically in line, numerically in rhythm. Cage's "night music," *She Is Asleep* (and maybe dreaming), is scored for wordless voice and prepared piano, and is a ritual murmuring of the unconscious comparable to Partch's aboriginal chants and to Giuffre's solo clarinet. Similarly, Cage's *Sonatas and Interludes* for prepared piano remind us of the Polynesian sounds of Partch's invented instruments, with an occasional hint of disembodied jazz, if the appropriately paradoxical expression be permitted. These pieces are highly musical and very beautiful, but Cage apparently came to think that their "chronometric" construction on ragas and talas was no less an evasion than the chromatic serial principle which he had already abandoned in rejecting European harmony. In any case he gave up humanly preordained structures and handed composition over to chance operations: the toss of a coin, the throw of dice, the noting of accidental imperfections in the manuscript paper. Though these methods produced some exciting noises (for instance, the Carillon pieces which sound like Japanese temple bells tolling a paean not to God, but to nothingness), they are in effect identical with the strict serialists' mathematically preordained order; both seek to free music, as far as possible, from subjectivity (the composer's, performer's and listener's) and from human error.

In later works such as the *Concert* for piano and orchestra Cage completes the composer's abdication. He no longer notates his material, but merely offers hints for improvisation. The succession and duration of the parts are dependent on chance operations, and also on the sub- or semiconscious reactions of the participants. Each performance is inevitably different, and while the texture of sound is comparable with that of Varèse, in that the instruments play microtonally in an infinite gamut of pitches, the chaotic amorphousness tends to be relaxed in effect, as compared with Varèse's impersonal order. Varèse's music seems to be beyond conscious volition, like Nature herself, whereas Cage's music, by this time, in fact *is* so, for the forest or the city street takes over from man.

While we can't help feeling that the loss of Cage's aural sensitivity is regrettable, he would consider our objection in the strict sense impertinent, for he is no longer concerned with "so-called music." Indeed, since each player is instructed to play all, any or none of the notes allotted to him, it is theoretically possible, if improbable, that a performance could result in complete silence: an ultimate condition which Cage has indeed realized in his notorious *Four Minutes Thirty-two Seconds* for piano. Clearly this is an end; it may also be a beginning, in that in possessing so completely blank an innocence Cage can be, like Gertrude Stein and Paul Klee, "as though new born, entirely without impulse, almost in an original state." However self-destructive such an attitude may be from our Western standpoint, it is interesting that there should be something like a post-Cage generation of composers in the United States, some of whom are literally a new race of composers in that they have never received, and have no use for, any training in the harmonic traditions of Europe. Certainly the degree of talent exhibited by this group is in no way dependent on conventional expertise. No orthodox training would be necessary to create Morton Feldman's *Durations,* which is scored for a number of instruments all playing from the same part, so that one couldn't hope for a more complete rejection of dualism. They play mostly single, designated pitches, but although they begin simultaneously they are free to choose their own occurrences within a given general tempo. Thus the instruments, in changing combinations, are "reverberations" from a single sound source. The tones are always isolated, immensely slow and delicately soft. Such simultaneous sounds as occur through overlapping of the durations are mostly unisonal or concordant. An infinitely slow drone on muted tuba, a third on muted string harmonics, sound as though the players are creating the tones out of the eternal silence, and we are being born afresh in learning to listen to them. Music seems to have reached the point of extinction; yet the little that is left certainly presents the American obsession with emptiness completely absolved from fear. The rarefied tenderness seems to have the property of making us saner, rather than more mad.

The element of renewal in Feldman's music lies in the fact that choice is once more very important; his isolated sounds are as scrupulously selected as are the isolated chords of Debussy, the composer with whom Feldman has most in common. A more widely relevant type of renewal may be exemplified in the graph pieces and "Available Forms" of another post-Cage composer, Earle Brown, who claims to have learned more from the painting of Pollock and the mobiles of Calder than from any musician, including Cage. His graph pieces (of which the most extreme is *December 1952* for any number and any kind of instruments) notate only high, middle and low registers and densities, and exist only in their mobility, while they are being made. They are not composition, but a stimulus to musical activity; they differ from Cage's later work in that they call for creative instinct on the part of the performers. Brown's later "open form" works precisely notate pitch, timbre and often rhythm, but leave to the performers or conductor the decision as to the order in which the sound events take place. Brown prefers to write for very large resources (his

Available Forms II is scored for ninety-eight instruments with two conductors who preserve independence during performance, though they have carefully rehearsed the sound events); thus, the sound of his music is remote from the hermetic tranquillity of Feldman, and is more comparable with the multiple-group pieces of Ives and Varèse than with the music of Cage. The human agency of the composer (who devised the complex sound events), of the conductors (who decide when and in what order the events shall occur), and of the players (who must play the notes as written, but not necessarily in temporal conjunction with one another) is immensely important. This is true even though Brown prefers to emulate the ambiguities, the "open ends" of Nature, rather than to impose his order on his material, which ranges from noise and "inarticulate sounds" to sounds produced by highly sophisticated musical techniques.

In reinvolving the performer in creation Brown is turning towards action, and in this resembles the composers who seem to have deliberately abdicated human responsibility. At the furthest swing of the pendulum from Europe's post-Renaissance obsession with the will, Cage and his disciples would free us from past and future, inviting us to enter an autonomous Now. Similarly, Robert Rauschenberg at one time painted completely white or completely black canvases, invoking the space, the nothingness within which we may perceive afresh the astonishingly disparate objects (introduced bodily into his later work) of the visible world. For Cage learning-to-hear, for Rauschenberg learning-to-see, are separate from action but not independent of it, since life must be lived in time. This is why "any relevant action is now theatrical," a belief which has been actualized when Cage and Rauschenberg have collaborated with the dancer Merce Cunningham to complement their aural and visual images with movement in time and space.

This movement, however, like the hearing and seeing, has no before and after. There is no expressionist purpose, only a "purposeful purposelessness," in the relationship between movement, sound and image in the work of the Merce Cunningham Dance Group. Thus, in *Suite for Five* the actions—now gay, now anguished, now grotesque—are as diverse as Nature herself; yet in being purged of causation they are purged too of the nag of memory and the tug of desire. This they achieve *through* their lack of relationship to Cage's music, which is even more devoid of progression or motor rhythm than is Japanese temple music. The softly reverberative sounds of the prepared piano, occurring at chronometric points dictated by chance operations, and separated by immense silences, really do cause one to listen anew, while Rauschenberg's almost blank costumes and decor help one to see the actions with unblinkered eyes.

This abstraction is preserved even when the work, such as the ballet *Crises,* seems to involve dramatic implications. Indeed, in this ballet the crises of the title are erotic; yet the actions between the man and four women evade climax. The music is Conlon Nancarrow's celebrated studies for three player pianos. The fantastic complexity of the polyrhythms, which machines can negotiate but which human beings couldn't, transmutes the sexy and nostalgic flavour of jazz and pop into loony hysteria. Yet the sounds preserve, through the mechanization, a disembodied detachment, which communicates itself to the actions. For all the violence of the gestures and the sleaziness of the atmosphere, we are released from our more inchoate appetites in simply accepting them. Even they can take their place with "the permanent emotions of Indian tradition." Merce Cunningham's *Solo* to Christian Wolff's pianistic explosions goes still further, for it induces a therapeutic calm from the neurotic twitch and spastic shiver that we've come to recognize, at least since *West Side Story,* as gestures typical of our world and time. Both the abstraction of the mechanical and the dadaistic release into an eternal Now recall Satie's *Parade;* small wonder that John Cage, himself a Beckett clown, regards Satie with admiration.

The ultimate, rediscovered primitivism of a Cage or a Feldman has parallels, we have seen, in the surrealistic trend in modern jazz. Most interestingly, it is also parallelled by mid-century developments in pop music. Thirty, or even twenty, years ago pop music was still commercial jazz, tied to the Sousa-Foster tradition of hedonism or escape. Today pop music seems, no less than "straight" music, to be affecting another kind of return *ab ovo,* to rhythm and to the most rudimentary line as incantation. The music of Cage or Feldman on the one hand, the Beatles and Bob Dylan on the other, may seem poles apart; nonetheless they have in common a distrust of the personal, of "individual" expression, and both attempt to return to magic, possibly as a substitute for belief. To neither does the Christian ethic, which implies guilt and conscience and the duality of harmony, seem relevant. In the music of Cage there is virtually no corporeal rhythm left; the Mersey beat has nothing much except corporeal rhythm. Yet both, by their complementary if opposite paths, effect a dissolution of Time and of consciousness.* In a very literal sense the rows of nubile young females who faint away at a Beatle performance have found the nirvana that Tristan was seeking, and the ecstasy of being "sent" becomes a communal and collective activity which is also a sundering of identity. The fact that young people dance *alone,* not with partners, to beat music is interesting in itself. They evade the togetherness of relationship with another person (a love relationship, however joyful, will also inevitably hurt) in order to enter into a collective unconsciousness. There's no coming together of individuals; their lonesomeness merges into a corporate act, and belonging to the group asserts one's livingness, such as it is. In this way the ritual value of the sound is inseparable from its musical nature. Its melodic and harmonic material is rudimentary, its rhythmic appeal obvious in its excess (contrary to popular opinion beat music never swings, only beats, for jazz-swing implies a subtle tension between metrical accent and melodic phrasing). The essential characteristics of beat music are that its phrases are very brief and are hypnotically re-

* "It is perhaps the essential character of consciousness that it is not just a picture of what is happening at one instant of time or an infinitely thin cross-section of process. Consciousness introduces the time-dimension as a reality, linking the no-longer-existing past with the actual present in what is called perception or recognition, and forecasting a merely possible future on lines influenced by wish and purpose. Process and purpose are thus inseparable in our minds from the beginning. . . . It is significant in this connection that the repressed unconscious mind is said to be 'timeless,' suggesting that the loss of 'span' is one of the factors in repression." (Ian Suttie: *The Origins of Love and Hate*)

F*

peated; that its rhythm is obvious and unremitting; and that its sonority is very loud. Through its rudimentariness, its unremitting-ness, and its loudness it provides a substitute for security, or a pre-tence that we, the young, in an insecure world, can stand—or dance—on our own feet.

One may doubt whether it is pervasively erotic, for the eroticism of jazz depends precisely on the swinging equilibrium between line and rhythm which beat music lacks. In this connection it is inter-esting that the musical origins of beat music were not in traditional jazz or even in the commercialized forms of jazz which were the pop music of the thirties and forties; rather, they were in the most primitive and rudimentary form of the country blues, which had begun not as a music of social (let alone sexual) intercourse, but as the solitary "holler" in the empty fields. Created by a deprived, dispossessed, alienated, persecuted minority, the country blues be-came the impetus to the mass-music of young people in a mass-civilization. We can trace the process whereby this happened by listening to some specific examples. Howlin' Wolf, yelling a field holler, attempts to "send" himself beyond personal distress by the monodic, incantatory repetition of a three-note wail, basically pentatonic, using techniques of pitch distortion and rhythmic ellipsis that have the remotest and most primitive ancestry. This folk tradition still survives in the urban blues, as we can hear in *Fare Well Blues* as performed by a white singer, Barbara Dane. The effect of this most moving performance depends largely on the fact that the "primitive" elements in vocal inflection and rhythmic displacement are at odds with the hymnbook-derived harmony of the blues guitar; the age-old monodic melancholy of the voice seems the more searing against the harmonic prison of "civilization." As folk art merges into pop, the prison, at least at a superficial level, has to be accepted. Two stages in this process can be observed in different versions of *Alabama Bound*. Leadbelly and Woodie Guthrie still employ primitive folk techniques of vocal production and rhythmic distortion, while at the same time subduing these wilder qualities to a regular beat and a simple *harmonic* pattern suggested by white vaudeville music, blackfaced minstrel music and hillbilly harmonica playing. The strange, disturbing hiatus between vocal and instrumental elements, typical of Barbara Dane's blues, has gone. This is still more the case in a typical rock 'n' roll performance, wherein the primitive blues has been metamorphosed into pop. Ray Charles's version of *Alabama Bound* is an excellent example. He preserves the blues inflection in pitch and rhythm, which gives the music its characteristic "lift," an intensity of feeling beneath the exuberance and bounce; we feel he knows what he's singing about when he tells us that he's banished the heebie-jeebies. Nonetheless, the drive of the music, scored for big band, is that of the powerhouse. The country blues, streamlined, seems to have entered the world of commerce.

Up to this point this tradition in pop music, stemming from a deliberate revival of the most primitive form of blues, has followed a predictable path, gradually increasing in sophistication and in technical expertise. With the appearance of the Beatles, however, something odd happens, which may not be unconnected with the fact that they are British, outside the main tradition of American pop culture. Rock 'n' roll music incorporated folk elements into conventions deriving from Tin Pan Alley, whereas the melodic, rhythmic and harmonic texture of the Beatles' songs is itself primitive; at least it has more in common with conventions of late medieval and early Renaissance music than it has with the harmonic conventions of the eighteenth century and after. Consider one of the Beatles' most celebrated songs, *She Loves You*. The key signature is the three flats beloved of pop convention; however, the opening phrase is pentatonic, or perhaps in an Aeolian C which veers towards E flat, and much of the effect depends on the contrast between the ascending sharp sevenths and the blue flat sevenths of folk tradition. Nor is the final chord of the song simply an added sixth cliché; or if that's what the guitar chord is, the melody suggests that C, not E flat, is the root. Again, *A Hard Day's Night,* the theme song from the Beatles' first film, has no conventional tonic-dominant modulations. Instead, it has a distinctively plagal, "flat" feeling, beginning with the dominant seventh of the subdominant. The tune itself is pentatonic until the chromatic

extension in the final phrase (which doesn't alter the harmony),
and the verse section depends entirely on alternations between the
tonic and the chord of the flat seventh (between C and B-flat
triads). After the double bar we have mediant substitutions for
dominants, while the coda phrase alternates sharp thirds with blue
flat thirds in a manner characteristic equally of the true blues, and
of the false relations of sixteenth- and seventeenth-century English
music. None of these features would be found in post-eighteenth-
century textbook harmony: the flat seventh-chord flourish in the
guitar postlude is strikingly similar to passages in the keyboard
music of Farnaby or Gibbons!

Of course this doesn't necessarily mean that the Beatles have ever
heard, or even heard of, medieval or Renaissance music, any more
than the peasant folk singer knew he was singing in the Dorian mode.
It's rather that their melody and harmony, welling up in their
collective subconscious, discovers authentic affinities with music of
a relatively early, less "harmonic" stage of evolution, and thereby
reinforces the primitivism of their rhythm. Even the noise of the
electric guitar, though in part commercially dictated because of the
sheer volume necessary to get across to vast audiences, emulates the
"primitive" sound of the multi-stringed Blue Grass banjo, a white
folk music. In their most recent discs (1965), the Beatles have,
indeed, employed far more primitive instrumental techniques,
imitating the guitar-picking styles of the most rudimentary country
blues and using an electronic organ to suggest harmonica, bagpipes,
jew's-harp and still more basic rural instruments. At first Ringo's use
of an Indian sitar in place of banjo or guitar was no more than a
pleasing new sonority applied to the Western-style tune *Norwegian
Wood*. On their latest disc, however, the characteristic Merseyside
electronic noises merge into sonorities and techniques that are specifically Eastern; and the Beatles couldn't do this so effectively if they
were merely picking up fashions from the sophisticated world. There
is a genuine connection between what is happening in pop music
and what is happening in "art" music and in jazz. The remarkable
song *Tomorrow Never Knows* begins with jungle noises very similar
to Coleman's or Coltrane's "free" jazz, and employs both vocal and

instrumental techniques which we may find both in Ornette Coleman and in Stockhausen! Interestingly enough, the words of the
song tell us to "Turn off your mind; relax and float downstream: it
is not dying. Lay down all thought; surrender to the voice: it is shining. That you may see the meaning of within: it is being." One
couldn't wish for a more unequivocal abnegation of Western "con-
ciousness"; and the disturbing quality of the music certainly suggests
that we're not meant merely to take it ironically.

Naturally enough, the Mersey sound has been, at least in its earlier
and cruder manifestations, commercially manipulated. Yet the impressive nature of their recent development suggests that it always
was the spontaneity and authenticity of the Beatles' return to "beginnings" that has given their music, no less than their characters, its
obsessive appeal, and has distinguished it from that of groups who
have made a more conscious attempt to imitate primitive models.
Moreover, it's interesting that when sophisticated composers such as
Burt Bacharach produce pop numbers, they exploit knowingly the
techniques which, in Beatle music, were instinctive. Bacharach's *Anyone Who Had a Heart,* made famous by Cilla Black, uses the same
mediant transitions and shifting sevenths as characterize the Beatles'
songs. There are more of them, in somewhat more surprising relationships, but the principle is the same, and equally remote from
post-eighteenth-century convention. Again, the tune itself has a
pentatonic tendency, while the irregular groups of repeated notes
suggest an affinity with folk monody, derived from the inflections of
speech. Perhaps there's even a link with folk tradition in the words'
and tune's simple, suffering, numbing resignation. It's the opposite
pole to the Beatles' bounce, but it isn't, like the Stephen Foster–
derived Tin Pan Alley ballad, self-pitying.

The intrusion of folk elements into the songs of a sophisticated
pop composer like Bacharach hints that there may be a growing
together of pop culture with the real folk-song revival movement:
a hint which is reinforced by the recent phenomenal success of Bob
Dylan. This American lad, after an abortive career at a provincial
college, wandered the country with his guitar, a new-style hobo,
writing and singing his own songs. Ray Charles, back in the days

of rock 'n' roll, lustily sang, the Beatles boisterously shout, Bob Dylan rustily croaks; this apparent decline in musical significance, however, is accompanied by a progressive increase in verbal significance. Dylan writes his own words, which are always *about something,* usually of urgently topical and local import. Quite often these words are of poetic intensity, resembling real ballad poetry, the nursery rune, or even on occasions the songs of Blake; they have to be listened to, if the experience is to mean anything. Whereas a typical Beatle performance may be totally inaudible beneath the screams of appreciation, a similar mass audience of young things will listen to Bob Dylan in a silence in which the proverbial pin could be heard dropping. Attention presupposes a rebirth of consciousness. Bob Dylan's primitivism, in succession to the Beatles', may mean a new start.

Basically, Dylan's music is far more primitive than that of the Beatles, or even the Rolling Stones. *The Ballad of Hollis Brown,* for instance, tells a (true) story of the poor white who "lived on the outside of town, with his wife and five children and his cabin fallin' down." His baby's eyes look crazy, the rats get his flour, bad blood gets his mare, his wife's screams are "stabbin' like the dirty drivin' rain." He kills his family and himself with a shotgun, and the song ends, "There's seven people dead on a South Dakota farm. Somewhere in the distance there's seven new people born." The tune of this ballad could hardly be more primitive, for it is entirely pentatonic and most of the time is restricted to four notes, while the guitar part oscillates between the tonic and dominant. The restricted vocal range, the obsessive ostinato, have a dramatic function, suggesting the numbing misery of poverty; the deliberately antilyrical, dead-pan vocal production has a comparable effect, which is by no means merely negative and deflationary. The primal simplicity of the tune and accompaniment carries its own affirmation, even resilience. The end isn't nirvana; life goes on, however insignificant one's personal destiny.

In *Masters of War* Dylan uses a similarly nagging pentatonic tune and reiterated ostinato to build up a cumulative fury. But not all his songs are musically as primitive as this. His social-satirical protest songs more commonly derive from white hillbilly style, rather than from the Negro blues. *With God on Our Side* has a swinging arpeggiated tune in slow waltz rhythm; Dylan's hiccups and hiatuses, and the occasional melismatic twiddle, point the irony of the words, which tell the bitter story of American martial history: "O the history books tell it, they tell it so well, The cavalries charged, the Indians fell, The cavalries charged, the Indians died, O the country was young, with God on its side." The song goes down through the Spanish-American War and the two World Wars, with an especially biting melisma for the Second World War, after which "we forgave the Germans and we were friends, Though they murdered six million In the ovens they fried, the Germans now too Have God on their side." After stanzas about the Russians, chemical warfare and the atom bomb, the song reaches its climax: "In many a dark hour I've been thinkin' all this, That Jesus Christ was betrayed by a kiss. But I can't think for you, You got to decide, Whether Judas Iscariot Had God on his side." The guileless tune, and the harmonica ritornelli which seem to come from another Eden, make the savagery of the words the more trenchant; it's not surprising that even in an "affluent" society, young people listen to Dylan croaking these words in an electrically tense silence.

In many of his songs Dylan adapts both the words and tunes of traditional folk ballads to contemporary ends. Thus, *A Hard Rain's Gonna Fall* is a version of Lord Randal: "O what did you see my blue-eyed son? I saw a new born baby with wolves all around it, I saw a highway of diamonds with nobody on it, I saw a black branch with blood that kept drippin', I saw a roomful of men with their hammers a bleedin', I saw a white ladder all covered with water," etc. *Who Killed Davy Moore?* transforms Cock Robin into an anecdote and parable about a calamity in the boxing ring, with social and political overtones. The mainly pentatonic tune is very fine, the words at once witty and scary, naturalistic yet with a flash of poetry when the boxer falls "in a cloud of mists." This isn't so far away from the authentic folk-revival tradition as represented by Joan Baez, who has her protest song *What Have They Done to the Rain?*, with its obsessive rhythmic ostinato, its plagal flatness which is possibly a mixolydian G. The fusion of pop and modern folk seems to be consummated when a Baez disc enters the Top Ten.

Many Bob Dylan tunes have been sung recently by folk singers such as Joan Baez, Odetta and Pete Seeger. The latter's version of *Davy Moore* is especially impressive, and interesting because he sings it not in Dylan's dead-pan, uninvolved manner, but with considerable passion. That he makes it a *dramatic* song-story is significant, since despite the Beatles' and Dylan's primitivism we know that the situation today isn't really the same as it was in primitive societies. Once having experienced knowledge and power, man cannot be entirely ignorant of moral choice; he's bound to ask, even if he's a pop artist dealing in myths rather than in personal expression, whether some myths aren't "better than" others. So the pop artist is inevitably an artist, once more making choices, using conscious techniques better or worse, *for* better or worse, as we can see from the Beatles, however spontaneous their creative origins may have been. What matters is how effectively he can learn to be reborn through the absorption of "preconscious" folk techniques, notwithstanding the commercial pressures he's submitted to.

Bob Dylan is said to be worried that he, the hobo troubadour, now nets an income of $500,000 a year. No doubt he is bearing up pretty well; if his art does so too, even as well as that of the Beatles, it may not be extravagant to say that youth's new world is winning through. In this context we should beware of the glib assumption that a capitulation to commercial techniques is necessarily a capitulation to commercial values. It's easy to say that Dylan's recent discs, employing electrically amplified guitar instead of the natural folk guitar and sometimes calling for the souped-up, big-band sound, corrupt his folk-like authenticity. Sometimes this is true, sometimes it isn't; and it is surely more, not less, "natural" for a folk singer living in an electronic age to exploit, rather than to spurn, electronic techniques. The folk purists are also the escapists; Dylan has proved that it is possible to be a myth-hero and an artist at the same time, and to carry the integrity of the rural folk artist into a world of mechanization.

There is thus a true parallel between a Dylan's desire for a rebirth, using not refusing the techniques of an industrial society, and the concern with a new birth of a Cage or a Feldman. It is interesting that the most insidiously haunting of all Dylan's songs should be a recent number, *Mr. Tambourine Man,* which, far from being a socially committed protest, looks superficially like an escape from life to dream. In a sense it is, for the tambourine man is a marijuana peddler; yet Dylan specifically says that he is "not sleepy," even though there ain't no place he's going to. Drug addiction is not, of course, itself a positive solution; but the song suggests that the impulses that have driven young people to it *could* have a positive outcome. We can sense this because the song is so beautiful. Like the tranced music of Cage or Feldman, it appeals for a different kind of commitment; it's a Pied Piper myth encouraging us to follow the unconscious where spontaneously it leads us, and this is most movingly suggested both by the wavery ballad-like refrain and also by the irregularity of the verbal and musical clauses which pile or float up, one after the other, like smoke rings. The metaphor of smoke rings actually appears in the verses which transport Dylan, a "ragged clown," beyond the "twisted reach" of sorrow. Release from the mind's tension, for Dylan no less than for Cage and Feldman, is a necessary step towards rediscovery; losing the self, in the ancient Biblical phrase, in order to find it, we are encouraged to forget "consciousness" today so that we may recharge our spiritual batteries for tomorrow. Such a pop song haunts us so disturbingly because its mythology plumbs unexpectedly deep; indeed, one might almost say that it not only links up with the extremism of Cage and Feldman, but also reminds us how the avant-garde has not been without effect even on the central, humanistic and Christian traditions of European music. Though this is unlikely to have been a matter of direct influence, it's an indication that, in Dylan's phrase, "the times they are a-changin'." In our final chapter, therefore, we must return to Stravinsky, to consider the later history of his retreat from humanism. Then we must discuss Benjamin Britten's two church operas as a

fusion of old values with new. This will lead to a consideration of
one of our younger composers, Peter Maxwell Davies, who is often
loosely grouped with the avant-garde, though his music has affinities
with traditions associated with both Stravinsky and Britten.

VII

Incarnation and Revelation:
The Promise of the Future

If we accept Stravinsky as the most "central" representative of twentieth-century music, though not necessarily as the greatest twentieth-century composer, we have to admit that he is representative in a paradoxical way. For just as he has expressed himself through a deliberate denial of what we are accustomed to call expression, so he has been representative by turning his back on most of the values and assumptions that have made us what we are. This suggests that we, too, are at least subconsciously distrustful of the beliefs in which we have been nurtured. The Stravinskian dubiety is also ours: which matters because his art's admission of dubiety is more honest, less afraid, than most of us can hope to be.

We have examined the nature of this dubiety in discussing Stravinsky's early, neoprimitive works. The ritual in those works, though cathartic and beautiful, couldn't be true; we could only act it, not live it, which is why the ritual had to be incarnated in the conscious artifice of ballet. That Stravinsky himself was aware that the burden of consciousness cannot be brushed aside merely by a recalling of the primitive springs of life is suggested by the fact that, in wartime works such as *The Soldier's Tale,* the theme of human guilt and responsibility makes a somewhat queasy appearance in a puppet-like parody of the Faust legend. Techniques and conventions from widely separated bits of Europe's "humanist" past are disturbingly reintegrated, while the primitive element becomes a conscious sophistication of twentieth-century jazz. The queasiness, even the cynicism, were serious enough in purpose and effect, and had positive direction in that they led Stravinsky to explore, in the "neoclassic" works of his middle years, his relationship to the great humanist tradition. Like his Renaissance and baroque predecessors, he took his themes from classical antiquity, rather than from Christian tradition, for he did not wish, at this point, to be concerned with a dichotomy between spirit and flesh. He started from those conventions whereby men of the baroque world had conveyed their belief that Man might be Hero, even to the point of divinity. In effect, however, he inverted the significance that these conventions had had at the time when they were created. We can examine this process in Stravinsky's opera *Oedipus Rex,* perhaps the key work in his long career, and the only one to make *direct* use of the conventions of baroque opera, wherein the humanist attempted man's deification.

A real heroic opera—and this applies too to Handel's oratorios, which are heroic operas on Biblical subjects—was simultaneously a ritual of humanism (a masque or State ceremonial) and a drama dealing with the perversity of man's passions, which makes paradise-on-earth a difficult ideal. Stravinsky preserves the "heroic" closed aria form and also the atmosphere of ritual ceremony. At the same time he admits that we can hardly belong to this ritual, any more than we could share in the primitive ritual of *The Wedding.* He symbolizes this by returning to the (authentically Greek) stylization of the mask, and by having the opera acted and sung in a dead language (Latin), interspersed with narration in modern French. The narration is done by a man in modern evening dress (in the original performance by Cocteau himself, the librettist). This smart, nineteen-twentyish convention becomes, in the hands of a master at the height of his powers, unexpectedly moving. It tells us that we, like the narrator, are cut off from the springs of passion and from the humanist's celebration; then gradually, as the tragedy unfolds, we come to realize that it is our tragedy after all. We may not be kings, great or noble as is Oedipus, but we too are subject to the destiny that hounds us; and it is only our pride that prevents us from seeing that destiny is the guilt within us all. From this point of view it is significant that Stravinsky chose, for this central work in his career, a myth that the more buoyant humanists of the heroic age had preferred to leave alone. For one thing, in its Freudian aspects, the myth stressed man's guilt, inherent in the fact of his birth; and Heroic man, though he made art out of the possibility of human error, was reluctant to admit that guilt could sully his divine pretensions. For another thing, the Oedipan myth contained another, immensely ancient strand, in which the theme of incest was less important than the revolt against patriarchal society, a desire to return to the embracing love of an earth goddess, Demeter. She was irrational, below consciousness, directly in touch with the magical mysteries. The theme we have repeatedly returned to throughout this book was already implicit in Stravinsky's opera, which deals directly with the ego's pride and also with the ego's insufficiency; and which links this insufficiency both with the "primitive" magic of his early works and with the mystical ritual of his later quasi-liturgical pieces.

After the spoken Prologue, in which Cocteau recounts the story in modern French, the chorus, masked like living statues, sing of the plague that ravages Thebes. They are the men of the city, but also Mankind, whose burden of suffering is a burden of guilt. The anti-expressive syllabic recitation, the ostinato patterns over chugging, B flat minor thirds, have affinities with Stravinsky's primitive phase, yet the effect is not one of orgiastic excitement. Indeed, falling minor thirds have always been a musical synonym for the domination of earth and therefore of death (consider the late works of Brahms); the feeling here is of almost claustrophobic constriction, of a submission to fate that may be equated with submission to death. Although we are not as yet aware of the significance of the twofold relationship, we sense, as we listen, that this music is complementary both to the primitive pieces and to the Christian liturgical works that, at this time, Stravinsky was composing for the Russian Orthodox Church.

In this grand, static lamentation there is virtually no harmonic movement, though there is much harmonic tension, created mainly by the telescoping of tonic, dominant and subdominant chords. There is a hint of very slow momentum as the chorus, in increasingly disjointed rhythm over nagging thirds, call on their King, Oedipus, to help them. Then, out of the prison of the falling thirds a prancing, dotted-rhythmed phrase is generated, and Oedipus, a high heroic tenor, sings in ornate coloratura, "Ego Oedipus"—I, Oedipus, will free you. Although the coloratura suggests the sublime assurance of the god-king, and derives from the ornamentation of Baroque opera, there is also a quality, in the high register and the oscillations around a fixed point, that reminds us of liturgical incantation. And Oedipus's freedom seems to be itself imprisoned, not only by the nodal oscillations of his vocal line, but also by a slowly revolving ostinato in the bass that chains down the clarinets' prancing arpeggios and reasserts the B flat minor obsession, against the voice's aspiration to C. Indeed, the fateful minor thirds continue intermittently, and are fully re-established in the *Serva* chorus, in which the men of Thebes ask their leader what is to be done that they may be delivered.

Oedipus says that Creon, the Queen's brother, has just returned from Delphi, where he has been to consult the oracles. Immediately, the B flat minor obsession is banished. Sonorous G-major chords from the chorus welcome Creon in hopeful luminosity; as they become ordinary men, looking towards their potential everyday activities, their music loses its monumentally tragic quality and becomes somewhat primitively Moussorgskian, for they, like us, are not kings. Creon, being at this stage a representative of the gods, sings a strict *da capo* aria, in which there can be no development since perfection is unalterable. But there's a certain ambivalence in his music, as there was in the heroic aria of the Baroque age itself. The middle section of the aria, touching on F minor, hints at the B-flat-minor obsession as it refers to the old, dead king, while there is something frenzied about the C-major assertiveness of the aria itself. The widely arpeggiated tune is crude, even cruel, with the brass-band vigour of early Verdi rather than the grandeur of Handel, and the rhythmic ostinato on four horns suggests a preconscious terror beneath the surface. The man-god complacence

carries all before it, however. After he has informed the chorus
that the oracles report that the murderer of their former king Laius
is among them and must be discovered, Creon concludes with a
tremendous C-major arpeggio: *Apollo dixit deus.*

Oedipus, as leader, responds to the challenge. He boasts of his
skill in solving riddles, which stands as a symbol of man's ability
to control his destiny through reason, and promises to save his
people by discovering the murderer. This aria, which is in E flat
(the opera's man key, as opposed to C major, which is the key of
the gods), is an almost hysterical intensification of his earlier ornate
style. Beginning with prideful, arpeggiated phrases which emulate
those of Creon, it turns into more emotionally agitated sevenths,
emphasizing in tipsy narcissism the word "ego" as it sweeps into
oscillating coloratura. Over the sustained E-flat bass the voice
resolves the fourth on to the prideful major third, but although the
music is superb in the strict sense, the chorus seem to suspect that
there is something a little phony about it. Their reiterated "deus
dixit tibi" phrase is metamorphosed back into the fateful minor
thirds, now screwed up a semitone into B minor. After invoking
the gods Minerva, Diana, Phoebus and Bacchus, they call on
Tiresias, blind prophet who sees in the dark, since he would be more
likely to help them than a human leader, however mighty. In
liturgically solemn, repeated notes and widespread arpeggio figurations, oscillating tonally between Man's E flat and God's C major,
Tiresias says that he will not, cannot, reveal the truth. Oedipus, his
imperturbability threatened, taunts Tiresias: whereupon, in a line of
immense, superhuman range, Tiresias announces that the king's
murderer is a king. For the first time the tonality hints—by way of
a C-major–A-minor ambiguity that merges into G—at D major,
with a resonant triad on horns reinforced by double basses in
octaves.

At the moment we don't realize the significance of this, for
Oedipus takes over the sustained D natural, only to force it back to
his man key of E flat. Yet though Oedipus has been ruffled by his
encounter with Tiresias, it marks a stage in his spiritual pilgrimage,
and his second E-flat aria is only superficially similar to the first.

Though the line is derived from his "superb" aria, it is now broken, chromatic, even fragmentary. For the first time he reveals his weakness, which is also his humanity, accusing Creon and Tiresias of plotting against him, bragging of his abilities as riddle solver and appealing to the chorus not to forget his previous triumphs. His proud line now carries harmonic implications that imbue it with pathos, even tenderness. Significantly, he ends unaccompanied, singing the *chorus's* falling minor thirds, and in C minor, relative of E flat and halfway to the god key which is C major. In seeing himself as one with the many he proceeds from pride to humility; he begins, tremulously, hesitantly, to accept fate and death in his music, if not in his words. It is interesting that, formally, this song is not a *da capo* aria, but a rondo in which the episodes change the destiny of the theme. His absolutism disintegrates, even while he tries to assert it. This is why the act can conclude with a Gloria, celebrating Jocasta's arrival in Stravinsky's "white note" diatonicism. The personal life of Oedipus's rondo-aria is banished; the ceremonial music that succeeds is related more to Stravinsky's music for the Russian Orthodox Church and even to his primitive works than to the harmonic ceremonial of a heroic composer such as Handel. Indeed, the chorus strikingly anticipates the *Symphony of Psalms*.

Oedipus's rondo-aria, which has more harmonic movement than any previous music in the opera, and the consequent Gloria, which has no harmonic movement at all, together make the axis on which the work revolves. The Gloria concludes the first act, and is repeated as prelude to the second, which follows the path to self-knowledge. To begin with, Jocasta pours scorn on all oracles. Her music hasn't the rigid, frigid panache that comes of Oedipus's desire for self-deification; it has a human, almost Verdian, lyrical sweep and a harmonic momentum such as Oedipus acquires only in his rondo. The key, G minor, is dominant of the godly C, relative of the fateful B flat; her reiterated syncopations and chromatic intensifications suggest an essentially human defiance. Defiance, in the F-major middle section of the *da capo* form, turns into insolent ridicule. To chattering clarinet triplets she points out how oracles often lie, and must do so in this case, for the old king was killed twelve years ago, outside the town, at the crossroads. The repeated eight-note figuration sounds panic-stricken, however; and when the *da capo* returns the syncopations and chromatics affect us differently, seeming to be dragging and anguished rather than defiant. At this point we realize that the minor thirds pad unobtrusively beneath the impassioned lyricism. She too struggles against destiny; and if, being a woman, she is more immediately human than Oedipus, she is also less heroic, and is not, like him, absolved.

Oedipus's assurance is finally shaken by Jocasta's reference to the past, for he recalls that twelve years ago he killed a stranger at the crossroads. Hypnotically, the chorus takes up the word "trivium," hammering it into Oedipus's mind. "Ego senem kekidi," he stammers, to a phrase that inverts the falling thirds, accompanied only by terrifying C-minor thirds on the timpani. This is the moment of self-revelation, when he sees that the guilt is within. At first the revelation leads to chaos, only just held in check by the rigidity of the ostinato pattern. Jocasta screams in wild 12/8 chromatics that the oracles always lie, while Oedipus sings in duo a strange, bewildered, broken lament, confessing his past history. So the mother-wife and the son-husband sing together, in C minor, relative of the man key E flat, tonic minor of the god key C major. On this a B-flat ostinato closes remorselessly, as Oedipus says that, though afraid, he must know the truth, must see the shepherd who was the only witness of the crime.

An anonymous messenger, agent of destiny, enters to reveal that Oedipus's reputed father, Polybus, has died, admitting that Oedipus was an adopted son. The messenger, being a low, unheroic character, sings a Moussorgskian peasant-like incantation, oscillating around a nodal point. The chorus takes up the words "falsus pater," stuttering, horror-struck; words, line, and rhythm are all broken, the harmonic movement gelid. Momentarily, when the messenger tells them that Oedipus was found as a baby on Mount Citheron, with his feet pierced, the chorus sing in modal innocence that a miracle is about to be revealed: he will prove to be born of a goddess. But the shepherd witness comes forward to reveal the truth. In a swaying arioso that, like Oedipus's *kekidi* phrase, inverts the falling thirds, he carries the music back to the obsessive B-flat minor. The shepherd's aria, accompanied only by two bassoons and then timpani, induces a state of trance in everyone except Jocasta who, now knowing that she is the wife of her own son, who was his father's murderer, rushes out.

Oedipus thinks, or pretends to think, that Jocasta has gone off in shame at the discovery of his lowly birth. He makes a desperate return to his early arrogance and sings a scornful Italianate aria over a bouncing bass. The key, F major, is the same as the insolent middle section of Jocasta's first aria, and perhaps it is not an accident that F is the dominant of fate's B flat. But the human impulse to dominate is frantic now, as is suggested by the jaunty vivacity of the dotted rhythm that takes us back to Oedipus's first appearance. The coloratura has here a kind of horrifying inanity, as though Oedipus is trying to cheer himself up, against all odds. The aria concludes in a cadenza of hysterical exultation, in wild descending chromatics that carry us, however, from F major to D minor. At this point the thudding minor thirds return, along with the hammering *kekidi* rhythm, and we realize that his exultation, though a mask, has not been entirely synthetic. Messenger, shepherd and chorus declaim the truth on repeated D's; woodwind and strings alternate to the *kekidi* rhythm in false relations between D major and minor; and Oedipus chants a brief arioso which, beginning in B minor over the pedal D's, miraculously transforms the falling minor thirds into D major on the words "lux facta est." Light floods his spirit as he decides to put out the light of his eyes; and like Shakespeare's Gloucester in *King Lear* he could say "I stumbled when I saw." So Stravinsky stresses the Christian implications that he can discover in the myth, and it is relevant to note that Oedipus's final arioso is closer to liturgical chant than it is to the heroic music he has sung previously. Or rather one could say that at the end he rediscovers the music that was implicit in his first utterance, which is now purged of egoism and self-will.

The transformation of the falling thirds into D major is the fulfilment of Tiresias's prophecy, which had also ended with a D-major triad. Then the triad had been immediately contradicted by Oedipus's E-flat egoism; now it is Oedipus himself who initiates the miraculous metamorphosis. The opera is dominated by the search for D major, which is the key of the inner light, and the tonal scheme of the work has a symmetry that is simultaneously musical and doctrinal. One can notate this in a kind of cyclical chart:

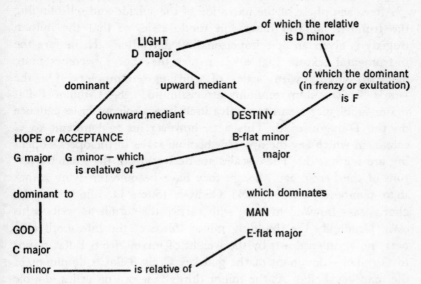

Stravinsky adheres to this scheme with consistency, and that he almost certainly did so without conscious intent emphasizes how instinctively he thinks and feels in ritualistic and "doctrinal" terms. The discovery of Light is the consummation of the tragedy, but an epilogue is needed to place the revelation in the context of our lives. So the visionary moment is followed by a trumpet fanfare in a tonally ambiguous region between B-flat major and G minor (see chart). The Messenger announces that Jocasta has hanged herself, and the chorus takes up his words, proceeding to tell us, in a sickening, lurching 6/8 rhythm, how Oedipus has blinded himself with a golden pin from her dress. The key is a compromise between C minor and E-flat major, for it is his and our humanity, not the moment of revelation, that we are concerned with now. The bass tends to oscillate around the E-flat pedal, but the vocal lines are tense with upward-thrusting chromatics and major-minor ambiguities. Significantly, the music refers back to the C-minor duo of horror and bewilderment that Oedipus and Jocasta had sung at the moment of discovery, for we know that we are involved in their doom.

After each phase of the narration of the suicide and self-blinding the trumpet fanfares return, in rondo style, so that the human tragedy is given an epic impersonality; and after each fanfare the instrumental texture that accompanies the chorus becomes more agitated, ending with scales of whirling semiquavers. On the words "spectaculum omnium atrocissimum," the C-minor–E-flat major ambiguity seems to resolve itself into a solemn brass cadence on the D-major triad. This acts, however, as a dominant to G minor, in which key the upward-shooting scales of the opera's opening are reinstated. (These scales are derived from the French overture of the heroic age, though they have become terrifying rather than pompously magisterial.) Oedipus totters in, blind, and the chorus says farewell to him, who carries their guilt as well as his own. Gradually the thudding minor thirds of the fate motif take over, now pulled down by the weight of sorrow from B-flat minor to G minor—dominant of the god key C, as B flat is dominant of the man key E flat. As the minor thirds fade out on cellos, double basses and timpani, the opera tells us that, though man is "dominated" by destiny, he may find his divine redemption. G minor is the relative of B flat, but also the gateway to light, which is D.

The Christian, rather than humanistic, implications of Stravinsky's heroic opera are fulfilled in the sequence of works that follows, most notably in the *Symphony of Psalms*, which has claims to be considered his masterwork. In this work he again starts from the baroque conventions of toccata and fugue. The similarity to baroque techniques, however, is no more than superficial, for the work shows little evidence of the baroque sense of harmonic momentum. Indeed, in so far as the themes tend to oscillate around a nodal point and the structures to be organized by linear and rhythmic pattern rather than by harmonic and tonal architecture, the *Symphony* is strictly comparable with some aspects of medieval technique, and the seemingly preordained or "doctrinal" system of key relationships is also in principle, if not in practice, appropriate to an age of faith. And here, in the marvellous lyrical expansion of the last movement, the faith is fulfilled, the music being at once an evocation of "the chime and symphony of Nature," and an act of worship.

The third phase of Stravinsky's career was already implicit in the *Symphony of Psalms,* which was, in turn, inherent in *Oedipus Rex.* This third phase begins with works such as the *Mass* and the *Cantata* wherein, starting from medieval texts, he consciously borrows medieval techniques also: the nonharmonic, nodal ostinato, the preordained, "doctrinal" serialism. His final acceptance of Webern's complete chromatic serialization is a logical extension of this neomedieval serialism. It has been frequently pointed out that Stravinsky does not employ his rows in a Webernian spirit but in a more literal sense, in much the same way as a medieval composer used his cantus firmus as the Word. The difference, of course, lies in the fact that the cantus firmus did have doctrinal significance which was intelligible to at least a fair proportion of the people who listened to the music. Stravinsky's Word, on the other hand, is a private invention, and since we do not live in an age of faith we cannot participate in a ritual, or at least not on the terms in which it is offered to us. One may question, too, whether Stravinsky's music has ever again achieved the lyrical fulfilment it reaches in the *Symphony of Psalms.* That work, which is certainly among the two or three supreme masterpieces of the twentieth century, is a revelation of God's love because the creator attains, in the last movement, to the love of God. In comparison, Stravinsky's later works seem to be in love with the idea of God, rather than with God Himself, and in this too he may well be "representative." There hasn't been a great religious composer since (in their different but complementary ways) late Beethoven and Bruckner; one would hardly expect such a composer, in the world we have made. Nonetheless, the great, central composers of our time have been seekers. Schoenberg, starting from an awareness of chaos and disintegration both within the psyche and in the external world, thought of himself as a Moses who tried, but failed, to lead his people into the Promised Land; Stravinsky, in *Oedipus Rex* and the *Symphony of Psalms*, admitted to the humanist's burden of guilt and had his momentary vision of redemption. In both cases, the creator started from man-as-he-is.

If a criticism seems to be implied in the previous paragraph, it is not a criticism of Stravinsky, any more than it's a criticism of Schoenberg to speak, as we did, of his failure. There is a deep allegorical significance in the fact that Stravinsky, our spokesman, should be in a sense a composer of denial. We know that although the rite has not always been, with him, an act of revelation, it has been a historical necessity. Like Webern, another composer who has sought revelation through denial, he came to accept as historical necessity the fragmentation of line and the disintegration of rhythm. Like Webern again, he must know too that something similar has occurred before in European history, at the expiring twilight of the Middle Ages, and that these late medieval linear and rhythmic contortions now seem grotesque rather than life-enhancing. They were not the creative essence of the Middle Ages, which had expressed supremely in Gregorian chant the fundamental human instinct for flow and continuity, following the heartbeat, but aspiring to an air-borne ecstasy. Yet the later dislocations were a "necessity," as was the imposition of an ever more rigid external authority, if we were to be rescued from chaos. Doubtless the twentieth-century dislocations are necessary, too; certainly we cannot doubt the probity of Stravinsky's "authority," even though, being man-made rather than god-given, its purpose and destiny are obscure. And we listen with the deeper respect because we remember that Stravinsky has shown us, especially in the work of his middle years, that even in our bruised and battered world the heart may still sing in the sustained lyrical period, the pulse beat in a rhythm that is not motorized, but fluid and compulsive as the sea. When it happens, it is both true and miraculous, for Stravinsky's "representative" significance lies in the fact that he is not by nature a lyrical composer.

Benjamin Britten is—too easily so, Stravinsky would probably maintain, though it's perhaps inevitable that the two most materially successful composers of our time should regard one another with a degree of suspicion. Those of us who consider both Stravinsky and Britten to be great composers (if less great than a Bach or Beethoven) may recognize that the key theatrical works in their respective careers are complementary. Stravinsky's *Oedipus* transmutes humanism, by way of an oriental abnegation, into a Christianity reborn; Britten's two church operas, *Noye's Fludde* and *Curlew River,* start from Christian assumptions, but use their medieval and oriental techniques to purge the Christian heritage of guilt. Both the Stravinsky and the Britten works represent a fusion of West and East, and in both cases the fusion is re-creative, not evasive.

Britten began his career with a rebirth, a work specifically called *A Boy Was Born,* written when he was still a boy himself. Despite the archaism of the texts and of some of the musical procedures, the essence of this work is its theatrically re-creative immediacy; a boy is born indeed, and in the thirty years that have followed Britten has never forgotten that Boy and Birth. The wonderful Hardy songs deal directly with the birth of consciousness which is also the death of innocence, and almost all his operas have the same theme. The limitation of range is part of the evidence of his genius, for in dealing with innocence and persecution he knows what he knows. The relevance of the theme of the sacrificial scapegoat to our time is clear enough: we are obsessed with innocence because we have lost it, and because we have lost it we persecute those who haven't.

The grandest statement of this motif is in Britten's first opera, *Peter Grimes.* The unhero is here a genuinely tragic figure: the Savage Man who, given different circumstances, might have grown to civilized consciousness. Deprived of love, however, he destroys the Boy who is his own soul, and is hounded to his death by the World. Similarly, *Billy Budd* is specifically about the agony of growing up. Billy is a child destroyed by his childishness, which becomes the *mea culpa* of his stammer; the opera tells us that we can't dispose of evil by a blind blow, provoked by the inarticulateness of the good within us. Among the chamber operas, *The Rape of Lucretia* introduces an overtly Christian note into its fable of innocence corrupted, and *Albert Herring* has the same theme, almost the same story, as *Grimes,* but with a comic instead of tragic apotheosis. *The Turn of the Screw* offers Britten's most direct and painfully involved statement of the childhood and corruption motif, while in *A Midsummer Night's Dream* it finds perhaps its most maturely resolved form.

All this being so, it is hardly surprising that Britten should, throughout his career, have devoted time to the creation of music for children, nor that his most extended children's piece, *Noye's Fludde,* should deserve to rank among his supreme achievements. The choice of a text itself, as so often with Britten, is evidence of genius, of a self-knowledge that finds what is needful for each occasion. Thus, the Chester Miracle Play is medieval and the common people with whom it deals are, despite the *intellectual* sophistication of medieval civilization, childlike at heart. On the other hand, the story is unambiguously a conflict, so that the piece can grow from (Orffian) ritual into music-drama, if not into full-fledged opera. Indeed, it starts from a direct admission of "humanistic" contrarieties; the congregation, including you and me, sing the well-known hymn "Lord Jesus think on me." This hymn is an appeal to Christ to restore to us purity and innocence, which if we're adult we've lost, or if we're children we're about to lose, in travelling through "darkness," "perplexity" and the Flood. We *start,* that is, with the consciousness of sin and earth-born passion, which we have to encompass before we can see "eternal brightness." Although the Flood is in one sense a destructive force, it is in another sense (as it was in Biblical myth) a necessary return to the unconscious waters.

So Britten sets the hymn as a rather wild march, a song of pilgrimage in which the pilgrims are the children, as well as everyone else who may be present in the church. The hymn's descending scale becomes a motif of affirmation ("think on me") throughout the opera, but the bass's mingling of perfect, god-like fourths and fifths with the devil's imperfect ones imparts a slightly savage flavour to the simple diatonic harmonies. The devilish, bitonal F naturals initiate the conflict—between good and evil, between guilt and redemption—which the drama is. When, in the third stanza, the words refer directly to the Flood, the harmonies become more chromatic. Possibly Britten intends these rather corny harmonies to remind us of the turnover in the stomach and the chill down the spine that the reverberating organ gave us, in the parish church, when we were young. Possibly it still does the same, for children who go to church; in any case, it tells them, as it reminds the grown-ups, of the Flood they must pass through, to reach maturity.

This is manifest at the start of the opera's action, for the congregational chorale introduces the Voice of God who declaims (not sings) over fourths that are both perfect and imperfect. He may be the maker of all things, but man, through the sin and guilt that Orff's pagan music has no knowledge of, has thrown God's blessings away. The theme of redemption is then introduced, because mankind may be saved through the agency of Noah's Ark, which will breast the Flood. Noah, who is Man, sings to summon his children to an act of work and worship. The modal E minor of the hymn (which we may think of as the key of pilgrimage) changes to a pentatonic simplicity, full of godly fourths and optimistic major thirds and sixths. This leads into a work song as everyone gathers for the building of the Ark: an Orff-like music of ritual action which becomes drama. The dancing tune which Noah's children sing is derived from his original call, and is still pentatonically innocent, at once medieval and jazzy in its syncopated rhythm, marvellously suggesting youth's equivocal eagerness and apprehension. So even in music as simple as this there is theatrical projection and character portrayal; while the rapid modulations, or rather shifts of key, are also a dramatic device to convey excitement. Similarly, a primitive contrapuntal ensemble becomes a vivid musical image for corporate action; this music is inseparable from physical gesture and mime, which is one reason why children enjoy performing it. Suddenly and dramatically, the music breaks off, at what seems to be a climax of solidarity, when everyone is about to work together, hammering and sawing and caulking to make the Ark that will save us all.

What disrupts this collective helpfulness is indeed the snake in the grass, the fly in the ointment. Sex rears its lovely head as Mrs. Noah, singing major sixths (D sharps) that create sensual (Wag-

G

nerian!) ninth chords, refuses to play any part in the labour of salvation. Instead, with her gossipping cronies, she breaks into a parody of the work song in rapid 6/8 tempo. Of course she's a comic character, but Britten's music makes evident that the attempt of the Middle Ages to laugh away the dualism of sex didn't lessen its impact. Noah tries to assert his authority, making one of the stock medieval jokes about shrewish wives. He doesn't expect her to take any notice, and in fact she disassociates herself from the building by sitting, with her gossips, at the side of the stage. The key abruptly changes from Mrs. Noah's mingled F-sharp minor and A major to F natural, and Noah initiates the building "in the name of God." The building song begins with God's rising fifths and is supported on an ostinato of fifths as bass, alternating between tonic and flat seventh. There is virtually no modulation, because this is ritual rather than drama. As a refrain between each stanza, however, Noah's children refer to the coming of the Flood, singing in four-rhythm instead of the ritual's triple pulse, and in increasingly full, emotionally involved harmonization which changes the F-major ostinato to minor. In this action-ritual, children are involved instru-mentally, playing open strings on violins and twiddles on recorders while the ostinato pattern is repeated; this beautifully suggests how the act of work and worship concerns us all, through the ages.

When the Ark and the action song are finished, Noah invites his wife, the perennial Outsider, to come in. She refuses, in a line that is more humanistically energetic than her husband's. In a canonic chase she parodies Noah's words which, to medieval people, seems not far from blasphemy, and is enough to provoke God to a second utterance. He orders Noah to take the creatures into the Ark, two by two, and little boys summon them with a fanfare of bugles. Again, Britten exploits, imaginatively, the music of our everyday lives. The first congregational hymn had been a noise such as we've heard in church, time out of mind; similarly, the bugle procession is a noise we can hear in the streets on a Sunday morning, a noise in which our own Willies and Johnnies may well participate. The march, in the bugle key of B flat, is all tonic, dominant and sub-dominant, and reflects with realistic authenticity (like the marches in the music of Ives) the tang and tingle of the noise we'd actually hear, wrong notes and all. Of course the wrong notes are right, because part of the innocence, and it is right too that there should be no modulation, which the bugles' simplicity cannot accommodate, apart from a brief shift to D flat for some of the wilder creatures ("beares, woulfes, apes and weyscelles").

Between each statement of the march tune various beasts and birds emit Kyries of praise and thankfulness (oscillating simply between the fifth and fourth). The creatures are "natural" but not "conscious," so there is a kind of celestial farce in the bugle march and the squeaking of mice and gibbering of monkeys. Only when Noah and his children and their wives (representing Mankind) join in a jubilant ensemble as they enter the Ark is there a change of mood and mode. The Kyries gradually grow from comedy to liturgical awe, from the rocking two-note figure into a beautiful pentatonic melisma. This melisma is rooted on G, which seems to be the key of harmony between man and God, and is the "relative" of the more disturbed E minor, which is the key of pilgrimage. There is no more than a touch of G major here; though when Noah once more orders his wife to come in "for feare lest that she drowne," he reminds her, and us, of the first hymn that had asked for Jesus's pity on our sinfulness. In apparent paradox, she too sings the same phrase in protesting that she "will not oute of this towne." But if there is Man's (and Woman's) stupid pride in her defiance, there is also a kind of courage. This may be why she is not finally beyond redemption; it's the Mrs. Noah in all of us that makes us human. Persistently, she sings sharpened sevenths against the hymn's modal flat sevenths. As humanist, she demands harmonic consummation, and throughout this dramatic exchange trills on a low D sharp (major seventh of E minor) repeatedly deny the tune its resolution into G. Mrs. Noah says to D-sharpish arpeggios over an E-minor triad, that she'd rather have her gossips than salvation, and sings, with the gossips, the Flood song, wherein the D sharps are aggressive over a lurching E-minor ostinato. Between the stanzas of the song, Noah tries to call her home, with the hymn's descending scale, to G major. But the D-sharp trills drive us back to the "lumpy," D-sharp-dominated ostinato. This, again, is an Orffian ritual piece that turns into drama.

The gossips say they'll sit there "regardless," and get drunk, their justification being the typically human imbecility that they "ofte times have done so." Habituation is all, and human pride becomes indistinguishable from hysteria. The sons take over from Noah, appealing to their mother in radiant parallel 6:3 chords, and with a humbly flattened, Phrygian version of the hymn phrase, drooping down to G by way of B flat and A flat. This flatness further counteracts the sharpness of Mrs. Noah's sevenths, and although her denials then grow frenzied, mingling D sharps with fiercer leaps and tenser intervals, she willy-nilly finds herself singing the hymn theme of redemption, as her sons bundle her into the Ark. She struggles, of course, and boxes Noah's ears, but the tide is turned and the hymn phrase sounds in fortissimo unison, not yet in the resolution of G major, but in the original E minor. With a sudden, miraculous shift to a sustained C-minor chord on the organ—a further subdominant flattening of the Phrygian G minor of the last reference to the hymn-tune, the D sharps finding rest in being metamorphosed into the E flats of the triad—Noah says that "it is good for to be stille." It is indeed, after the fury and the mire of human veins, and the stupidities of the human will; now the redeeming Storm can work its way.

The Flood takes the form of a passacaglia, with a chromatic, rhythmically restless theme in which a falling third expands to a fourth and then to a godly fifth, only to wind itself back to the original drooping third. Though it generates the storm's excitement, the passacaglia theme is also God's Law which is beyond change, and again the piece is action as well as music. The drama is epic, concerning not individual men, but man's fate through successive generations. Child recorder players and open-string fiddlers place the epic in its present context, as they emulate wind, waves and flapping rigging. The animals panic to rising and falling chromatics, until gradually everyone begins to sing, over and through the passacaglia, the hymn "Eternal Father, strong to save." This Victorian tune includes the falling scale figure of the first congregational hymn, but also a rising *chromatic* scale to express the urgency of our appeal to God. Britten manages to suggest that this chromaticism is both a part of our heritage (we've thrilled to it as long as we can remember), and at the same time something that has been discovered during the slow chromaticizing of the storm. The passacaglia bass persists as the congregation joins in the hymn, but disappears during a triumphant repetition with full organ and a descant of boy trebles. After we've achieved, with God's help, this victory over darkness, the storm can subside. The various storm incidents are heard in shortened form, in reverse order over the declining bass theme, now dominated by pedal G's on drums. The passacaglia closes in a profound calm, with an ostinato of spattering raindrops, played on suspended mugs and piano. The tonality is poised between G and the subdominant C.

We still don't know precisely what the calm signifies, nor does Noah, who sends out the Raven and the Dove, the black bird and the white, to spy out the land and the waters. The point of this Christian mythology would seem to be the interdependence of good and evil: only through the Raven is the Dove apprehensible, and we must pass through the Flood to attain redemption. The music for the two birds is, anyway, closely related. The Raven dances to a fast waltz, played on the humanly emotive cello; it is chromatically and rhythmically unstable, veering now this way, now that. There's an E-ish flavour to its tonality, for the Raven is still a pilgrim; yet his line is lyrically songful, and we hear the passacaglia theme again as he flickers off into the distance. This recollection of God's will carries the tonality flatwards towards the dominant sevenths of A flat. This hovers on the brink of G-major peace as the Dove, represented by flutter-tongued recorder, flies after the Raven in a graceful waltz that seeks to resolve the Raven's chromatics into rising diatonic scales. Tremulous dominant sevenths, repeatedly harking back to A flat, exquisitely suggest a mingling of ecstasy and awe, even fear, in the approach to G major bliss. When the Dove returns, alighting on the Ark, he brings our redemption in the shape of an olive branch; a transformed version of the passacaglia theme (in G with an E-ish flavour) becomes a melody, not a bass, while Noah sings simple but noble fourths and fifths as he tells us that "it is a sign of peace."

God's voice speaks quietly in forgiveness, bidding the creatures to go forth and multiply. Sleepily, the tonality sinks to a subdominant pedal C, reminding us of that earlier subdominant triad that made it "good for to be stille." Over the pedal C, the bugle-call key of B flat softly intrudes, and the animals and humans leave the Ark, two by two, singing B-flat alleluias. The syncopated theme reminds us of the first work song, of which it is, indeed, the spiritual consummation. Gradually, it is metamorphosed into a joyous ensemble, until the music changes back from drama to ritual, with tolling bells and modal flat sevenths accompanying God's benediction. G major finally comes into its own as the key of peace, uniting man with God in the last hymn, "The spacious firmament on high." This tune includes the first hymn's scale figure in rising, and in its original falling, form, both now in unsullied diatonicism. Ritual bells and bugles continue to sound in B flat, the major relative of G minor, which would seem to be Nature's (preconscious) key. They remain unaffected even when everyone sings Tallis's hymn in G-major canon, for the creatures are what they are, eternally unchanging in their relationship to God's cosmos, whereas Man alone can progress from E minor to G major. The final pages are magic ritual in the ringing of B-flat bells and the blowing of B-flat bugles, and at the same time are the end of a human drama in the final resolution into a quiet, low-spaced, infinitely protracted G-major triad.

What is here achieved in childhood experience is explored at adult level in Britten's later "parable for church performance," *Curlew River*. In a programme note to the first performance Britten tells us that the seed of the work was sown when, in 1956, he witnessed two performances of the Japanese Noh-play, *Sumidagawa*:

"The whole occasion made a tremendous impression on me, the simple touching story, the economy of style, the intense slowness of the action, the marvellous skill and control of the performers, the beautiful costumes, the mixture of chanting, speech, singing which with the three instruments made up the strange music."

If he was to create a Noh-play himself, however, it would have to make contact with the Western world he lived in, and was heir to. How this might be possible was suggested by one of the odd coincidences that happen to genius.

For the Noh-play that Britten saw tells a tale that is close to Christian myth, and closer still to the personal myth that has dominated all Britten's work. A mother, desperate in grief, is searching for her lost son, slain by the barbarian; in a vision she sees him reborn. So Britten's myth of innocence, of persecution and of the sacrificial scapegoat, reappears, but with one significant difference. In *Peter Grimes* the hero is the Wild Man, the barbarian who, having lost love, destroys the boy who is his own innocence. But in *Curlew River* the persecutor doesn't even appear, his story being narrated retrospectively. The central characters are the suffering mother and the boy himself, who, in momentary vision, is restored from death. The duality of persecution and guilt is absolved.

The action is transferred from medieval Japan to an early medieval church in the English fens, which is justifiable, since English morality plays were probably performed in a style more comparable with a Noh-play than with naturalistic drama. We begin with ritual, with monks singing the plainsong hymn *Te lucis ante terminum*. The duality of harmony is thus rejected. This remains true throughout the work, since the instrumental and ensemble textures are monophonic or at most heterophonic, one part doubling another at the unison or octave, with occasional variations at the fifth or fourth, over slow (because numerically complex) patterns on percussion. When the monks have assumed the garments of the characters, the drama can begin. A Traveller asks the Ferryman to carry him across the river that divides the Western Country from the Eastern Fens—a symbol of separation and also, perhaps, of the division between flesh and spirit. Each character has certain (mostly stepwise) motives associated with him, and also his own instrument which, however, usually plays melismatic extensions of the vocal phrases. Thus, the Ferryman has a chromatically altered, agitated version of the plainsong theme, and the horn, thrusting or floating this melody across slow percussion, acts the gestures of rowing. The

Traveller, because he's travelling, covers more melodic space, though his Brittenesque thirds, accompanied by arpeggiated harp, tend to be stilled, rendered hieratic, by the infinitely slow reverberation of drone-chords on the chamber organ. Here and throughout the opera the chamber organ is used with magical inventiveness, in a manner comparable with the eternity-drone in both medieval and oriental music. While the Ferryman explains to the Traveller why people are gathering to celebrate the "special grace" of the boy's death, the chorus of monks sings the Curlew River's song of separation. Derived from the plainsong theme, in an undulating heterophony of parallel seconds, this reappears as refrain throughout the opera.

When the Mad Woman enters (sung by a man, with female mask), the music returns to a premedieval phase of consciousness, becoming pure line which is also gesture: song that merges into pathogenic speech, and into the glissando yell or sigh which are the heart's core. Her first phrase (perfect and imperfect fourth, and major seventh) is woman's grief, but also the curlew's call, here represented by flutter-tongued flute. Britten thus achieves an extraordinary equation between individual passion and universal lament. The instrumental line becomes a disembodied extension of the half-articulate cry that hurts too much to be borne; it's almost as though the woman's voice is her suffering humanity, and ours, while the flute is our yearning for spiritual grace. Only Janáček, among earlier opera composers, has used instrumental figurations as an extension of the voice's "gestures," though Britten's use of the technique is more radical, since he relies on nothing except line and rhythm. This is evident in the arioso where the Mad Woman tells the story of her loss and her pilgrimage from the Black Mountains. Her voice and its instrumental echoes stutter in septuplet repeated notes, fading into glissando moans, as she gropes back into the past. The Ferryman and chorus jeer at her, parodying her melodic gestures, but the savage mockery is silenced by the flute's metamorphosis of the woman's stutter into a song of lyrical longing. The curlew's cry, over a shimmering harp drone, becomes the Eternal Beloved and, prophetically, the lost boy. The Ferryman allows the Mad Woman to board his boat with the Traveller.

While the boat moves, infinitely slowly, to harp and string glissandi over an organ drone, the Ferryman tells the story of the boy who died, in almost-spoken recitative. The chorus's Kyries remind us of the Christian connotations of grace, which we may have forgotten in being carried, with the Mad Woman, to our remoter ancestry. Weeping over the tale of the boy destroyed by the barbarian, the woman reveals that she is his mother, and breaks down in frenzy, "crying in the empty air," since "the nest of the curlew is silent with snow and the lamb is devoured by the carrion crow." She begins her arioso with a whimpering figure of undulating seconds. It doesn't grow into winging lyricism, as her stuttering figure had done earlier, before she knew the truth. She seems to end in despair when a terrifying yell on the word "grave" admits that her search seems to have led only to death. But encouraged (at last) by the monks, she does achieve a painful lyrical consummation, and prays for her child's soul in a version of the river song of separation itself. The monks join in with the *Te lucis* hymn, creating a heterophonic, not harmonic, ensemble, over a timeless ostinato of organ and bells.

At this point one may experience a fleeting moment of intellectual doubt. After all this intensely "realized" suffering, are we to be offered no more than a mumbling of monks, a tolling of bells, a piping boy? Of course we're not, for the miracle happens not on the stage but in Britten's music. The woman hears the curlew's cry, her original motive of fourths and sevenths ecstatically liberated; the boy's spirit appears in a vision, and vanishes in a skitter of piccolo bird-song, with the plainsong theme as ostinato on horn and double bass. Vanished, the boy sings in English, telling his mother to go in peace. She transforms her original grief-broken stutter into a wildly triumphant Amen; her passion is consummated, and the priests resume their vestments. Innocence has indeed "outshined guilt." Britten has left *Billy Budd,* and even the expiation of public guilt in the *War Requiem,* far behind. He has created his first indubitably tragic masterpiece, and it may be, with the possible exception of *Oedipus Rex,* the only tragic music-drama of our time.

This hasn't entailed a sudden *volte-face* in Britten's development;

G*

we can see the beginning of his relinquishment of harmonic progression in favour of melismatic line and ostinato patterns in *A Midsummer Night's Dream,* which is a comic complement to the tragedy of *Curlew River.* He has gone back, first to the Middle Ages, then to a more savage antiquity, in order to go forward, as has Tippett in the recent linear phase of his work, not to mention the avant-garde composers we have discussed. Yet Britten has arrived at this point not through any wilful rejection of the West but through the pressure of human experience that went to create the cycle of his operas. It's a tribute to his strength that he can, at the height of his fame, spiritually and creatively "begin again."

If we can see the superficially improbable collocation of Stravinsky and Britten as a central tradition independent of, yet related to, the avant-garde, it is interesting that the younger composer of our time who seems most likely to achieve major stature has something in common with them both. Peter Maxwell Davies, like Britten, seems to have an intuitive understanding of English medievalism which, being a retreat from "consciousness," is also a rediscovery of innocence. So it isn't surprising that Davies should have achieved, while teaching at Cirencester Grammar School, such remarkable results with children, encouraging their creativity in the process of discovering his own. *O Magnum Mysterium,* the first full-scale work that Davies wrote for the Cirencester children, specifically deals with the Christian mystery of the Puer Natus, the Boy and the Birth. While the instrumental sections in this work *could,* with their tolling bells, reverberating gongs and fragmented cantus firmus, be pagan music, like that of Orff or early Stravinsky, the sung movements couldn't, not because they have Christian words but because they are, or become, harmonic.

The three versions of the refrain carol are, from this point of view, interesting. We first hear the tune as pure monody: a treble solo like plainchant, yet different too, because the pervasive stepwise movement is occasionally disturbed by more complex intervals, especially by the *diabolus* of the tritone. This gives to the monody an oddly moving precariousness, the more so because it is sung by children's voices, sharp and clear in line, without emotional vibrato. The sound, like the medieval texts, is innocent; yet the tonal precariousness makes the line also fragile and forlorn, so that if the music induces an incantatory serenity, it also hints at the perils flesh is heir to, as we grow into "the pain of consciousness." It's about the Boy's birth and, like most avant-garde music, about the necessity for *our* rebirth. At the same time the nervosity of the line reminds us that we are, and the Boy was, born into a "world so wylde," and the sexual undertones of the poems' references to "bobs of cherryes," "balles," "pennys" and "tennys" are probably present in the music's harmonic texture too.

Compared with Orff, the homophonic part-song versions of the carols imply an embryonic consciousness. The parts move in a restricted compass and in very close harmony, revolving (like plain-chant) around nodal points; the tritonal tensions which they create are the more disturbing because the melodic phrases are, in themselves, so brief and simple. It's as though the music were half eager, half reluctant, to escape from the innocence of the monodic state, and this must be why children, growing through puberty, could recognize it as peculiarly their music. Being at once innocent and slightly painful and "lost," it is relevant to twentieth-century children and to all of us who need to rediscover the youth of the heart. This is why Davies's children's music (like Britten's) is inseparable from his adult music; he is justified in saying that the children's part of *O Magnum Mysterium* is completed only by the grown-up organ fantasia which, though more difficult, is not a different kind of activity. This helps us to understand why the Christian theme inherent in Davies's music is meaningful independently of his belonging to the, or to any, Church.

In his earlier "adult" works Maxwell Davies was apt to employ the serial processes he had learned from Webern in a somewhat doctrinaire spirit, though most of his early music has more in common with medieval cantus firmus and proportional metre than with Viennese chromaticism. He also followed the late medievalists in literally destroying semantic communication by splintering words into detached syllables, and if the "Gothic desperation" was the (squawking) swan song of the Middle Ages, Davies's early music, like that of Stockhausen and Nono, may be part of the swan song of post-Renaissance Europe. With him, however, it's also a case of *reculer pour mieux sauter;* it's significant that, despite the medieval affiliations of his work, he also passionately admires Monteverdi, who created an (operatic) *Musica Nuova.* Monteverdi musically initiated modern Europe, transforming the linear techniques of theocracy into the harmonic techniques of humanism. Davies worked the other way round, recreating harmony in lyrical and melismatic monody; yet the point is that harmony is not denied in the process, but rather intensified. The early music of Davies tended to be, in its jittery tenuity, inadequately auralized; in the beautiful *Leopardi Fragments,* however, he sets fragmentary words by a neurotic poet of Europe's decay to music which fuses medieval and primitive elements with techniques derived from Monteverdi. The new texture, at once rich and simple, is both regenerative and heart-assuaging.

The later works involving chorus and instruments, such as the *Veni Sancte Spiritus* (which is hardly a children's piece, though written for the remarkable Princeton High School choir), explore similar techniques on a more extended and impressive scale. Here we can see how serial and canonic devices are used not to destroy but to define a harmonic texture, as they were in early Renaissance polyphony. This is why the texture of the music, despite the intermittent fragmentation, seems to have more in common with Stravinsky's *Threni,* or even with the *Symphony of Psalms,* than with post-Webernian fashion. The elaborate mensural writing and the partiality for monodic writing, as in the ecstatically fine-spun cantilena of the "O lux beatissima," exist alongside, and often help to create, the increasing density of harmony. And while the music's quavery intensity is a product of our time, it becomes affirmative in total effect. The hiccuping alleluias admit muscle and sinew as well as spirit, inducing a joy related to that of the jazz break; the tender "Dulce refrigerium" uses doctrinal canon to attain harmonic resolution. In being a "middle path" composer as compared with Boulez or Stockhausen, Davies faces up to the problem of temporality, and to its human implications. His most recent large-scale work, the *Second Fantasy on an In Nomine of John Taverner,* is by modern standards a very long work. It makes a new sound, if one less startlingly new than that of Messiaen's *Chronochromie* or Boulez's *Pli selon Pli.* Beyond the newness, however, this sound has human significance as an unfolding of melody in time, a coruscation of lines and tensions, a precarious resolution of conflict. There's evidence here that the humanistic forms of an opera, on the all too human theme of betrayal which is inherent in Taverner's life, may be well within Davies's grasp. Such an opera would, one suspects, have affiliations both with *Oedipus Rex* and with *Curlew River,* and despite its ritualistic flavour would discredit the fashionable assumption that our humanity, which is all we have, isn't worth the having.

This is what one comes back to if one attempts to speculate about the future of music. We have seen that a part of the revolution in twentieth-century music has been a return to the unconscious and to levels of being that have affinities with those of primitive societies, and that this is probably a much more significant matter than a mere escape from our perplexities. Marshall McLuhan has suggested that just as the Elizabethans were poised between medieval religious, corporate experience and our modern individualism, so we "reverse their pattern by confronting an electronic technology which would seem to render individualism obsolete and corporate interdependence mandatory." Our ordinary perceptions and habits of behaviour are being remade by the new media, and we are finding the process both painful and chaotic because our heritage is of little help to us in dealing with the oral and aural (rather than literate and visual) civilization which may be latent in the new technology. Modern physics envisages a simultaneously existent past, present and future in which human consciousness may be the only moving element; and the modern physicist may have more in common with religious, medieval man, with the mystics of oriental cultures, with the alchemists and even with the magicians of primitive societies, than he has with the post-Renaissance rationalist. In considering composers from Debussy to Stockhausen, we have noted that artists have for years been intuitively aware of how radical a change this is.

If most of us have failed to grasp the nature of our metamorphosis, the reason may be that the visual chronology of Renaissance tradition has tied us to the conception of a historical past. This was irrelevant to primitive oral cultures, and may be equally so to our future.

The world is becoming a smaller place as our awareness of "space" grows larger; we can no longer think of our Western arts as autonomous. Developments in pop music cannot be isolated from what is happening in "serious" music, and the West's veering towards the East and the primitive can be understood only as complementary to the East's need of the West. The future of civilization is inseparable from what happens to, for instance, the emergent African nations, and this is as true in musical as it is in social and political terms. At one level the Africans' conflict between their indigenous traditions and their desire to catch up with Western Europe seems incapable of resolution. The ancient musical traditions (which we call primitive because they are nonharmonic, though they are rhythmically far more complex than ours) belong to an aural and oral culture and can have no valid relationship to the literate traditions of the West. Their attempts to pretend that they have a past and present comparable with ours thus tend to end in unconscious comedy or bathos, for their mock-Bartók (or mock Stravinsky, Webern or Berio) pieces sound jejune compared not only with the real thing, but also with their own native music. Yet one can understand the motives that prompted these inexpert, pseudo-sophisticated imitations: it is no longer adequate, or even relevant, for African composers, living in their new macadamed cities, to create tribally functional music in the old sense.

One can, however, pertinently point out that the new African art composers may be on the wrong tack; and can indicate positively that there is another aspect of Western culture—jazz and pop—which might have a more authentic relationship to African traditions. This isn't merely because there's an African fundament to what has become a Western art, but also because jazz and pop, being improvised and performing rather than notated musics, have affinities with an oral rather than literate culture. The admirable series of recordings made by Hugh Tracey for the African Music Society demonstrates how a generation of often highly skilled, virtuosic performer-composers is arising who exploit, with charm and vigour, the natural affinities between the music on which they were nurtured in their village, and the "commercial" music which radio and television have brought to their changing world. Similarly, an African jazzman such as Dollar Brand, in spontaneously fusing traditional African and Cape Coloured music with the Chinese, Moslem, Indian, European and American music heard in the streets, has created a musical eclecticism that breaks the barriers between classical, jazz and pop music, as well as between races. In musical significance the achievements of these men far exceed those of any African composer of "art" music; and the music tends to be best when the merging of traditional African elements into modern beat is closest. It is no longer possible to segregate the elements of African tradition—white hymnbook harmony, Negro gospel shout, primitive piano boogie, Italianate opera, pop beat. This may have bearing not only on the history of music, but in a wider sense on the story of twentieth-century civilization.

For it is not only the "emergent" consciousness that learns. We in Europe, we have seen, may be recovering some of the qualities of a primitive civilization, learning to live, as J. C. Carothers has put it, in the implicit magic, charged with emotion and drama, of the oral word; and it is not fortuitous that Carl Orff is reluctant to allow children to begin musical studies in his school if they have already learned to read and write. This is not because reading and writing are to be deprecated, but because first things must come first; indeed, in rediscovering the "rite words in rote order" we should remember that James Joyce's revoking of our remote, Finn-like, fishy, calibanistic ancestry is also a Wake and awakening. Our reborn primitivism has to contend with, not to evade, consciousness; having thrown up a Shakespeare or Beethoven, we cannot pretend they never existed. It is significant that one of the most "central" traditionalists of our time, Bartók, should have affiliations equally with the static "present" of Debussy and with the Becoming of Beethoven. Similarly, if "statistical" serialism and coin-throwing chance seem equally to discredit the human, they are balanced by a Boulez's or a Stockhausen's attempt to preserve human impulse within the relativity of time-space, and by indeterminacy which can be, in Boulez's words, "a liberation from robotism in an oppressed creative universe, weighed down by the petty abuses of power."

From this point of view our latter-day history is perhaps already implicit in the Orpheus myth which, we observed in our first chapter, had so obsessive an influence on Renaissance man. It was man's power, through his arts, to affect, even to control, Nature that was celebrated in the first phase of the story. The second phase looks like an extension of the first in that, through his arts, man seeks to conquer even Time and death, reversing the gods' decree. There is, however, another strand in this part of the tale, whereby Euridice becomes not only a representative of the social world and of marriage, but also an earth-goddess (Persephone, Demeter?) whom Orpheus can find only by entering the dark labyrinth. She may even merge into the Eternal Beloved, the anima to his animus, a part of the search for a human "wholeness" which his *looking back* betrayed. For his betrayal he is, in the third phase of the myth, torn to pieces by the Maenads; the White Goddess has been metamorphosed into the Terrible Mothers. The Mother Goddess is pre-Oedipal, a legacy of our infantile history, "unboundedly good," in Ian Suttie's phrase, to the young child, yet also "utterly terrible, in that her displeasure is the end of all good things and of life itself." Even so, Orpheus's dismembered head sings on, prophesying to the winds: an image which seems peculiarly relevant to the artist of our time, who has undergone a comparable dark pilgrimage.

Yet this is not an entirely adequate image for the modern artist; whether or not we still live in a Christian civilization, we cannot escape the implications of our Christian heritage. The matriarchal cultures fell before the aggression of the guilt-ridden religions which "must needs atone for sin and propitiate the outraged father by compelling others to worship him." So although Christianity had garnered much of its mythology from pagan sources that had stressed human wholeness (which linguistically has the same root as haleness and holiness), it came increasingly to emphasize division at the expense of unity. Into its preconscious Eden it introduced the duality of sex and of choice. Whereas in pre-Christian cultures the White Goddess and the Terrible Mother had been accepted as complementary faces of the same life-instinct, Eden's serpent, twined around the Cross, became a means towards consciousness. To be conscious is to be aware of difference—between self and not-self, life and death, love and hate, flesh and spirit. Only through the war of Cain and Abel, and of Esau (the hairy one of the earth) and Jacob (the hairless one of the spirit) can we hope to achieve again wholeness in union with God. In so far as the new primitivism, whether as manifested in the work of Boulez, Cage and Stockhausen, of Britten and Stravinsky, of Ornette Coleman, or of the Beatles and Bob Dylan, may evade the strife inherent in consciousness, it may evade too our human responsibilities. But this does not alter the fact that some such healing of division within the psyche has been necessary before the new life can be born.

Having attained our rebirth, we should not forget, as Francis Bacon put it, that "the knowledge which induced the Fall was not the natural knowledge of creatures, but the moral knowledge of good and evil, that they had other beginnings, which man aspired to know; to the end to make a total defection from God and to depend wholly upon himself." This defection would be at once a tragedy and a triumph, as was foreseen by Shakespeare, who foresaw most things. In *The Tempest* his Prospero is post-Renaissance man, drunk with knowledge and power, able to reverse the seasons, make brave rivers run retrograde, bring the dead to life, split the atom, blow us all up. Scared at last of the power he hasn't the wisdom to use, he burns his book and casts his wand back to the ooze of the unconscious from which it came. But this is not, and cannot be, an opting out, only an admission that there are things both without and within man's nature which can never be finally mastered. We cannot "know ourselves" unless we can first recognize and accept the fish-like Caliban within us, who was (we recall) an offspring of the Moon-Goddess. Only when we have said, "this Thing of darkenesse I Acknowledge mine" (which may be the task of a lifetime), may we hope to enter into and to possess our brave new world. In so far as it is valid, the "new primitivism" is probably not so remote as we might think from Beethoven's desire to submit his rational faculties to intuition and to the "electrical" springs of his nature. Though there is not likely to be another Beethoven, his music, especially that of his third period, is still immediately pertinent to our future. And his words are a still-valid statement of the identity between human and divine, between flesh and spirit, which has been the theme of this book:

"Man cannot avoid suffering, and his strength must stand the test. He must endure without complaining, *know* his own nobleness, and so again believe in his own perfection: that perfection which the Almighty will then bestow upon him."

A CHART OF RELATIONSHIPS

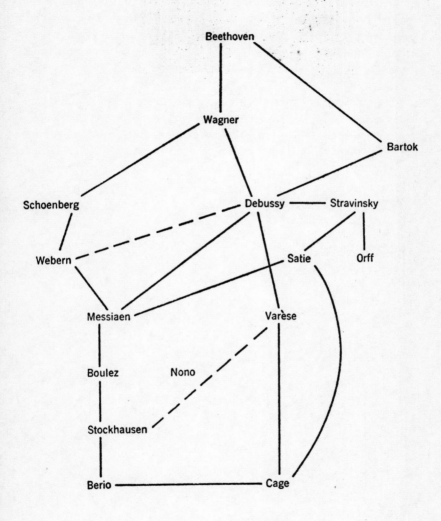

A CHART OF RELATIONSHIPS

A Note on Editions

of the works analyzed in detail

All the works of Schoenberg and Webern are published by Universal Edition

Debussy's *Pelléas et Mélisande*	Durand et fils
Satie's *Parade*	Edition Salabert
All the works of Orff	Schott and Co.
Stravinsky's *The Wedding*	J. and W. Chester
All the other Stravinsky works	Boosey and Hawkes
Messiaen's *Cinq Rechants* and other works	Rouart Lerolle
The works of Boulez and Stockhausen	Universal Edition
The works of Varèse	Ricordi and Co.
The works of Cage, Feldman and Brown	Peters Edition
Berio's *Circles* and other works	Universal Edition
Britten's *Noye's Fludde*	Boosey and Hawkes
Britten's *Curlew River*	Faber Music
The works of Maxwell Davies here discussed (His later music is published by Boosey and Hawkes.)	Schott and Co.

Glossary

added sixth (Debussyan). A chord consisting of a major triad with the sixth degree of the scale added (e.g., C-E-G-A).

Aeolian (mode). A scale represented by the white keys of the piano beginning on A.

appoggiatura. A dissonant ornamental note, especially common in eighteenth-century music, which resolves on to a concord, the dissonance taking the stress.

aria (da capo). A characteristic form of the eighteenth century, consisting of a melody often of 16 or 32 bars; followed by a middle section in a related key (usually the tonic minor or the relative major); and rounded off by a strict repetition of the first section, usually with additional, often improvised, ornamentation.

arioso. A passage of declamatory or recitative-like character which is none the less to be sung or played lyrically: i.e., halfway between recitative and aria.

atonality. Music without a defined key centre.

augmentation. Restatement of a theme (or rhythm) in longer note values.

blue notes. Flattened thirds and sevenths occurring in the blues, within major tonalities; though to describe them as "flattened" is misleading, since they are survivals of vocally modal ways of singing which conflict with modern instrumental tonality.

break (in jazz). An improvised cadenza-like passage, "breaking" across the beat.

canon. Strict imitation of a single theme in a number of different parts. Canons may also be by inversion (the sequence of pitches turned upside down, so that a rising sixth becomes a falling sixth) or, more rarely, backwards (starting at the end of the theme) or backwards and inverted.

cantus firmus. A pre-existing melody, usually plainsong, used as a basis for a composition. The other parts may or may not be related to the cantus firmus.

chromatic. A scale consisting entirely of semitones; known only in western music.

density (harmonic). A great deal of harmonic activity occurring in a short space, as in Bach's or Schoenberg's music. In this sense Debussy's music is seldom harmonically dense, and Carl Orff's never!

diatonic. Usually applied to the equal-tempered major and minor scales of western Europe.

diminution. Restatement of a theme or rhythm in shorter note values.

dirt (in jazz). Singing or blowing off-pitch, and in other ways exploiting noise, rather than "musical" sound, for expressive purposes.

dorian mode. A scale represented by the white notes on the piano starting on D.

fugato. Imitative passages in a musical texture, though the imitation need not be strictly canonic (see canon).

gagaku. Ancient Japanese court music of high sophistication.

gamalan orchestra. Balinese and Javanese bands of percussion instruments, some pitched, some unpitched.

heterophony. Literally, music in heterogeneous parts, put together without reference to their harmonic implications. Most commonly heterophony consists of different versions of the same melody sung or played simultaneously.

hocquet. A device in late medieval music whereby a passage is broken by rests, regardless of the words. The term is derived from hiccup.

homophony. Music in homogeneous parts; i.e., normally with a tune at the top and the other parts accompanying harmonically.

isochronous motet. A late medieval form in which one part (or more) has a preordained rhythmic pattern which is adhered to throughout, though the pitches change.

just intonation. Singing or playing in the "natural" scales derived from the harmonic series, not in scales artificially fixed by keyboard instruments tuned in Equal Temperament.

klangfarben. A fragmented style of instrumentation especially associated with Webern, whereby each note of a melody may be given a different instrumental colour.

leitmotiv. A short theme associated by Wagner with particular characters or ideas, and developed symphonically.

Machaut, Guillaume de. Late medieval composer, c. 1300–1377.

mediant. The third degree of the scale.

melisma. An ornamental passage, especially in oriental and medieval monody; strictly speaking, on a single syllable, though the term is used for any decorative arabesque.

microtonal. Interval smaller than a semitone.

mixolydian mode. A scale represented by the white keys of the piano starting on G.

mode, modality. The fundamental tonal formulae of music, derived from the behaviour of the human voice, independent of artificial systems of tuning.

monody, monophony. Music in a single line of melody.

organum. A medieval form of part singing, mainly in parallel fourths and fifths.

ostinato. Melodic figure and/or rhythm insistently repeated.

passacaglia. A composition built over an ostinato, usually in the bass and usually in triple time. Especially favoured by composers of the baroque era.

pedal note. A note sustained throughout a developing musical texture, usually though not necessarily in the bass.

pentatonic. Five-note scales; the most rudimentary of all the modes, and the commonest all over the world, because most directly derived from the Harmonic Series.

Perotin. Medieval composer, chapel master at Notre Dame in the twelfth century.

plagal cadence. A progression from subdominant to tonic.

polyphony. Literally, music in many voices; in current usage, music in more than one voice.

ritornello. In the seventeenth century, a short instrumental piece played recurrently during the course of a stage work; later it was applied to the instrumental interludes between vocal sections of an aria or anthem.

rondo. A musical form based on the recurrence of a theme, each recurrence being separated by an episode. In later developments of the rondo, what happens in the episodes tends to modify the theme or its harmonization; this type of developing rondo may be called incremental.

serialism. In chromatic serial music as used by Schoenberg, each note of the composition (chords as well as melodic lines) must be derived from a preordained sequence, or "row," of the twelve chromatic semitones, either in the row's original form, or inverted, or backwards, or backwards and inverted. The serial principle is extended by later composers (Boulez, Stockhausen) to rhythm (or rather metrical proportions), dynamics and timbre (the allocation of notes in the series to different instruments). Though never carried out systematically before the twentieth century, serialism is not a new principle. The medieval cantus firmus acts as a (nonchromatic) row, medieval isochronous motets are rhythmically serial, the ragas and talas of Indian music are more like melodic and rhythmic rows than they are like scales or themes.

subdominant. The fourth degree of the diatonic scale, or the key associated with that note.

tonality. Strictly speaking, the relationships between tones that are inherent in acoustical facts, so that the term covers all scale systems, or rather formulae, from the pentatonic to the chromatic. In practice, however, the word tonality has become associated with the tempered diatonic (major and minor) scales of European music in the eighteenth and nineteenth centuries. The terms atonality and pantonality are used to define the breakdown of that system.

triad. The "common" chord of three notes based on the tonic note with the third and fifth.

tritone. The interval of the augmented fourth or diminished fifth (e.g., B to E sharp or B to F natural). In the Middle Ages it was known as the *Diabolus in musica* because it tended to destroy tonal order, being difficult to sing as a melodic progression and harmonically inimical to the perfect fifth which, to medieval people, was a musical synonymm for God. (Scientifically, the fifth is the most perfect of harmonic relationships after the octave, which is hardly a harmony at all.)

Index